IT'S WRITTEN IN TH

• Capricorn men make
fidelity you're after)

• Libras are notoriously attracted to beautiful men—
don't expect monogamy!

• Taurean lovers may have inspired taste in bedroom
furnishings, but may be less than inspired in bed

• A Cancer/Taurus love affair is one of the most immediate and lasting pairings in the zodiac

Here, back just in time for the gay 90s, is *the* defin-
itive guide to gay love and its relationship to the stars.
In this completely revised edition, author Michael Jay
will show you how a knowledge of your astrological
nature can lead you to a new "best buddy" or a love
that's heaven-sent. Let GAY LOVE SIGNS be your
guide to achieving happiness.

MICHAEL JAY has been a student of astrology for
over twenty years. He is perhaps the most well-known
astrologer within the gay community, having written
the weekly column "Cocktail Astrology" for the *New
York Native* during the mid-1980s.

GAY LOVE SIGNS

The New Astrology
Guide for Men Who
Love Men

Revised Edition

Michael Jay

A PLUME BOOK

PLUME
Published by the Penguin Group
Penguin Books USA Inc., 375 Hudson Street,
New York, New York 10014, U.S.A.
Penguin Books Ltd, 27 Wrights Lane,
London W8 5TZ, England
Penguin Books Australia Ltd, Ringwood,
Victoria, Australia
Penguin Books Canada Ltd, 10 Alcorn Avenue,
Toronto, Ontario, Canada M4V 3B2
Penguin Books (N.Z.) Ltd, 182–190 Wairau Road,
Auckland 10, New Zealand

Penguin Books Ltd, Registered Offices:
Harmondsworth, Middlesex, England

First published by Plume, an imprint of Dutton Signet, a division of
Penguin Books USA Inc.
Published simultaneously in Canada.

First Printing, July, 1990
15   14   13   12   11   10   9   8

℗ REGISTERED TRADEMARK—MARCA REGISTRADA

Library of Congress Cataloging-in-Publication Data
Jay, Michael.
    Gay love signs: the new astrology guide for men who love men / by
Michael Jay. — Rev. ed.
      p.   cm.
    ISBN 0-452-26431-6
    1. Astrology and homosexuality.   2. Gay men—Miscellanea.
3. Love—Miscellanea.   I. Title.
BF1729.H66J39   1990
133.5′83067662—dc20
                                                             89-49603
                                                                  CIP

Printed in the United States of America
Set in Times Roman
Designed by Nissa Knuth

Acknowledgments
"That's What Friends Are For"

The original version of *Gay Love Signs* was dedicated "to the one I love," but this edition requires a fuller account and a deeper dedication.

Arn Gabel needs recognition for the long days and nights we spent racing toward deadlines. Marjan Mozetich was composer-in-residence and musical midwife. Larry and Helene Hoffman were the first to see the potential in the idea and see it to commercial fruition.

The book was a passport for me. It took me to Key West and a new life with loving friends. It was there that I met Rusty, who taught me the truth of a Cancer–Leo relationship. He introduced me to Courtney, whose friendship I continue to cherish.

And now from Florida to New York, where Gary and Beth sustained me as only family can. Thanks to Lloyd "Buddy" Mailander, who suggested I write a column for the *New York Native,* which was magically offered me. Thanks to the fans of "Cocktail Astrology," who restored my faith, and to Richard Cytowic, who supported my craft. To Jamie Leo, who led me out of the wilderness of West Fourth Street and out into the city. To Leonard Perlson, who loaned me his gallery to do consultations in the meat market, and to Douglas Stone, who gave me shelter in the Pines. To Patrick Daniels, who gave me bed and breakfast, and to Laura Tilden, who gave me someplace to go in the morning, and to David Ehrlich, who sustains me with his erudition, admiration, and sense of humor.

And always, above all, to Arlene, who was there at the beginning of everything and is forever in my heart.

This is truly dedicated to the ones I love.

XOX,
M.

CONTENTS

x CONTENTS

INTRODUCTION

Gay Love Signs was originally written to provide astrological information about relationships for gay men from a positive point of view that would celebrate the love between men. I wrote this book because there wasn't anything like it, straight or gay, i.e., a book on astrological relationships that actually details all one hundred and forty-four possibilities between signs, each section written as a personal message for the one born under that sign. No "love-sign" book, before or since, has given such complete information on the matchups between signs.

Gay Love Signs is the first astrological guide that understands the unique personalities, acknowledges the preferences, and explores the potential happiness of gay life. The original version was written in 1979, when a whole universe of possibilities seemed open to gays—socially, politically, culturally, and sexually. Things have changed.

The bright hope that was part of *Gay Love Signs* has been dimmed by the specter of disease, by the sad loss of so many loving and talented people, by the heavy hand of political repression, and by the worldwide threat of religious fundamentalism. The party may be over, the music may have a different beat, but the need to celebrate ourselves remains undiminished.

As we have all been touched by our troubled times, the value of love, of loving one another, has actually increased. As a culture, gay people and their friends have learned more about caring, about treasuring the moments we spend together, about the lives we build together. Out of adversity we can see a new spiritual dimension in gay culture that can be an example to all people.

This book is about love—about the lessons of love within the framework of the knowledge of astrology. It is also about sex—within the context of falling in love. It is about caring for another person, about making commitments to learning and teaching and sharing as part of a loving life.

And in the dedication to life there is a dedication to enjoying sex as an expression of caring, to celebrating the triumph of love over death and of joy over selfishness. All relationships represent a faith in the future. This book is meant to encourage and honor that faith.

A NOTE ON METHOD

Gay Love Signs is based upon analysis of the properties associated with the Sun signs, natural elements, and ruling planetary combinations. This method provides accurate general information on the patterns to be expected in a relationship, but there will be many modifying factors when specifically applied. The major factors involved in Sun-sign analysis are the personality needs and goals of the individual, rather than the emotional nature (Moon sign).

Sun-sign analysis is not meant to provide prescriptions for action, though it can permit insights into the basic issues that underlay any relationship. There are instances when specific combinations may seem negative, though value judgments are difficult when dealing with the entire spectrum of potential human relationships. Some couplings are obviously better—or worse—than others, and the standards are not objective. If you are happy with your lover and this book says that you should be miserable, then you should thank your lucky stars. If your current lover makes you miserable and *Gay Love Signs* says that the aspects are favorable, then there are personal planetary placements that are obviously incompatible. In any case, the answer to the apparent contradiction lies in the fact that we are each unique manifestations of the possible archetypes symbolized by the zodiac. The stars do not compel; they only indicate.

THE ASTROLOGICAL SIGNS

Aries	March 21–April 20
Taurus	April 21–May 20
Gemini	May 21–June 20
Cancer	June 21–July 20
Leo	July 21–August 20
Virgo	August 21–September 20
Libra	September 21–October 20
Scorpio	October 21–November 20
Sagittarius	November 21–December 20
Capricorn	December 21–January 20
Aquarius	January 21–February 20
Pisces	February 21–March 20

These dates are approximate; they may vary a day or two, depending on the year of birth.

ARIES
March 21–April 20

♈

Symbol: The Ram
Ruling Planet: Mars
Color: Scarlet
Metal: Iron
Natural House Rulership: First House, the house of
    personal expression and the physical body
First House Traits: Love of physical activity and
    preoccupation with self
Motto: "I am"
Nature: Cardinal sign (leadership)
Element: Fire sign (spiritual)
Qualities: Competitive and adventurous
Capacities: Leadership and intuition
Personality Key Words: Daring, passionate, and
    courageous

MAXIMIZING YOUR ARIES POTENTIAL

"If you've got it, flaunt it!" No other sign of the zodiac believes this egocentric maxim as fervently and as innocently as you do, Aries. You are the newborn consciousness of the ego in the sign of spring and the House of the Sun. You embody the original force of life. No wonder you feel like the leader of the pack—you are!

Aries' strong self-image is the source of your charm and your sex appeal. Your childlike energy and enthusiasm are admirable and very attractive, but you can easily get carried away with yourself. Aries' symbol is the Ram, which you imitate by leading with your head—charging impulsively without considering the consequences. Your romantic and daring nature can be endearing and boyish in its naïveté but childlike when you initiate things you don't complete. Your combination of ego involvement, passionate sex drive, and sense of adventure can easily lead you to become the master of the weekend love affair. The strength of Aries is in the sprints and hurdles, not the marathon, of love and sex.

You have the power of the Sun—combined with Aries' ruler, Mars—giving you the ability to come on strong. The thrill for you is in the pursuit more than the conquest. Fortunately you have also been endowed with an indomitable spirit that allows you to play the game of pursuit and conquest with a real feeling for the adventure involved. You know that sex is fun, Aries, and having fun for you means no guilt, no shame, no blame. You can be fun-loving and carefree in your self-absorbed attitude toward sex, but Aries' blithe spirit can cause a lot of frustration for your lovers. If you can convert some of your abundant passion into simple compassion, you'll find your relationships will be as lasting as they are exciting.

Men who don't respond to the implicit challenge in your open manner and easy familiarity are just not your type. Sometimes you come on too fast and too hard. You are bound to be rejected by someone who is not secure enough to cope with your aggressive personality. If he is sensitive to your Aries vibrations, he'll know that playing with a Ram means butting heads and competing to decide who is going to be in charge.

You thrive on the adolescent, athletic spirit that you sense in the search for love and sex. You enjoy competing, and losing at your own game doesn't crush your spirit. Rejection won't send you slinking home to write another chapter of cosmic self-doubt in your diary. No, the Aries ego is more likely to be surprised than hurt! Your pride might be bent out of shape, but you can always count on picking yourself up, dusting yourself off, and starting all over again.

This dauntless energy comes from the masculine-aggressive powers of Mars. It's a mixed blessing, though, Aries, because the Mars call to attack head-on leaves you with no time to learn the lessons implicit in momentary setbacks. The strategy of continuous frontal assault is really no strategy at all. It can leave you on the brink of physical and mental exhaustion.

When you reach that point of butting your head against the fence with no results, you are saved by the influence of your Sun in Aries. It gives you the strength to discover a new interest that will allow you to abandon your futile efforts without losing face. Someone new and exciting, or some new situation, will challenge your imagination and you'll be off on a new adventure.

Not only are you emotionally equipped to handle the passion and trust of love, but also you have the energy and drive to do it with flair. You need sex to keep your Mars batteries charged and recharged. You can let yourself be led off on a series of extravagant episodes in the search for sexual gratification, seeking the thrills of the perfect Saturday night.

When you fall in love, as you do in your usual impulsive way, it can be like shooting stars. Your declaration of passion can amaze the heavens with its intensity, but it won't last long unless you feel positive ego-reinforcement or a real challenge from your partner.

Your Man of Life will have to be somebody who accepts you for the very qualities that seem to make you a less than ideal partner. The man who shares your bed will have to share your high opinion of yourself without being completely submissive to your drive for dominance. Your search for love is basically romantic. You want a fellow Prince Charming whose adoration will be worthy of you. It's no challenge for you to accept the admiration of a pussycat. When you make the mistake of choosing a mate who is too passive in the face of the onslaught of your Aries ego, you can quickly become overbearing, bored, and on the prowl for another prince—a real one, not just a Puss-in-Boots.

Your straightforward desires for good times and lots of sex can make you insensitive to your lover's feelings and needs. Your sunny personality and lack of introspection can make you intolerant of your partner's moods, dismissing them as trivial. It might not occur to you that his depression may well be caused by your own impulsive actions in the first place. You can use your charm, wit, and enthusiasm to lift his spirits. If you want to keep a lover, you have to learn to give of yourself in more than superficial ways.

You can easily fall into the trap of being sexually demanding of your partner without concern for his needs and desires for satisfaction. Ultimately you will find yourself having less and less to share with your mate, and sharing the best of each other is the key to a lasting love affair. For you, Aries, overcoming selfishness is the true path to maximizing your radiantly attractive personality. Your great generosity can go a long way toward balancing your usual preoccupation with yourself.

The one thing you can't handle is a restrictive relationship. Aries likes to be his own man, even when he's in a rewarding partnership. You have to be able to relate to others as an individual, not an extension of your lover. Your best mate will be someone who is willing to accept your masculine role playing and appreciate your open, honest personality and your drive to initiate, whether it's sex or ideas. Short separations will increase your interest, as each reunion is a way of recapturing your initial sexual attraction, and when you're apart, a little flirtation on the side is not going to mean the end of your relationship. Overcome your jealousies by promising to be truly together when you are with each other.

As the first sign of the zodiac, you also represent the seed of consciousness, and therefore your potential for growth is unlimited. Other less aggressive signs—the shy Cancers, the conservative Capricorns—may see you as a show-off. While you may promise more than you deliver, you'll never fail from lack of trying. Arians do not have the enmeshed complexities of other signs. This freedom gives you an acute awareness of the importance of surface impressions. That's why you are so fearlessly up-front about who and what you are. Most likely you never had to agonize about coming out; you were just "out," doing what comes naturally—but with style.

Stick with your energetic and exuberant style, Aries, and it will take you through a life filled with social and romantic adventure.

ARIES & ARIES

Man to man, this can be one of the most challenging partnerships in the entire zodiac. It is difficult for two Rams to keep butting their heads, expending energy, and getting nowhere; but if you are willing to be open about yourself and your own ego, there is a great deal you can learn from an Aries lover.

As masculine Fire signs, you are both driven to dominate, compete, and express your needs for ego gratification. If you get involved in a loving relationship, trust and understanding are the keys to overcoming your mutual potential for selfishness. Your clashing egos will always be an issue, but you are both perverse enough in your Arian ways that you enjoy a stormy affair. Your tempers are short but your tempests short-lived. Though Arians are intense, they lack stamina, so your arguments don't last long, you don't hold a grudge, and problems usually can be resolved on a physical plane once you two get into bed. Heated arguments leading to heated sex is a common Aries-to-Aries phenomenon. You are passionate men—and passionate in more than a sexual context. Your needs and desires become urgent forces that carry you along on waves of energy.

As fascinating as you find yourself, in turn you will be fascinated by another Arian. Your mutual attraction has great magnetic force as you both attract and repel each other like alternating current. Often the spark between you two will be physical. Across the room or across the street, Arians react to each other's sexual vibrations in a totally masculine way—like two buck Rams who are simultaneously drawn to each other but challenge each other because of their innate masculine natures. The potential for tension is obvious. You are both bold, direct, assertive people and may well be too much of a strain on each other's nervous systems.

But an affair with another Aries can mean a magical encounter if you are aware of the way you can complement each other to double your fun. Arians represent "young souls" because they are the first sign on the Wheel. Arrogant about your powers and eager for the loving care and respect of others, both of you want to be acknowledged as "number one." Constantly trying to prove yourself usually means a life of adventure. When there are two of you together, you can expect the unexpected—crisis and passion, surprise and disaster. Your extravagance with money will lead to anguish, but it will often be balanced with miraculous windfalls.

All of the flash and dash of an Aries-to-Aries romance will come to burnt offerings in the end if you don't learn some of the valuable lessons you must teach each other. Look in the karmic mirror that he is to you and see both the beauty and the blemishes. Your worst traits—your overaggressiveness and selfishness—come from the insecurity of wanting to be the best but not knowing if you are really good enough, equating attention with love. You both crave affection that is demonstrative and physical. You must display your caring to each other—through physical contact, little presents, and surprises, as well as strong shoulders to lean on, even to cry on, when your high energy levels leave you both mentally exhausted.

If you want to keep him, you will have to show him that you care enough to bend—sometimes—to attempt to share your victories, and to seek a common challenge to work on together, rather than competing with each other for the attention of friends or strangers. If you really want to express your care and affection for him, then you must honestly praise him. Remember that you expect recognition for *your* good points as well.

The process of loving another Aries can be a form of self-love, requiring you to examine yourself so that you can know what you want to communicate with others. Of course, the typical Aries–Aries love escapade is so full of alarms and diversions that there is little time or energy for serious self-appraisal. Arians feel more than they analyze, and as long as there is that feeling of stimulation between you two, the relationship will thrive.

Arians don't like compromise. They tend to interpret it to mean alternating victories rather than a meeting of minds. There is always the scent of challenge in the air between you and another Aries lover. If you give in to him when he least expects it, you'll keep his interest by keeping him off-

balance. Avoid being predictable, especially as a lover, and
this stellar combination can light up your life.

ARIES & TAURUS

If you are involved with a Taurean man, you have probably
noticed that his attitudes about sex are very different from
your own passionate, masculine impulses. For one thing, he
doesn't think about sex as much as you do. Though the Bull
is a masculine symbol and an obvious representation of a
stud, Taurus is ruled by the feminine planet of Venus. Now,
Venus may be the goddess of Love, but as the ruler of Taurus she imparts a very practical and receptive attitude about
sex.

Aries looks upon lovemaking as an almost spiritual act.
Taurus appreciates sex on a very practical level as one of
the most pleasurable of human necessities, like eating. You
would be willing to pass up a good meal for some good sex,
but your Taurus man would rather have the meal first, and
maybe a nap, and then slip between the sheets for some
long, slow sex that trails off into the night. Practicality is
not your strong suit and not likely to be a virtue that you
look for in a lover.

Your great strength in this relationship is your Arian energy. Each sign of the zodiac has a certain amount of sympathy, even admiration, for the qualities of the signs that
precede or follow it, and while you both can benefit from a
long-term affair with this Mars–Venus mating, it will probably not be very calm. The Ram will butt heads anytime,
but the Bull has to be provoked before he will charge. When
you attack, your aggression is usually an expression of your
basic impatience. On the other hand, the Bull has plenty of
patience. When he puts down his horns and begins to paw

the ground, he is angry. Aries' nature is to enjoy excitement, and sometimes you will stir up trouble just to make
things a little livelier. Unfortunately, easygoing Ferdinand
the Bull doesn't like to be disturbed. You will have to be
committed to periods of adjustment, negotiation, and re-
definition, which may quickly dampen your enthusiasm for
any Taurus lover.

On the positive side, Taureans are the embodiment of patience, and this is the one most important virtue for Aries
to acquire. Your Taurus will be patient in your demands for
attention and give freely of his constructive criticism in
helping you to work out your frustrations. Don't let your
ego get in the way of listening to his advice. Just as your
instincts are often right, he has the power to be perceptive
in his reactions. If you can learn to accept criticism with
grace from your Taurus man, you are probably in love.

Your casual attitude about money is more than likely to
arouse his criticism. Taureans don't appreciate the charm of
extravagance. They are willing to spend money only if they
have "something to show for it," or if it involves personal
comfort. Your Taurus lover is more likely to be annoyed
than amused by your generous impulse to give surprise gifts.
He will like them if they are practical, but your presents are
gifts of emotional inspiration rather than an expression of
your lover's needs. It will be hard for the normally passionate Aries to accept the fact that his Taurean lover would
rather have received a new pair of socks than a gold neck-
lace, especially when he suspects that you had to use your
credit card to buy it. Taurus natives are not against materialism, but they see possessions as symbols of security. He
likes to own things that express solid taste and comfort,
rather than trends.

The bedroom of your Taurus lover may be tastefully furnished, but he may not be imaginative in bed. As an Aries,
you like to assume an aggressive, masculine role. You tend
to seek men of similar sexual preference, since you enjoy
the challenge of man-to-man sex. Taurus is a feminine sign,
and the language of the zodiac denotes that he naturally be

the receptive one in any sexual pair. While he may prefer you to be the aggressor, you are likely to lose interest in him as a sex partner unless he offers you more of a challenge to whet your appetite. You can awaken his sexual potential with your passion. He will be willing to experiment in bed if you take the initiative, but you must work him up to a fever pitch of passion first.

After passion, may one discuss fidelity with Aries? Yes, for as long as you may be involved with a Taurus, he will assume fidelity as a condition of the relationship. He likes things to go along on an even keel, and he won't rock the boat by arousing your jealous streak. If he likes the status quo, he won't mind your occasional lapses as long as you are discreet.

An Aries–Taurus love affair is often fraught with difficulty because both of you are so close to each other on the karmic wheel that you don't have enough perspective on each other's personality needs. You will find that he infuriates you with his practicality, passivity, and stubbornness, but you will love him for his receptivity and sensuality and genuine concern for your welfare.

ARIES & GEMINI

The Air of masculine Gemini fans the Fire of masculine Aries to produce a blazingly active combination. This is a magnetic relationship held together by the force of your energies in proximity. As a Cardinal sign, your urge to initiate ideas can act as a focus for the more diffused mentality of the mutable Gemini.

While the initial attraction to you may have been physical, your Gemini lover will appreciate you as a man of stimulating ideas too. You and Gemini are most likely to meet over a sparkling conversation. Your mutual attraction, both physical and mental, will be obvious to you. The difference between you lies in your emotional needs. The relationship you have with a Gemini may ultimately lack enough satisfying emotional dimension for you.

Even though the potential for emotional disillusionment is present, the path to that point of awareness is usually paved with exciting adventures for you and your Gemini. His mental energies complement your sheer physical energy. The combination leads to good sex, good times, and good friendship.

A Gemini loves to experiment, and your Aries instinct is to be a pioneer—in matters both social and sexual. The Gemini flair for the casual, for the impromptu moment, will delight your Arian spirit. You will marvel at the ease with which he gets into the flow of events, people, and ideas. His Mercury ruler keeps him changing while your Mars keeps you charging.

As a couple, you have the potential for an extensive social life. He wants to be on the go even more than you do. You may move your residence, visit friends, take weekend jaunts, and entertain with panache. Your relationship will seem to be held together by the centrifugal force of your whirlwind activities.

Astrologically, Gemini represents your Third House. It is the sign of mental energy, brothers and sisters, short trips, and creative inspiration. As masculine signs, both of you could develop a very fine pal-brother relationship. Friendship is of vital importance to a Gemini, and you are likely to have been friends before you became lovers, and will probably continue your friendship even if the romance should fail to be permanent.

Your Gemini lover has a highly developed sexual imagination and a rich facility for fantasy. An Aries can learn a great deal about being a more interesting lover by going along with his Gemini guy's fantasies.

Aries and Gemini have good potential as a successful and dynamic duo, but there are dangers you should know about.

Your high energy levels and your well-matched spirits of adventure can easily lead to overextension. Both of you may find yourselves committed to more than you can accomplish, especially where money is involved. You are both free spenders, and your love affair could founder from an extravagant life-style.

The major difference between you lies in your emotional natures. As an Arian, you are more emotional than he because you are more ego-oriented. Your Gemini lover may get so involved with the velocity of events that he won't pay enough attention to your need for reassurance. This lack of sympathy will stem from his comparative lack of emotionalism. Gemini is intense, but it is mental rather than spiritual intensity. He is sexy rather than passionate. At times he may seem cool and rational when it comes to sex and lovers.

Because you are friends, he will be true to you as a friend. But as a lover, you are dealing with a spirit that is even more promiscuous than yours. Your natural jealous streak will short-circuit this affair unless you are willing to accept his wandering ways. This particular aspect of the Aries–Gemini combination makes it more likely that you two will have an exciting relationship and be occasional lovers, rather than a long-term couple. After a while on the Gemini–Aries merry-go-round you may lose your Aries Fire exuberance. Your energies will be scattered, leaving you feeling tired and unsatisfied.

Gemini's duality is expressed through his ability to turn his interest on and off, thriving on the energy as if it were alternating current. Gemini can be both conventional and eccentric, and while you are attracted to the unusual aspects of his personality, you may not find the rich emotional life that you crave.

Your excess of energy will accumulate tension that results in lengthy argument; however, an Aries will accept vehement differences of opinion from a Gemini without losing his temper. And if you are really involved with your Gemini, you will find these differences of opinion stimulating rather than alienating. You should attempt to reach an understanding early in your partnership. Go along with Gemini's desire for open friendship and decide that you can agree to disagree without spoiling your love for each other.

ARIES & CANCER

This combination mixes Fire with Water, elements not generally known for their compatibility. Your daring Arian spirit will not likely complement Cancerian caution. Cancer may be attracted to you physically, but the prospects for a mutually satisfying love affair are remote, even though you two have this common karmic lesson to learn: Love comes to loving men. The Crab and the Ram also share a common need for affection without fear of rejection.

And yet the Ram is really out of his element on the shore of Lunar sensitivity, whereas the Crab darts between the tidal moods. If you first met during one of his up moods, there was probably an instant sexual attraction. He is as ready and eager for sex as you, though he is not as overt about it. A Cancer will expect the other man to be the aggressor, but he may turn the tables on you once you're in bed.

Your most compatible traits are your desire for success and your bravery. Neither trait is usually connected with a satisfying romance. Another propensity you both have is romantic wanderlust. While you tend to be very open about your urges to seek experiences outside the relationship, Cancer is more likely to be deceptive about it.

As Cardinal signs of the zodiac, you are both leaders and look for the limelight. You can inspire him to be more self-confident and daring. Perhaps you can learn from him the value of being more spiritually relaxed and involved with long-range planning. A Cancer buddy may teach you the value of caution. He will show you depths of sensitivity and swings of mood that defy your powers of comprehension. He doesn't necessarily want you to understand or sympathize, as long as you are willing to be affectionate and reassuring. If you want this love to last, you can try to use your natural exuberance and good humor to lift him out of his moods. You can tease and cuddle him. You can even tickle him—but never laugh at him.

Sexually he can be very exciting. A Cancer man thrives on affection, and he responds with an impressive display of passion. You can be as sexually demanding as you dare with him, as long as you are extremely affectionate. He is a champion at foreplay and can keep you on the edge of orgasmic combustion for longer than the usual Aries can stand it. If he is willing to submit to your aggressive sexual instincts, it will only be in return for a deep feeling of protective affection from you. While he enjoys sex for the thrill of orgasm, he also sees it as a covenant of affection. As his lover, you must be willing to make your Cancer less fearful of life's ups and downs.

While you thrive on life as a roller coaster, Cancer wants the stability of the tunnel of love. He isn't comfortable with extremes, which is why his own emotional diversity causes him anguish. You may further his insecurities because you are the type who can force conflict into a placid relationship just because you want some action. In his eyes you don't have enough access to your emotions. You may not be very tuned in to his moods, nor very tolerant of them. A Cancer man may be an exciting sex partner, but you might find him to be too worrisome, too indirect, and too subtle for you.

Aries and Cancer share a common need for emotional security from their love lives and sexual relationships. At the same time you both find it difficult to provide security for others—and ultimately for each other. Cancer is a receptive—or feminine—sign, and he has a desire to hold on to things, situations, and people. He is likely to take your relationship more seriously than you do. He is so sensitive that you are bound to hurt him. Yet it would be rare for him to leave you unless he felt totally shunned. You will have to be the one who takes the initiative in ending the affair.

If you can keep your encounters with Cancers on a social plane, you can have some thrilling experiences. You will both have to be free, however, to find emotional and ego reinforcement from more compatible signs of the zodiac.

ARIES & LEO

Man to man, this combination of masculine Fire signs can only be described as "hot stuff"! The noble Lion of Leo has the broad vision that can make constructive use of your Arian energies. As lovers, the Lion and the Ram are capable of providing each other with the fundamental ego support that you have been seeking. Leo's ruler, the Sun, brings out the best in you. You will be stimulated to be creative, to excel, to please. If you ever give yourself completely to another man, he will probably be a Leo.

A Leo lover will admire your aggressive nature, yet he will be able to encourage your natural charm, as a balance to your more impulsive attitudes. At your initial meeting he will bring out your feelings of romance, instead of your lust for pursuit and conquest. Your masculinity can be matched easily by a Leo in his prime. Aries will usually be willing to acknowledge that Leo is the King of the Zodiac. You feel secure enough to relax your macho instincts and release some of your latent receptive feelings.

As Fire-sign buddies, an instinctive trust already exists between you. You are willing to let him see your vulnerability, and Leo will respond warmly. His vanity may even be humbled by your trust and faith. You are likely to be inspirational to him, energizing his talents and thus earning his admiration.

When Aries and Leo get together as sex partners, Arian passion plus Leonine affection equal a sex life that is dynamic, theatrical, active, and open to experimentation. He will want to assume a dominant role, and you will be intrigued by your willingness to submit to him. The more you flatter, praise, and extol his prowess in bed, the more you will incite him to ever greater heights of sexual pleasure. To keep him at his best, you must tell him how much you love him and why. He will require these assurances from you because he values the adoration of his lover above that of anyone else. It's Prince Aries and King Leo fulfilling each other's egos through their sex drives.

This Mars–Sun attraction can also signify a very exciting social life. Together you are bound for good times—even grand times, if you can afford it. Aries and Leo both enjoy lavish entertainment and the adulation of crowds. Leos tend to be frugal when it comes to necessities, but they are extravagant with luxuries. You are both fond of giving and receiving presents. Your parties will be legendary.

You find Leos naturally attractive because you are both Fire signs and have a sympathetic trine relationship within the zodiac. If you continually stroke his ego, he will become condescending, confusing your open admiration of his noble qualities with an admission of your inferiority. The result will be a quarrel in which you attempt to assert your refusal to be taken for granted. Arguments between Aries and Leo will be intense, followed by passionate sex and ultimate forgiveness. You will be able to tell when the climate of affection is clouding over. It is usually caused by lack of attention. If either of you feels ignored by the other, you become very demanding about small issues and unimportant matters.

A Leo lover will provoke your anger and then he will act hurt. If he feels neglected, he will try to arouse your jealousy and yet he will feel guilty about flirting. Your temper display will dissolve his insecurity and absolve his guilt feelings at the same time. On the other hand, if he should discover you being indiscreet in public, he will take it as a personal humiliation. A confrontation will follow—once you are home. Leos are very conscious of public relations and seek to pick the right time and place for moves, which is consistent with the Leo image. A Leo man will find it very hard to handle your more impulsive and impatient outbursts.

Don't be jealous if you find that he has a collection of mementos from a former lover or two. Leos are sentimental, and his attachment to these things is romantic but not personal. He is memorializing the feeling of being loved rather than idolizing his old lover. Leos like to be monogamous. If you should find him in someone else's arms, the affair between you is probably over and he is shopping for a new lover.

If you can muster your Aries bravado and stand up to his ego when it is petty and demanding, as well as admire him openly when he is generous of spirit, you may find an ideal love affair in this combination.

ARIES & VIRGO

Virgo men are under the influence of Mercury in a feminine Earth sign. He will have to be a very special guy to be receptive to your aggressive Mars personality. Sexually you two come from different worlds. Aries associates sex with the body and the personality, but Virgo tends to look upon sex as lack of control. The unifying contradiction in this combination is that you are both idealists, searching for your vision of beauty and truth in sexual attraction.

Virgo is the sign of service, and a devoted Aries can learn the meaning of selflessness from him. You generously assist friends in need and expect thanks and acknowledgment in return. The feeling of earned gratitude is important to your ego. Virgo will be just as eager to help others, but he does not really expect thanks. He is a little too cynical and critical of his friends, even though he does not hesitate to give his time and talents.

An association with a Virgo will have to make you more open to analytical advice and intellectual criticism if it is going to last. You can counter some of his negative attitudes by reminding him that perfection does not equal happiness.

Virgo is the sign of the Virgin, representing perfection and purity. Your Virgo lover won't be a virgin, but he is a bit of a puritan in his sex life. He cannot abandon himself to love the way you can. You can use your Aries drive to sublimate your ego through stimulating sexual activity, but Virgo has a difficult time suspending his critical faculties, even in bed.

If you are currently involved with a Virgo man, he may well be older than you, since it makes him feel more secure to associate with those who seem socially or sexually less experienced than he. He wants his criticism and analyses to be accepted without challenge, and he gravitates to those men he feels will be receptive.

Intellectually a Virgo will appreciate you for your honesty, frankness, and innocence, as well as for your refusal to accept defeat or pessimism. By the same token, he will not be thrilled if you express your sexual demands with the same forceful strength. Your sexual appetite is something that he will want to control, but he can only do that by giving you real satisfaction. He may let you take the lead, but he may not follow through. Too much reticence in bed will smother your passion and arouse your urge to wander.

If you two can give each other positive reinforcement in other ways, he won't be intolerant of your desires. If he feels love for you, he can love you in a very pure and ideal way, with no strings attached and no need for you to prove yourself to him continually. What he may not understand is that you like the challenge of a lover who demands proof of your affection and passion.

And a Virgo's criticism will arouse your Arian temper. You may begin to resent his detachment and demand that he give you more positive attention. What you want is more passion, more madness, more abandon than Virgo can supply. Though he may be a perfectly good sex partner, you want a lover who is also affectionate and physical and reassuring on a moment-to-moment basis. The force of your extroversion and impulsiveness may make him feel inadequate. The result will be that you will feel emotionally immature as a response to his lack of enthusiasm.

On the positive side, you may find yourselves confiding secrets to each other, things you would never tell anyone else. If you can share a trust in each other, then you see values in your union that can go beyond the idiosyncrasies of your personalities. If you are involved in a business together, it can be a very trusting and mutually beneficial relationship, even though he is usually not very much better at managing money than you are. Aries' energy and Virgo's practicality can mean excellent income-producing projects. He can help you organize your impulses toward solid achievements. You may be able to free his spirit sexually if the other elements of his life seem secure to him, but his attitudes about sex are still more intellectual than emotional.

Aries and Virgo are most compatible if Virgo has a Fire sign as his ascendant.

ARIES & LIBRA

You will find yourself at home in the arms of a Libra, another masculine and Cardinal sign. He is your complementary opposite in the zodiac, directly across the Wheel of Life, ruled by Venus, the natural mate of Mars. Just as

Aries represents the force of the ego, Libra—the Balance—represents the spirit that allows two egos to interact as a successful relationship.

Your Libra lover is endowed with all of the refinements and nuance implied by the Balance in matters of taste and judgment. He may earn his living at almost anything, but he is very conscious of the aesthetic environment and his ability to enhance it.

Aside from his obvious good taste, you are attracted to his friendliness and kindness. You admire his fair and logical habits of mind and wish that you could acquire some of the same traits. But you can become agitated and impatient with Libra's inability to make decisions. The lesson you can learn from him is to evaluate before acting. If he was the one who first approached you when you met, it was only after having observed you for some time, deciding on your apparent merits and responding to your obvious availability. If you were the initiator, it was because you like the way he looked and followed your impulses to see if he would respond.

Your physical attraction to each other could lead to exciting sexual experiences. Mars and Venus are born lovers. They are the twin symbols of physical love. With masculine Libra you have found another man who enjoys sex in the same way that you do: hot and heavy, yet lighthearted. You are joined in your mutual appreciation of beautiful sex with beautiful men. Libra's love of beauty keeps him on the alert for love, yet his sense of balance allows him to handle his sex life without losing his cool.

A Libra lover can give you a better sense of balance about your own personality. Since he is conscious of your public image, he can help you to see yourself as others see you. If he wants to encourage you to clean up your act, let him have his way. A Libra will certainly know how to package your best features. At the same time he will respect your individuality and your need for freedom. A Libra man knows how to treat his Aries lover with tact and affection, thereby avoiding your Mars temper. He can even teach you how to slow down your impulses and control your drives enough to savor them.

In this combination you are the one with the most energy. Venus is basically indolent, and Librans would prefer not to have to act on matters. He can become a vacillating person who winds up languishing in emotional lethargy. You can use your Mars energy to rev him up, to get him moving, and to act on his ideas. An Aries partner can always advance the career or image of his Libra mate by encouraging him to make the most of his talents. You will have to remember that he doesn't have your energy level. He likes a leisurely pace and tires more easily than you. Even with your dynamic assistance, he still needs regular rest to maintain an active schedule. Don't lose what little patience you possess and accuse him of laziness.

Libra is a romantic. Despite his easygoing attitude, he is really looking for a knight in shining armor. An attractive Aries will usually fill the bill for Libra's well-tuned sensibilities. Like you, he needs reassurance through affection. Tell each other often how much you mean to each other. You can be sure he will delight in your surprise gifts, and he will be even more touched if he knows you spent more than you really could afford. Luxury-loving Libra will never reject extravagance as a token of affection. He will see your impetuous nature in a romantic light. Your natural lusts make him feel sexy, and he enjoys being easily aroused. The more elegant the surroundings, the more ardent his sexual response. If you really want to impress him, take him away for a dirty weekend at the most luxurious hotel in the city.

An Aries–Libra match can be a mutually satisfying experience, with good indications for two-way support. Despite his roving inclinations, Libra can be quite dedicated to living as a couple with another loving man. He trusts his sense of balance, his taste, and his aesthetic standards to help him find his ideal partner. If you can learn to be patient with his indecisiveness, you will find many rewards in your love affair with a Libra.

ARIES & SCORPIO

Scorpio is known as the sign of sex, and Aries recognizes it immediately. These two signs have the potential to unite in some wildly active encounters. If you are involved with a Scorpio, it will have a much more profound effect upon you than upon him. Scorpio is a feminine sign, ruled by masculine Pluto.

It means that karmically he is very heavy and intense compared to the youthful spirit of your ruling Mars. Scorpio is the Scorpion, but he is also symbolized by the combination of the Snake and the Eagle. He has the power to hypnotize you like the serpent in the garden and to carry you to great heights like the mighty eagle. The Scorpion, the Snake, and the Eagle are very deeply involved with the mysteries of sex, death, and transformation. Emotionally this Water-sign lover can get you in way over your head.

Through their innate sexuality, Scorpios are among the great lovers of the zodiac. Even straight guys find them appealing (and disturbing). Your jealous nature is not very compatible with a Scorpio's need for sexual sensation. Your own sex drives are so simple compared to his that you may become a docile lamb, fascinated by your overwhelming attraction to him. Your Scorpio lover has a very strong will, and you may find yourself sexually bound to him by ties you do not understand but also feel powerless to dissolve.

If you are looking for kinky sex, you have come to the right place with a Scorpio. You will find that he is a sensation freak, relishing new sensual experiences. In turn, he brings out your hidden desires, which keep you spellbound and highly aroused. If you have ever had fantasies about leather and love, this guy may well be your dream come true. If you are a relatively inexperienced Aries, you can learn a great deal about the varieties of sexual expression from a Scorpio. He's tried just about everything at least once!

As long as you satisfy him sexually, he will be faithful to you, but he is so attractive to others that your jealousy is bound to be aroused. Don't try to boss him around or bully him. He simply won't stand for it. Your Arian personality assets in this relationship are your open desire to be liked, your uncomplicated and generous instincts, and your lack of deception. A Scorpio lover will feel that he can truly relax with you, and you should encourage him to let down his guard and be less secretive. He tends to keep a very tight rein on his emotions, and he will expect you to keep your aggressive streak in check.

A Scorpio lover will demand a lot more tolerance and patience from an Aries man than you are usually willing to put into any relationship. If you want it to last, if it's really love, you will be willing to sacrifice your independence to the force of his stronger will.

Your Scorpio prince has old General Pluto as his ruling planet, endowing him with stealth, guile, and cleverness in personal affairs. If your Scorpio man is untrue to you, you may never know it. Your planetary champion, Mars, is brash and bold in fending off attacks to your ego, but he is no match for Pluto. The basic message is that Aries may not be karmically experienced enough to keep a Scorpio lover in a mutually supportive relationship. In your naïve way, you may get in much deeper than you can imagine.

The combination of Aries and Scorpio leads to an all-or-nothing situation, an experience that you will both remember for a long time. As a long-term affair, the pitfalls are too great for your innocent Arian desires. When it begins to go bad, cut it off immediately and don't look back. Otherwise the pain of separation will be even worse than the trauma of being together. If he should feel that you have wronged him, he will never forgive you; but if he feels that you shared love together, he will never forget you, either.

ARIES & SAGITTARIUS

You will find that there is a natural and mutual attraction between you and Sagittarius, the Archer. Like you, he is a masculine Fire sign and enjoys the excitement of a challenging partner. His ruling planet is easygoing Jupiter. In combination with your Mars energy, the planetary indications are for a hot coupling. Aries and Sagittarius may develop a fine relationship based upon your sexual experiences together, but in a long-term relationship you may become disillusioned as deep differences in your personalities are revealed.

But the beginning may be glorious, adventuresome, and stupendous! You and Sagittarius are likely to find many things in common, especially your sex drive. Your shared enthusiasm will be expressed in spontaneous affection for each other. This can be a very good psychological experience, with few clashes of personality. Your Sagittarian man is less ego-oriented than you; he won't get emotionally involved in your ego games or ego claims. Neither of you is capable of sustained anger, because it cramps your natural styles. You and your Sagittarius lover are too interested in good times to have an emotionally demanding relationship. You both want love to be lighthearted rather than heavy-handed.

Arians and Sagittarians share the same attitudes about partnerships: You want them to be open, free, fun-loving, and independent. You are both drawn to sexual adventures but are able to be honest about your individual needs. Maintaining open and frank communication will mean that neither hurt nor anger will have an opportunity to fester. Jupiter has gifted him with a degree of self-confidence and a philosophical outlook that is capable of blunting the thrust of your Mars aggressiveness. Disputes between you will not be emotionally wounding, since there will be too many good things happening for you to dwell on your differences.

The aura of excitement that surrounds an Aries–Sagittarius pair is a combination of your energy and his gambling spirit. If you want to travel, a Sagittarius makes a wild and crazy companion, whether you decide to hitchhike or take the Concorde.

Speaking of travel, a Sagittarius likes to roam a bit on his own. His wanderings will summon all your powers of tolerance (usually not abundant in Aries), because if you display jealousy and suspicion, he will lie to you and further invite your anger. When Aries' uncontrollable jealousy clashes with Sagittarius' uncontrollable wandering, it could be the end of your love affair. A Sagittarian will not deliberately deceive you or himself about love. He will not easily commit himself to a serious relationship unless he is honestly ready to settle down. You may well come to feel that any long-term relationship between you would not be to your mutual advantage.

Jupiter is the planetary symbol for the principle of expansion, but with Mars as a companion, the situation could become reckless. He will tend to encourage your plans and ideas, but that same encouragement may cause you to act too quickly and on too grand a scale to be successful. A Sagittarian will often share your extravagant streak and innocent selfishness. The result can be a partnership in which you get very wrapped up in yourselves rather than in each other. As personalities, you may become mirrors of each other's traits and attitudes, rather than windows to each other's souls. For a while the pleasure of his company, of your compatibility, may cause you to confuse parallel play with a mutually supportive love.

Every Arian has a similar mission or path toward fulfillment in the scene of the zodiac. Patience, tolerance, and selflessness are the qualities you need to acquire and experience for personality growth. While a Sagittarian does reinforce your good points, he doesn't have enough of a modifying effect on your weaknesses. You are bound to have many good times with him as your companion and lover, but your bouts of excess will leave you exhausted and unsatisfied. If you are looking for true love, Aries, it should be in a relationship that allows you to develop more selfless behavior. If you have a Sagittarian lover in mind and are willing to devote your energies to becoming less selfish, you two may combine in one of the best pairings in the zodiac.

ARIES & CAPRICORN

The Ram of Aries finds that his Fire-sign instincts and energies become sublimated by the preponderance of the Capricorn Mountain Goat. While you are off in the meadows of experience, he is relentless in his ascent up the mountain of ambition. His planetary ruler is Saturn, and the lesson he learns from the Lord of the Rings is that frivolity does not lead to success. While you may crave success because it means recognition, a Capricorn works toward his goal because he desires security as the substance of happiness. His drive to succeed is as strong as his will to survive. Your charming and congenial Arian nature may give a Capricorn man something to cherish beyond his concern for advancement.

The key word here is *cherish*, rather than anything more passionate or sensual. As lovers, you are not likely to send comets shooting across the skies. In fact, an Aries–Capricorn relationship is usually better as a business relationship than as a love match. You two are joined through your shared ambition and spirit of idealism rather than by sexual attraction.

If you are willing to be receptive, a Capricorn can teach you about practical approaches to your goals. In return, your playfulness and wit can make him laugh more often. He has a fine sense of humor, but he tends to take things too seriously, including sex. A Capricorn likes to appear rather straight and dignified, but he has more unconventional desires that you can help explore. He enjoys earthy and unrestrained sex as a release for his usual conservatism, but he may feel too inhibited to express his secret desires. Capricorns are often very tender lovers and will respond handsomely if you just get in there and butt away at his libido!

A Capricorn lover or partner can help you to mature by having a calming, supportive effect upon you. You will sincerely believe that he has your best interests at heart in managing your affairs. He would be a rare and maladjusted Capricorn if he were to disappoint you in that respect. Through his influence, you take more care when planning projects instead of rushing headlong into things.

Astrologically, Capricorn represents your Tenth House, accenting career, ambition, and goals. A Capricorn can activate your sense of responsibility toward your goals in life. You can come to value caution and prudence as virtues. Even though you may not yet have learned how to practice these virtues, you may be impressed by how well your Capricorn can use them to his advantage.

If you like older men, a Capricorn lover may be the man you are looking for. Capricorns seem to shine in their later years, getting better and better as they get older. In many cases they also get sexier, because the security of success in middle age has left them feeling free enough to relax their inhibitions. You can liven up his sex life with your youthful Arian enthusiasm. The potential exists for a strong union between Aries and Capricorn. You can provide the action and he can supply the depth.

On the other hand, the average Mountain Goat is awfully serious for the normally frisky Ram. You may be impressed at first by his image as the strong, silent type, but that won't be enough to maintain your interest for very long. If you are a typical Aries, you will see a challenge in attempting to penetrate his cool exterior. You may well be successful in your mission, but the rewards for your efforts may not be as great as you imagine. Most Capricorns operate at a much lower emotional level than you do. His restrained attitudes may make you feel silly, trivial, and foolish when you compare yourself to him. Such comparisons will wound your ego, even though the hurt will be self-inflicted.

Socially, Capricorns tend to be much more reticent than Arians. He won't like any displays of public affection, and the implied challenge will force you to insist that he march arm in arm with you in the local Liberation Day parade. As a compromise, he will probably suggest sending a check to a gay-activist organization in your area. You will want him to do both, but if you push him to go against his natural conservative posture, he may do neither.

In the end you may justifiably feel that he is more devoted to his career, his ambitions, and his family than to you. If you're not made to feel like the number-one object of his affections, you won't want to remain involved with him for very long. There is a warm and sexy side to every Capricorn, but it is not often revealed for an Aries to enjoy.

ARIES & AQUARIUS

Aries the Ram and Aquarius the Water-bearer will manage to be friends as well as lovers, if not during your initial encounter, at least afterward. You share your masculine, positive, and optimistic attitudes, feeling a common attraction. Aries usually recognizes the best of himself in an Aquarius lover. You will find that you both get a thrill out of defying the expectations of conventional society, even within the gay culture. When the fiery masculine aggressiveness of Mars joins up with the masculine Air forces of unpredictable Uranus, it can mean an exciting time with no holds barred!

Despite your tendency to be possessive, you may find yourself attracted to his freedom-loving nature. An Aquarius will usually make it clear that he prefers to live on his own, even if you should become lovers. You may agree to his wishes because his independence makes him more challenging and more interesting. As long as you can restrain your imagination from convincing you that he is leading a double life, you will be willing to love him without becoming jealous. Unfortunately, he likes to circulate with such a wide group of acquaintances that your suspicions are bound to be aroused.

The rapport between Aries and Aquarius will be expressed in a desire to confide in each other. For this reason you may be friends—if not lovers—forever. To a typical Aquarian, friendship is more valuable and personal than sexual involvement. He feels that good friendships are to be treasured above all things.

The average Aquarian man is curious about sex and loves to experiment. Given Aries' pioneering spirit, the two of you could engage in a very enjoyable sex life. In fact, you will have to keep him amused as a sex partner if you want to sustain his interest. Avoid sexual predictability or he will get bored and be out looking for some excitement. With unpredictable Uranus looking over his shoulder, he's liable to find it in the most unusual situations!

Remember that you are governed by physical energies and Aquarius is a mental sign. Even though he may be a very complex personality, he won't match your speedy exuberance. You tend to be a romantic and fling yourself into each encounter, while the typical Aquarian is not as physically demonstrative as you would like and tends to be intellectual in situations and relationships when you would normally be emotional. Since he is unpredictable, you may feel that you never really know where you stand with him. An Aries can easily imagine that there is more to a relationship with an Aquarius than really exists. With an Aquarius lover you may indulge in your potential for self-deception, leading to disillusionment.

The kind of love and ego support you are seeking may not be easy to find with an Aquarius. Astrologically, he represents your Eleventh House of friendship and though your experience with an Aquarius may enable you to broaden your social connections, ultimately it may lack the intense emotional dynamics that you thrive on in your love affairs.

Aquarius thinks before he acts. Sometimes his thought processes seem so complex that he is never able to act with conviction. This element of detachment is a way of cushioning his ego from the insecurities inherent in his Uranian planetary rulership. He may allow his intellectual attentions to become so diffuse that you can't feel any of the affectionate reassurances that you need from a lover. A long-lasting affair will be difficult to sustain, but the attraction and trust is there for a very fine friendship with an interesting sexual dimension.

ARIES & PISCES

As the twelfth sign of the zodiac, the Fishes of Pisces represent the repository of all of the sensitivity of the preceding eleven signs, including yours. Aries is the first most basic energy force, and Pisces is the last and the most evolved. Technically, the Ram is way out of his depth in the Water sign of Pisces. And yet there is a certain level of fascination that you share with each other as neighbors on the Wheel of Life, which can make for a rewarding, though complex, relationship. You both can share your deep-seated ideal of an intense and purifying sexual experience.

The feminine, receptive nature characterized in Pisces will make him impressed by your Arian masculinity and aggressiveness, as long as you don't get too carried away in your macho role. Pisces is willing to be swept away by your energies and impulses. Your ego benefits from the feeling of importance you get from his admiration. He implicitly challenges you to be your utmost self. A Pisces man will allow an Aries lover to play out all of his romantic fantasies, and you will both relish it.

Though Arians are normally more compatible with the other masculine signs of the zodiac, Pisceans are the one feminine, passive sign with which an Arian man will feel comfortable. A Pisces man will enjoy his Arian partner assuming a dominant role because he turns his receptive inclinations into effective sexual fantasies. You will be turned on, in and out of bed, by the way he looks up to you for your supposed strength.

If Aries represents pure ego, then Pisces is the incarnation of pure humility. The connection between the two apparent opposites is sex. You both can use your sexual experiences as keys to the deepest parts of your personalities. You are a very open and nondeceptive person, but Pisces is the sign over your Twelfth House—secrets and things hidden from ordinary perception. He may symbolize something hidden from you or within you, probably the humility and selflessness that you need to balance your psyche. You and your Pisces lover may share your innermost secrets.

This combination of signs can provide you with positive kinds of ego support and gratification. He will be willing to let you be the center of attraction and he won't be jealous that other men find you attractive. You have the potential to complement each other without compromising or disrupting your individual attitudes toward life. From him you can learn that there is virtue in taking the path of least resistance, the opposite of your usual Ramlike instincts. From you he can learn the value of direct action. He can be your anchor and you can be his sail.

On the negative side, a Pisces won't really understand your faults. He can become so involved with your fantasy persona as a sex partner that he will become carried away by the force of events. He will let you run with the ball even though you are acting irresponsibly. In response, you may give in to your worst impulses and bully him, allowing his natural passivity to encourage your most overbearing and selfish attitudes. His admiration for your masculine qualities may involve a great deal of self-deception on his part, and he'll let you get carried away by your own ego image. In his soul Pisces knows that the path to self-actualization comes through letting go, but letting Aries have his way all the time is like speeding downhill without brakes!

The potential is here for a real master-slave relationship. His humble nature can stimulate your least attractive domineering urges. At the same time you feel a need to be challenged. That need is the dynamo that keeps your energies high. Without it you can fall into pattern behavior and lose interest.

You will find that he is much more sensitive than you are to the anxieties of everyday life. A Pisces man can be brought to tears for reasons you find impossible to fathom. You must be willing to allow him time on his own to recharge his more delicate psychic batteries. He lacks your emotional energy, and you mustn't push him into confrontations with you or with himself. Pisces is a gentle soul, and if you can learn to treat him gently, you can open up whole new areas of your own consciousness as a loving partner.

LOVING YOUR ARIES MAN

If you want to find an Aries man, you are very likely to run into him at sporting events, since he exults in the spirit of competition. You may also find him anywhere there is a masculine atmosphere. Aries is a casual type and prefers informal settings that allow him to feel comfortable and secure.

The typical Arian fantasy can be simply described as "basic butch." He has always wanted to make it with a cowboy or a sailor or a steelworker because these stereotypes complement his own masculine image and ideals. If you can stimulate any of these macho-man looks, you can always attract an Aries.

Aside from costume codes, you can usually interest an Aries through a direct, up-front approach. The correct type of eye contact is often enough to encourage an Aries to approach you. Don't be shy if he doesn't respond right away. The Kinsey Report on homosexuality reveals that the one fear gay men have most in common in initiating sexual encounters is that they won't know what to say! Don't worry about Aries in this respect. He is a good conversationalist, especially if you are willing to discuss a topic in which you share a mutual interest—him. Let him talk about his interests, be prepared to flatter him, and you will quickly find the way to his heart.

Aries men are tuned in to their own sexual wavelength and rely on their desires. He is a very sexy man! Arians expect sex to be a total physical release, sometimes to the point of noninvolvement in your pleasure. He can naïvely assume that you must be enjoying him as much as he is enjoying himself.

An Aries man can be very sweet and boyish in his innocent desire to be generous and loving. He knows that he makes mistakes, but they are errors of impulse and exuberance. He is rarely scheming or deceptive and is earnest in his desire to be liked and appreciated. He will always respond positively if you praise him and assure him of his worth. It is within his nature to be aggressive and overbearing, but it is because he is insecure, not because he is power-hungry. Though he is susceptible to flattery, you should not give in to pampering him. An Aries will like it if you are willing to stand up for yourself and present him with a bit of a challenge. But don't ever try to convince him that he is totally wrong or that he has dishonest motives for his actions. Such imputations will leave him hurt and very angry!

Under his macho exterior the Aries man is longing for an ideal romantic love. This charging Ram can become a docile lamb under the influence of a warmhearted lover who will protect him from the pressures of the outside world. Arians have such abundant energy that they are prone to nervous exhaustion. He needs a lover who can help him to cool out.

The typical Arian man is controlled by his passions. Sex is integral to his happiness and necessary for his ego, but he needs the certainty of freedom in a relationship because he values his independence. If you are in love with an Aries man, you may have to reconcile yourself to allowing him to follow his romantic urges.

Conversely, paradoxically, and selfishly, he can be a jealous and demanding lover. An Aries may become childlike, even infantile, in his demands on your time and your independence. His worst displays are often signs that he is feeling neglected. He needs much attention and reassurance that he is the number-one man in your life and that you truly love him. An Arian may blow hot and cold, driving you to absolute distraction with his ego games. At some point he may doubt your love because you don't show him enough obvious affection, yet he may turn around and become inconsiderate of your needs because he feels secure enough to take you for granted.

He wants you to hold him in high esteem, to acknowledge him as the very best. Extravagant Aries delights in pleasing you with surprises and presents. In turn, he loves to be surprised with symbols of your affection for him. Don't ever forget his birthday!

Arians love the out-of-doors, even though they are very much city people. Hiking is a favorite outdoor activity because it allows for sex al fresco, an Aries fantasy favorite. But if you take a long vacation, don't go off with him to some remote rural retreat, no matter how romantic it may seem. He is a city boy and will shortly become restless for the bright lights and busy nights.

Boredom is lethal to an Aries, and he will not hesitate to look for greener pastures and more exciting meadows if your relationship seems to be getting bogged down. Keep it light-hearted. Arians believe in miracles and the flash of inspiration. If you keep him guessing, active, challenged, and aroused, you will find yourself in the midst of a first-class love affair. As you can probably tell, an Aries lover is not going to be very stable, but he will be exciting, exasperating, and very sexy!

TAURUS
April 21–May 20

Symbol: The Bull
Ruling Planet: Venus
Color: Green
Metal: Copper
Natural House Rulership: Second House, the house
of money and possessions
Second House Traits: Desire for material security
and love of comfort
Motto: "I have"
Nature: Fixed sign (organizer)
Element: Earth sign (material)
Qualities: Strong values, conservative, sensual
Capacities: Management of creative projects
Personality Key Words: Practical, sensuous, and
possessive

MAXIMIZING YOUR
TAURUS POTENTIAL

Taurus combines an obviously masculine image of the Bull with the indisputably feminine archetype of Venus. With the softness of the Goddess of Love as your guiding spirit, the aggressive instincts of the Bull are truly well domesticated. Just as Zeus appeared as a white bull to woo Europa, you have the power to attract others with your stability, strength, and gentle charms. Your strength comes not from the brute power of the Bull but from the receptive capacities of Venus when integrating sensation and stimulation into creative patterns.

You are the first Earth sign, born with a growing awareness of the material nature of the world. With Venus as your guiding star, you find yourself given to the pleasures of this world, but in a practical, earthbound way. Good food, comfortable surroundings, stable relationships, and sensuous sex are the cornerstones of your desire.

Taurus is also a Fixed sign, indicating that you tend to stand firm and solid in your goals and beliefs. You much prefer the comfort of predictable routine to the uncertainty of surprise and change. Your emotional stability is in direct proportion to the stability of your environment. For this reason many Taureans have the long-range dream of a cozy house in the country, someplace where you can be surrounded by treasured possessions, cuddled in the arms of a longtime lover.

As a Taurus, once you have reached a level of maturity in which your goals become defined, you are endowed with the patience and endurance to see things through to their successful completion. Of course, the ultimate extension of determination is stubbornness. It can be the quality that turns your strength into weakness. Though you are not impulsive, once you have committed yourself to a project, you are definitely committed and nothing can get you to stop. This stubborn streak is an aspect of your possessiveness. Taureans need to "possess" those people, ideas, and things that are held to be worthy and important. It is difficult for you to part with anyone or anything that you have come to cherish.

As a consequence of your innate Taurean conservatism, you hope to find a consistent lover who will "settle" the question of sex and companionship, once and for all. Even though you may have been disappointed in the past by short-lived affairs, you believe in a lasting and permanent love relationship as a practical necessity rather than a romantic ideal.

Your practical, down-to-earth desires for a lover who will serve your physical and emotional needs tend to make you a little short on passion, but Taureans more than compensate with consistent and sincere devotion toward their partners. Your fantasies are sensual and languidly erotic rather than pornographic. You would rather be snuggled up with your Man of Life on a down-filled sofa, basking in the embers of the fireplace, than having wild, abandoned sex with some beautiful stranger in an exotic situation.

Like Ferdinand the Bull, you prefer the creature comforts of your own meadow, more than the tension and passion of the arena. You find nightlife too superficial and chaotic for the kind of life-style you hope to establish. Taureans are more likely to meet compatible lovers through business or in social and cultural gatherings involving music, the visual arts, or gourmet delights—all the Venus-oriented activities associated with the pleasures of good company.

Taureans are rarely total strangers to the world of Earthy sex, but your ultimate goal is a stable relationship in which your sex life is an integral factor in your feelings of fulfillment. No simple quest in these mad times, Taurus, though one you have the power to pursue through your persistent devotion to your ideals.

Venus, in her Earthy mode, has endowed you with an animal magnetism that is the reactor core of your sex appeal. Other men, even straight men, find you physically attractive. Women appreciate your charm and grace and find you very attractive because they sense your sympathetic traits. You are likely to be seen as a warm personality rather than a "hot" man. Your stability, sincerity, and sense of humor are magnetic qualities that will attract the kind of person you are looking for to share your life.

Taureans have strong paternal instincts. You see yourself as a good provider, and you're generous, though not extravagant, with your lovers. You pride yourself on the practical nature of your life-style and expect your lover to adopt your patterns. Often you will find a younger lover particularly satisfying. You will enjoy initiating him into the comforts of "the good life." In return, you expect him to appreciate your solid virtues and provide you with physically satisfying and emotionally undemanding sex. But your enjoyment of sex will be greatly enhanced by a lover who will gently initiate you to new varieties of pleasure, making your bond of intimacy stronger than ever.

On the day-to-day side of things, you are very conscious of money and moneymaking, and you prefer saving to spending, unless it's for a practical purpose. Taureans are often successes in any field of creative management or finance. You have a tendency to channel your excess sexual drives into your career, but you should take care to avoid becoming "married" to your work.

Your love relationship can lose its affectional basis if your drive for success leads you to neglecting your lover. The influence of Venus can make you complacent, allowing you to take your lover for granted. While you are working overtime to provide that rose-covered cottage in the country, you may find that the love you expected to reside in your sylvan retreat has simply melted away.

Though you are normally possessive of your lover, you

won't feel jealousy as long as you believe he is fundamentally committed to you. You won't fear that someone will take him away from you unless he gives you just cause to be suspicious. But if you see the order you have patiently established in your life slipping into emotional chaos and insecurity, you will finally see the red cape and lose your temper. In the heat of your anger you will convince yourself that you would rather live alone and feel secure than to be coupled with uncertainty, instability, and emotional trauma.

You may dust off your recording of "I Will Survive" and show him the door, but your righteous indignation may begin to weaken when you realize that you haven't been able to throw away the flowers he bought last week, even though they have wilted and look terribly untidy. You should remember that materialism, possessiveness, and selfishness are the obstacles that you Taureans must overcome if your spirit is to soar.

Fortunately Taureans are good students who pay close attention to the lessons of experience. You have the magnetic powers of Earthy Venus to bring out the very best in people. You will find that as you expand your emotional consciousness, your personality will continue to grow and blossom as profusely as the roses that twine around the cozy cottage of your dreams.

TAURUS & ARIES

You find yourself physically and mystically drawn to this Fire-sign man in a way that you can't quite explain. Aries the Ram represents matters in your Twelfth House: hidden meanings; unseen causes; and sacrificial service. You see him as glamorous, sexy, and somehow mysterious. Taurus will feel drawn to Aries in subtle ways, feeling both threat-

ened by his impetuous nature and protective of his vulnerability. Despite his bravado, you instinctively sense his
underlying insecurities. As Aries is the sign immediately
preceding Taurus on the Wheel of Karma, you have sympathy for the lessons he must learn in the evolution of his
personality.

Taurus will certainly appreciate the refreshing candor,
honesty, and uncomplicated motivations of the typical Aries
man. His energy, initiative, and imagination are qualities
you find admirable in their nobility and lovable in their egocentric naïveté. His eternal adolescent spirit brings out your
paternal instincts. You enjoy playing the Dutch uncle and
giving wise counsel, but he is likely to anger you when he
doesn't follow your advice.

Aries travels through life on an emotional joyride that you
may come to appreciate, in spite of your more cautious and
conservative outlook. Your Ram buddy can encourage you
to be more adventuresome, more optimistic, and more self-
assured. Unless you are constantly trying to rain on his
parade, he will look up to you as a source of stability, reinforcing your own opinion of your virtues. Aries will get
Ferdinand the Bull out from under the placid shade of the
cork tree and encourage him to gambol in the meadows of
experience. A bit more spontaneity in your life will go a
long way toward making you a warmer and more versatile
personality. Aries has so much energy from his solar ener-
gizers that he can certainly spare some for you to charge
your own psychic batteries.

Just as you can benefit from him showing you the value
of being more optimistic and open to new ideas, you can
influence him to moderate his restless drives into more productive channels. He can teach you how to live in the present, and you can initiate him to the enduring values of the
past through your appreciation of art and culture. Aries can
also use some insight into the importance of the future. As
a Cardinal sign, he is great at initiating ideas, plans, and
schemes, but he often lacks the perseverance and organizational skills to follow them through. You can add your

Taurean practicality to his Arian impulses to create a dynamic partnership in love or in business.

When it comes to playing roles in bed, Aries will normally be the aggressor, and your receptive Venus-ruled sex drive will respond fervently to his Mars-ruled enthusiasm. It seems like he's always primed for sex, and though you are slow to become aroused, he will stimulate your more passionate instincts and increase your potential for physical enjoyment. With an Aries partner you can become a more imaginative lover.

The typical Aries sees sex as a compulsion, but your Taurean inclination is to regard sexual intimacy as a pleasure rather than an overwhelming passion. He can be very satisfied with numerous brief and intense sessions of lovemaking, just as he can exist happily on a diet of fast food. With your gourmet tastes, you prefer sexual encounters to be more languid, sensual, and savored. Obviously you two will have much to give to each other as lovers if you let your partner moderate and exhilarate your expectations.

There is not a great deal of room for compromise between the Ram and the Bull when they are not actively working to be adaptive, mutually supportive, and understanding of each other. Taurus tends to be stubborn and Aries tends to be impetuous. While you are digging in to hold your ground in Earth-sign preparation for trench warfare, Aries will reach for his flamethrower and leap over your fortifications to do what he damn well pleases. You may feel emotionally overwhelmed by his energy, impulsiveness, and minor tantrums. As your Twelfth House influence, Aries can stimulate deep feelings within you that lead to confusion about your emotions and goals. At first you may withdraw, passively counting on your patience to see you through. Finally, what you once saw as naïve courage will appear to be merely foolish and childish obstinacy, and you will erupt with earthquake-like tremors of anger.

A relationship between Aries and Taurus works best if you are part of a larger social or professional group that will allow him the social contacts he needs and provide you with mutual interests outside of your emotional involvement. He needs an active social life and won't be willing to be domesticated by you or for you, unless he feels totally secure in the ego gratification you can provide for him. Without reassurance he will begin to look for solace in other relationships and become untrustworthy.

There is a hidden potential for cruelty to each other in this Fire–Earth combination of impetuous Mars and stubborn Venus. Don't try to smother him with your possessive, stable Earth instincts. Love him for the man he is and appreciate the little boy that is his spirit. You can never bend him by your force of will, but you can nurture the best in Aries by unreservedly demonstrating your love and affection.

TAURUS & TAURUS

Earth sign to Earth sign and man to man, Venus is exalted with such a complementary partner. It's wonderful and comforting to meet someone with a steady job, sensible values, good taste and manners, and a sense of humor. At last you have met a man you can respect, and it can lead to a tender, gentle, and rewarding love affair.

Of course, it won't be love at first sight. Even if it is, you will both want to get to know each other before you become sexual partners. If you're sure it's love, then the Taurean strategy is to proceed with caution. This Taurus–Taurus combination can develop into a loyal and devoted mating with the potential for a sensuous sex life that will be your deepest bond.

When two Taureans discover each other in a loving encounter, they can create a world of their own. Your mutual sensuality and sense of propriety makes for a very private relationship in which your sexual compatibility has the power to smooth any troubled waters. Since you are both possessive by nature, this can be a very strong bonding, and third parties are not a threat to your harmonious patterns. Taureans crave emotional continuity, and you both are willing to blend your desires into a long-term partnership, since the dividends of the investment seem well worth it to your practical instincts.

Taureans share similar attitudes about sexual pleasure as well. You both prefer sex in bed at the end of the day, after a leisurely meal and a relaxing evening. It's the cherry on the sundae, the ice cream on the pie of your mutual affection. Neither of you enjoys being rushed into sex, and you like to linger in its warm glow long after the peak of orgasm. Taureans love the sheer indulgence of sexual appetite, as they do with all other appetites. The two of you have the mutual potential to encourage each other to overindulge in food, acquisitions, or sex. If the image of you and your lover becoming two chubby food junkies, strung out on cherry cheesecake in your overstuffed apartment, doesn't amuse you, then your practical, sensible selves will know when to take a break. Overindulgence is a sign of insecurity for Taurus, and if your buddy is too obviously into second helpings of the charlotte russe and complaining that the cleaners has shrunk his trousers, it's time for the two of you to have a serious talk about what could be making him feel unloved.

There are several possibilities. You are both Fixed signs and easily take each other for granted. You assume that everything is just fine as you settle into your predictable patterns. Your basic conservatism can allow the development of habits that are not emotionally satisfying for either of you, and yet your possessiveness may impel you to go on for years, refusing to admit that your relationship may be a mistake. The only thing Taureans hate more than being wrong is being proved wrong!

Lovers born under the sign of Venus are essentially placid. It makes you easy to get along with, but it can also mask

developing discontent, giving small disagreements an explosive potential. Your stubborn streaks are your biggest
obstacles, since they obscure your ability to see the other
person's point of view. Yet you both pride yourselves on
"being fair."

Your common sense and your love for each other will
allow you to forgive those words spoken in anger and frustration, but they will be difficult to forget. It takes a kind
word and an admission of your emotional vulnerability,
which only he understands, for the two of you to gently retie
the bonds of love that only Taurus can share so deeply with
another Taurus. If you count your lucky stars, Venus will
be there to notarize the balance sheet and seal it with a kiss.

TAURUS & GEMINI

When Fixed-Earth Taurus the Bull meets Mutable-Air Gemini the Twins, it can mean double the fun or double the
trouble. In most cases it depends upon you and your ability
to learn how to loosen up under his ever-changing influences.

Sometimes Gemini will be as inspired as the Morning
Star, other times as melancholy as the Evening Star, but
usually the Twins combine a unique blend of both elements
into a completely different persona. In your Fixed way, you
like to know where you stand—or rather, you know where
you stand: with both feet on the ground. In his Mutable
Mercury way, he doesn't care where you stand, because he
isn't interested in anything that isn't moving. If you want to
be rooted to the spot, he'll let you hold his kite string while
he flies away.

You will be attracted to him for his obvious charms; he's
a clever conversationalist, enthusiastic and optimistic. As

Gemini is the next sign of the zodiac after Taurus, you sense
that you have lessons to learn from him. Your problem may
be that his Airwaves are so jammed with signals that you
may never get the message. It seems like he is always changing channels just as you were beginning to pick up the plot
line. Your frustration leads to mistrust, and you will wonder
if the whole Gemini Air show isn't just a put-on. In that
case you will wisely decide that there is little prospect of a
long-term partnership and save yourself the emotional
trauma of trying to catch your Gemini genie in a bottle.

Even if he is not a very likely candidate for your Man of
Life, there is much you can gain from the Twins' companionship that will make you a better lover, friend, and a more
integrated personality. The influence of his many-faceted
imagination will allow you to rethink some of your Fixed
Earth mental "eternal truths." To Gemini's way of thinking, the only thing that is permanent is change. No Taurus
is going to find that a comforting message, but it is a most
valuable one. You can achieve a sense of freedom and an
elevation of spirit that will assist you in completing your
karmic task: rising above the cross of matter and materialism.

A Gemini lover is not going to get you to renounce your
need for physical pleasures and join an ashram, but he can
get you out of your security-oriented rut. You will have to
learn to appreciate the unexpected instead of dreading it.
Keeping up with Gemini will mean experiencing new levels
of energy and enthusiasm and broadening your outlook.

In return, a Taurus can teach a Gemini to be more practical and less superficial. You will never be able to force the
Twins into a sedentary life-style, but you can encourage him
to appreciate the fact that life has depth as well. The two of
you could strengthen your bond by studying or taking a
course together, which will give you the opportunity to
jointly focus on your mental powers. Your association could
well lead to your mutual financial gain, since Gemini represents your Second House, involving money and posses-

sions. The Twins' ideas and inspirations can lead to success in business when directed by Taurus' organizational skills.

As lovers, your sexual and emotional needs are very different. Your sex drive is much more Earthy and intense than his. Gemini indulges in sex for its fantasy and mental stimulation rather than for his physical and emotional satisfaction. You will resent his apparently casual attitude and lack of passion. As a bed partner, you will find the Twins to be "very, very good when they are good, but when they are bad they are horrid."

As an Air sign, your Gemini guy is more interested in mental stimulation rather than in emotional or material pursuits. His naturally detached attitude will hurt you because you feel more than he does. You will interpret his Mutable nature as a lack of commitment and consideration. Ultimately you will not trust him with your affection. The Twins are too restless for the Bull, and Mercury makes them more flirtatious than Venus is willing to tolerate.

Learn to love your Gemini friend for the exciting and broadening experiences he will bring to you. Like a small boy emptying his pockets after a day of discoveries, he will always be finding diamonds in the dust. If you can see the "diamonds" and overcome your urge to dismiss them as mere pieces of broken glass, then the dizzy Twins may be doing you some good, after all.

TAURUS & CANCER

There is an undeniable attraction between Taurus and Cancer the Crab. Cancer is the Cardinal Water sign, creative and elusive and as moody as the tides. Your Cancer man is ruled by the Moon and it makes him receptive, highly sensitive, and emotionally vulnerable in a way that you will find endearing—and even irresistible. Your sexual interest in him will be stimulated in direct proportion to your perception of his thoughtfulness, quick sense of humor, and sensuality.

Like you, he tends to be a homebody who is at his happiest in pleasing surroundings. Together you can create a haven of emotional security based upon your mutual appreciation of art, music, travel, entertaining, and friendship. Cancer influences your Third House: the areas of family ties, intellect, and education. Your shared powers of perception and communication indicate a strong and enduring friendship that should survive even if you do not become lifelong lovers.

Cancers are usually good cooks, and the two of you will delight in giving dinner parties. Taurus and Cancer tend to equate nourishment with emotional security, and feeding your friends in festive surroundings becomes an act of love and devotion. Since you are both highly motivated by the need for security, money will be very important in your relationship. As a business couple, there is unlimited potential for success. He will have Cardinal-sign-inspired ideas for increasing your earnings, and you have the Earth-sign capabilities to carry them through to completion.

The depth of your caring for each other will certainly extend to your sex life. Your Taurean physical need for sensual pleasure will be fulfilled through his Cancerian need for sex as an emotional release. There is great tenderness here as your warm and protective instincts provide him with the feeling of security that he craves. When the Bull and the Crab fall in love, they play for keeps; you will both be able to satisfy your powerful urges for love and affection.

A common desire for harmony will allow you to compromise in the face of conflict better than many other couples. There is the power to give each other tender understanding and good advice in times of personal crisis. Though you may find him to be overly sensitive and sometimes emotionally evasive, his moods will change quickly with the passage of the Moon. Through your patience and under-

standing, you can learn how to become much more in touch
with your own feelings.

When misunderstandings do occur, the Taurus–Cancer
combination has several positive factors going for it. First
of all, you are friends. Neither of you can bear the idea of
being unkind or unfair to those you love. Underneath all the
brooding and sulking, you both have a marvelous sense of
humor that can provide some much-needed perspective.
Your disagreements can linger and fester because you both
tend to be too shy and too devoted to preserving harmony
to bring differences out into the light of healing examination. Don't let your love be poisoned by the accumulation
of old hurt and disappointments.

Though it happens rarely, when you do fight, it takes a
long time for your wounds to heal. He will be too hurt and
traumatized to apologize, and you will be too stubborn to
say "I'm sorry." In the end, it is much more meaningful
to a Cancer if you declare your unchanging love and affection for him than for you to admit you were wrong or offer
an apology. You will have to learn to be more flexible in
working at this relationship because Cancer will always
sidestep the issues rather than face your anger or disapproval.

Cancer men will be faithful and ardent lovers as you provide for their emotional need for security. Take care that
you don't let your sex life become mechanical or prosaic
and he will provide you with abundant physical affection
and comfort to match your emotional support.

Despite your many accomplishments as men of talent and
recognized achievements, you both crave security and affection. The rulers of your signs, Venus and the Moon, have
combined to bless you both with the power to assuage each
other's fears. If you use these powers to help each other to
become mutually strong instead of mutually dependent, you
will have found the key to happiness in love.

TAURUS & LEO

Fixed Fire-sign Leo is ruled by the Sun and symbolized by
the Lion. This guy really believes that he is the king of the
jungle and expects deference to his royal prerogatives. It's
rarely love at first encounter, since your own Fixed-Earth
outlook finds Leo's regal posturings to be arrogance per-
sonified. Though you will find him physically attractive,
your practical and sensitive instincts can be somehow
offended by his extravagant personality.

When you find yourself fascinated by a Leo, there is definitely the promise of sexual pleasure and a kind of emotional security. Physically the Bull and the Lion can be very
compatible, as the generous impulses of Leo's Sun rulership
warm up your Earth-sign nature. Your sexual experiences
together can be luxuriant, providing a comforting retreat
from the pressures of your active social and business affairs.

A Leo lover will appeal to your sense of values since he
is loyal and generous to his partners. A Taurean will enjoy
basking in his favor and kindness. You are both sexy men,
oriented to sensual pleasures. Under the best of circumstances you will satisfy each other with sexual fulfillment,
emotional security, and the encouragement to succeed.

Sexual activity is essential to the Lion's ego image. If you
want to please him, you will learn to become a lover of
some imagination and style. It is an extravagance you can
well afford, and Leo will be pleased that you are making a
special effort just for him. Your lovemaking will be both
sensuous and intense.

For all his airs and arrogance, your Leo lover is basically
insecure. He needs confirmation of his ego to keep his positive spirit recharged. The Leonine qualities of hope, confidence, and pride can be maintained with compliments and
loving attention. You will have to soft-pedal some of your
possessive traits and allow him to show off in public. Royal

Leo needs the adulation of crowds that he usually receives in social gatherings. Actually you won't mind showing off this charming man in public as long as it's understood that even without a leash, he is your pussycat. If you let Leo have his royal appearances, he will not be unfaithful to you. Honest praise of his virtues and reaffirmations of your love will always keep him coming home to you.

While Taurus is often content to let Leo have the glory, you won't allow him to become overbearing with you. He is driven to dominate any relationship, and you may well find his regal pretensions to be conceited, ostentatious, and trivial. In conflicts the Lion takes a commanding and condescending attitude that will bring out every instinct of the Bull. You will punish him by withholding the admiration he needs and demands. When he points out your Taurean obstinacy, you will attack his Leonine vanity. The degree to which you are capable of wounding each other makes it difficult to talk things over. When the storm finally blows over, verbal apologies will be rare. Instead, through his lovemaking he will show you he still cares, and you will express both apology and forgiveness by being a receptive and responsive partner.

No doubt by now you understand that this is an astrologically tense relationship. Although there is stress and friction, there are also rewards for overcoming adversity. Since you are both romantics with sentimental leanings, your devotion to the ideal of love can lead you to become more flexible personalities. Leo's expansive nature can increase the scope of your own vision and allow for more confidence in making plans for future accomplishments.

When the chips are really down, Taurus and Leo can join forces with a courage and determination that will deepen your affectional bond. Leo will want to be your kitten in shining armor, always taking up your cause in moments of crisis or depression. He may well come to idolize you for your stable and calming influence. Despite his damnable streak of conceit, if he loves you, he will treasure your support and good opinion above all else.

Don't deflate his ego too often with your Taurean sense of humor. He can be so full of his own self-aggrandizement that he becomes pompous and laughable, but don't overreact. Remember, Leo is a Fixed sign and he takes himself as seriously as you do! If you treat each other with love and affection, this can be a long-lasting, rewarding love affair that will allow both the Bull and the Lion to develop the most noble aspects of their natures.

TAURUS & VIRGO

Virgo is the sign of the Virgin, ruled by Mercury in his "feminine," or responsive, role. You will recognize an Earth-sign buddy in Virgo, but his qualities are Mutable, making him more unpredictable than a Fixed sign like Taurus. You will find that you share basic goals, outlooks, and desires.

Earth-sign men are able to share a fundamental trust that allows for personality development and personal growth. With a Virgo companion you can be stimulated to discover more about yourself because you feel secure enough to express your feelings without fear of rejection. You will find this man interesting, both mentally and physically.

Virgo is a sign of sensibilities. He may not a Virgin, but he does have an unsoiled and pure ideal of perfection. Because you will want to please him (and avoid his more critical attitudes), you will strive to be at your best and live up to his high opinion of you. He will share and admire your practical Taurean instincts. The Virgin and the Bull are both sentimentalists, and your romantic attraction will be your enduring bond—above and beyond your sexual needs.

When it comes to loving and the physical expression of your mutual desires, it will be up to you to overcome some of your natural passivity. Taurus can gently take Virgo by the hand and lead him to the joys of sensual pleasure. This man is not casual or relaxed about the intricacies of sex; his passion is moderated by his worries about his performance as a lover. Fortunately you have the powers of Venus to encourage him to enjoy Earthy and uninhibited sex. It will have to be accomplished with the skills of body language, since physical intimacy is a deep and silent experience for Earth signs. You will have to restrain your Taurean sense of humor and refrain from making sex a laughing matter or the subject of coarse jokes. Virgo's refined sensibilities will be offended if you do.

Since Mutable signs tend to be adaptable and flexible, this should not be a stressful romance. Emotionally and sexually he is less demanding than you. Taureans may feel frustrated by Virgo's apparent lack of emotion, but you should not interpret his reticence as disinterest. If you attempt to force him to be more responsive, he will respond to your bullying with sarcastic criticism. As it is, Virgos are prone enough to point out the faults and inadequacies of others. If you can make him feel more secure and relaxed by being easy-going with him, he will temper some of his more critical attitudes.

Taurus has a built-in tolerance for Virgo's idiosyncrasies. You will appreciate his innate curiosity for the mental stimulation it provides. A Virgo companion will increase your enjoyment of the arts and culture by increasing your critical understanding. You may find that your own ideas are clarified under his influence, giving you a new confidence in your creative talents.

A love affair between Taurus and Virgo is normally stable, solid, and integrated. The Bull and the Virgin share qualities of passivity, caution, and integrity. No fireworks, but a meeting and mating in friendship, resting upon your implied understanding of each other's virtues. When conflicts do occur, you will summon your Taurean patience to weather the storm, though neither of you is given to outbursts of temper. The problem may be that your stubborn silences will cause him to become a nag. Disagreements will usually become stalemates between your obstinacy and his self-righteousness.

When you two settle down together, he will be the one who looks after your love nest, since he finds comfort only in neatness and you tend to be rather casual about such matters. If you let him get compulsive about "yellow wax buildup," you will both be miserable. Focus your combined energies on more rewarding social and intellectual activities and you will find a level of happiness and comfort that only two Earth-sign lovers can share.

TAURUS & LIBRA

Libra is a Cardinal Air sign, symbolized by the Balance, or Scales. His ruler is also Venus, but it is Venus as an Air element, denoting a man of inspiration rather than your Earthy physical inclinations. Venus as the ruler of Libra is more aesthetic, more speculative, and more imaginative than the Venus of Taurus.

A Libra man has definite standards of physical beauty when it comes to choosing a partner, whereas you would be just as happy with someone who made you feel good. The initial attraction between you will be physical, though you will find him intellectually interesting and he will appreciate your warm humor and forthright manner.

A Venus–Venus combination means a shared love of beautiful possessions and harmonious surroundings. Any home the two of you settle in will be comfortably and taste-fully appointed. The main difference between you in this area is that you are a Fixed sign, and once you have ac-quired nice things and placed them in your environment, they become fixtures. Libra, on the other hand, is always tinkering with everything, always adjusting the balance. Normally such indecision would drive a Bull to rage, but the blending of your Venus rulers mean that you will treat each other with courtesy and respect. Your common goal is a peaceful, harmonious, and regular life-style.

You will admire his mental agility, and he finds much to like about your sense of values and stability. Play on these open lines of communication to insist that your relationship has firm rules early in the game. Otherwise Libra will keep changing the rules or inventing new games as he goes along. Make the best use of your strong points—sincerity, a sense of humor, and simple common sense to bring him down to Earth. This charming, airy fellow needs your practicality and patience to provide him with the tranquillity he seeks.

The Venus of Libra endows him with an innate optimism that is just the right antidote for your darker moments of insecurity. The qualities of this Air-sign lover can lighten your heavy Earth-sign nature and keep you from becoming a stick-in-the-mud. There is a danger that your natural passivity, combined with his Libran tendency to procrastinate, can lead to a general malaise that will leave you both unhappy, undirected, and out of harmony with each other.

Fortunately Libra influences your Sixth House, the area of service. Your desire to take care of him will be a strong and loving element. By the same token, Libra finds that he is always eager to do favors for you. Your karmic tie is to serve and care for each other to your mutual benefit.

For the sake of harmony, you might find yourself avoiding discussions of his more disturbing habits. His extravagance, his lack of drive concerning success, and his lapses into wishful thinking are all matters you find detrimental to the wonderful potential you see in him. Too much patience with a Libra may only encourage his worst excesses. If you don't speak up, your romance will begin to drift aimlessly and founder on the rocks of mutual misunderstanding.

Sexually, the Libra man has a light touch. He is devoted to ethereal fantasies and fancy variations as a lover. You may find that you need more physical contact and Earthy sensuality to attain emotional security and sexual satisfaction. What he may lack in the area of intensity can be compensated for in frequency.

Libra is a social butterfly, and though you may prefer quiet evenings at home, you will have to allow him the freedom of his social and intellectual pursuits. Provide for your mutual social life by using your home to give sumptuous dinner parties and develop a reputation as stimulating hosts.

Should the two of you feel threatened in a stagnating relationship, there will develop a growing competition between you, and a coarseness in your manner toward each other that your Venus ruler will find intolerable. You will feel completely bored by his constant need to make and remake minor decisions, and he will accuse you of being a penny-pinching drudge. But if your love is strong, the karmic ties between Taurus and Libra will allow for a feeling of sexual interest, personal fulfillment, and unselfish devotion.

TAURUS & SCORPIO

A Scorpio lover is under the influence of Pluto, planet of the mysteries of sex and regeneration. His qualities are Fixed-Water, making him emotionally deep. Bulls are not known for their abilities as swimmers, but you feel yourself drawn to this magical man by his penetrating gaze. Since you are opposite signs on the Wheel of Life, you will feel that he has qualities you lack, just as he feels that you have virtues he needs.

Despite the potential for harmony, this will never be a tranquil mating. The toll of your emotions may be high, but the experience will be exciting and passionate. If you are still yearning for your peaceful meadow, stay away from Scorpio! Of course, you may not be able to resist. He is an undeniably attractive character who can make you feel as if you are on the verge of a whole new stage in your life.

If you set your heart on a Scorpio lover, you are going to need all of your Taurean patience and endurance. You will have to summon up the resources of tolerance, unselfishness, and compassion if the relationship is to succeed. Scorpions tend to be jealous, suspicious, very private people. Pluto lacks Venus' light touch in most things, and if you focus your sense of humor on him, he will be hurt. When Scorpions are wounded emotionally, they don't sulk or pout; they retaliate. In a love affair with a Scorpio you will have to practice more tact and compromise than with any other sign. This relationship requires constant care, attention, and adjustment.

Given the karmic ties between these two Fixed signs, if you are going to fall in love at all, it will not be any casual matter. Scorpio brings out your most intense physical desires, indicating passionate lovemaking. Scorpio men find sexuality to be an unfathomable mystery, which they feel compelled to explore. Though he is jealous, you are not flirtatious and will give him little cause for suspicion. In turn, he will be a faithful lover as long as you provide him with the emotional satisfaction he hungers for.

Scorpions are more passionate and vulnerable than Taureans—on all levels. A Scorpio lover will make you feel more self-confident. The heavens know that you will need to be strong when conflicts arise between you! Though Scorpio may be seething inside with self-reproach, outwardly he will be cool, brooding, and sarcastic. After a quarrel, reconciliation will be difficult. Taurus and Scorpio instinctively know how to hurt each other more deeply than many other lovers.

Avoid situations or confrontations with Scorpio that involve apportioning blame and granting forgiveness. The process will only lead to deeper wounds. Unlike some other lovers, you will not be able to resolve your differences through transcendent sex and tender lovemaking. When your Scorpio lover is hurt or angry, he knows better than to try to make love. Allow him to retreat into the depths of his Fixed Water. Time alone will heal his wounds, but make it as easy and shameless as possible for him to return from his strategic retreat. Reassure him that your arms are eager to receive his passionate embraces whenever he has recovered. Should a Scorpio seek solace in the arms of another man, you can bet that your relationship is over.

Easy harmony in love between Taurus and Scorpio is not to be expected. This is an active relationship and a constant challenge. The reward for your hard work will come in moments of passion that exceed your fantasies and will convince you that your love was truly meant to last.

TAURUS & SAGITTARIUS

Sagittarius is the sign of the Centaur, aiming his arrows at the heavens. He is ruled by Jupiter, the planet of good fortune, and you may well thank your lucky stars for meeting this mythological creature. Unlike the other Fire signs, you will find that the Mutable qualities of this amiable fellow excite your sexual and emotional sensibilities.

Venus and Jupiter share a love of good times, good food, and good sex. You will provide the sensuality and he will contribute the excitement. Though he is certainly passionate, he is also warm and engaging. Since he likes to roam the Earth in search of new sensations, the Centaur rarely develops deep emotional attachments. Your biggest disappointment may be that you do not feel he is willing to reciprocate the devotion you feel for him.

The Bull will have to realize that Centaurs are not domestic creatures. It will not be easy for you because Venus combines with expansive Jupiter to cause extravagant emotions in you when you fall for a Sagittarius. His boyish optimism may bring out your maternal instincts, but be careful not to smother his innocent dreams. If you want to keep him and nourish the best in him, you will have to encourage his idealism. Centaurs instinctively shy away from pessimism, so support him by being an attentive listener rather than bursting his balloon. Taurus can come to value the Sagittarian spirit of independence for the wonderful quality it really is without feeling hypercritical or threatened.

In any Taurus–Sagittarius relationship you are dealing with the forces of stability (you) and the forces of expansion (him) in a very delicate balance. Your Centaur lover will be more extravagant in things, both material and spiritual, than you. Don't try to keep up with his frenetic pace and throw yourself into projects you can't finish. Your strength in this combination is in the Taurean ability to maintain your own identity as a stabilizing presence. Don't try to change him or restrict his activities. No amount of confrontation or nagging is going to make him more responsible or more sensitive to other people's needs. If you try to keep him on a short leash, he will become Sagittarius the Archer, wounding you with bitchy barbs of stinging sarcasm. He represents a challenge to you that can best be met by being true to your own personality, as he is to himself.

Sexually, you find him to be very exciting. You have the chance to learn a great deal about the pleasures of uninhibited sex and playful lovemaking from your Centaur. He is greatly stimulated by his partner's erotic responses, and if you learn to become more expressive as a lover, he will even intensify his efforts to please you.

Conflict may arise over the issue of money and how to use it. Your sensible fiscal plans are in direct opposition to his desire to distribute funds hither and yon like Johnny Appleseed. Fortunately the potential is here for both of you to work out a very profitable business arrangement. If you handle the organization and allow him to tackle the fund-raising and promotion, the results could lead to great success.

The influence of Jupiter will spin you out of your rut and point to new directions in your life and work. In return you can keep your Sagittarius partner on a more even keel by watching over him when he takes off on one of his adventures. The Centaur loves to roam free, and travel is important to his life-style. Adventures abroad with a Sagittarius buddy will be lively opportunities to expand your horizons. En route through life with him, you will come to understand how this man can be kind and loving without being especially sensitive or responsible. The contradictions in this jovial lover may drive you wild with confusion but will keep you fascinated.

Taureans are drawn to Sagittarians by a force that they don't quite comprehend. In many ways he is the Don Quixote of the zodiac, eternally tilting at windmills. If you love him, you will become his Sancho Panza, always interjecting your solid common sense but knowing that you will probably be needed to pick up the pieces no matter what. If you can filter all of his reckless enthusiasm through your sense of humor, this will be a lasting and enjoyable love.

TAURUS & CAPRICORN

The Mountain Goat of Capricorn can be a true Earth-sign mate for the Taurean Bull. You are both reserved and moderate personalities, cautious with your commitments because of your mutual search for security. As a Cardinal sign, he will take the lead in matters pertaining to the steady growth of your love into a stable relationship.

Capricorn is ruled by Saturn, planet of restraint and executive direction. When he comes under the influence of Venus in Taurus, the indications are for shared sympathies in education, the fine arts, and romance. The confluence of your Earth-sign natures will allow you to work willingly for each other, as well as the permanence of your union.

As lovers, the men of Taurus and Capricorn prefer fidelity, but you are both willing to forgive momentary lapses rather than destroy the bonds between you that transcend sex. Once you feel committed to each other, you will have the power to overcome obstacles without serious trauma. The trust you share allows you to relax and let down some of your defenses. Fundamentally both signs crave affection but find it difficult to express their needs. In love with each other, the lines are open.

Since you are more sensual and emotional than Capricorn, you can help him to release his desires through the physical expression of your affection. Conversely a Capricorn lover will moderate your emotions, making you feel more mature and secure. Your romance will provide each other with much understanding, loyalty, and devotion.

Since Taurus is more demanding of sexual stimulation and gratification, you will have to encourage his sexual interest without making him feel pressured or inadequate. Your loving patience may help him mature into the sexy man he has kept repressed. Best of all, Taurus, you have a humorous perspective about sex that will give him a new outlook on a subject he has previously taken much too seriously.

Despite your immediate rapport, neither of you is likely to rush into a relationship. According to your Earth-sign wisdom, good fortune is the result of hard work and you won't value anything that comes easily. Saturn's influence will cause you to take a long-range view of the future you want to build together. This is good for you because you will feel stimulated to broaden the scope of your interests in reading, education, or career matters.

Taurus may even feel somewhat pressed by Capricorn's prodding for self-improvement. He can be so persistent that you may feel "herded" and somewhat resentful. Both of your are stubborn and resistant to change and external control. Remember, your influence on him is to stimulate creative and open feelings. If you take this affair too lightly, you will hurt him deeply. The saving virtues of both signs are your patience and perseverance, creating strong aspects for harmony. Reconciliation after a dispute will not be difficult, since you both understand that you have each other's best interest at heart.

Security is the ultimate goal of both the Bull and the Goat, and emotional and financial security are certainly indicated in any Taurus–Capricorn partnership. When you two are unhappy, you may become miserly materialists to compensate for the emotional starvation you are unable to express. Though you are certainly no spendthrift, he is even more conservative with money than you are. It will shock you that he should ever accuse you of extravagance, and yet he might, if he is feeling insecure.

The secret to your mutual happiness is to show much love and admiration for his virtues. A Capricorn lover will strive to give as much as he feels he receives, so don't take him for granted no matter how self-sufficient he pretends to be. You have found a man who will be a dependable friend and lover, seriously devoted to your welfare. As he gets older, Saturn shines on him and he gets even better—more confident, more optimistic, and much more sexy. Taurus, this may actually be the man of your dreams!

TAURUS & AQUARIUS

Despite what his symbol implies, Aquarius the Water-bearer is a Fixed Air sign, making him both eccentric and eclectic. He is ruled by enigmatic Uranus, planet of surprise and instability. The Bull and the Water-bearer can have a harmonious relationship, especially if there is a business aspect to your mutual attraction.

Aquarius represents your Tenth House—ambition and aspirations—even though when you first meet, you may feel bashful and he may seem detached. You may even be inclined to distrust him, since he seems superficial in his social contacts and attitudes. You are indeed more conservative and conventional than Aquarius, but remember that he is also a Fixed sign. It means that he is just as stubborn as you are, and has integrity—even if you don't agree with all of his standards of behavior and thought.

The influence of Uranus in your life will force you out of your neat patterns of behavior. Through an Aquarian lover you will meet unconventional people who may advance your career in unexpected ways. For you to expand beyond your carefully constructed life-style is not a comfortable process for Taureans, but the experience could lead to much success and future security.

Together, the Bull and the Water-bearer can achieve a blend of practicality and freedom that will allow you to develop as individuals, without restrictions. If you want the love affair to last, you must be willing to make intellectual, rather than emotional, concessions for the good of the relationship. You have the power to stimulate his creativity by showing him how to put it to practical use. Aquarius will reciprocate by teaching you to appreciate the value of spontaneity and flexibility in dealing with life. As you may already know, this can be an exhausting and unpredictable relationship. If you really want to remain devoted to the status quo in your life, then you should not set your heart on an Aquarius lover.

The Water-bearer's natural eccentricity will undermine your need for security. He values his individuality above all else and will not be willing to submerge it for the sake of your emotional needs. Since he lacks your more romantic leanings, an Aquarian may be an interesting and amusing pal but not the lover you really require. The incompatibility between you is based upon lack of communication. Taurus, you will find this to be an emotionally fragile affair in which the slightest upset could blow it all away.

Sexually, you will have to be the one to encourage a response from him, since his interest in sex is rather abstract. His Airy Uranian nature is very different from your Earthy Venus desires. Aquarians don't like a great deal of physical contact, and you will have to use all of your sensual powers to get him to value communication through touching and feeling. He prefers verbalization during sex, lights on, mirrors—anything that removes it from the physical level and projects it somewhere else. Aquarians also tend to be emotionally secretive, and you will not appreciate that at all.

Any Taurean who expects an Aquarian lover to be dependable is setting himself up for disappointment. His devotion to being unashamedly unpredictable and nonconformist strikes you as phony and unnecessary, and you have to let him know it. When it comes to confrontation, you will accuse him of courting chaos in his constant search for stimulation and he will attribute your materialism to vanity. Then you will really see red!

You can certainly learn to enjoy the way he can stimulate your individuality and originality. Take good advantage of the powers you can develop in an Aquarian association to advance your career ambitions. If it is truly love, you will be much more tolerant of his unusual approach to life. After all, sometimes he can be such an idealistic fool that your protective instincts are aroused. Don't try to dull his natural sparkle by scouring it with the steel wool of your disapproval and you may find much to love in your Aquarian man.

TAURUS & PISCES

Pisces the Fish is a Mutable Water sign, influencing your Eleventh House—friendship, hopes, and wishes. Ruled by Neptune, this Water baby is a bundle of sensitivity who will respond intuitively to your need for sensuous and romantic love. Since he is sometimes emotionally timid, a Pisces man may appreciate your possessiveness for the security he needs in a loving relationship.

Karmically, Venus and Neptune make for an easygoing pair. Pisces' Water enriches your best Earth qualities and enhances your virtues. Normally a Taurus would be hesitant to trust his affections with a man who can be as elusive and changeable as Pisces, but you feel different with him. In many respects you will perceive him as the gentle, sexy romantic you have been searching for.

Since Pisceans are sexually receptive types, you will be stimulated by his appreciation of your sensuous and affectionate manner of lovemaking. If you can curb your more demanding instincts, he will blossom into a lover of delicious technique. Your steadying influence in most things not only will be comforting to him but also give him more self-confidence.

The sign of the Fish is highly sensitive. Though not as moody as Cancer, he is given to periods of emotional confusion that will surely try your patience. Both Taurus and Pisces have a potential for pessimism and brooding. Venus and Neptune, when they are both feeling down, can drive each other to all manner of extremes in behavior. Fortunately you are endowed with the power to charm and reassure him out of his periods of depression. If you should focus your temper on him, he will shy away to seek comfort in escapist adventures. Don't try to force him out of his moods. He merely needs time to work them through and integrate his feelings. Contemplative solitude is a way of calming his nerves.

When a Pisces gets on your nerves, though, you will see him as a drifting dreamer. He needs direction and you have the ability to encourage his more creative efforts, but you can't force him to your way of thinking. Taurus is dedicated to the tangible world and its practical applications and consequences; Pisces is not. Your concepts of truth are fixed and finite, but Pisces views the Universe as relative. Direct attempts to pin him down will only cause him to be evasive. You will have to overcome some of your stubborn opinions and become more flexible and sensitive to your Pisces lover.

You are bound to be exasperated by the Piscean tendency to spend money on nonmaterial things such as taxi fare and tips. Normally he will be happy to let you assist him in taking better control of his finances. Let him spend his money any way he likes, but help him to keep his accounts, and be ready with sound Taurean advice when he seeks it.

There is a wonderful capacity in the Taurus–Pisces aspects for a true and lasting friendship. He is the one Water sign that is happiest when taking the shape of its vessel or running in its channel. Taurus is the Earth sign that most easily and graciously provides a solid framework for Mutable Pisces. Here is the man who will gladly share your country retreat, insulated from the cares of the world by your loving protection. He will touch the spiritual aspirations that lie beneath your Taurean materialism. This allows him to trust you and causes you to respect him despite your different approaches to life.

Your Pisces lover is a man who can benefit from your ability to put the confusion of life in order with sound common sense. In return for the security of your love, he will expose you to new vistas of imagination that increase your sentimental attraction. Your first impressions of each other may be filled with misgivings, but familiarity breeds contentment and true affection when Taurus and Pisces join forces as loving partners.

LOVING YOUR TAURUS MAN

If you want to find a Taurus man, look for him wherever there are pleasant social gatherings, especially those involving music. Whether a symphony concert or a disco, music definitely has charms to attract him. Since he can be a social climber, the more elegant and refined the setting, the more likely you are to meet a Taurus man. Taureans are usually looking for love, rather than a quick fling. Stable and enduring romance is his biggest turn-on.

While he certainly has the capacity for Earthy sex, he is not usually the aggressor when you first meet. He will want to feel that he has accepted your advances rather than submitted to you. The difference may be subtle, but it is important to him to feel that he has control of his life. If you come on too strong, you will drive him away.

Taurus men are honest and forthright fellows who like to live lives of order and comfort. He is a materialist, and his possessions are an important statement of his goals in life. He needs symbols of security and achievement to be happy. He is not susceptible to personal flattery, but if you compliment him on his taste in clothes or praise the way he has decorated his apartment, he will feel that you appreciate him in the way in which he has chosen to seek recognition.

Taureans have a natural sense of humor, especially when they feel secure within their social setting. If you meet him at a small gathering or in the company of friends, you will see him at his charming best. He may be a bit insecure in large and noisy scenes, but if he finds you attractive, he will suggest that you two meet another time so that you can get to know each other better. Take your cue from him and don't try to rush him into bed. He likes to be courted, to feel that you are interested in his personality as well as his other charms.

When you go out together, he will respond beautifully if you go to a good restaurant. Taureans are very susceptible to classic seduction scenes: soft lights, fine wine, soothing music, plump pillows, and seductive conversation. He loves to receive small tokens of affection, but extravagant presents offend his practical nature. Taurus is a generous sign, and he will get much pleasure from giving you little gifts— usually practical ones. Always make a fuss over things he gives you, not for the object but for his kindness and consideration.

Taureans often make their living in management fields because of their organizational skills. They are dedicated to their jobs and are rarely irresponsible, even when in love. Don't pester him with calls at the office or try to distract him from his sense of duty where his career is concerned. If he doesn't feel that you respect his need for professional advancement, he will reject you as a friend or lover.

This man needs to keep his professional, social, and sexual lives separate and in harmony. In love, he is a very private person and will not broadcast the details of his personal life. Though not necessarily in the closet, he may worry that his private life will adversely affect his professional advancement. Money is the tangible proof of his success and the guarantee of his security. Without financial peace of mind he is very unhappy and pessimistic about his future.

Taureans are protective and possessive. Evenings at home engaged in domestic pursuits may not be your cup of tea. If you want him to be more social, you will have to be subtle in your suggestions. If you make an issue or force a confrontation, he will become stubborn and angry. He is willing to tolerate things about you he doesn't especially like for the sake of your relationship, but don't take advantage of his desire for domestic harmony.

Taureans are men of moral values. He has a strong sense of right and wrong and prides himself on his fairness. He may be set in his ways, but his habits are based upon high ideals. Taureans are gentle, romantic souls in spite of their efficient exteriors. He can easily slip into predictable patterns of behavior and may take his lovers for granted. Most of all, he needs to trust you with his love, but he needs to learn that others need demonstrative affection in order to love.

Encourage him to engage in physical activity; with his sedentary habits, he will start putting on the pounds. He is usually a good dancer, and it is a form of activity and entertainment you can both enjoy. Get him to take short trips to the country. Long walks through the meadows and woods will do wonders to lift the burden of the world from his shoulders. Whenever you want him to become putty in your hands, give him a massage. Focus on the neck and shoulder muscles and you will feel the tension and worry flowing out of him as he surrenders to your loving touch.

Most of all, he needs to feel appreciated by his lover if he is to be secure in any relationship. If you take him too lightly or are too flippant about the matters he prizes so highly, he will lose his equilibrium. When a Taurus is emotionally confused, his temper is short, he eats too much rich food, and he loses his charming sense of humor. As a potential lover, the man is a blue-chip stock that will provide dividends forever if you let the investment slowly appreciate over the years.

Someday he will achieve his longtime goal of moving to the country. He values the simple pleasures of life that are rich in spirit and untainted by the vanity of superficial gratification. Taurus wants and needs a long and lasting love to make his world complete. If you are willing to commit yourself to his ideals of permanence and perseverance, Taurus can be the pot of golden love at the end of the rainbow.

GEMINI
May 21–June 20

♊

Symbol: The Twins
Ruling Planet: Mercury
Color: Orange
Metal: Quicksilver
Natural House Relationship: Third House, the house
    of communications
Third House Traits: Desire for information and love
    of stimulation
Motto: "I think"
Nature: Mutable sign (adaptation)
Element: Air sign (mental)
Qualities: Inquisitive mind, experimental, and alert
Capacities: Awareness of ideas
Personality Key Words: Restless, inventive, and
    intelligent

MAXIMIZING YOUR GEMINI POTENTIAL

Gemini is ruled by masculine Mercury, the planet of mental communication. The Mutable Air qualities of your sign are symbolized by the Twins. That doesn't mean you are schizophrenic, but it does mean that you are tuned in to more than one level of awareness. As you already know, the duality of your sign makes life exciting and interesting. The combination of intense interest and the ability to distance yourself from your experiences is often confusing to your friends and lovers because they can't always keep up with your pace.

Conversation is your forte. Some of the highlights of your life have come in all-night gabfests or long-distance telephone calls. Though you may talk up a storm, you can also be a good listener and a keen observer. People feel your interest and warm up to you quickly, often speaking easily and confidentially to you on your first meeting. You can be a natural "bartender," listening to any interesting talk. By the same token, you can be a valuable member of a gay peer-counseling group or community-information service. You follow the influence of Mercury to keep information moving in all directions. No subject is taboo, and no issue is ever really settled when there is so much to be studied, analyzed, digested, and disseminated.

Curiosity is the motivation for your wide range of activities. You may not always be sure of what you want, since your Air-sign nature makes your mental energies so diffuse and dispersed. You tend to be a very quick study, even a dilettante, since your restless spirit beckons you to follow each clue as you discover it.

In your career, social, or sexual life, a similar pattern may be apparent. Not that you bore easily, you are just readily stimulated and eager for new experiences. Sometimes you are like a voracious computer, hungry for input. Your research may not always come up with original ideas, but they are clever in the unusual ways you combine your influences and come to interesting conclusions.

You always have an opinion, no matter how little data you may have. You come up with instant readouts rather than reserve judgment until all the facts are in. Should new information prove you wrong, your belief in the eternal flow of new ideas is merely confirmed. You are always willing to give advice, though you don't try to force your opinions on anyone. Your role is to facilitate, not to administrate, the information. If others fail to take your advice, you don't dwell on their lack of receptiveness, because you are not emotionally involved with your knowledge.

Your Air-sign talent for multiple awareness indicates that you enjoy life on many levels, but others may feel that you don't take anything seriously. Your constant flow of witty conversation and fund of eclectic knowledge give people the impression that you are superficial. Actually, Gemini, superficiality is not an inaccurate description of your talents.

You are intellectually promiscuous by nature. You learn something from every man you meet, and you are an eager student. Geminis are particularly fond of talkative, responsive sex partners who express their own needs and desires. While one Twin gets down to the business of pleasure, the other one is taking notes.

Pornographic movies, magazines, and voyeurism of all kinds appeal to your thirst for knowledge. You are stimulated mentally rather than sexually by the endless variations on poses and positions. Your lovers benefit from your studies, since you are capable of becoming an accomplished sexual technician. Your Mercury urges you not only to gather information but to disseminate it as well.

Security is not the primary goal in your life while there is so much variety to stimulate your active mind. If a lover should become too serious, too possessive, or too intense, you feel trapped. Freedom is essential to your happiness. You can question the value of ever having a monogamous relationship when you find it so easy to meet interesting men.

When you do fall in love, and that's L-O-V-E love, you fall like a ton of bricks, like a house of cards. Real emotion upsets and confuses you, causes you to doubt your light-hearted, capricious self-image. When you get into a love affair, you are curious about understanding your attraction rather than being wildly turned on sexually. You want to know everything about the other person. As you arrange dates, engage him in conversation, drop him notes, he will get the idea that you are interested in getting to know him more intimately. If you are a typical Gemini, you are really excited and flustered at the idea of any real emotional involvement with another man.

Making commitments is difficult for you, even when you think you are in love. Part of you wants to learn how to surrender to your emotions, and another part of you questions the difference between love and intellectual fascination. Your sex life is firmly rooted in fantasy; you can't always distinguish between the real man and a dream figure. The more intelligent, expressive, and creative your lover, the happier you will be as a Gemini in love.

GEMINI & ARIES

The Ram is a Cardinal Fire sign and he will want to take the lead, in and out of bed. He is likely to find the Twins exciting and stimulating playmates. Your fund of inspiration and ideas keeps his pioneering and adventuresome spirit at peak performance. Aries' generous impulses will allow him

to be tolerant of your vagaries and diversions because he
will be fascinated by your wide range of experience.

Your scintillating conversation will spark his imagination.
Together you can engage in a social life that keeps you close
to the edge of exhaustion yet feeling very satisfied. All the
indications are for energy, variety, and pleasure in an affair
with Aries.

Aries men do not have the urge to settle down into one
long relationship any more than you do. He is a creature of
physical passion who attracts you by his animal magnetism.
His intense sexuality may be more than you can handle, but
if you let him have free rein, he will give you a continuing
course in new approaches to erotic experience.

The danger in this buddy-buddy situation lies in the potential for rivalry between you on all levels. You can drive
yourselves to the brink of emotional and financial disaster
by trying to outparty, outdo, and outrage each other. Aries
is a competitive man who will try to rise to the challenge
posed by your quick shifts of activity and interests. Your
Air qualities can fan his Fire nature to white-hot intensity.
Despite your enthusiastic natures, you are both high-strung
and lacking in emotional stamina. He can make love all
night, but it will leave you a nervous wreck. Since neither
of you is a good money manager, these periods of divine
excess will leave you broke and bitchy. Work on combining
your strengths rather than opposing them.

A relationship with an Aries can develop into a lasting
friendship after the first flash of intensity dies down. You
two always share something to talk about. Your shared in-
timacies will keep the bond between you alive and vibrant.
Vacations together will be exciting adventures on the open
road as you sample the delights of new cities full of new
faces.

Aries stimulates your creative urges. When you are involved with him, your analytical drives are channeled into
writing or clarifying your ideas. Arians will respect your
intellectual gifts. You should learn to value his honest emotional qualities, since you lack his passionate devotion to

feeling. Both Aries and Gemini can be devoted to causes that affect their lives. As gay activists, you would make a dynamic pair. The intensity of this commitment, combined with your communication skills, could energize the movement.

Aries likes to be the dominant partner, and your strong need for independence could lead to conflict over plans, directions, and goals. When it gets too heavy, you will normally absent yourself from the scene long enough to cool off before he goes into Arian meltdown alert. Your analytic powers have probably clued you in to the fact that he's prone to be in a bad temper only when he's feeling insecure. Encourage him to verbalize his insecurities rather than focusing his emotionalism on you. Emotion is a mystery and a curiosity to you. An Aries lover will keep your normally restless attention longer than most other signs. The problem may be, if you are typical of the Gemini Sun-sign influence, that your interest is in analyzing this feeling of affection rather than giving in to your feelings. This is the one way in which your selfish Twin prevents you from going beyond analysis and into experience. There is always that element of emotional self-voyeurism that prevents Gemini from coming to grips with feelings, except on an intellectual basis.

A Gemini–Aries love affair has so many other intensities going for it that you will understand when he seeks emotional fulfillment outside your relationship. Both of you will feel that you may have parted as lovers but will remain loving friends.

Gemini and Aries both have the power to keep introducing new elements into a partnership that keeps it stimulating. The aspects are good for an intense love affair and a lasting friendship based upon your physical attraction and shared aspirations.

GEMINI & TAURUS

Fixed-Earth Taureans represent a dilemma for the Mercury Twins within you. One part of you says, "This warm and sensual man attracts me with his depth and wit." The other Twin sings countertenor to the refrain "Boring and bullheaded materialists turn me off!" Which one is he? Which one are you?

The answer, as in most perceptual dilemmas, is both. When he is responding to your vibrant intellectual energies, he comes alive under your Mutable Air influence. When he is reacting to your scattered impulses, Taurus becomes confused and stubborn. When the Bull is feeling insecure, he retreats to his materialist symbols for support. Your Mercurial need for independence causes him to question his need for deep roots, as expressed in Taurean habit and routine.

Gemini has the ability to function with a degree of routine as format, but the content must be constantly shifting. Explain to your Taurean lover that sex at the same time and place in the same way, no matter how affectionate, provides you with no stimulation. For a Gemini it would be like seeing the same movie every day at the same time in the same seat. Taurus will argue that it would be fine to have a regularly assigned seat and appointed time at your favorite movie theater.

What you should understand in any relationship with a Taurus is that all the sharp edges you attempt to polish with your intellect are the same rough spots in life he attempts to bury with systematic organization. Being forced to think fast makes him nervous and full of self-doubt. It would be alright if he simply trusted your superlative skills of quick study and instant readout, but the stubborn cuss won't admit that any quick decision can be anything more than a tentative hypothesis.

Sometimes he's like Goldilocks, trying on all of the three bears' creature comforts until all the apparent options have been considered. Only then does he feel that anything is "just right."

Taurus will reveal his depth of knowledge under the influence of your clever mind. You will feel relaxed because he doesn't keep turning your conversation into a seduction scene. Taurus is serious about love and sex and doesn't want to feel that he has made a commitment unless he sees the potential for a lasting relationship. Your little notes, phone calls, and unexpected invitations will flatter him and appeal to his romantic idea of courtship. You can leave him dizzy with the pace of visits to galleries, lectures, concerts, and parties that you encourage him to attend with you.

Money is the outward symbol of stability and achievement for Taurus. But your interest in money is limited to your desire to spend it on travel, clothes, and entertainment. You see your expenditures as investments in your personal development, but he thinks you are irresponsible and frivolous. You'll allow him to advise you on the most advantageous ways of budgeting since it can give you a secure foundation for your freedom, but you will resist his criticism.

When the time comes for loving, try not to be too quick and casual about sex. Taurus leans toward sensuality at an even pace rather than at your usual blitz approach. His affectionate lovemaking will calm your nervous energies, though it will take some adjustment on your part. The reward for Gemini will be a feeling of pampered protection from a solidly sensuous man. You can learn to concentrate your mental energies as you observe and analyze the success he has attained by being attuned to his feelings, as well as to the thoughts and words of others.

On the other hand, you will not be pleased by his monolithic opinions and his possessiveness. You thrive on a diversity of ideas and acquaintances that may cause him to accuse you of being superficial and flirtatious. Your flash and dash makes him feel insecure because he can't find a proper emotional response to your quicksilver enthusiasm.

When a Taurus is insecure, he becomes suspicious, mistrustful, and disdainful. You will have to learn to compromise if you want to keep him as a lover and friend. This may be difficult because compromise calls for constant effort, and you will resent having to divert this energy from your unceasing quest for knowledge through experience. You will manage to avoid the scenes and tears of recrimination if you keep your lighthearted wits about you. If you have truly come to understand each other as loving men, Taurus will understand that the Gemini butterfly is a beautiful creature, capable of turning the nectar of wonder into the beauty of knowledge.

GEMINI & GEMINI

A double-Gemini love becomes an automatic foursome. A porn epic featuring two sets of twins is bound to be jam-packed with every variation you can imagine! After all, there are some strong powers of imagination and fantasy projection at play when Gemini meets Gemini. The physical and mental attraction between you creates an exciting force field of infinite potential.

Gemini rules the arms and hands. If it is love at first sight, you will probably find the first handshake almost as exciting as the first kiss. Holding hands in public or walking arm in arm, a gay Gemini couple are often willing to risk adverse reactions from straight society, but there is a youthful exuberance about your carryings-on that renders them innocent and above any criticism.

Fortunately Geminis are no strangers to criticism. You are often the target for implications of superficiality, but they cannot (and should not) dampen your spirits. Your life-style will continue to change and grow as long as you live. It's the wonderful gift of freedom that keeps Geminis youthful and optimistic.

In a close relationship with another Gemini, you should get intelligent feedback from your eclectic collections of ideas and information. When you get together at the end of the day, it will be like two little boys emptying their pockets of all the wonderful things they have come across on their wanderings. And talk! You and he will be the proverbial couple whose conversation in a restaurant keeps all the adjacent tables lending at least one ear to what you're saying. Your mischievous Mercury influence lends itself to gossip, and combined with your dramatic flair, it could mean that dessert is a really "deep dish."

You will find that your Gemini lover has an innate grace in his responses to you, intellectually and sexually. He is physically capable of fulfilling your fantasies. Erotic experiments can be the core of your physical bond. When you're making love, there is the thrill of group sex because it can be so exciting and so changeable. Lights on, please, to better observe and appreciate the action with all of your senses.

In the acts of love, he is both participant and observer. You both feel the thrill of watching and of being watched. This added impetus to sexual performance makes your intimate moments together very intense. In a Gemini–Gemini relationship the predilection for lightly held emotions is no detriment. It means your loving commitments are normally free from jealousy, fear, or suspicion. You can trust your lover to be himself without suspicion. You can trust your lover to be himself without feeling threatened by compulsive emotional demands. Your openhearted arrangement allows for the freedom Geminis need to survive and prosper.

Conflicts over infidelity will be rare unless he is secretive or dishonest. Neither of you can resist being flirtatious because it's part of the Gemini charm. If you are really in love with him, you will be happy to limit your philandering to your imagination and realize fantasies with each other instead of actualizing them with others.

Though you may trust each other, Gemini buddies will not take each other for granted. You both believe in the principles of change and the constant flux of all things under the Sun. If it is love, your relationship will never be static. Geminis are always experimenting, probing the boundaries of experience. Your relationship will be no exception. If you two "settle down" to a predictable routine, your love may be in danger of suffocating from lack of Air-sign inspiration. Remember, Geminis are Mutable Air and the doldrums of boredom are deadly to your breezy sensibilities.

When your solar batteries are depleted and you are feeling insecure, a Gemini–Gemini love can seem futile. You may feel shanghaied on a love boat that is all sails, with no anchor and four pairs of hands on the tiller. Your dynamic energies as a couple may lack direction, giving full rein to impulse, curiosity, and chaos. As a result, you can feel dissatisfied and begin criticizing your mate.

Money can be a source of insecurity and dispute, since you both tend to let financial matters slide as long as you have enough to spend on your needs. Funds, like caution, are often thrown to the winds when two Geminis join forces. A passion for fashion and entertainment will place constant demands on your budget.

Disagreements and disaffections tend to be short-lived in a Gemini love because you are both changing. A little patience may be all you need to overcome your problems with each other. Since you are rarely down on yourself for any shortcomings, you will be just as lenient with your Gemini lover. It won't be hard to forgive and forget because there are so many more stimulating things on your mind. Mutual goals, established in your open-ended Gemini fashion, can give your love endurance as well as enthusiasm.

GEMINI & CANCER

When your restless Gemini Mercury begins to long for a home and security, your need for a more mature love could be perfectly met with a Cancer man. His Moon-ruled moods may leave him feeling insecure, but Cancer's fund of affection will overcome both of your periods of temporary instability. Your tendency has been to shy away from security, fearing restrictions on your vital need for freedom.

When your Cancer lover wants to put your intertwined initials on the towels, you may resist the urge to pack up and go to New Guinea. If it's love, you will be willing to stay with him forever, however long that may be. Cancer has so many virtues that you admire, you are willing to accept his need for you without feeling threatened.

Cancer and Gemini share the gift of gab, the power to entertain with lively minds and vivid imaginations. You genuinely enjoy one another's company. Your ever-shifting intellectual focus is complemented by his emotional fluctuations. By the same token, he will be sympathetic to your flights of fancy, even tolerant of your restless need for change. When your mental intensity drives you to the brink of distraction and nervous fatigue, your Cancer lover has the maternal instincts to comfort your overloaded circuits and cool off your impending Air-sign insecurities in the warmth of his loving arms.

Cancer tends to cling to the objects of his affection, and he will care for you as a precious possession. If you learn to love this patient soul, you will feel liberated rather than restricted by his feelings for you. His tender sympathy will be truly comforting in those moments when your Gemini wanderings leave you feeling lost and alone.

The protective affection in his lovemaking will act as a buffer between you and the pressures and insecurities of the outside world. Your sexual union should be exciting and fulfilling. Cancer men are ardent lovers who will intuitively respond to the imagination and fantasy element you provide as a partner. Your intellectual flexibility and his emotional shifts allow for sexual experiences together that are always changing, so don't be shy about introducing him to your most erotic fantasies.

You will also share intimacy on the intellectual and social levels. With a Cancer lover you will feel inspired to new achievements and exposed to new stimuli. You can make important new contacts that change your life. A dashing group of creative friends and acquaintances will keep you happy. Families and neighbors are highlighted in a Gemini–Cancer combination. Your relationship will grow and thrive as you bring others into your circle. Cancer can become a retiring homebody without your encouragement to enjoy parties, outings, and short trips. Travel experiences can be wonderful adventures with him as you bring out his latent desires to join you in exploring exotic places.

Problems between you arise from the same source as your strengths: the power of change. Since you are both men in flux, mentally and emotionally, there are times when your shifts are out of sync. The resulting feelings of estrangement are almost insufferable. He may feel his most possessive and clinging at a point when your most important need is for the freedom to pursue a special interest on your own.

You may feel impelled to give up everything in search of the new and different. Your Cancer man holds on to everything he cherishes—people, objects, or relationships. His comfort and well-being depend upon the familiar. Gemini can learn the importance of enduring values and deeply felt emotions from a Cancer lover.

Patience is the key to loving your Cancer man. Don't overreact to his mood changes, and don't probe too deeply for emotional reports from him. He often finds it difficult to verbalize his feelings. Allow him the freedom to experience these feelings on his own if he chooses to. Coax him out of his darker moments with humor and affection. His lovemaking may be most intense with you when he feels most insecure; it's a Cancer man's instinctive way of expressing his need for love and a way of showing you that you shouldn't feel responsible for his gloomy interludes.

Cancer is a Cardinal sign, and Mutable Gemini will look up to him for his originality and his intellectual sensitivity. He will show you the value in letting a good idea get better before acting upon it. By the same token, he likes to have his money earn a little interest before he spends it. Curb your impulses to give Cancer extravagant presents. He will be much more impressed if you use your imagination to give him a small symbol of your love and understanding.

Despite all your love and understanding, there is the potential for a love affair with a Cancer to be transitory. You drift apart as you grow into new worlds of achievement and new circles of acquaintance. The parting will be neutral, natural, and full of the affection you have learned to reciprocate. You have the tendency to be casual about relationships, but an affair with a Cancer will be a profound experience. If it comes to you after you have matured, it may be the lasting love of your life.

GEMINI & LEO

When you fall for Leo the Lion and his golden charms, the potentials for love are unlimited. Your restless intellect and his creative energy combine with typical Air and Fire intensity. The possibilities are for a permanent and passionate relationship to develop from your affair with a Leo.

He is under the influence of Fixed Fire. Like the proverbial burning bush, he is aflame with energy and drive, but he is not consumed. You are surprised and intrigued that you have to work hard to keep up with him, and it can be a real challenge. Leo has the strength and character and discrimination to focus your abilities. Changes will be significant. For once you have met a man who sets a pace that makes you want to slow down and settle down. Ideas, travel, and intellectual stimulation are all intense experiences for you in a Leo love affair.

He loves the limelight, and your social life should be filled with personal appearances at which you are expected to shine as brightly (almost) as he does. You may resent Leo's command performances turning you into the court jester, but he wants the rest of the world to admire your virtues. Leo will encourage you to read, write, and expand your horizons because he sees your extensive potential and wants you to display your talents.

He will be extravagant in his gifts, and you will both live high on the hog, if you can possibly afford it. Fashionable clothes, trendy resorts, and lavish entertainment could be the order of the day for a Gemini–Leo couple. You recognize your karmic ties and relish your friendship in tender moments as he squeezes your hand just before you board the Concorde for Carnaval in Rio. Gemini fantasies can come true with a Leo lover.

His Leonine nature is certainly evident in his passionate and affectionate approach to sex. Praise him for his sexual powers and he will purr like a kitten in your arms. Don't allow your Airy nature to distance you from him while making love. Your fantasies must center on him or he will become jealous and suspicious. Leo wants all of you to focus on the event when it comes to sex. If you are not responsive, he will begin to feel inadequate. When Leo is insecure, he will be driven to insufferable bouts of vanity and jealousy.

Leos tend to become emotionally committed to, and dependent upon, their loves. You may find his dependency too restricting and too intense to bear. You don't want the responsibility of maintaining his ego. You can hurt him by deflating his pride with humor, though he will usually be responsive to your glib wit. His emotional needs and demands will confuse and frustrate your analytical mind. As you become more flippant, he will become more arrogant and domineering. Arguments between you can become contests, with sarcasm and displays of temper that can destroy the trust you have built up together.

Your need for freedom will conflict with your desire to please him. His need for devotion will be frustrated by his inability to command or predict your restless energies. You share the power to perceive each other's needs but may be simply unable to provide for them. While blithe-spirited Gemini may accept the revelation that this is not to be a lasting love affair, poor Leo will feel personally responsible. Ending affairs is never easy for him because he leads with his heart, not his head.

If you can, let him down gently or he will be truly broken-hearted. Leo's pride and passion may lead to unpleasant scenes as he tries to recapture his frayed dignity. Just as he wants you to share his love, he will want you to experience his pain. Wounded lions are a dangerous element loose in the jungle of hurt and bewilderment. Appeal to the warmth of your friendship and to his generous spirit to make him understand that you have needs that neither you nor he can control.

Leo tends to be sentimental and nostalgic, while you are always attracted to the newest, the next, the latest. He will teach you to be more selective in your interests; always to go for the best, finest, highest goals. His noble spirit will enrich your life. You can encourage him to be less fixed in his opinions and more open to the world of wide experience. There will be a glittering social life that can expand your potential for advancement.

You are fascinated by his creative personality. If your free-ranging intellect acts as an influence to make him more flexible, he may be able to win your love forever. If you feel the need for intellectual and romantic adventures outside the relationship, the chances for permanence are not good. In either case you will become a better person and a more creative personality through a Leo love.

GEMINI & VIRGO

When Gemini meets Virgo, the heavens and the Earth are joined under the influence of Mercury the Communicator. You broadcast the messages and he refines them, pulsing them through the cables to get them to the widest possible audience. The modest instincts of the Virgo man will slow you down. On a positive level, he stimulates you into thinking about future long-range projects and material security. Unless you are old enough to appreciate it, a Virgo love may not be wise for you.

There is the possibility you will be drawn together through your friends, family, or business contacts. At first he may seem a bit conservative for your tastes, but there are indications of creative energy and ambitious undertakings. Writing, speaking, reading, films, or television are highlighted when Gemini and Virgo join forces in business or love.

The first flush of your attraction can be an enjoyable period of activity and investigation. Getting to know each other will be the beginning of a spirited friendship rather than an intense series of seductive encounters. Sex is not at the core of your reactions to each other, but sexuality will not be a difficult accommodation if you remember that Virgo is slower and more considered in his manner than Gemini.

You can benefit by the association with a materialist who can provide practical understanding and criticism. You may chafe under his scrutiny, but he sees through your illusions and gives you the advice of a friend. You have similar inspirations but different methods. Misunderstandings can come from lack of respect. Your Virgo lover may feel that you never stop being flighty and dizzy with change, and you may feel that he never relaxes, enjoys life, or stops being hung up on perfection.

Use your charm to gently lighten his serious nature. You know that he is clever, and surely he could learn to laugh with you in delight at the foibles of the world, rather than fret about things he cannot control. If he loves you for your best qualities, your Virgo man will not mind your need for lighthearted freedom. He will understand your need for variety and stimulation and even selfishly appreciate a break from your incessant activity. Virgo needs time alone to soothe his nerves. Otherwise he becomes critical, bitchy, and no fun to love.

When it comes to fun and love, the prospects for excitement depend upon you and your imaginative ways of introducing him to pleasure. There are many times when sex is an unnecessary distraction for both Mercury-influenced signs. When this happens, you are usually too excited mentally about some fabulous idea. Virgo is often too preoccupied with some problem or task to look upon sex as anything more than a duty to himself or to his partner. Gemini–Virgo lovers use their sexual interaction as a way of proving to each other (and themselves) that they still have the power to arouse and satisfy each other mentally, through physical expression.

It sounds a little complex, but there are the Twins to worry about, the chaste attitudes of the Virgin, plus the dualities of Mercury Air and Mercury Earth. Mixed emotions, insecurities, and difficult obligations result from your Sun signs and are expressed sexually. Voyeurism may be an important part of a Gemini–Virgo search for stimulation.

You interact most effectively with words and ideas. When the relationship is not going well, they will be the daggers you throw at each other. You can talk rings around him—with flash and dash, shadowboxing with sarcasm when you find him too stodgy and dull. He will zoom right through your little tornado with devastating criticism you never suspected him to be capable of thinking, let alone expressing!

And all over what? Your frivolity and fickleness or his criticism and banality? Is it due to a breakdown in communications and the nervous strain of maintaining this difficult but rewarding relationship? There are obligations in a Gemini–Virgo love that keep you together simply because separation becomes unthinkable. It may have to do with business or family pressures that would mean abandoning everything and starting a new life if you and Virgo were to dissolve the ties that bind you. As you get older and more mature, a lasting love relationship with Virgo is possible. You will stimulate each other on a mental plane, and sexuality will not be a burden to your communication. He will be more tolerant of your flirtatious nature, and he'll appreciate the artistic company of your eclectic circle, along with your irrepressible youthful qualities. You will value his solid abilities to manage the smallest details of your mutual concerns, which will give you a secure freedom as a base for your continued exploration of experience.

GEMINI & LIBRA

Air signs attract and the Airy Venus of Cardinal-sign Libra will certainly be attractive to your Mercurial tastes. He has an indefinable style that excites you. Though not classically handsome, he has a look that is unique enough to stimulate your Gemini mind. In conversation you will find him clever and responsive, indecisive but very charming.

You are both dual signs. The Balance reflects his own potential for dealing with complexities. Where the Twins want to experience everything, the Scales seek to evaluate experience through balanced values. Libra likes to think he practices moderation in all things. While he strives for this ideal he goes through incessant decision-making processes, always weighing and shifting the elements in his environment. You will see how he can appreciate your own inability to make up your mind. The difference is that he yearns to settle each issue once and for all, but new data is always coming in for appraisal. You can teach your Libra lover to relax and accept the fact that life is constantly changing.

Changes of scenery, exciting friends, and influence in the world of art and media are highlighted when your life becomes entwined with a Libra lover. Encourage him to focus his energies beyond the ordinary. You may have to select his daily wardrobe to save time and effort for more worthy intellectual pursuits.

Pursuing each other could be the best part of your relationship. He represents your Fifth House: love and sex. You will be eager to bed this man, and he will not be shy in returning your lighthearted but lustful suggestions. Don't be too Airy, because a Libra love could be one of the most compelling attractions of your entire life. Don't begin to play ball with his affections unless you are willing to go the whole nine innings.

If you decide to go the distance, the indications are for a brilliant coupling. Together you project the image of men of accomplishment and enjoyment. The aura of good fellowship surrounds you as his inclination for harmony helps channel your Gemini impulses into positive results.

You may meet at a point in your lives when neither of you desires a permanent lover. A casual relationship will be difficult, especially if you enjoy the experience of meeting him sexually. Your Libra buddy can provide passionate sex that excites you to the heights of your physical capacity. If you follow his lead, he will stimulate you to responses that will leave you both delighted as you switch roles to suit your moods.

Beyond the lure of sex, a Libra lover will also stimulate your need for affection and romance. They are important elements in your love, even more than sex, when it comes to a long-term association. The inner grace of your romance will be reflected in your environment. *Tasteful* and *fashionable* aptly describe your life-style with a Libra lover. Fresh flowers, good books, travel, and entertainment will make demands upon your budget, but you are both more interested in using money than accumulating it. You spend for new ideas, educational interests, or travel. He uses his money to purchase luxuries and comforts necessary to his sense of equilibrium.

Under Libra's influence you feel less restless and more content with life. But when things between you are not good, you may look upon his Libran judgments as attempts to strip you of your power of imagination. At this point he will resist your Gemini entreaties to come and play. You will believe he thinks you are silly, flighty, superficial, inverting every one of your strengths into weaknesses. But not for long. Your love for him will allow you to be adaptable enough to rearrange your illusion so that he can perceive the Balance once again.

He is usually tactful and courteous, desiring harmony in all things. If you wound him with a verbal outburst, he will not retaliate or escalate the unpleasantness. Libra will point out the inaccuracies of your judgment, the logical fallacies involved, and suggest a compromise based upon his analytical observations. His "old-smoothie" routine may not prevent a quarrel, but it will leave a door open to reconciliation. After you have blown your top you will realize that the issues are not really crucial to the love you share with this graceful charmer from Venus.

When you fall in love with a Libra man, together you can achieve an Airy blend of timeless qualities that will enrich your lives forever. Even if the pressures of life bring you to a parting of the ways, the experience of his graceful love may well become the standard by which you learn to judge all others.

GEMINI & SCORPIO

Gemini Twins provide the duality of your dynamic personality, but Scorpio finds himself enmeshed in the symbolism of triplicity. He is the Scorpion of sex and death, the Eagle of transcendent aspirations, and the Serpent of forbidden knowledge—quite a potent combination. You live in different worlds and are not likely to come across each other unless you are brought together by family or business connections.

His Scorpion magnetism comes from his Fixed Water qualities of deeply felt emotion. Your curiosity is activated to find out what it is he feels, what mysteries lie behind his penetrating gaze. The karmic fact that you will never plumb the depths of his emotional intensity will not deter your interest. A perpetual puzzle always keeps you interested. Remember, though, that Scorpio plays for keeps, and there are some games he won't play at all.

Though you project charm and wit, a Scorpio man will zero in on your sexuality. If he wants you, he wants you totally and will focus his intense desire on you, oblivious to your clever chatter. The effect can be hypnotic. Some-

thing you don't understand is happening. The wind in your
sails begins to slacken and you feel yourself being drawn
into a whirlpool.

At first you will revel in the mystery of this new adventure. He, too, will find you curious, unable to get you out
of his mind, and eager to get you into his bed. Yet he does
not seek to use you for mere sexual gratification. He feels
a deep desire to serve you somehow, to express the intensity
of the devotion he can feel.

Under his influence you can finish important projects. He
teaches you the power of single-mindedness as a means to
success and excellence. At the same time this strong, intense man comes to you for advice and wants you to feel
that you have his confidence. You are intrigued by this role
reversal, since you are usually the one who seeks to gather
information rather than dispersing wisdom. But then, it is a
rare and difficult relationship you are letting yourself in for,
Gemini.

Scorpio appeals to you for help and offers you devotion
and protection. Often you share an interest in the occult or
mystical subjects. Your sexual attraction to him will be powerful, but you must remember that he is possessive in his
love. Sex with him can be like a drug: some kind of compelling and exotic high. His ruling planet, Pluto, makes him
deeply serious, and sex is no exception.

Attempting to keep your relationship on a lighthearted
basis will not be acceptable to him. Scorpios are jealous,
even suspicious. Your freedom will be curtailed. The sex
may be fabulous, but that is never the be-all and end-all of
a relationship for Gemini, even in love. You need more
mental stimulation to keep you involved with another man
for any length of time. There are communication problems
with a Scorpio lover that prevent his real nature from revealing itself to you. Of course, you do the same thing with
your glib Mercurial illusions. He will get all the surface he
can handle, but you don't reveal your emotions because you
are not used to dealing on that level of expression.

This fascination-without-communication can make you

feel uncomfortable and insecure. Sometimes you feel like you are drowning, struggling for air. Your attempts to free yourself will cause him to feel hurt, betrayed in his affections, and even violently emotional. When he is in one of these states, he may become unpleasantly rough in his lovemaking or, exercising Plutonian self-control, withdraw from sexual relations altogether for a while.

When he's down on you, your spending habits, your friends, and your superficial interests will all come under criticism. You will respond with a few analytical observations of your own on the nature of his character faults. As you do, his Fixed Water will slowly become frozen into ice. It's an ill, cold wind that will blow between you when you have come to the end of your compulsive journey in the maze of a Scorpio love affair. It may pile up drifts of resentment that obscure a potential for a good relationship as friends or business associates.

At least you have the bruised but unbroken optimism inherent in Gemini to carry you out the door and out of his life. You may wish you had been able to convince him of the importance of a little emotional distance, but don't blame yourself or him. You were both being true to your Sun-sign needs. How could he expect you to trade your independence of spirit for his intense sexuality and heavyhearted devotion: this is too restricting to the Gemini.

When you remember how quiet and gently sensual he was when he fixed his gaze on you in the throes of love, you may feel a tug of nostalgia for those exciting erotic moments. But survival of spirit overcomes sentiment for you, Gemini. Now it's time to get back to the surface and get into your water wings or hop on an airplane after having probed the deep, dark seas of Scorpio's love.

GEMINI & SAGITTARIUS

Sagittarius is another dual-sign complication for your own Twin dualities. He is half horse and half man, all basking in the lucky vibrations of Jupiter. Usually depicted as the Archer, he aims his arrows into the Air with his Fire-sign intensity. One of the Centaur's arrows may just lodge in your heart and become as difficult to dislodge as Cupid's own darts.

Remember, your signs are opposite on the Wheel of Life. If you are mature enough to handle the obligations and rewards involved with the Sagittarian principles of steady expansion, idealism, and abstraction, this can be an open, fulfilled, and beneficial experience. The potential for creative freedom exists in your mutual love of the unexpected. Your status in life may improve through your Sagittarian lover because aspects between you involve contracts, obligations, public relations, and partnerships. Your Mercurial ideas can become moneymaking propositions as the financial rewards from Jupiter's influence encourage your acceptance of responsibility.

As opposites, you admire the qualities in his character that you, yourself, lack. If he is his normally extroverted Sagittarian self, you will be impressed with his enthusiasm, warm sincerity, and idealism. There is an instant spark of communication between you that is the signal of recognition. Both of you sense the potential for some empathetic companionship when you meet. You share your Mutable qualities and incite each other to engage in some flashy and dashing escapades as pals or lovers.

Sagittarius has many of your youthful qualities. He is optimistic and intelligent. He loves to travel, rarely willing to consider settling down until he has roamed the world. You will also find him charming, though perhaps a little blunt. He is an honest soul, but sometimes he embarrasses you with his lack of tact. His naïve version of the whole truth can rend the veil of illusion you artfully spin with your threads of imagination and conversation. When it comes to talking, your Airy breadth of interests intensifies his Fiery inspirations to create a fire storm that could scorch the planet.

Imagination and enthusiasm give your partnership a magical aura of excitement and energy. Lucky breaks can come your way that mitigate the potential for confusion with a Mutable-sign Centaur as your companion. Somehow speed seems of the essence when you join up with him. The relationship may be pleasurable and rewarding but too intense to endure the test of time. Opposites do attract, but in any polarity there is tension.

His Mutable urges impel him to seek respite in emotional stability and affection. Your Gemini fund of talents is usually low on these two particular items. When he realizes he can't depend on you to fulfill his emotional needs, he will not be averse to accepting romantic dalliances. Both of you have wide circles of friends and acquaintances. The opportunities for infidelity are usually great, and the temptations are more than your exploratory natures can resist.

Competition with a Sagittarian lover can drive the two of you to incredible binges of overindulgence. You can degenerate into a restless searching for new highs. As you neglect your intellectual and spiritual development, you will find yourself blaming him. And when you become sarcastic with your Centaur lover, he will shoot it right back to you honestly and bluntly—aimed right for the heart.

If things begin to break down, you will find him becoming more abstract and philosophical. Sagittarius will retreat into his idealistic mode, unable to be reached on your glib and charming wavelength. The Centaur will get the urge to travel again and broaden his horizons. Colorado—or Katmandu—may be calling him. Absence will revive the fondness in your hearts that has been buried under the tensions of keeping up with each other in a difficult relationship.

Once he's gone, you will both feel the exhilaration of freedom. A vacation may be just the breather you need to refurbish your energies, though you are more likely to head for Key West than an ashram in the Rockies. When you return from your journeys, there will be enjoyable hours of special stories that only you two friends can share with ultimate delight. You may find that you have gained a new breadth of vision, a respect for idealism that has strengthened your character. You can thank lucky Jupiter for the lessons learned from a Sagittarius lover.

GEMINI & CAPRICORN

Dutiful Capricorn will intrigue you in an inexplicable way because stern Saturn is not normally compatible with your happy-go-lucky Mercurial influences. There is something sound, even reassuring, in his Cardinal Earth manner as he relentlessly pursues his path up the mountain, picking his way with the sure foot of the Mountain Goat.

Capricorns are supposed to be restrained, and Geminis are supposed to be more interested in the mind than the body, but your aspects indicate that sexuality will be the core of your relationship. It may not be the greatest sex you've ever had, but you are particularly drawn to him as a partner. There are many reasons why you may not be interested in him emotionally or socially, but you are drawn to him in a fated relationship during the first blush of your meeting.

It won't be animal magnetism drawing you together across a crowded floor that prompts your first meeting. Normally the Twins and the Mountain Goat live in such different environments that you are rarely aware of each other. But once you have been introduced by friends, family, or business associates, the attraction may be activated. You may impulsively decide that his arrival in your life is a message, a symbolic moment in time that is calling you to investigate the world of this mountain man.

As he becomes your latest hobby, you will find that he takes life much more seriously than you do. Saturn is all about rules, restrictions, and obligations. Sound like fun? Well, it could be. Very often these men are involved in various forms of art appreciation or patronage. He can introduce you to a circle of interesting and well-placed people in creative fields. Capricorns are in their prime after forty or fifty. By then they have achieved the material success that made them so single-minded and uptight as young men. Once they have attained material security through their typically painstaking efforts, they relax and enjoy life. Saturn rules time, and time is very kind to Capricorn. He is one man whose sex life actually improves with age.

It you meet at the right time in your lives, there is much benefit to be derived from a May–December love with a frisky old Goat. Travel can be accented in a way that will be pleasing and exciting to both of you. He will enjoy the meticulous tasks of preparation and execution of details for a trip, leaving you free to add the notes of exploration, discovery, and excitement in a new or different environment. As an attractive and scintillating travel companion, you increase his sense of prestige and accomplishment. In return, he will be gentle, considerate, and comforting to you.

When it comes to comfort, both Gemini and Capricorn will find that sex releases them from the pressures of the daily world. You feel relieved and reassured because he is not a man of intense passion. A demanding emotional relationship is not suited to either of you.

If it's a loving arrangement, the planets indicate that he will expect you to serve him in some way. He will value your energy, your youthful spirit, and your alert attention to the things he has to teach you. The values placed upon the Capricorn virtues of achievement, stability, and gracious aging will become apparent to you.

While there are subtle ways in which your affair can develop into devotion, there are also obvious differences between you and a Capricorn lover that will be difficult to overcome. If there is anything he wants from a lover, it is commitment—in return for security. You already know that security and commitment are the two things that can start you packing your bags. Your love may come with a warranty that broken hearts will be mended but never with a lifetime guarantee on his investment.

A Capricorn lover will keep his frustration to himself, but his silence will be enough to let you know that he is feeling cold, alone, and empty. All he really needs is a big hug and a declaration of love, respect, and affection. But you are not easily physically demonstrative. By the same token, when you are feeling down, you want him to talk to you and verbalize his love. Yet he is never comfortable expressing his emotions outright. The result is a falling-off of communication, which leaves you both unfulfilled but not unsympathetic. Often you will remain loyal friends, even if your love does not stand the test of time.

GEMINI & AQUARIUS

Air-sign lovers make dynamic partners, and Fixed Air Aquarius is no exception to the rule. Ruled by Uranus, the planet of eccentricity, this man has the potential to keep you stimulated and activated beyond your wildest fantasies. Why? Because he will combine his wildest fantasies with your own to create a magical festival of delights.

His nature is symbolized by the Water-bearer, spilling the substance of spirit from the jar of experience. He is often zany, but your own Mutable Air frequencies will never cause you to question any of his unpredictable antics. Like jamming musicians, you find that you have the power to "riff" off each other and make some very far-out music. From bebop to New Wave, a Gemini–Aquarius love can be an experience to beat the band.

No isolated duets when you two guys get together, either. His wide circle of odd friends and unusual acquaintances will fascinate you. He's into humanitarian causes, and you could well meet at a fund-raiser for his favorite movement; or first see him on a float at the Gay Pride parade; or on roller skates, being pulled along behind the biggest motor-cycle you ever saw. Your first impulse will be to get to know this wild and wonderful stranger.

It won't take long to make his acquaintance. Aquarians are usually open and friendly, easy to converse with, even fun to argue with sometimes. Like you, he has a free-ranging intelligence; and you will be stimulated to learn, discover, and experiment. He flouts convention, and you will join in laughing at the hang-ups and foibles of straight society. As a couple, you will bring joy, laughter, and excitement to your friends and to each other. Amusements and entertain-ments can be the ever-shifting foundation of a Gemini–Aquarius love affair.

Youthful enthusiasm permeates your relationship. Sex is playful and extensive in its experimental diversions. Emo-tions are not so complex here, but fantasies are both head-ing into hyperdrive as you two zoom out to the far reaches of the Universe on flights of orgasmic ecstasy.

This relationship has a built-in tolerance that will allow both Gemini and Aquarius the freedom needed to manifest your personalities. *Empathy, fraternity,* and *compatibility* are the key words that characterize this ever-changing love affair. You will combine your talents in travel, education, philosophy, and creative efforts. You feel encouraged to ex-tend yourself into new areas of endeavor. Gay activism may become the focus of your interest under his influence. Aquarius urges you to seek a greater understanding of your world and to discover new meanings for your talents.

His is a Fixed sign, and therein lies the chief difference between you and your lover. Exciting and experimental as he may be, he has definite ideas about life that he will not change. He is a man of principle, despite his unpredictable nature. He believes in freedom and friendship. A devotion to truth makes him tolerant of the Gemini urge to be true to your personality.

Clashes between you and your Aquarian lover are verbal gems of wit and wordplay with stormy undertones. Neither of you is afraid of Virginia Woolf. There are no deep emotional issues involved with Air signs, but there is much surface tension. Money will always be a worry, as his influences will make you more likely to spend more than usual. Your arguments are over common interests rather than points of essential difference, squalls rather than hurricanes. Since neither of you is particularly reliable or dependable, little outbursts are inevitable as lines of communication get crossed and recrossed. Often there are times when he will seek solitude. As a Fixed sign, it is difficult for him to apologize.

Should your love affair dwindle due to the pressures of your life-style, the communion between you and your Aquarian should still be a lasting phenomenon. There is so much you value that only you two can share. Should subsequent love affairs or happenstance drive you to each other's arms again, it will be as fast friends. Each of you will represent a kind of "home" and safety to each other, no matter where you may roam.

GEMINI & PISCES

A Pisces is doubly loaded with the possibilities implied by your mutual dualities. The Twins meet the Fishes in a confusing combination of Mutable Air and Mutable Water. Mystical Neptune keeps inquisitive Mercury from getting all the facts in a love affair with a Pisces man. Similarities exist on a superficial level, but your motivations are very different.

Your first meeting should result in your powers as a conversationalist being matched by his skills as a good listener. It may not sound terribly stimulating for some signs, but you appreciate an interested audience as only a compulsive communicator can. His sensitive eyes, even though as furtive as yours, make you feel relaxed and confident. Though his emotional life is complex, he is not demanding in a relationship. Pisces is the sign of service and sacrifice. A loving man born under this influence will be affectionate and tolerant with you, but it will still be a rather tense arrangement.

Your common love of art, culture, and beauty will bring you together and be a source of renewal for your relationship. Pisces also shares your dislike of boredom but lacks your social and mental energy to overcome moments of lassitude. While his emotional level is high, his energy level is low. Your Mercurial enthusiasm lights up his life with charm and humor. Your time together can represent a rest and refuge from the normal pressures you both feel. The problem is that there is often more going on beneath the surface than you are used to perceiving.

Pisces men share your own qualities of elusiveness and evasion in the face of direct questions. You are mentally agile under Mercury's influence and create little diversions to stimulate your imagination through exaggeration and embellishment. You tend to cover up your superficialities, but your Pisces lover is trying to hide the fact that he is vulnerable. Neptune gives him powers of mystification that obscure issues as a means of survival. He is sensitive but lacks your powers to analyze what he feels. Your own tendency to be ever-changing confuses and fascinates him.

Fantasy is an important element in your lives, but at very different levels. You seek to explore fantasies and incorporate them into your actual life. Pisces keeps his fantasy life to himself and expects you to respect his privacy. Don't be too curious about his daydreams or pry into their substance. Making them ''public'' will only make him more vulnerable and decrease your chances for happiness.

He is the kind of guy who would take an extra job to help you raise money for a career project, do your laundry and shopping to give you more time to meet a deadline, and have a hot meal ready when you come home from a long day. It may sound pretty cushy, but your pussywillow Pisces will demand that you reciprocate by living up to your ideas and sticking to your guns.

A Pisces lover is not possessive or jealous, preferring you to need him in ways beyond desire. Neither of your Mutable natures requires passionate physical sex for a satisfying partnership. Fantasy fulfillment is an important element in your sex life, but you will have to take the lead in a subtle Gemini way.

Let your Pisces lover set the tone of your lovemaking. Learn to read his body language, his Neptunian clues. You can reveal your repertoire of sexual experience and information by accurately responding to his sexual moods. You need the mental challenge of figuring out what will please him, and he needs the element of variety to increase his sexual involvement. His emotional needs will spark your mental responses.

The best aspects of your sexual experiences indicate that it will be an energy exchange for both of you. As lovers, you will become more intense. Sex will be one way of attempting to get on to each other's wavelength.

A Pisces lover can give you a new perspective on your abilities. Under his influence you will learn how to turn your inspirations into realities where career is concerned. Where love is concerned, Pisces cannot free you from the multiple layers of illusion and deception that can coalesce like fog banks on the shoreline of your love for each other.

LOVING YOUR GEMINI MAN

Your Gemini man is an entertaining and charming bundle of enthusiasm, inspiration and intelligence. A bird of bright plumage, he will never sing in a gilded cage. Freedom is the key to his happiness and success. If you are secure enough to accept the love of a wandering minstrel, a Gemini man will provide an exciting and rewarding experience for you.

Communication is the essence of his archetype. His restless mentality compels him to explore that which catches his interest. Gemini is the classic "social butterfly." Meeting new people, engaging interesting strangers in conversation, and exchanging ideas and influences through friends and acquaintances are his devotions in life.

Like the youthfulness he symbolizes, he desires to know and experience without commitment to any prescribed course of action. On one level it leaves him open to charges of superficiality, but it also allows him the potential for unlimited growth. It is true that his desire for breadth over depth makes him seem emotionally shallow. Gemini is capable of many simultaneous social and romantic contacts, just as he is able to read several books at one time. Each interest or fascination receives his undivided attention—but not forever.

You will meet many Gemini men if you are involved in the media, the fashion industry, or any activity where communication and quick ideas are in demand. His intelligence is restless, his sexuality diffuse. If he finds you attractive, a Gemini will rarely come on to you sexually. He turns on the charm and wins your confidence through his intimate conversation.

The Gemini man's sexual interest is connected to the degree of mental stimulation he receives from you. If he likes your mind, he will want to get to know you physically as well. He needs someone to talk to, and if that person can also provide him with sexual pleasure, so much the better. If not, he can be content for long periods with an active circle of friends, supplemented by an active imagination.

If you come to love one of these elusive Twins, be aware of his duality in all things. He may seem dizzy, flighty, and altogether untogether, but it is usually a smoke screen for his feelings of inadequacy. If he seems silly to people, it is because he feels no responsibility to be serious. Security holds little interest for him in a love affair. Consistency can equal boredom for a Gemini. If you let your life-style get too cozy, too regular, or too predictable, his mental wanderlust will compel him to roam.

The range of his activities can be truly amazing. Usually Gemini has had many jobs, and his résumé is a study in eclecticism. He's always striving to be on top of the scene. Fashion, style, and current trends are his areas of expertise. Gemini can develop and discard a look faster than any other Sun-sign man.

If you want to keep him, you have to keep him interested. A Gemini lover will encourage you to expand your own horizons in an effort to keep up with him. Surprises delight him. Take him to places he's never seen, keep finding new stimuli, and he will be happy and content in his own frenetic way. Gemini's tendency is to dominate the tone, rather than the specifics, of a relationship. He will agree to let you plan your evenings together, but he will expect you to keep the calendar filled with activity.

Imagination is the key word where Gemini's sexuality is concerned. He is stimulated by suggestive situations and pornography. If you get him to express and act out his imaginary sex life, you will find him an exciting partner. Variety is his middle name. Any new wrinkle you introduce into lovemaking will intrigue him. Geminis are fond of all manner of gadgets and toys. As in all things with this Mercurial man, let your imagination be your guide.

The dual nature of his Sun sign makes him both participant and observer in most things. It's this indefinable element that signals his lack of total commitment. Sometimes you feel as if he's only half listening; the other half is busy formulating his next question. He can be single-minded in his attention but not for long periods. His strength is in the sprint, not the marathon.

Travel is a great stimulant to him. He delights in new people, places, and situations, which makes him great fun on the road. Visit cities rather than going on camping trips or to isolated cottages by the shore because he is easily bored, even in an exotic setting, if he isn't getting new data and feedback all the time. A Gemini man is usually good at language, and foreign travel will challenge and excite his urge to communicate.

Unexpected gifts will be greatly appreciated by a Gemini lover. Books, magazines, avant-garde accessories, and theater tickets will all find the way to his heart. A month in the country is more than he can tolerate, but a relaxing day trip or weekend will help calm some of his excessive nervous energy. If you want to care for his needs, you should find ways to slow him down periodically, or he might work his way into nervous exhaustion.

Gemini's Mutable nature makes him adaptive and flexible. He'll try anything once, even a possessive and restrictive love affair. It won't last long, and the memory of its lessons will confirm his other investigations in life. You will hold on to him only by keeping the bond between you as open as possible. If your arms are there to hug him rather than hold him, if your communication is meant to stimulate him rather than scold, he will always return to you after a flight of fancy. A Gemini wants to feel needed, but only for his inherent virtues. If you try to pin him down, you will lose his marvelous essence and his love. If you keep the options open, this roving bee will always deliver the honey.

CANCER
June 21–July 20

Symbol: The Crab
Ruling Planet: The Moon
Colors: Pale blues and greens
Metal: Silver
Natural House Relationship: Fourth House, the
    house of home and family
Fourth House Traits: Desire for emotional security
    and regard for the past
Motto: ''I feel''
Nature: Cardinal sign (leadership)
Element: Water sign (emotional)
Qualities: Cautious, intuitive, and sensitive
Capacities: Creative leadership, perceptive planning
Personality Key Words: Imaginative, romantic, and
    tenacious

MAXIMIZING YOUR CANCER POTENTIAL

Often referred to as the Moon Child, the Crab is characterized as a Cardinal Water sign, governed by the tidal flow of
emotions associated with the Moon. As a Cardinal sign,
your instinct is to lead with your creative intelligence and
wit. At the same time, however, your innate shyness holds
you back. You question yourself, weighing your need for
affection and recognition against your fear of rejection, rid-
icule, or failure. Cancer is a reflective, receptive, passive
sign, and you respond to the phases of the Moon in your
approaches to life and love. Your powers of subtle perception can make you moody, but if you go with the flow,
you will find happiness and success in life's endeavors.

Extreme sensitivity is both your prime talent and your
biggest obstacle in developing a successful personality. You
are intuitive, but the shifting sands of your moods cause
you to doubt your ability to act upon your feelings. You
need a sound affectional continuity in your life to give
you emotional security in a sea of change.

Cancer is blessed with the power of intuition. If you see
someone who attracts your interest or attention, you will
file him away in your memory. Your paths will mysteriously
intersect in the future, almost as if you had willed it. Often
these chance encounters will reveal important associations
in your life. In similar ways, your partners are "chosen for
you." You can't really define the man of your dreams because you perceive him as a feeling rather than a look. If
you can learn to trust your inner voice, you can be carried
along on some very enjoyable and enriching appointments

with destiny. Though the children of the Moon instinctively know that you should follow your heart, there is the problem of maintaining enough self-confidence to follow through. The security of a loving relationship can be the missing element that gives you enough faith in yourself to become a creative and happy person.

Worry and doubt can nibble at your consciousness like the tides eroding the shoreline of self-confidence. Your imagination is so finely tuned that you can fall prey to unwarranted paranoia. A glance, a sigh, a hesitation, or an overheard remark can etch itself in your brain and send you either into gloomy despair or delicious rapture.

You are most likely to meet your lover through friends or common interests than through the diversions and vagaries of social encounters. Finding a lover will have an enormous effect on your life. The welfare of those you care for is as important to you as your own well-being. You are the one in your crowd who always arrives with chicken soup (or its equivalent) in an emergency. It is this very quality of devotion that may be too much for some lovers to accept. Cancer clings to relationships, to symbols of love, even after they have outgrown their positive potential. If you smother your lovers, you will stifle the very affection you crave.

You like to take the lead in lovemaking, but at the same time you wait for your partner to signal his desires. With a more aggressive man you may not have the strength to articulate what you really like, so you simply follow his course of action. You can become caught in "the pleasure trap," giving satisfaction to your lover but remaining curiously unsatisfied yourself. Your lovemaking is sensuous and affectionate, but affection need not mean passivity.

Many Cancers live too much in the past, failing to take advantage of the present. You keep your secret hurts and fears to yourself, and yet you long for a lover with whom you can be open and vulnerable. When your need for intimacy is frustrated, you withdraw into yourself rather than expose your insecurities. Clinging to negative feelings will not serve you or your lover's best interests.

You need a man who is willing and able to reassure you about your worth and dignity. He will need intelligence and good humor to still your fears and wipe away your tears. When your romantic, sensitive, and emotional feelings are activated, the pressure comes out in your eyes. The ability to cry is a naïve virtue and an important release, but don't overindulge yourself. Fortunately your Cancerian ambitious streak should leave you little time for wallowing in self-pity while there is work to be done.

Your drive for success is fueled by your desire for recognition and your need for security. Caution is evidenced in the Crablike way of approaching objectives indirectly. You never make a frontal assault in love or business. You like to work behind the scenes until all of the elements are in place for you to take proper credit for your achievements.

Cancer men are nest builders and collectors. You need a secure and comfortable base of operations. Too much comfort, however, can dull your creativity, narrow your imagination, and thwart the success you crave. You need a stimulating environment to really shine at your brightest. If you are secure enough in your home and in your love life, then you should be able to meet challenges with verve and gusto. Travel, business contacts, and creative triumphs are indicated when the pressure is on, Cancer!

The combination of sensitivity, imagination, and showmanship makes for a potentially exciting career. Life in the limelight keeps you glowing, and success is indicated in the entertainment, public relations, or communications industries. But no matter how dazzling your professional life becomes, home is always where the heart is for you. At the end of a day you need a place of repose, a well-stocked kitchen, a small circle of intimate friends, and a man to hold you and love you in the quiet of the night!

Though Cancer is often characterized as frugal, you can be lavish in giving love and in accumulating the symbols of affection that give meaning to your life. Material success can never be an end in itself for you, unless it provides the security of love as well. Holding on, holding back, and becoming overly dependent in love will not keep you afloat on a raft of hope and faith that leads you to a future filled with creative experiences. Just as the oyster creates a pearl from its tears, you have the power to transform fear and longing into serenity and beauty.

CANCER & ARIES

Aries men are ruled by macho Mars. Their Cardinal Fire qualities are not usually compatible with your own Cardinal Water nature. You both want to be leaders, but he is often too impulsive for your more subtle instincts. Cancers are attracted to the overt masculinity of Arians, and the aspects of your Moon rulership and Mars indicate physical desire.

Aries is the aggressive type who is easy for you to meet because there is no ambiguity about his intentions. You could be swept off your feet by this dashing buck Ram. His own bravado makes you brave enough to throw caution to the wind, or, in this case, to the flame of his promises of passion.

The promise will be best kept if you limit your expectations. Aries isn't necessarily looking for a full-time lover. Though he might need a man who can take care of him, he will not be able to provide you with the kind of reciprocal security you crave. A commitment to an Aries relationship could become a very one-sided arrangement in which you submerge your own needs in order to provide for him. The end result would be a feeling of frustration, which will cause you to be melancholy, nagging, and prone to outbursts of temper.

Dependency is often aspected in your relationships. With

Aries, you are likely to become dependent upon him. Though it may initially flatter his ego to feel that you can't live without him, he isn't really able to accept that kind of responsibility. In the first blushes of love he may be willing to accept the role of protector to your tender soul, but it cramps his style too much for his own comfort. Aries needs to be free in a way that precludes taking on your problems or being home on time for dinner.

If love begins to grow between you and Aries, it will be more tempestuous than you can usually handle. Sometimes he will pick a fight just to keep the waters stirred up. Arian emotions are much more volatile than your own subtly shifting feelings and perceptions. He may hurt you without realizing how sensitive you are.

Remember that Aries' primary devotion is to his own ego. Your love may cause you to feed his ego, to your own detriment. The aspects between Cancer and Aries indicate that you will not be able to reconcile your shy, cautious emotional needs with his impulsive, pioneering spirit. In order to survive, you must learn to be more self-assertive with an Aries lover. In turn, you can teach him to be more considerate in his actions.

Aries enjoys frequency and friskiness where sex is involved. Power, presence, and control will be issues if you two are regular sex partners. Aries wants sex often. While you can keep him dangling forever with exquisite foreplay, he may not be able to restrain his Fire-sign urge to explode. The cuddly, buddy-to-buddy sex you like is only possible with him occasionally. It all depends upon how well you communicate your mood and your need for affection.

Cancers are not up-front about stating their feelings. Arians are not noted for their sensitivity to others. Your moods will be a mystery to him, and he doesn't have the patience for puzzles. When it becomes too frustrating to deal with an Aries lover, you will have to do your crying alone. Tears evoke a form of confusion and insecurity in Aries that is too emotional for him to confront.

If you find your Aries love affair drifting from tears to

temper to tantrum, you should learn how to let go. The Crab will instinctively hold on until he loses a claw rather than release his grip. It is most likely that Aries will call it quits before you do, anyway. He is not afraid to admit failure in love and forge ahead to the next adventure. It is an Aries trait you should observe with all of your Cancerian perception and intelligence. If you fall into gloomy brooding over the past, your potentially bright future will never be realized.

The problem with the Ram and the Crab centers on the differences between Fire and Water as astrological qualities. Nevertheless, if you and your Aries lover are tuned in to your inner natures, you may understand that you do have things in common. Aries and Cancer have similar goals, similar insecurities, and similar desires for affection. You will both be wiser, stronger, and more loving from the experience of a Cancer–Aries romance.

CANCER & TAURUS

If you find yourself falling in love with Fixed-Earth Taurus, it won't be long before it becomes something more serious and lasting than just an affair. Venus is his ruling planet, and he loves being in love, especially if the man in question values security, comfort, money, food, and sex.

Well, Moonbeam, what are you waiting for? You are probably responding to your sensitive perception of his unhurried nature. The Bull doesn't like to be rushed into anything or overtly seduced. When you're dealing with Taurus, your movements should be slow, deliberate, and reassuring. You can gain his confidence and prevent him from charging. Your waves of Cardinal-Water inspiration present no threat to his Fixed-Earth stability. There is harmony here, and a peace of mind that can even transcend your moody Lunar lows. So take your time getting to know him and you may end spending a long, long time together learning, growing, and loving with a Taurus man.

Since your signs have inherently compatible aspects, you probably have warm associations with other Taureans in your family or in your past. He has a powerful memory as well, and Cancers have likely been close friends for whom he has equally fond feelings. You are predisposed to friendship, since Taurus represents your Eleventh House: friends, hopes, and wishes.

Neither of you reacts very well to change, especially unexpected ones. You can get so involved in security and routine that sudden successes will depress you rather than cause elation. It may seem strange, but your mutual tendency is to worry, even in the face of good fortune.

His love of luxury makes you unnaturally extravagant with your money and your time. In your desire to please him, you lavish him with gifts and attention, which does not serve your own best interest. Taurus has the reputation for being practical, but he can turn a blind eye to spending when it comes to creature comforts. It would be typical of a Cancer–Taurus couple to live frugally when it comes to necessities so that they have enough money to spend on luxuries.

Living in the lap of Taurean comfort can be the worm in the apple, the fly in the ointment, and trouble in paradise— if you lean back and let it all bathe over you. Remember, you are a Cardinal sign and you achieve only under a challenge to your intellect. Taurus is not aggressive enough to give you the challenge to succeed. You will have to be the motivator and initiator, or else your cozy contentment is in danger of becoming frustration as you find yourself drifting aimlessly on a placid sea of routine.

Taurus has a built-in admiration for your creativity. He wants you to take the lead and is willing to give you all the support you need. He has the stamina of the Bull and enough perseverance to help you make your dreams come true, if

you articulate your wishes. Your Taurus lover will work hard
for you and with you, but the direction must come from
your own inspiration.

A similar situation prevails when it's time for lovemaking.
Though you will find him to be a cozy and cuddly lover of
luxuriant pace and great capacity, you will have to bring the
imagination into the bedroom—and I do mean bedroom. It's
about the only place in which he is willing to indulge in
sexual pleasures. Cancerians are able to enjoy sex on bear-
skin rugs, beaches, or sofas, anywhere that's private and
comfortable. Taurus tends to be conventional. He is no
prude, just a creature of habit with simple, but ample, sexual tastes. You can deal with this by being patient and inventive and not forgetting your sense of humor. Little trips
will add spice to your sex life because he responds to a
change in surroundings. Exotic situations may lead to more
exotic sex. You two rarely discuss sex. Overcome the communication barrier by leaving a well-known "joyous" gay-
sex manual on the breakfast table with a marker at a page
that appeals to your imagination. As long as he has some
advance warning and some idea of what is expected, he will
try to please. Don't be surprised or hurt if he laughs about
exotic sexual treats. Enjoy his Earthy sense of humor, but
don't stop what you're doing!

When Taurus displeases you, it will be short-lived and
easily reconciled. On some issues you simply may have to
agree to disagree. Though he is possessive, you don't mind
the security of being his prize possession. His practical sensibility contrasts well with your imaginative sensitivity. No
other Sun-sign partner can allay your fears and insecurities
as well as your Taurus man.

When the chips are down, there is never any question of
your mutual loyalty and commitment to the survival of the
relationship. Though you have a large and eclectic circle of
friends, you always act as a team. The stability and affection
you share is often widely admired as a paragon of male
relationships. The auguries are certainly here for a love of
lasting quality and amazing grace.

CANCER & GEMINI

Cancer is emotionally and intuitively attracted to the Gemini Twins. Since he is the sign just before yours, Gemini looks up to you for information on his next level of karmic experience. By the same token, you have an intuitive sensitivity to his motivations because, on the same karmic level, you have already been through the Gemini experience.

The influence of his planetary ruler, Mercury, increases your desire to communicate with Gemini. Not only does he stimulate you with his witty conversation, but also you feel at ease in his company. Gemini represents your Twelfth House: secrets. You may find that he becomes your confidant.

If you are in love, you will be willing to trust him with some of your secret vulnerabilities. This can be a gesture of intimacy, but it is also a Cancerian way of avoiding the pressures of idolization that you sense developing in him. You protect yourself by revealing that the idol has feet of clay. Of course, if he really has a case for you, Gemini will be just as impressed by your humility!

Gemini in love will feel fascination but not deep emotional commitment. His Mutable-Air and your Cardinal-Water qualities can blend to create projects and think of ideas that look so good, you are forever chasing after them. Be true to your cautious Cancerian self and don't get swept away by this breezy charmer. Air and Water create no solid framework on which to hang your mix of imagination and experimentalism.

You are fortunate if your Gemini affair happens when you are young. A Cancer–Gemini combination has an appropriate feeling of adolescence about it. If you are older, a May-December love could add a revivifying note of youth to your life. Gemini men are so wide-eyed and eager that they make ideal young lovers. Your best maternal/paternal instincts are stimulated in your desire to protect and advance him.

Your need for emotional security and commitment conflicts with Gemini's free-ranging quest for experience. With a Gemini lover it will never be dull or boring. The problem is that your clinging nature could inhibit the extension and expression of his intellect. When he doesn't have much to say, it may be due to the restrictions he feels from your protective and possessive attitudes toward him.

Without variety in your own life you can become lethargic and melancholy. A Gemini lover can provide that variety if you let him..It will mean letting go in order to hold on—a Zen paradox for Cancers in love with Geminis.

Variety combined with fantasy are elements he brings in abundance to your sex life. Your imagination is capable of responding to his sexual fantasies and focusing them into lusty realities. No need to feel inhibited with a Gemini partner. You must remember that he is prone to ecstasy rather than passion. Sex is a physical and mental activity for Gemini, not an expression of emotion. Gemini is both participant and observer in everything. Even in the most intimate form of sexual sharing he cannot give you a total emotional commitment.

Accept the fact that your motivations are different but not incompatible. Despite his superficiality, Gemini has a breadth of vision that you can appreciate and enhance. Encourage his curiosity rather than being a wet blanket. Sometimes you feel that it's a one-sided love affair or a triangle between you and him and his Twin. Your despairing mood will lift when you recall the feeling of lightness and joy he imparts to your sensitive spirit.

The thrill of discovery powers his Twin dynamos and keeps his imagination charged. Travel often brings out the best in your relationship. You prefer a modicum of comfort, but Gemini will be willing to backpack it for the sake of adventure. Gemini and Cancer can be a pair of happy, loving gypsies on the road.

Gemini may be adorable and fun, even when he is being

his most manic; but the pace he sets may be too wearing on both of you. Eventually you may be drawn apart, but if your love has fulfilled its potential, you will have learned the power of letting go with grace. There may even be a drop of relief among the tears you shed when it is all over. You will smile again when you realize the best part of your Gemini love affair is that you have both increased your understanding of love in ways that will make better lovers in a brighter future.

CANCER & CANCER

Crab to crab, claw to claw, two Moonbeam lovers can cling to each other like clones as you wander hither and yon along the beach of life. As with all same Sun-sign relationships, you have the potential to reinforce all your mutual strengths and weaknesses. Your highs are rapturously high, your lows abysmally low. But the wonderful power of his sense of humor will combine with your own to make the best of the worst times.

The initial attraction is easy, trusting, and intuitively sexual. Your feelings tell you that this will be an enjoyable experience, even if it doesn't go beyond the physical magnetism that pulls at you like the tides. If he pleases you, your longing for true companionship will urge you to take the risk. It will not be difficult for you to open up to him once you sense his patience and caring.

You can meet a Cancer buddy at any of the places you usually frequent—beaches, art galleries, museums, the theater, or through close friends. The attraction will be strong, but so is the fear of rejection; Cancer Crabs approach each other with cautious, sideways moves. You are sensitive enough to be aroused by the way he seems both eager and shy. A little furtive eye contact and a reassuring smile are enough to set your imaginations buzzing on the same wavelength.

Time your approaches to the tentative mystery of the New Moon. As the Moon waxes, so will your own Moonbeams begin to glow in each other's reflection. Seduction scenes will follow with delicious results. Delicious means food, and both of you know that the way to a man's heart is through his taste buds. A Cancer with an empty fridge is as lonely and unhappy as a Cancer with an empty bed. Nourishment equals love for you, and his love can be as rich and filling as a fine meal. Rather than competing in a culinary contest from the outset, invite him to dinner at a cozy bistro, someplace that serves small portions of exquisite cuisine. The meal should leave you just satisfied enough to appease your appetite but leave room for other hungers once he comes back to your place for a nightcap.

Given your natural caution, the seduction scene could go on into the wee, small hours until you are both so relaxed that you fall easily and naturally into each other's arms at the slightest physical contact. You will discover that his erotic imagination physically complements your own. You two can tease, tickle, and tongue each other to the point of no return, then go back for more. Your lovemaking will transport you to new heights of erotic enjoyment; his goal is to express the depth and intensity of his emotions.

Your Cancer man is a Cardinal sign and you like him to take the lead in bed because you want to please him and then bask in his reflected enjoyment. Well, he feels the same way. Unless you are going to make love all night, one of you will have to take the matter into his own hands and guide the other to the next step on the stairway to the stars. Variety is essential to his sexual well-being, and fantasy games and dress-up can all be extremely pleasurable with gently affectionate Cancer as your erotic playmate.

Both the need to lead and the need to serve your lover can create mutually dependent confusion when you fall in love with a Cancer. Making decisions can be very difficult as each of you undercut your dominant instincts for fear of treading on the other's feelings. Your goals for personal achievement may go unrealized as you concentrate on your mutual needs for security. Crabs are tenacious, and both of you collect and retain things long after they have become necessary or useful. Hanging on to symbols of security and continuity will keep you feeling stable and settled, but it may not be very satisfying if you get bogged down in a miasma of domestic routine.

You need to be drawn outside yourself and the tight bond of your relationship. It's important to stay anchored in the world of real events and physical reality or you will drift among the tidal pools endlessly. You can become familiar, too comfortable with him, to bother maintaining sincere communication.

Aside from the sulking, pouting, and occasional shouting, there is a great deal of joy to be gained with a Cancer lover. Money will rarely be an issue as long as you have plenty of it. Fortunately the indications are here for success and security through financial advancement. Don't worry about being an underachiever. Worry can destroy your love with a Cancer man.

Like most same-sign loves, it can be heaven and hell, depending upon how well you know yourself and how much you like what you see of your own best and worst potentials in him. It all depends on you and the love and faith you allow to shine forth, letting much-needed optimism and confidence into your lives.

CANCER & LEO

Surprisingly and delightfully, bold, arrogant, and egotistical Leo the Lion can be the pussycat of your dreams. It may seem paradoxical that your shy, cautious, and self-effacing instincts should respond to his Fixed-Fire qualities, but there are many opportunities for love as your Moon rulership reflects and mellows his powerful Sun-struck personality.

You can take a few lessons from his flair for the dramatic and become more active, even dynamic, in the way you present yourself. Leo can bring out the best in you, even if he sometimes does it for his own aggrandizement. Your intuitive sensitivity tells you that his proud and overbearing nature is the outward expression of his own insecurities in searching for love and affection. Even when he is being a show-off, or unreasonable in his demands for continual stroking of his vanity, you have a built-in tolerance for his emotional excesses. Despite the hectic life the two of you may lead, Leo has a stabilizing influence that can comfort you in the midst of your Cancerian moods of insecurity. You are capable of giving each other the kind of tender, loving affection that you crave in order to become complete personalities.

Cancer is the embodiment of the primal mothering instinct, providing the security of hearth and home with nurturing affection. Leo is the Brother Sun to your Moon, defending your home and advancing your mutual interests in the world. Though he may rally forth to knock 'em dead in his role as king of the jungle, alone with you he is warm, kind, and generous; longing for the serenity and comfort only you can give him. Though he must play the role of powerful king, you are at your best ministering to his passions, maintaining your love with care, wisdom, and affection.

Leo represents your Second House, the house of income and possessions. Abundant success is indicated as your material advancement receives a boost from his urgings to come out of your shell and present your talents to the world.

A Cancer–Leo couple attracts the attention of others through the magnetic illumination created by the blending of the Sun and Moon. When out in public, you literally sparkle in the company of each other and your circle of dynamic friends. Both of you love to see, and be seen, at cultural events. You can develop a reputation as generous hosts and fabulous guests. The primary social event of your calendar is probably his birthday. Leo will be his most regal and his most gracious in presiding over this royal command performance. You will lavish him with symbols of affection and the adoration of a glittering assemblage of friends in commemoration of his special day.

Special days can lead to special nights. Good lovemaking is the true heart of the matter in a Leo love affair. Your receptive qualities are the perfect complement to his own aggressive sexuality. He is a man of passion who will stimulate intense desire in you. Leonine lust becomes transformed by Cancerian affection into loving and fulfilling sex.

Don't let your feelings of dependency keep you from asserting your own sexual needs with a Leo lover. Though he normally doesn't like to be the passive partner, you can get him to play the passive role and enjoy it—if you are clever. You are a more inventive and imaginative lover than he is, and you can show him many new delights and pleasures if you treat him patiently and gently. If you praise him exorbitantly for the pleasure he provides you in any particular sexual act, his pride will overcome his resistance to the passive role. The more you praise him, the more he will be aroused to heights of sexual abandon.

He will return your sexual favors by being loyal and faithful, and he will expect the same from you. Infidelity is a threat to his need for primacy. Leo has to know for sure that he is number-one in your life. Fortunately you prefer to be monogamous and center your life on your home and your lover as the firm foundation for your personal advancement. You can soothe and comfort his excesses of passion in the same way that he can alleviate your fears and worries.

Let him know that the warmth of his love is important to you, and any complaints are only based upon your desire to care for the most important man in your life. Flattery will get you everything with Leo, but it must be sincere. As you honestly list his good qualities you will convince him that you truly do care for him, as well as reminding yourself of how wonderful he can be.

Leo is an optimist, a gambler, and a showman. With him as your lover you have positive experiences in travel, adventure, and your career that you would never try on your own. Each new fear that is overcome makes you more capable of being independent but more willingly devoted to sharing the future with him as your loving partner in life.

CANCER & VIRGO

Though only a Virgin in the symbolic sense, your Virgo lover will be pure of heart in a down-to-earth way. After all, he is Mutable Earth and ruled by Mercury the communicator. Unlike the grand and airy messages of Air-sign Mercury in Gemini, Virgo signals are about smaller things, practical things, the details of life and love that can bring order and security to your occasionally mixed-up feelings.

Your initial meeting will not be charged with sexual overtones. Virgo is a private person and you will be attracted by his polite manner and reserved charm. A Virgo will grow on you rather than come on to you because he shares some of your own native caution regarding love and commitment. Your reticence stems from your emotional insecurity, while his comes from a need for emotional distance and detachment.

Despite his reserved nature he is agreeable, and your own Moonbeam charms are enough to relax him. Spend some time together out-of-doors. A walk in the woods or along the shore will give you the opportunity to get acquainted and indulge in silence without being embarrassed. If you sparkle too much for him, it will make Virgo feel uneasy. Lay low and be a good listener. Your elusive and indirect approach will gain his confidence enough to make him more than just agreeable, if that is your goal.

You will be the one to make the first move. The sexual potential in your relationship is more important to you than to a Virgo man. He will willingly be bedded by you, but only after he has been won over by your intelligence and wit. Visits to the theater or museums will impress him, especially when you join him in a critical discussion afterward.

While he may be down-to-earth in a practical sense, Virgo is not Earthy. Ribald humor is not amusing to him. He's about as clean-cut as they come these days. Given his Mercury-endowed youthfulness, he may affect a Joe College look that brings out a few of your old varsity fantasies.

Virgo is not above a few sexual fantasies of his own, but they tend to be very precise, even to the point of fetishism. Virgos are masters of detail in a way that is very different from your own diffuse sexuality. You tend to throw yourself into sex and play it by ear, letting the tides of passion come in succeeding waves. Virgo is much more programmed in what he wants and how he wants it. You can try to get him to be more imaginative as a lover and encourage him to trust your creative tastes as a partner.

One way to get him into bed is to get him into the shower. Usually he will want to shower before and after sex, anyway, so you might as well start warming him up with some slippery, soapy body contact. Rub him down with a fresh, fluffy towel; Virgo loves to be groomed. Make sure you have clean linens on the bed. The crisp feeling of fresh sheets is definitely an erotic sensation for him.

His Mercurial tendency to observe and criticize is very different from the kind of imaginative spirit embodied by Cancer. He wants all of the facts and details, not impressions and interpretations. When you fall into one of your moody phases of the Moon, he will insist upon a thorough analysis of its cause, effect, and cure. While you may be comforted by his prescription of two multivitamins washed down with some herb tea, you will also feel isolated by his clinical attitude toward an emotional situation over which you have no control.

Even when he is picky, finicky, critical, and all too cool, there is a bond of friendship between your astrological aspects. Virgo represents your Third House—communication—and implies enough variety and interest to keep you working at the relationship. The one trait you two share in abundance is worry. You are agitated about things on an emotional level, and he frets on a material plane. You should combine your interests in a project that can allow you to focus your concerns in a constructive way.

Virgo is the Sign of Service, and he will want to care for you by making your life as smooth as possible. You like to cook and he likes to clear the table and wash the dishes. He's a marvel at parties. While you are mixing drinks or pontificating on the secret of your crudités dip, Virgo will be making sure everyone has ashtrays and coasters for their glasses.

When the situation gets out of control, he becomes cynical and sarcastic, criticizing you for minor faults and petty issues. You respond with some emotional outbursts that are neither gentle nor sensitive, but scathing in their bitchy wit. Virgo doesn't hurt you so much as he disappoints you in focusing on the mundane when you offer him the mysteries of the Moon. Don't be too hard on him. He is just trying to protect you in the only way he knows how.

Should your affair be able to resist the strains of worry and tension, your friendship is the firm ground that allows you to overcome the confusion and disillusionment that can result from a Mercury–Moon love. Your Water qualities enrich his Earth nature and keep it from drying out. His practical powers of analysis can keep you from getting carried away with your own emotions. Together you are a blend of spirit and matter that can exist together in true harmony and loving security.

CANCER & LIBRA

Cardinal Air meets Cardinal Water when you find your Moonbeams shining on a Libra lover. Ideas? Inspirations? Style? Glamour? Trend with no end? If you want all that, you get it with Libra. It's a brainstorm a minute when you jump on the Scales of Libra's balancing act.

Keeping your balance won't be easy with this man in your life. You are men of ideas. His inspirations are mental and yours are emotional and intuitive, but you are both supercharged in each other's company.

Nevertheless, the general aspects between your Watery Moon and his Air-sign Venus are not harmonious. You can be swept off your feet by his romantic nature but may regret it later if you abandon your natural caution and commit yourself too soon.

If you are interested in him, overcome your reticence and secrecy by confiding your feelings. Libras are not emotional by nature, and if he is able to accept the fact that you feel you are falling in love, then he will begin weighing his impressions to see if he is able to return your commitment. It is very difficult for you to be open and honest about your feelings, but it is the only way you can possibly have a relationship with a Libra man. The most valuable part of a Libra experience for you will be in learning to articulate your needs.

The chances for success in a Cancer–Libra pairing are much better in business than in love. Libras are usually masters of acumen who can combine with Cancer's talents for any kind of artistic endeavor, whether it's a gallery, a design studio, or a talent agency. But even in a successful business there is natural tension between the two Cardinal drives of Cancer and Libra. You are more concerned with being secure than he, and his ideas make you somehow apprehensive.

Libra represents your Fourth House: home and later life. Cancers make Librans want to settle down and concentrate on domestic virtues. You will urge Libra to accept more responsibility and to live up to the potentials you see in him. The influence of Venus can make him lazy or complacent, so he needs a lover who will accent his interest in achievement and prestige. There are times when he seems so passive that you become more aggressive than is natural for you.

Passivity and aggression may also be problems that upset the harmony of your sexual relationship. He is usually adaptive, eager to please, and unhurried as a lover. Your Cancerian sexual traits are very much the same. Both of you are willing to comply with each other's needs, but you don't really come forth with what it is you want to do. There are times you want him to be more aggressive and he just lies back luxuriating in your touch and absorbed in his fantasies. Like the other Air signs—Gemini and Aquarius—fantasy, rather than emotion, is the mainspring of his sexual desire. Voyeuristic elements, such as mirrors, will definitely excite a Libra in bed. If you can articulate your own erotic needs, he will be willing to comply—Librans never say no if they are aroused enough—but he is not sensitive enough to intuit your desires from your manner, mood, and body language.

The potential for mutual fidelity is not high in a Cancer–Libra affair. He is too attracted to beautiful men. Libra's commitments can be very shallow, and you will not be willing to accept a man who wants a home and a partnership but doesn't take responsibility for your relationship. Your moody periods will be incomprehensible to him, and he will be intolerant of your emotional needs if you become too demanding. Libra won't hang around to comfort your tears, either. The need for affection may well drive you to seek out a new love.

A relationship with a Libra man can work, but you both have to want it with all your heart. Patience with his Air-sign need for freedom can help to see you through. Compassion for your Water-sign emotions is Libra's task. You can both become so wrapped up in your own concerns that there is no real love left to share. It isn't the comforting and indulgent partnership that either of you dream of. It calls for dedication, sustained effort, and a sincere desire to make the relationship work.

Keep it light, open, and casual as long as you can. Learn to make the best of a fun-loving affair and let Libra take the lead in making a commitment to true love.

CANCER & SCORPIO

The Fixed-Water intensity of a Scorpio man blends with your own Cardinal-Water emotions to form a powerful attraction. The influence of his planetary ruler, Pluto, reveals emotions within you that excite and even fatigue you. The deep sexual attraction you feel for him certainly is exciting, but the possibility of fulfillment is also frightening.

Scorpio men are sexuality incarnate. When you first meet, you see it in his deep-set eyes, fixed in their gaze. When he makes eye contact, this man is not teasing. He doesn't flirt because he realizes that sex is more than a game. His eyes make promises, pose challenges, and have an altogether hypnotic effect on you. Your first instinct is to run away, but the promise of such intense sexuality and the challenge of coping with his power combine to force you to surrender.

You feel like you are jumping feetfirst into a deep pool of dark water, giving yourself up to a mystical experience that could lead you to either heaven or hell. After your first sexual encounter with a Scorpio man you may feel that you don't care whether it's angels or devils, as long as you can spend eternity with him as your lover.

It sounds like a lot of purple passion, but the power is definitely in your charts. Scorpio represents your Fifth

House: love and sex. If you are ever going to find a man who is willing to take all your loving and return it in a way that fills all your capacities to receive, that man will probably be a Scorpio.

Scorpio influences the aspects in your chart that indicate travel, excitement, and variety. Be prepared for surprise weekends in exotic places, passionate sex beneath a jungle Moon, and the call of the wild that echoes in his Scorpio spirit.

Scorpio is a man of strength, power, and subtlety who can take care of you in any circumstance. If you listen to your intuition instead of wondering who is going to feed the fish and water the plants when he whisks you off to Tahiti, you'll know that you can trust a Scorpio lover. In fact, you can trust him more than you can trust yourself. He doesn't have your Moon-influenced vacillations. Don't be evasive or coy with a Scorpio lover, or it will make him suspicious of your affections.

Scorpios with suspicions are dangerous creatures. When you are insecure, you feel inadequate. When he is insecure, he wants to sting the source of his unhappiness. He shares many of your own emotional frailties, but he has much more powerful defense systems. The Crab seeks the shelter of his hard shell to avoid pain, but the Scorpion lashes out to meet pain with strike-force capacity. Jealousy is the negative expression of his intensity as a lover, just as affection is the positive expression of his powerful feelings. As long as your secretive tendencies don't cause him to be suspicious, a Scorpio lover will lavish you with all of the affection and devotion you can possibly handle.

Invite him to dinner at your place. Cook for him. Candlelight and wine will make his eyes sparkle and your heart beat even faster. It will be hard not to rush through dinner, so you should prepare an easy meal.

The rest of your gourmet experience is limited only by your imagination. Each of you can provide a rich emotional outlet for the other in a Cancer–Scorpio love. You feel protected by his inner strength, and yet, your Water-sign sensitivity allows you to perceive his secret vulnerability. You have the ability and the need to show him the constant affection he craves. It gives his intense and mystical energies a positive direction that brings out the best in his Scorpio personality.

But when you are feeling distant, it's a cold and chilling situation. Tempers will rarely flare, but the coming of the Ice Age is not accompanied by cataclysm; it's a slow and exorable process of impending disaster. Insecurity can drive each of you into escapism of all kinds. Fortunately the extreme harmony indicated between Cancer and Scorpio allows you to be more open with each other than with anyone else. It will be possible to forgive, and even forget, your disagreements, because they seem ultimately trivial compared with the quality of your love.

CANCER & SAGITTARIUS

The sign of the Centaur is characterized by Mutable Fire-sign qualities that are difficult to reconcile with your own Cardinal-Water instincts. If you become emotionally involved with this freewheeling rover, your whole attitude toward life, love, and security will undergo some radical shocks.

Jovial Jupiter is the ruling planet of Sagittarius. He is endowed with an independent spirit, high idealism, and a happy-go-lucky manner that takes little or no account of your own Moon-ruled sensitivity. The Centaur is prone to a restless inspiration that can make him charming and exciting, but not dependable. The Centaur finds romantic attachments too restricting. Your own needs for security and emotional consistency in a relationship can be too demanding for a Sagittarian to cope with. Coping is the constant

theme in a love affair with a Sagittarius man. His tendency
to be blunt or tactless can hurt you deeply, unless you are
willing to make constant allowances.

At first meeting you will be attracted to him by his sense
of humor and his appealing gift for conversation. The Centaur likes to talk about himself, but he's done so many
things, been so many places, that he is rarely boring. If the
chemistry is there, you'll realize that he finds you fascinating, and in turn, this will stimulate your own desire to know
you are wanted. You have to realize that he is experiencing
fascination and not devotion. Take it light and easy, Cancer,
or you will lose any control you might have over the course
of a joyride on the back of a Centaur.

These mythical creatures are rovers. The Centaur doesn't
travel in a herd, and he will have none of your regard for
your family, or the friends you have developed. If you force
him to engage in sentimental associations, he will be so
blunt, outspoken, and outrageous that you will be hurt and
embarrassed.

You tend to want a man who will cuddle and coddle you
into overcoming your insecurities. Sagittarius may not coddle you, but his open, honest, and naïve bluntness will give
you an objective mirror in which to consider your faults—
as well as your strengths. Though you react very badly to
criticism, he doesn't intend to inflict pain with his quiver of
Sagittarian arrows. If it's really love, and not just some kind
of dependency, you will be thankful to have someone who
can help you be more honest with yourself.

A Cancer–Sagittarius affair can be strong medicine for
you but also a tonic in the development of a stronger personality. In some way he will want you to be more concerned with taking care of your health. You may be the
chef-de-cuisine, but he is interested in diet and healthful
activity. You will be encouraged to engage in some form of
physical fitness, if only to avoid his stinging jokes about
your being pleasantly plump.

The Centaur is a Fire-sign man, and his sexual appetite
is varied and intense, rather than warm and sensuous. He

would rather have impulsive sex three times a day than have one long, sensual session. Nevertheless, the sexual attraction between you is very strong: your imagination is stimulated by his rough-and-ready attitude about sex.

You can give him a better appreciation of sensuality as an important element of sexuality. You can lead him into the labyrinth of the mysteries of sex, since you aspect his Eighth House, the house of sexual mystery and secrets. The Centaur may well learn to be a better lover through you, but it is likely that he will want to spread the good word. The emotional and sexual commitment you are willing to make to him will not always be rewarded by fidelity. He will be faithful to you as a friend, but Sagittarius will rarely tolerate a restricted relationship.

His roving spirit of adventure makes Sagittarius an exciting travel buddy or on-the-road romance. Just don't expect the love affair to last back home once the luster of wanderlust has worn thin in more domestic surroundings.

Holding on can cause you to risk too much without the promise of any emotional reward. Letting go may lead to a friendship that will benefit both of you in the long run. A Sagittarian lover can help you to see yourself more clearly, giving you the strength to carry on. You will be a better person for knowing him, loving him, and leaving him free to follow his heart.

CANCER & CAPRICORN

Cardinal-Earth Capricorn knows where he's going and how to get there. Your own Crablike indecision causes you to look up to him. Up is the right direction when you are looking at the Mountain Goat of the zodiac. He is heading for the top, and your intuition tells you that you can dare to join him in his climb.

Capricorn is the sign opposite yours, and you represent traits and potentials for development that complement each other. Together there is a feeling of wholeness that gives both the Crab and the Goat a unique sense of satisfaction. You have much to teach and much to learn when you join forces with a Capricorn man in a loving relationship.

A meeting between you and the Mountaineer will not result in mad passion. Capricorn never falls head over heels in love. It will take time for your relationship to develop. Capricorn is ruled by Saturn, the planet of Time and Order. Your Moon-ruled inspirations will respond to the security of understanding that comes from him. If you feel ready to be serious about a relationship, then the Capricorn man is for you.

The Mountain Goat aspects your Seventh House: partners, pairings, and dualities. He has the qualities you need in a lover—stability, determination, endurance, and reality. In return for the anchor of his values your Moonbeams unfurl the sails of Lunar changes, receptivity, reflection, and dreams. He needs you to lighten his load with your gentleness and sense of humor. Together you can represent a combination of feeling and reason that makes for a solid and loving relationship.

Though he may seem outwardly cool and controlled, you sense the inner softness and longing for affection that he conceals in his steadfast determination to be serious. You understand his need for financial security as the necessary foundation for emotional security. As lovers you will both work hard to achieve the success that will allow you the peace of mind to enjoy each other without worrying about the possible disasters tomorrow may bring. Capricorn shares your feeling for the past and the meaning it has, in terms of emotional continuity. The family is very important to him and he respects the value of familial relationships. You are both generous and parental with your intimates, dispensing emotional support and sound advice.

The physical expression of your mutual attraction shows similar aspects of romantic intensity. You can add the necessary touches of voluptuous eroticism to enhance his strong sex drive. Cancer can teach Capricorn the joys of ecstasy on a lasting basis. One of the best things about Capricorn is that he gets better and better as he gets older. Physically, emotionally, and sexually, he is the best investment in the zodiac. If you want a relationship founded on continuous development and devotion to the principles of achievement, this is your Man of Life.

Encourage him to be physically and verbally affectionate with you. Remember, the Goat is a loner and not accustomed to the niceties required with another man around, especially a sensitive Moonbeam like you. Your emotional extremes make him feel confused and inadequate. Be lavish in the gentle expression of your love and he will respond in kind. Be Crabby and complaining and he will become a severe and condescending critic. Capricorn does not have your quick wit, clever tongue, or vivid imagination, but he has a strong and powerful intellect that can reduce you to a quivering mass of Jell-O when you get too carried away.

Cancers are traditionally attached to the maternal principle of nurturing through loving care. You can serve that function for Capricorn by softening his hard edges. He does not sparkle in crowds and usually avoids glittering social events. Small gatherings in your home, surrounded by symbols of material comfort, will bring out the best in his conservative nature. Quiet times together will be the very best times. It's only in those special moments that he is willing to relax, to reach out and show the vulnerable tenderness in that Capricorn heart that beats beneath the vest of his three-piece suit.

Changes make him insecure unless they are well discussed and thoroughly planned. You won't be able to get him to take off on a spur-of-the-moment weekend jaunt unless you have firmly planted the idea in his mind and covered all of the necessary arrangements. It's a lot to go through for a supposedly spontaneous adventure, but you must assuage his practical side if you want to encourage a little romantic abandon.

It is always give-and-take between you, but it's an ongoing process that can lead to beneficial growth. He needs you for the very qualities you have to give in a loving relationship. You need him for the very same reason: Because the love you have to share is the promise of fulfillment written in your stars.

CANCER & AQUARIUS

Aquarius is called the Water-bearer, but what he carries is more like stardust or Moon mist than water. His ruling planet is Uranus, which makes everything about him surprising and suggests a strange meeting of Fixed-Air enthusiasms and Cardinal-Water inspirations.

An Aquarius lover will activate your imagination but also stimulate your apprehensions. Your social life will be a kaleidoscope of activity but to the detriment of your home life. You are looking for someone to share life, but the Water-bearer wants to share his life with many people for many different reasons.

You will be fascinated by his social, intellectual, and sexual eccentricities, but you are disturbed by his Air-sign lack of emotional commitment. His motivations are intellectual, while yours are emotional. The situation seems fraught with instabilities as you cling to the emotional past for your value structures and he looks to the intellectual future as his perceptive guide.

Your initial contact with an Aquarian will be an unusual situation, a truly chance meeting through tenuous acquaintances or someplace you've never been before. He likes people and he enjoys getting to know them. At first meeting you may find yourself strangely fascinated by an Aquarius man. He represents your Eighth House: the mysteries of sex, death, and regeneration. A common interest in the occult may even bring you together. His psychic interests center on his powers of perception, rather than your receptive quality of intuition.

If you are turned in to your Moonbeam reception station, you will pick up his Aquarian wavelength. Sex is only a means to an end for Aquarius. His goal is to make mental contact. You will enjoy each other as partners but for different reasons. Frankly, sex is more important to you. As a Cardinal sign, you will probably be the more demanding sex partner. It's a position that you enjoy on one level but would like to feel was reciprocated by your partner. When your moods impel you to be sexually receptive, an Aquarian man will not pick up on your yearnings. If you verbalize your needs, he will interpret your need for love as a sign of possessiveness.

When the Water-bearer feels closed in, he rebels. Since he is a Fixed sign, he will resist feeling dominated. If he thinks you're trying to restrict his freedom, an Aquarian can become stubborn and maybe even more eccentric. Flashes of quick anger are not unlikely. His behavior can become very unpredictable, leaving you confused and completely up in the air.

Your own moodiness is just as incomprehensible to him. He will not be interested in those things that he cannot intellectualize, but he enjoys the challenge of coping through his mental agility. The only moods he doesn't know how to cope with are those that require solitude. Aquarius will want an explanation at moments when you prefer to be alone. At the times when you most need a big silent hug, he will be looking for a way to mentally crack your Lunar code.

The potential is for excitement, not emotional communication, in a Moon–Uranus combination. Along with all the other excess baggage that Aquarius distributes in his eccentric journey through life, money flows through him like a sieve. You've heard of turning lead into gold, but

Aquarius has taken it one step further and changes gold into experience. It's a mystic transformation whose value eludes you, to say the least.

In fact, the value of an Aquarian love relationship will elude you completely, unless he has enough Water-sign or Earth-sign aspects in his chart to make him more receptive to your emotional needs and material interests. An exciting weekend of offbeat experiences is more likely to happen between you than a long-term love affair.

Still, it can be a very strong and enduring relationship and will seem karmically fated in some way. This relationship is aspected favorably when you have sought each other out for your strengths rather than for your needs. The meeting of your powers in some eccentric combination causes you to join forces in a dynamic love that produces strange new harmonies, defying convention. If you are looking for a one-of-a-kind love affair, you may have it with the Aquarian man. Together you can create a music of the spheres that neither of you has ever heard before.

CANCER & PISCES

The sign of the Fish makes Pisces men natural Water buddies for Cancer Crabs. He represents the Mutable Water of the Ocean and is ruled by the planet Neptune, mystical Lord of the Sea. Your Cardinal qualities give you the power of the tides to move and affect him through the harmonious attraction between the Moon and Neptune. It is easy for you to fall for this subtle man of dreamy charm and gentle sexuality.

Your powers are reflective and his are absorbent. Pisceans have theoretically participated in the experiences of the previous signs and are ready to be transformed to another cycle of being. They understand the existential nature of the Universe, but the knowledge gives them little comfort. You will find that you want to be his shield and rock and that he is willing to serve you.

Pisces knows how to give of himself better than any other Sun sign. He is a good listener and you will feel flattered by his sincere attention to what you have to say. Though you are both secretive and sensitive, you will reveal your vulnerabilities to a Pisces with ease. You feel safe from harm in his presence, not because he is strong and protective but because he is simpatico. He accepts your problems, your fears, and your hopes, lightening your burden with patience and serenity.

You can sense much of this in your first encounter. The attraction between Cancer and Pisces has all of the relentless force of the ocean tides behind it. You will follow your Cardinal instincts and take the lead in initiating a relationship. You will charm him with your wit and imaginative conversation. No need to rush into anything with Pisces. Once you two have established your bond of mental and emotional communication, a satisfying sexual communion will develop naturally.

Both the Crab and the Fish are emotionally vulnerable and impressionable. On a positive level this relationship heightens your perceptive powers and presents new opportunities to develop your character and your career. Pisces aspects your Ninth House: journeys, philosophy, profound mentality, and new horizons. Your intellect and your ability to detect, promote, or initiate new trends is accented in association with a Pisces lover.

If you lack direction in a Pisces love affair, the potential for negative development can become manifest. Instead of communicating your brightest hopes and creative insights, there is the danger of becoming lost in the fog of gloom and doom. When you both slip into a low period, the depths are cosmic. You can talk one another into escaping to the netherworld of drugs, alcohol, and self-pity. If you consciously dull your wits, the Crab and the Fish will become truly lost at sea, fumbling for love through a thickening haze of melancholy.

Your Cancer inclination is to evade depressing or threatening issues, but Pisces will absorb them, dive into them. Pisces is responding to his Neptunian urge to release his ego into universal experience, but you can keep him closer to shore through your sense of humor and the comforting release of sex.

The comfort, affection, and emotional satisfaction gained in your sexual union is better than any drug you can administer. You are both aroused by the needs you sense in each other and the power you feel in fulfilling those longings. Sex is a deep and meaningful experience with a Pisces lover. Your imagination is more erotic than his, but he is willing to follow your direction to creative lovemaking at its most stimulating. His desire to please you is boundless, and you engage in feats of mutual affection that will leave you bathed in wave after wave of pleasure. Compliments will increase his confidence and double his sexual pleasure and yours! Don't get carried away with his pliable manner in bed, taking advantage of his willingness to give pleasure. Pisces has the potential to become a slave of love, especially to a loving master.

Usually there is no need for domination in a Cancer-Pisces love, though there are areas of conflict in which you will take the leading role. Don't be angry with his laissez-faire attitude about money. Keep the accounts in order as best you can and leave him enough room to maneuver. Arguments between you may be frequent, but they are at a mundane level that does not touch the foundation of your love. Periods of hurt are often due to slights so minor that only you two supersensitive guys can pick them up. Fortunately your physical attraction can overcome your mental and material clashes. Sex is the soothing and satisfying experience that says "I'm sorry and I love you" every time.

You are men of secret sorrows, combined with a love of beauty and wisdom. You have the power to reinforce the most creative aspects of your personalities. You both value the security and enrichment of a loving home and close friends. Confidence will develop in the atmosphere that you share in a Cancer–Pisces relationship.

LOVING YOUR CANCER MAN

A Moonbeam lover can be exhilarating or exasperating, depending upon the phases of the Moon. As a Cardinal Water sign he wants to take the initiative, but a basic fear of rejection holds him back from striving openly for the recognition he craves as a creative personality. You will have to be willing to give him plenty of love as an assurance of his own worth, and encouragement to seek the success that is obvious in his potential.

On one level he wants a lover who will take care of him, but he also has a strong maternal instinct that impels him to devote himself to your welfare in myriad small ways. The same impulse makes him possessive, even smothering, in a relationship. You have to be attentive to his nurturing or he will feel that his affection is not returned. When he is feeling loved and needed, there is no end to the cooking, intimate dinner parties, and sensual lovemaking he will provide.

Cancers are true romantics with a strong nostalgic streak. He collects mementos and souvenirs that evoke his fondest recollections. His strong memory inclines him to the study of history, romantic novels, and an inability to let go of anything he has learned, whether beneficial or harmful.

You will meet him at his best in any situation involving art and culture. Museums, galleries, and prestigious social events appeal to Cancer's love of beauty and need for harmony. At the early stages of an affair you should exercise caution in committing yourself to a Cancer love. He sizes up every congenial man as a potential partner for life.

The Cancer Man of Life is warm, kind, considerate, intelligent, and sexually devoted to his partner. He wants a man who will support him emotionally and be receptive to his Cancerian need to protect and nurture his lover. His moods are rarely long-lasting and are easily dissipated by stimulating his irrepressible sense of humor—but no teasing these sensitive Moonbeams!

Cancer's quick wit and lively imagination make him a thoroughly enjoyable companion. Though he is devoted to the idea of home, he needs the stimulus of change to keep his spirits out of the emotional doldrums. Short trips and surprise gifts will delight a Cancer man because of the thoughtfulness they express. Lavish gifts, like lavish praise, embarrass him. In fact, he will prefer constant physical assurances to occasional material expressions of your love.

A Cancer man is a responsive and imaginative lover who will accept your direction as he intuits your needs. Once you express your fantasies or desires, he will indulge with gusto, adding new creative touches to your most pleasurable moments. He wants to express the depth of his emotions, and he takes sex very seriously.

Cancer men like variety in their sex lives. He will not continually accept either passive or active roles, preferring to adapt to his own mood or to the needs of his partner. As long as he feels emotionally secure, he will always welcome new elements of sexual experience.

Tenacity is the word for Cancerian feelings, and winning an argument with him is much worse than losing. If he wins, he will immediately apologize for everything and may even concede or adopt your point of view. If he loses, he may sulk for days; not because he begrudges your triumph, but because he resents his own weakness and failure to convince you.

Loving patience is the key to keeping him happy. You can tell him that you are there when he needs you, but you understand that there are times in which he needs to be alone. When he is ready, sometimes after a few tears and a long walk, he will return to you with a little present and in need of a big hug.

If you refuse him affection as a means of disciplining him, he may become hysterical in his need for loving caresses. Though he is faithful and monogamous by nature, the need for love will drive him into the night. In his worst moods he can easily become a martyr of love, selfishly using other men and submitting to all kinds of sexual indignities as a confirmation of his poor self-image.

Don't let your Moonbeam lapse into bad habits. When he is feeling insecure, he can cook and eat himself out of his extensive wardrobe. Overindulgence is his weakness, physically and emotionally. To counteract this tendency you will have to indulge him with your solicitous affection. He can be emotionally demanding, but there is much to be gained from giving in to his love.

Cancer men are talented and creative in their approach to life and their drive to succeed. Money is very important to his sense of well-being. He will work hard to reach the top; financial security is a hedge against his fear of being alone. He needs more faith to sustain him, and he really wants to place his faith and trust in you. Cancers will cling to relationships long after they have ceased to be of positive value. He is better able to accept the pain of a futile affair than the dark uncertainty of tomorrow alone. If things go sour in your relationship, you are the one who must bring it to its end.

Leaving a Cancer lover may be as difficult as leaving home. It will have to be either a long, slow process of mutual discussion and frank emotional openness, or a quick and surgical cutting of the ties. Cancers are secretive creatures. He may also feel that your journey together has come to its end, but he is unable to express such a powerful emotional situation—even to himself.

You can improve a Cancer lover by encouraging him to keep the lines of communication open at all times. You might even be able to overcome his reticence by setting up a confessional period when either of you can speak the truth without having to face each other. It can be a time with no blame and no shame. It will clear the air and calm the waters in a way that will make your love stronger.

If you come together with your Cancer lover and close your eyes, hold hands, and speak the truth of your deepest feelings, the need for love may sweep you both off your feet and into a passionate embrace. When his mind is free of his fears, your Cancer lover can be the most loving man in the zodiac.

LEO
July 21–August 20

♌

Symbol: The Lion
Ruling Planet: The Sun
Color: Yellow
Metal: Gold
Natural House Rulership: Fifth House, the house of
    creative self
Fifth House Traits: Desire for ego confirmation and
    love of devotion
Motto: ''I will''
Nature: Fixed sign (organization)
Element: Fire sign (spiritual)
Qualities: Magnanimous, flamboyant, and inspired
Capacities: Presentation of creativity
Personality Key Words: Generous, dignified, and
    ardent

MAXIMIZING YOUR
LEO POTENTIAL

You are the Sunshine of the zodiac—a real Golden Boy. The Fixed Fire-sign qualities of Leo make you devoted to the principle of life as an expression of your ego-oriented personality. You want your life-style to speak for you, to embody your creative imagination and need for recognition, admiration, and acclaim. The vibrant power of the Sun radiates your Leonine dignity and passion, attracting other men to your warmth and power. The intensity of your desire, the generosity of your spirit, and your drive for creative self-expression are the most potent gifts that the Fixed Fire of Leo the Lion bestows upon you as the child of the Sun.

Your basic goals center on your ability to dramatize the Leonine need for confirmation of your talents. You feel that you are innately worthy of respect and admiration from the world. You have a flair for the dramatic, enjoy the best things life has to offer, and inspire others to have faith in your ardent personality. You are very demanding of attention, but the magnanimous qualities of your royal sign also make you loyal and devoted to those who accord you your noble due. Your sense of dignity gives you a strong ego, which allows you to maintain a sunny optimism and faith in your future.

Leo's flair for personal style translates to success in any field in which the public can be exposed to your drive and imagination. In return you want recognition for your talents. Leos don't want to work behind the scenes because there isn't enough glory. You like to be out front, projecting your creativity and basking in acclaim. Acting is a typical Leonine activity, or any other field in which there is the opportunity for applause, glamour, and self-expression. You must guard against being too extravagant or your positive charms will become negative factors that drive away the creative and sensitive people you seek to attract.

The power of the Lion's love is sometimes overwhelming. You want total attention, devotion, and passion from any man who becomes your lover. Though you love the adulation of the crowd, your Fixed-sign nature impels you to look for a stable love that will allow you the rewards of one man to whom you will be able to devote your precious love. You expect fidelity from him as an acknowledgment of your superior ability to satisfy his need for passion and security. You like to feel protective rather than possessive toward your lovers.

Leos do everything in the boldest way possible. You are a snappy dresser—not trendy but with a focus on quality and things that stress your best features. Your talents for creative inspiration and for attracting attention combine to create an almost irresistible image of self-confidence, even arrogance. You have a way of stimulating other men to live up to your standards of excellence, whether it's in business, pleasure, or creative endeavors.

In keeping with your kingly tastes, you like to live an active social life that focuses on you as the main attraction. Leos often arrive at social events with a party of friends and admirers as a ready-made "court." You survey the scene before entering a room, waiting to be noticed and recognized as you decide where to place yourself. You tend to pose in social situations, to make yourself look as good as possible. You want others to approach you, because underneath all that sunny self-confidence you fear rejection. You love the glitter of opening night or chic restaurants—situations that allow you to see and be seen in a flamboyant setting.

You are looking for a love that expresses your need for quality, devotion, and personal pride. The magnanimous Leo spirit needs to give love as much as to receive it, with lavish displays of affection. You are direct and open about your needs, especially when it comes to love. Leos believe in loyalty, and you want a love in which you can place your

total faith. Your gambler's instincts, combined with your
optimism, tend to make you a bit of a romantic. You believe
that true love may be just around the corner, so it's important always to be at your best.

Cupid's darts of desire can hit at odd moments, causing
you to be unfaithful if you already have a lover. A man with
your flair is bound to be tempted by the flattering attention
of other men. Your dalliances will be very discreet because
"cheating" is incompatible with your dignified self-image.
Furthermore, you are genuinely distressed at—if not deterred by—the fear of hurting your lover. Your guilt will
result in some extravagant present that says a silent "I'm
sorry and I love only you" to the man who rules your heart.

The lover you choose will express the same personal care with
which you choose all of the aspects of your life. As a Fixed
sign, you prefer to stick to those things, places, and people you
have come to value as up to your standards and reflective of your
taste and style. When you have decided to commit yourself to
another man, you want him to be someone you are proud to be
seen with, who will complement your life-style. Ideally he will
look up to you for your most admirable qualities and reinforce
your own best opinions of yourself. You don't want a man who
will restrict your freedom or social life, even if it's because he
wants you all to himself. By the same token, you should be
careful not to be overly possessive or too demanding. It is easy
for you to have attractive partners, but your ideal lover is the
man who is home when you get there and cuddled in your arms
when you wake up in the morning.

The power of the Sun in Leo gives your personality much
charm and creative drive. You handle your life and your
loving with a grace and style that can attract all the recognition, affection, and success you crave. A lover you can
depend on will be the crowning glory of your life, but you
can be domineering and predatory in your attitudes and
manners. When you lead with your heart, you are bound to
get hurt, but you have the ability to heal quickly and the
faith to continue the quest for the true love that brings out
the finest in your noble nature.

Tender passion and affection make you capable of overcoming your most arrogant and conceited insecurities. You will never need to demand recognition when you use your radiant charm to express yourself. Friends and lovers will come forward to return your warmth and reinforce your bright image. Happy rests the head of Leo who wears the crown with grace, generosity, and affection. When you falter, it is always with the best of intentions. When you succeed, you share your joy from the bottom of your generous heart.

LEO & ARIES

When your solar energies shine on Cardinal-Fire Aries, the outlook is definitely hot! His ruling planet is masculine Mars, and your own aggressive instincts are highly stimulated by those men born under the sexy sign of the Ram. Arians are keen competitors and like to play hard and fast in the game of love. If you are looking for a real man-to-man relationship, Aries is the right guy for you.

You will appreciate his open and cheery approach from the moment he catches your eye. Aries is a born flirt and will easily attract your attention by making his intentions crystal clear. Your aloof manner will challenge his free-wheeling nature. Aries will come on like an excited puppy, forcing you to loosen up and enjoy his boyish charms. When you feel like the king whose crown is heavy with responsibilities, Aries will appear as the happy prince who calls you away from your regal cares to frolic in the courts of love. Not that Aries is a courtly lover, by any means; he is too unpolished, too rough-and-ready to write poetry or send flowers. What you see is what you get with this lad.

You will love his need for your approval, recognition, and respect. Aries men are natural admirers of Leos and they can inspire you to live up to their high regard for your talents. He doesn't have your breadth of vision or your organizational skills, but he will promote your talents and advertise your abilities to the whole wide world. Aries lovers will stimulate your most noble ideals.

There is great creative potential in a Leo–Aries love affair. You must be careful, though, of an overwhelming compulsion to attempt too much without a solid foundation. Arians don't plan, they act. You will be sympathetic to his naïve energy and his courage, but don't let your more responsible Fixed-Fire qualities get carried away by his Cardinal-sign impulses.

But do let yourself be carried away in bed with your Aries lover. When you share your passion, you will reach new heights of expression in fiery lovemaking. He will go from the charging Ram to the gentle Lamb at your command. Though not usually versatile or creative lovers, Aries' explosive techniques appeal to your Leonine sensibilities. As much as you require admiration, he needs to be cherished. Aries will come to you bursting with desire but also longing for the security and emotional tenderness that only you can provide.

Your egos are both enormous and require constant reaffirmation. With an Aries lover, the more you love each other, the more you love yourselves in a reciprocal blend of mutual desire for affection and emotional support. It can make for a sparkling and glamorous combination.

Aries aspects your Ninth House—concerning journeys—and travel should be in the offing as you branch out into new, adventurous directions. Arians love to explore new cities; your lives will be charmed with wonderful experiences together on the road to anywhere. He stimulates your desire to get out, to be seen rather than resting on your laurels. There is no time for sentimental reminiscing with an Aries lover.

If the joy and excitement begins to pale under the drain of insecurities, Aries will panic, pout, and seek other men as an affirmation of his power. You like the fact that other men find him sexy, since it reflects upon your taste; but, on the other hand, you can be too possessive of an Aries lover. He will rebel and you will roar with rage, but your generous spirit will allow you to forgive your Aries lover for an occasional discreet indiscretion—especially if he is properly contrite.

If sexuality has the power to divide you two, it is also the magic potion that will always bring you together again. Remember that he thrives on excitement. If you let your life with him fall into neat patterns or predictable sexual habits, he will feel unwanted and unneeded. Since he really does admire you and want to serve you, let him know how much he means to you. He is never better than when you need him. Aries will give unselfishly of whatever he possesses to those in need, despite the fact that his is the most self-centered of all signs (except for Leo!).

It won't be an easy love affair, but you will always fondly remember an Aries man who has touched your life. Despite his faults, you sincerely admire his courage. Just as you learn to be more active and engaged by his energy, you can give him a greater insight into spiritual grace, natural nobility, and breadth of vision. The best qualities between you are mutually shared and admired. The potential for growth, happiness, and true love are there in abundance when you fall for an Aries man.

LEO & TAURUS

A Taurus lover puts your Fixed-Fire qualities into conflict with his Fixed-Earth attributes. The immediate sexual attraction may well give way to a period of testing each other's willpower. In the face of your extravagance and downright arrogance, Taurus will be conservative and simply stubborn. The resolution could be a relationship based upon two independent personalities admitting their mutual need for love and affection from a man they can respect.

Taurus has a sense of honor and a devotion to principle that touches your noble spirit. You will like his poise and his air of self-possession, not to mention his physical attractiveness. The Bull of Taurus is ruled by Venus, and she endows him with a subtle sexuality that appeals to you. No need to be coy with him, but don't expect a positive response if you come on with too much Leonine flash and dash.

He is an Earth sign, into simple pleasures and creative comforts. Dinner in a good—but not extravagant—restaurant should work for starters. He needs time to warm up to people, and his pace is slow and deliberate. Overcome your urge to bed him immediately if you want his attraction to develop. All of his Fixed conservative instincts tell him that the exuberant and extravagant Leo is not to be trusted. You have to demonstrate the nobility of your affections if you want a Taurus lover.

Good food and good music are the aphrodisiacs that stimulate Taurean men to thinking of other, more sensual pleasures. An evening at home, exploring his record collection, could result in further explorations that lead to some very satisfying discoveries. Satisfaction, more than passion, is the keynote of your sexual compatibility with a Taurus lover. Both of you like your partners to come to you, stimulate you into bestowing your sexual favors. But as the Fire sign, you usually are the one who makes the first move. Venus gives him the power to be receptive and highly responsive as a lover, once you indicate your desire. He is deeply physical in his need for love and will want to feel totally immersed in your warmth and passion. Together you are capable of combining languid sensuality with exuberant passion in a sexual union that becomes a total body experience.

Taurus men like sex on a regular basis, with few surprises. No midday sessions, no fantasy trips, and no kinky scenes for these salt-of-the-Earth types. Fortunately you also enjoy this same kind of predictability. However, beware of taking your lover for granted, because it can be a source of dissatisfaction between the Lion and the Bull. You can fall into a rut that stifles your creativity and threatens your freedom of spirit. You need freedom of action for your expansive personality, and Taurus can be possessive, even jealous.

Affection is the prescription for unhappy Taureans. Leo rules the heart and you have plenty of warm and generous affection to bestow on your lover. Don't let his sedate nature allow you to fall into bad habits and forget to express your feelings. Taureans are emotion-ruled, if not outwardly emotional. His concern for material possessions, money, and comfort are all complements to his desire for emotional security. Without it, he becomes calculating, possessive and boringly set in his ways. He will go along with your more flamboyant life-style and even enjoy himself as long as he feels warmed by your affection and regard. Denial of affection will spell the end of a Leo–Taurus relationship. There is natural tension between your signs, making sincere display of affection the only means of overcoming your differences.

Taurus aspects your Tenth House: career and public standing. Wealth and status are important matters to both of you, and your mutual talents for organization may well pay off with financial reward. Taurus will manage the money well to allow you a truly luxurious life-style. He won't take chances because he lacks your gambler's instinct, and he will increase your prosperity.

Taureans have patience, but they don't extend it too easily to Leos who are arrogant and conceited. He will understand your need to shine in public, to play to your courtiers and dazzle the crowds with your radiance, but he will not tolerate such pretentions between you. Taurus wants his lover to be down-to-earth with him when you are alone together, and the only thing that counts is honesty, sincerity, and loyalty, eternal values for both Taurus and Leo.

Keeping a Taurus lover happy can be as easy as stopping to think about how your actions will affect him. When you take off on your own egocentric path, you lose some of the substance and solidity you get from his loving. When you two are at your best, the relationship can be even more than men in love. It will be "loving gentlemen." A little old-fashioned, perhaps, but also a little wonderful.

LEO & GEMINI

There is never a dull moment when you link up with the Mutable-Air sign of breezy Gemini. You will be mentally stimulated by him, and your optimism—combined with his curiosity—make for exciting and involving experiences that will be long remembered. You will have to cope with his duality, since Gemini is symbolized by the Twins. Gemini's lighthearted spirit may confuse and hurt you with his apparent lack of commitment, but his youthful enthusiasm always warms your heart.

Gemini men are ruled by Mercury, planet of communication and the closest heavenly body to your own ruling Sun. The combination indicates active ideas, travel, speculation, and publication. Social contacts are highlighted, and Gemini lovers will introduce you to a whole new circle of admiring acquaintances. You make a dynamic couple that others find extremely attractive. Remaining faithful to each other will be difficult under the pressure of so many diversions. Emotional commitment is not Gemini's strong suit, and he may disappoint your needs for a truly loyal partner.

You will be delighted by a Gemini lover in many other ways. Gemini men inspire you to trust your instincts and go for the big gamble, the grandstand play, the royal gesture. The plans you make may not always be practical, but they are drenched in optimism and shimmering with potential. Leo and Gemini represent the magnetic attraction of creativity and intelligence.

The dynamic blending of Fire and Air leads to a new level of intensity in your lives. Just as Air feeds Fire, Gemini will stim-

ulate your creativity and allow you to have the spotlight your
ego requires. He knows exactly how to praise you, flatter you,
and show you in your best light. Gemini recognizes your noble
virtues, and in return you feel protective and generous toward
him. Even though his carelessness and his lack of emotional
commitment may exasperate your sensibilities, you will feel a
karmic tie that keeps you fascinated.

This fascination should be apparent on your first encounter. He likes to flirt and to circulate in any social situation.
Gemini will chart his way around the room until he meets
a man who interests him intellectually or who stimulates his
fantasies. You have the power to do both. Though you think
of yourself as the aggressor, you really like it when others
come on to you. Gemini will confirm your suspicion that
you are basically irresistible.

Sex with Gemini will be easy and enjoyable, but you can't
expect a strong commitment or passionate depth. Follow his
lead and keep your association lighthearted. It will allow
you all the freedom you need and plenty of affectionate admiration. You usually like your lovers to be rather predictable, but Gemini will keep you passionately stimulated by
his spirit of experimentation. Let his fantasies carry you
along to new levels of enjoyment. He will make you the star
in his erotic attempts at infusing sex with a theatrical dimension. He will talk, exclaim, and urge you on with expressions of his pleasure in your passion.

Though your Gemini lover may try your patience, the
tolerance you exhibit toward him is indicative of natural
compatibility between you. On one level you don't mind his
many interests outside your relationship as long as you feel
that they are worthy. The problem with all of this mutual
admiration and understanding comes in reinforcing each
other's worst excesses.

Gemini aspects your Eleventh House: friendships, hopes,
and wishes. Your innate optimism is given a boost. There
will be rewards for your career coming from the new people
you meet through Gemini. Since Gemini is your biggest fan,
he will tell everyone what a superb person you are. His

roving intelligence and quick wit will supply you with interesting social companionship and creative inspiration.

But remember, you are the Fixed sign, and practical organization must come from you. It is essential that you maintain a sense of responsibility in the face of Gemini's youthful exuberance. The combination of your strengths will moderate his charming weaknesses to create an exciting and loving affair with a Gemini man.

LEO & CANCER

When you meet this enigmatic charmer, his Cardinal-Water Moon influence will activate a mysterious magnetism within you. He seems so much like you, but at the same time so very different—softer, quieter, but hauntingly similar. What you feel is the magic of dawn and the melancholy of sunset—the blending of your Sunshine and his Moonbeam.

A Cancer love affair combines the majesty of those moments of inspiration and repose symbolized by the meeting of the Sun and the Moon. He reflects your energy and radiates it back to you through his own mellow sensibilities. You understand the strength behind his feelings and realize that he senses your vulnerability. In a way you have no secrets from each other, and yet a haunting aura of mystery surrounds your attraction to him.

Your sexual attraction will be no mystery as he intuits your interest. There is no need to puff and strut for a Cancer man. He will naturally come to you with gentle encouragement. If he is interested in you, he will be attuned to your slightest suggestion, so don't overdo it. Cancer men are supersensitive and shy away from emotional involvement until they are sure of their feelings. Cancers always look upon their male acquaintances as possible lovers.

It would be a rare Cancer man who could turn down the opportunity for an affair with an attractive character like you. On the same level you find him glamorous and worthy of your attentions, but you may be unsure of the potential for a relationship. You may only be aware of a craving to possess and unravel this intriguing character. The aspects indicate a clandestine element in a Cancer relationship that draws you to him and enfolds you two in a private world of shared confidence. The intimacy in a Leo–Cancer love affair is the core of its existence and the saving grace that ameliorates your differences.

Cancer men are moody, ruled by changing feelings that they can neither control nor fully comprehend. Your generous heart understands that he needs comforting rather than doses of reality to overcome his insecurities. Intellectually he knows that feeling alone or hurt may have no relation to being alone or hurt, and yet, he may still be lonely or sorrowful when the Moon tugs at his subconscious.

There are times your Cancer lover needs to be by himself, to wait until his feelings pass, like clouds before the Moon. Soon enough his humor will return and he will again become his charming, warm, and loving self. In return for your consideration he will lavish you with affection. A beautiful blending of "masculine" sensitivity and "feminine" strength characterize a loving arrangement between the men of Leo and Cancer.

When you are feeling down, unrecognized and unrewarded for your talents, no other man can hold you in his arms and soothe your fevered feelings like a Cancer lover. He will go all the way in caring for you when you have gone into one of your sulks, and his imagination knows no bounds when he sets his mind to pleasing you. Don't waste his wonderful gifts by taking him for granted or he will jeopardize even the security of the home he loves so dearly for the affectionate attentions of another man.

When you make love, you bring a transcendent dimension to your intimacy. Each caress, every kiss, rekindles thoughts of kisses longed for or caresses fondly remembered. Make the first move and he will always be receptive to your amorous advances. A Cancer man can be shy or embarrassed about his strong sex drive until the object of his affection indicates reciprocal desire. Once shyness is overcome, you will both flourish under the creative and imaginative challenge of alternating roles during lovemaking. The experience will be emotionally intense, releasing tension, fear, and worry.

Sex is the mystical force that cements the cracks in your relationship. When the words can't come fast enough to express your overwhelming need for each other, your minds and bodies can speak for you. There is so much creativity, sensitivity, and intelligence between the unlikely Lion and Crab couple that there are no obstacles too great to overcome.

Leo and Cancer can be the most loving of men, especially in love with each other. A long and happy love affair will lead to a life of spiritual, affectional, and sexual devotion that flows between you like the radiant glory of the Sun and the Moon.

LEO & LEO

Set your controls for the heart of the Sun and fasten your seat belts in a mating of two Fixed-Fire Lions! Rough-and-tumble playmates as young men, generous companions as mature lovers, you are both men of distinction. True romantic affection for each other may grow if you don't let your egos get in the way.

As your Sun-sign buddy he shares your best and worst traits, and you inflict them on each other either to the point of frustration or to new levels of tolerance and self-awareness. Giving equals getting, and you will get back all of the affection you give to a Leo lover. You can admire each other endlessly in a narcissistic arrangement that works to your mutual benefit. If you rise above your childish urges to compete for attention, you can match each other with desire, passion, and the ability to love and be loved. The aspects indicate a combination of creative drive and stimulating amusement if you relax and let the stars take their course.

Two Lions may not be enough for a "pride" of such creatures, but your Leo lover will make you feel proud indeed. You will delight in showing him off and will strive to make him feel equally proud of you. In conjunction, the power of your Sun energies adds sparkle and polish to your already dynamic personalities.

Instead of urging the whole world to look at you, it will be enough to see your reflection in his eyes, to feel his arms around you, to revel in his warmth, to catch his wink from across a crowded room, knowing that all is well in the Kingdom of Leo. At the best of times you are a blend of affection and creativity that radiates positive energy. Powerful people are drawn to you, and there is a high potential for social advancement and career success.

There is also the possibility of confusion when energy levels are so high. You may mistake the glitter of glamour and recognition for the gold of real achievement. You can become very extravagant with a Leo lover. Too much luxury, impulse spending, and gambling on the future could leave you depleted and disillusioned, financially and emotionally. The romance can blossom quickly and fade just as quickly, if you don't nourish it with commitments to long-range goals that give you solid prospects for the future.

You want to do everything on a grandiose scale that reflects your opinion of yourself and of your lover. Expensive presents, fine restaurants, and high living seem natural expressions of the exuberance of your feelings when in love with a Leo man. Remember that the greatest gifts you have to give each other are devotion and affection. The sign of Leo rules the heart, and no one in the zodiac has more love and courage in his heart than a Leo man. You will want to protect your lover and advance him with the same spirit of generosity you perceive emanating from him.

Instead of endlessly mirroring your personalities, stand side by side and combine your power to project it out into the world. Face-to-face with another Leo can lead to conflict and confrontation, questions of primacy, and contests of superiority.

When two Leos fall in love, there are bound to be royal displays of temper. They always lead to equally intense reconciliations, which will end in soothing lovemaking that returns your relationship to the peaceable kingdom of Leonine love. Sex is the way to make him purr like a kitten after the roar of the big cat. Be gentle, tender, affectionate, and playful with a Leo lover. He will respond in kind. He likes regular sex with creative intensity, but nothing too unusual. You will both want to be dominant but also are willing to be submissive to a man you consider your equal and your partner. If you ever learn to willingly accept the passive role, it will be under the gentle touch and tender love of another Leo. Once your orgasms have irradiated your bodies, the two of you will be tangled in each other's arms like setting suns, glowing into the approaching night of sleep. Morning will often find you ready for another session of intimate relaxation. As the Sun rises, so will your desires to rekindle the flames of the night before.

Good sex, good times, and grand adventures can occur with a Leo lover. Attention, affection, and admiration are the three keys to happiness for you and another Leo man. They unlock the doors of generous love and show the way to a bright future, if you focus on mutual goals rather than individual demands for immediate ego gratification. If you give your heart to a Leo lover, you will receive one of equal value in return for your unselfish devotion.

LEO & VIRGO

Careful Virgo can take a dim view of your flamboyant personality. He is characterized by Mutable-Earth qualities, and his restless Mercury-ruled intelligence will stimulate both practical ideas and unwanted criticism. With a well-timed remark that pierces your shining armor like a poisoned arrow, he can make you feel like you are wearing the Emperor's New Clothes.

A brief and secretive affair is more likely than a lasting and loving relationship with a Virgo man. Unless he has some sympathetic Fire-sign placements in his chart or emotional Water-sign influences, you will not be able to arouse his passion or admiration. These Virgos are practical men who pride themselves on their control. Your deeply felt emotions are looked upon by him as unnecessary affectations. He will worry about your health, plying you with vitamins rather than soothing you with affection. The most important things in your life are beyond his urge to analyze, criticize, and evaluate.

And yet there are certainly chances for compatibility if he respects you and feels you understand the objective nature of his intelligence. He may secretly admire your creative fire and breadth of vision, just as you are impressed by his efficient, capable sensibilities in practical matters.

A Virgo man needs you to be serious, calm, and considerate of his tender feelings. The perpetual excitement, clutter, and glitter that surround you may be too much stimulation for him to cope with every day. If he loves you anyway, a Virgo man will go to great lengths to create a safe haven for your refuge and repose. He will be tolerant of your excesses and willing to care for you in a truly devoted manner.

If the attraction you have for him ripens into love, it will be because you feel you have much to gain from a Virgo lover. He will stimulate a positive interest in security and domestic responsibilities. You may feel that it is time to settle down, and if you do, Virgo will be a true helpmate in life.

This domestic security and financial tranquillity is fine for a while, but your basic flamboyance is still at odds with his innate prudence. Virgo cautions moderation in all things, and yet there are times when your creative energies are overflowing and you have to go for broke. When you feel too restricted by his solicitous attitude, your rebellious instincts cause you to make a dramatic gesture that will distance you from the whole Virgo scene.

A Leo–Virgo love affair needs plenty of space and lots of fresh air to prosper. Just as you can feel trapped by him, he can feel possessed by you. The combination of your Sun and his Mercury can lead to an intensity that creates too much heat and not enough warmth. Mercury impels the Virgo man to feel free to roam, to exercise his critical intelligence in new directions. Your Fixed-sign temperament inclines you to be possessive of your lovers, and he will not be happy with your attempts to keep him fixated upon you, your life, and your interests.

You can both hold on to each other only by being willing to let go, relax your inhibitions, and communicate your needs for affection. Sex is not the driving passionate force in his life that it can be for you, Leo. Don't overwhelm him with your passion or your personality if you want to become lovers with a Virgo man. He needs to be tenderly tantalized. He wants you to be a gentle and devoted companion rather than a raging passion machine.

Making the most of your capacities for generous affection, you can initiate a Virgo man to the joys of male sexuality. You can teach him how to celebrate love if you first make him feel relaxed and secure. If you are too aggressive or demanding, his participation in sex will become mechanical and prosaic. A frustrated and insecure Virgo will submit to your overpowering desire, but the relationship that develops will be devoid of the loving affection both of you crave.

But sex in the shower will definitely turn him on. All that lather, herbal scents, warm water, and natural sponges make the act of love seem as clean and as pure as his nature requires. He's probably going to want to shower before and after lovemaking, anyway, so you might as well take advantage of it.

After sex it's bedtime for him. No lazy afterglow or pillow talk or tender caresses after the act is over. Not unless you gently communicate the pleasure he can give you through a deeper physical involvement. He is not uninvolved, but very subtle and even embarrassed when it comes to understanding his own sexuality.

Virgo aspects your Second House: finance and possessions. He can help you attain material advancement, but he will not pay you homage or render flattery. You will have to work hard to earn his compliments and his love. If you are patient, there are definite rewards when your sunny optimism blends with the tender devotion of a Virgo to form a lasting companionship between two men of mature values.

LEO & LIBRA

The Cardinal-Air qualities of Libra men attract you through their clever versatility. His ruling planet is Venus and he finds your sunny optimism and dramatic flair very appealing. Your Fixed-Fire intensity fascinates him and opens the channels of communication between you.

Sparkling conversation will set the tone of your first meeting. You will bask in his attentive interest in what you think, and he will be stimulated by what you know and how you present yourself. Librans are true devotees of beauty, and a handsome Leo is already halfway there the minute Libra sets eyes on you. He wants the best and appeals to your sense of superiority. You, too, appreciate the finer things in life, and an intelligent, stylish Libran lover can be one of the very finest things in your life. The aspects indicate a natural and easy friendship that can develop into an intense love affair.

Extravagance is a key word in describing a Leo–Libra relationship. Both of you possess luxurious tastes and habits that are further stimulated when you are together as social and sexual companions. Each of you has art, fashion, and entertainment high on your list of necessities. You will both spend your last dollar for fresh flowers rather than see it go to pay a debt. If there is trouble between you, it will be when you are broke or over your heads in debt. When you two are down to your last daffodil, you both believe that tomorrow's mail will bring the windfall you need to carry you through.

If you are men with established incomes, the future can be as bright and exciting as your creative imaginations. Libra is a trendsetter and a trendspotter who will know just how to package your best features to increase your career potential. You are the brilliant organizer who can direct his ideas and propel them in the public eye. You make a stunning couple and will insist upon boxes at the theater, the best tables at restaurants, and generally making a finer-than-fine impression.

The distractions and temptations of an active life-style, however, can be very wearing on your relationship. Since both of you are such attractive personalities, you will be subject to the pressures of flattery and flirtation from other men. You are more likely to be stirred by jealousy than he, and also annoyed by his lack of jealousy. Your need for ego gratification can drive you to becoming a flirt yourself, if only to let Libra know you want him to want you and to show it. If you don't express your feelings, the relationship can degenerate into a contest of tiny infidelities until there is no respect left on which to base your love.

When your Fire-sign temper is aroused, you go either hot or cold. You will rage with injured pride or radiate icy indignation when you feel that Libra has gotten out of line. Fortunately he has the power to balance your temporary disharmony. You are willing to listen to his explanations and accept his logic. Libras are not above flattery to achieve their objectives, and you are not above conceit when it comes to soothing your ruffled passions. Libra knows just the right strokes to keep you happy.

Your differences can easily be resolved by clearing the air in an intense conversation, followed by some equally expressive sexual communion. Venus brings forth all of the erotic and sensual passion you can give to a Libra man. He can anticipate and satisfy your aggressive need for a unique blend of abandon and tenderness. Though there is a certain Air-sign delicacy and fantasy detachment with a Libra lover, he appreciates your lusty desires, your masculine drive, and your boyish need to cuddle. Librans are sensual voluptuaries who appreciate and revel in creative and erotic lovemaking.

Libra aspects your Third House—communication and variety—leading you off on a quest for social and romantic adventure, but you can burn yourselves out, deplete your emotional and financial resources, and then wonder what happened. Therefore a solid, stable, comfortable home environment is essential to your mutual well-being. Occasionally spend time together in quiet pursuits, such as an intimate dinner with a few friends, instead of a night out. You are active men who need time to recharge your energies in restful company. Relax and enjoy the simple pleasures of sharing your thoughts, your presence, and your heart with the man you love.

Savor each other for the rare and precious treasures that you are. A fine romance will grow in harmonious surroundings while you continue to fascinate each other for a long, long time. As the years go by, a grace and poise gives your relationship a glow that will be the pride and envy of your friends.

LEO & SCORPIO

If you are attracted to a Fixed-Water Scorpio man, you had better fall like a ton of bricks into complete, total, abandoned, submissive love, or else forget it. If you try to dally with this Pluto-ruled beauty, you will be sorry. Scorpio is a synonym for serious and Pluto is the planet farthest from the Sun, which makes him as far as one can get from your sunny, optimistic energy. A Scorpio man will make you come to him, and you are attracted to his smoldering sexuality and intrigued by his power to summon up your desires. Your curiosity is aroused by the magnetic power in his eyes, which express the promise and the warning of Scorpio's inner nature: This man is deep, very deep.

Your symbol is the Lion: golden, regal, direct, and easily recognizable. His many symbols are not always obvious. Scorpio is sometimes the Scorpion but also can be the Serpent of forbidden knowledge (sex) and the Eagle of transcendence. Getting to know him and understanding which elements of the astrological bestiary are operating will not be easy.

There is nothing easy or natural about Leo and Scorpio getting involved with each other, socially or sexually. The aspects between your signs indicate tension and challenge. Rewards come only as the result of hard work and the patience to endure difficulties over which you have no control. You will probably know very quickly whether or not this affair is going to work. As you get to know each other your Fixed-sign natures will establish and define the points upon which either of you will not budge. If you can arrive at an understanding without much trauma, then there is a good chance that there are deeper levels of compatibility. It will help if he has a Fire sign rising or other Fire elements in his chart.

The problem comes from the intensity of your basic differences as Fire and Water signs. Scorpio is much more internal, secretive, sensitive, and suspicious than you, but with an added mystical power. Both of you expect very high standards from those with whom you associate. Be aware of the need to control and how it operates in your lives. Leo and Scorpio both believe in commitments that oblige and manipulate others to follow suit. When either of you has a commitment to an ideal—or to a relationship—there is a totality and intensity that most other signs could not live up to. You expect a higher standard of behavior from your lover than from anyone else because he is an extension of your ego. Scorpio expects the same from the men he loves, but because it is a confirmation of his ability to influence them.

Your emotional nature allows you to fall in love with someone and not know why, except that he makes you feel good. Scorpio's karmic mission is to plumb the mysteries of sex. Even if a permanent relationship becomes emotionally confused, the memory of sex will linger on. Your romantic nature combines with his erotic power to reach new levels of passion. He creates an intensely serious mood of sexuality that envelops you. On the other hand, you impress him by the joyous, sensuous, delicious attitude you project about sex. If each of you gets off on the other's style of lovemaking without feeling insecure, then there is enormous potential for sexual fulfillment with a Scorpio man.

Sex is an unpredictable quantity with Scorpio. Sometimes he blows hot and heavy; other times he seems too preoccupied to be very interested. His complexity can be overwhelming and incomprehensible to you. Your sexual blending indicates hot-blooded passion and primitive desire. Affection comes only after passion has been spent. Sex, as an aspect of discipline and ego withdrawal, can be very exciting for both of you, though you definitely prefer to be the dominant partner. You will act out the role of being conquered, but you will never play the willing slave. It's one of the aspects of your Leo personality that appeals to Scorpio.

Scorpio aspects your Fourth House: roots and tradition.

You look up to him for the enduring values he holds, but you rebel against the way that tradition can stifle creativity. You will be able to provide him with the warmth and generosity of spirit he truly needs to complement his psychic weight. If you two can share your power to protect and nurture each other, the intensity of your love can span the farthest reaches of the galaxy.

LEO & SAGITTARIUS

All of the Fire signs get off on one another, and Mutable-Fire Sagittarians are no exception. These men give off a certain spark, an aura of inspiration that appeals to your own sunny optimism. When you fall in with a Jupiter-ruled Centaur, you combine your Leonine gambler's spirit with good luck.

Lucky breaks always seem to come for Sagittarius. He will even be bold enough to say that meeting you was one. The Centaur is also known as the Archer, and his blunt verbal arrows leave bruises. Even when he means to send a compliment, your Archer lover may reach for a left-handed zinger instead. Remember, he is a dual sign, half man and half horse. His compliments may come wrapped in remarks that would seem sarcastic coming from anyone else. When you announce a great idea or new realization, he may say, "That's very interesting. You know, I used to think that!" Instead of taking this as an insult to your Leonine wisdom, you will be delighted to find something else you have in common.

He thinks about everything under the Sun with a restless curiosity you find youthful and appealing. The Centaur likes to roam, both physically and mentally. He usually has had many partners; surprisingly you may not be jealous, and even more amazingly, he may be willing to accept a mo-

nogamous arrangement with a Leo lover. Your generous
spirit and creative intellect keep him interested; you spark
his imagination and activate his sexual drives in a way he
will find very satisfying.

Meeting the typically gregarious Sagittarian is easy and
fun. He is never at a loss for opening remarks and usually
will hand you a clever line that amuses you—and pierces
your regal pose just enough to let you know that he is hip
to your Leo vibrations. You admire his cheekiness, allowing
him liberties that ordinarily you never would tolerate. The
promise of variety, amusement, and romance will lead you
to mutual interests and significant experiences that cement
your emotional bond with a Sagittarian lover.

The physical and sexual rapport between you indicates
that you will find much stimulation and contentment in each
other's arms. He will try anything once, just for the sake of
the experience. You can give free rein to your erotic imagination with a Sagittarian man. He will respond with an
intensity that sends you both beyond the moons of Jupiter
and coming back for more. The typical Sagittarian lover has
a collection of sexual techniques that approaches the encyclopedic in its range.

An afternoon on horseback will be an ideal outing with a
Sagittarian playmate. The feel of muscular flesh between
his legs will be totally exhilarating, and the stimulation of
being in the saddle will be reenacted later when you fall
exhausted—and excited—into bed. Any other form of outdoor activity—hiking, cycling, camping—will all bring out
the best in his sparkling personality. The Centaur's spirit
needs a lot of experience. He loves making love alfresco,
and a picnic will satisfy any number of hungers on an ex-
cursion to the great outdoors.

You want to be at your best with him, throwing caution
to the wind in an attempt to keep him continuously dazzled.
Sagittarius aspects your Fifth House: sex, love, and variety.
You feel an enormous boost to your creative responses. Unless one or both of you have some Earth-sign elements in
your chart, there can be a spirit of recklessness that puts a

lot of tension on your relationship. You have to accept the responsibility of knowing where to place your energies so that they will have the maximum effect. Your Leonine instincts can lead you to be a show-off with a Sagittarian lover. Don't be too impatient or you will waste all the lucky breaks that can come your way.

Your Centaur is an idealist, and you will have to be careful not to become too wrapped up in unrealistic urges that lead nowhere. He doesn't love as deeply as you do. His lack of ultimate commitment can cause you to become bossy and arrogant in a vain desire to control the situation. A Sagittarian will always reject attempts to tie him down. Your demands will seem pompous and arrogant to him, and he will retaliate with stinging sarcasm that seriously undermines your faith in his love.

The Centaur can never be truly domesticated, and frankly, you wouldn't want him to be. Independence of spirit is essential to his charm, intellect, and emotional security. You both have the optimistic belief that all of your experiences lead to maturity. Keep that faith and you will keep each other content in a lasting love affair that allows for satisfying personal growth. Locked within the mythical personas of the king of the jungle and the magical Centaur are the two men with powerful desires that can blend well and result in a relationship filled with very real passion, devotion, and unusual opportunities for happiness.

LEO & CAPRICORN

The men of Cardinal-Earth Capricorn are aptly symbolized by the Mountain Goat. You will be impressed by his ambition, dedication, and serious attitude toward life. Saturn rules these men of achievement, and you will have to adopt a more responsible course if you want to share your life with a Capricorn lover.

He is impressed with status, and your regal demeanor will attract his desire to associate with men of distinction. If you come on all flash and dash, he will wonder whether there is any substance to your royal display. Underneath his solid exterior he may long for some of your warmth and confidence. If he comes to love you, it will be for the generosity he sees in you. Capricorn will certainly admire the scope of your vision and the golden quality of your dreams.

The men of Capricorn use their ambition and dedication as a cover-up for their shyness and insecurity. The demands of their careers and need for financial security keep them from emotional commitments. He is afraid that romantic or emotional distractions will not be stable enough, or as rewarding as he hopes. Rather than be hurt, disappointed or vulnerable, he keeps his shoulder to the wheel. You can charm him away, but you shouldn't trifle with him. There is a tender, gentle, and understanding lover beneath his Earth-sign practicality.

He envies your ability to be a public personality, to shine like a real star in social situations. Don't come on too heavy with the Mountain Goat or he will shy away. Remember, the path to the top of the mountain of success is narrow and difficult, and he has already accepted the possibility, even the probability, of going through life as a loner. If you confuse him with too much Leonine sparkle, he will recoil from your intensity to the security of his lonely road. Capricorn is worth cultivating and courting; don't expect him to fall at your feet in surrender to your passionate personality.

You share an interest in all forms of culture, especially music and the theater. Both Leo and Capricorn are status-conscious, and you will please each other with evenings that combine intellectual and social stimulation. Capricorns like to mix pleasure with duty; often you will meet a Capricorn through his involvement in a political or social-service organization. It is easy for him to relax and enjoy himself if he also feels respon-

sible at the same time. Your own noble tastes will find many
ways to appeal to his refined sensibilities.

The seduction scene should be refined—soft lights, classical music, and suggestive and luxurious surroundings will
arouse his deep passionate instincts. Capricorn men have
sexual stamina enough to be completely satisfying if you
give them enough time. He needs the power of your warm,
affectionate, and playful lovemaking to stimulate his physical desires. Once you get him going, there will be endless
erotic rewards for your patience. Though socially and publicly restrained, his Earth-sign qualities allow him to ''get
down'' to a completely uninhibited sex life. When you are
alone together, he will trust you enough to release his pent-
up physical urges in straight-on, man-to-man sex that leaves
you feeling totally consumed. Your erotic imagination is
turned on by this Jekyll and Hyde routine as your Capricorn
banker-by-day turns into a biker-by-night!

You share the need and capacity for love and affection,
but while you wear your heart on your sleeve, he keeps his
buried deep inside. Only your generous spirit can kindle his
tender emotions.

Capricorn aspects your Sixth House—service—and he will
want to serve you and your interests in some way. As a
Cardinal sign he is a man of ideas that have sound, practical, Earth-inspired foundations. You can take those ideas
and organize them into brilliant activities with your Leonine
flair. As business partners you can make a great deal of
money; you can achieve new levels of serious endeavor with
a Capricorn lover to assist you.

He hates waste or extravagance of any kind. Overspend-
ing on ''needless'' luxuries is one Leonine trait he can't
tolerate. Accept and acknowledge his primacy in practical
matters, and he will accord you the same in matters of creativity and imagination.

The relationship between a Leo man and his Capricorn
lover is a combination of affection and respect, tempered
by the delicate dynamism that exists between the expansive
principles of the Sun and the restrictive principles of Saturn.

You can make it work if you lavish all your affection on him. When this man feels that you are interested in his emotional security, he will begin to live up to your expectations. A Leo–Capricorn love affair is marked by a spirit of determination that mellows into a true romantic attachment—an achievement worthy of you both.

LEO & AQUARIUS

There is usually quick and intense attraction when you come in contact with your opposite Fixed-Air sign, Aquarius. His unusual approach to life and his flashes of inspiration will intrigue your big-cat curiosity.

There isn't much time for courtship when you two find each other. The energy of your Sun is combined here with the Aquarian rulership of Uranus, the planet of surprise. Aquarius is symbolized by the Water-bearer. Actually he is emptying the jug of ideas in his attempt to expose and analyze. You live a much richer emotional life than he does, though you are both passionate men. You require endless affection and attention, and he wants constant stimulation. An Aquarian lover will give you plenty of attention, since he finds you intellectually and spiritually interesting; but you may not get all of the affectional feedback you need.

With an Aquarius lover you can learn to deal with opposition intellectually, rather than emotionally. In a certain sense Aquarius has got your number and can be relentless in stripping away mask after mask from your personality. You rise to the challenge and stay creatively charged when in love with an Aquarius. You have to be on your toes at all times.

Aquarius' love of the eccentric and unorthodox certainly includes his sexual preferences. As in other aspects of his life, he is stimulated by intellect rather than emotion. He sustains sexual passion through variety and experimentation. It is important for him to get warmed up to lovemaking. You will have to take the initiative in getting him to respond sexually, but once he is worked up, his erotic energies are amazingly eclectic.

Aquarians refuse to tolerate boredom, and you may be unable to get the kind of restful, reassuring, and rejuvenating feelings you require from lovemaking. Sex is a way of soothing your nerves, but his insistence on continually changing sexual activities leaves little room for you to relax and enjoy your intimate moments. He will want to try out various toys and unusual positions in his quest for playful sex.

You will have to be willing to let an Aquarian lover have free rein if you want to keep him loyal to you. Since he aspects your Seventh House—partners—he will be predisposed to being a faithful lover. Try to offer him your affection and friendship without restricting his independence. He should be willing to accord you the same kind of freedom. The possibility is here for a truly "open relationship," based upon mutual respect and a commitment to friendship.

A problem can arise from your feelings of inadequacy or lack of emotional fulfillment in an "open" arrangement. You need more than a friend or intellectual companion to keep you happy. Leo needs devotion to confirm his self-image, and Aquarius doesn't really communicate that feeling to you. The result could be a search for more affection in other romantic encounters. Aquarius may not be jealous, but you may feel guilty, anyway. You want to be faithful, but you have emotional needs that he may not be able to satisfy.

Though Aquarius is a Fixed sign and wants to have a home base, he is devoted to his wide circle of friends and the need for enriching experiences. If you try to restrict his activities, rebellion will ensue. He can become cool and detached or erupt in sudden anger. Often your conflicts will be resolved through intensely stubborn arguments that simulate your sexual desires. The arousal of physical passion during confrontation can lead to mutual sexual surrender.

An affair with an Aquarian man will be hectic and unstable, even though you learn a great deal about yourself through the way he reflects your opposite-sign characteristics in his Uranian mirror. You learn the power and value of your generous nature to bring out the best in his wide-ranging intelligence. In return he gives you a new objectivity and an appreciation for the values of nonconformity. The combination of your astrological natures can lead to a union that keeps you both youthful and attractive. You are resourceful men, strengthened by your relationship and ready to take on the future with an aggressive optimism.

LEO & PISCES

Your need to dominate your lovers can prove beneficial in combination with a Mutable-Water Pisces man. He is symbolized by the Fish, swimming in circles. Your Sun-powered warmth, affection, and sense of direction can provide his Neptune-ruled dreaminess with a new sense of creative expression. Where others may find you too arrogant in your demand for attention, Pisces will find strength in your generosity and willingly offer you devotion.

A Pisces man can activate your most tender feelings. Your protective affection will provide him with the emotional security he needs. He will express his admiration and appreciation in a manner that balances your differing natures. He is more intuitive and emotional than you, but you are more rational than he. The combination can lead to a new spiritual strength for both partners. There is romance, but it is tempered by practical considerations and the development of hidden talents.

You will find yourself mysteriously drawn to him, since Pisces represents your Eighth House—sexual magnetism. Pisces has the power to attract you and to keep you without making demands. You will woo and conquer him sexually, but you may not really feel in control of the situation. It's as if his unconscious charm seduced you into seducing him. Both of you respond to compliments, and fortunately there is much for you to admire in each other.

Pisceans are often good dancers. You make an attractive pair on the dance floor, but don't be too inhibited to dance at home to more intimate rhythms. Close-contact dancing is always a good preliminary sexual move with a Pisces man. After he has languished in your arms to the slow beat you can carry the same physical experience to the bedroom. You will definitely be the sexual leader in this relationship. A Pisces lover can be very passive to your Fire-sign passions and needs. Sometimes you need more of a challenge to arouse your interest than Pisces is able to supply. There is the danger of developing a relationship that will express your need to command and his need to sacrifice, without nurturing your mutual need for romantic affection.

Good sex with a Pisces lover has the quality of erotic dreams of illusory but intense sensations. You can consummate your Leonine passions any way you like, since he will adapt to your style of lovemaking. Remember, he is a subtle and sensitive lover who will respond to sex by becoming totally passive and emotionally withdrawn. The gentler you are, the more he will trust you. The more he trusts you, the more capable he will be of sustaining the physical passion you require from the man you love.

Even though there is an aura of devotion between Leo and Pisces, jealousy may be an issue that comes between you. Your strong emotional ties will lead you to covet each other and to feel threatened by flirtations. He will fear the loss of his protector while you will rage at the possible theft of the object of your most intense affections. Leave the surface impressions to the gossips and keep your faith in each other. Neither of you can resist basking in the attention of others, especially other attractive men. Let the enjoyment go no deeper than an ego boost, and there should never be any need for deception or jealousy.

You may well find that in your relationship you can break

through to new areas of accomplishment. Books, publishing, writing, filmmaking, and television are all fields that yield to positive Leo–Pisces cultivation. Material success can be combined with an interest in the occult or transcendental sciences.

This is not an easy relationship because of the differences in your emotional levels. Pisces needs time alone to sort out his sometimes jammed Neptunian airwaves. He is so sensitive that he needs periodic retreats to clear his mind and refresh his spirit. Stay close to him, but give him all the freedom he asks for to keep himself properly in tune. He won't resort to sulking unless he becomes resentful of your arrogance or overbearing demands upon him. Be there when he needs you and let him know that your heart is his to command, and he will never abuse your trust. Pisces is not as pliable as he seems, and you can hurt him without realizing it, unless you are constantly attuned to the need for balance in your relationship.

Leo in love with Pisces can turn insecurities into mere fantasies as your Sun energy shines through the mists and fogs of Neptune mysticism. You can bring him out of his watery confusion while he can temper your energies with new awareness and sensitivity. You can be well served and well loved with a Pisces man to share your life.

LOVING YOUR LEO MAN

If you can imagine Tony the Tiger, Garfield, and Morris the Cat as gay men, you can spot a Leo in a crowd. Look for a Leo wherever you find bright lights, handsome crowds, and creative energies. They have a fondness for the theater and for spectator sports. They prefer play to exercise, and you are more likely to meet a Leo man on the tennis court than a jogging track or in the weight-training room. Art events interest him as much as art itself, so look for Leo at the opening or preview night at museums and galleries, rather than on a quiet afternoon there. Leos are often involved in photography—as collectors or as photographers or sometimes as models. If you have occasion to deal with promotional or administrative people in cosmetics, sportswear, hairdressing, or fashion accessories, you will probably meet plenty of Leo men.

Attracting a Leo's attention is not difficult if you appeal to his self-image. He prefers other men to come on to him because he is a cowardly Lion when it comes to risking rejection. No matter how noble, dignified, or arrogant he may seem posing there against the bar, he is afraid that he may be turned down, that he won't get some sign of interest from you. A wink, a nod, or a smile will be enough to rouse him from his reservations about crossing the room and meeting you. A little bit of encouragement can go a long way with a Leo man. He likes to be admired, and he will purr like a kitten at compliments. Leos are attracted to beauty and enticed by curiosity, so you should look your best to catch his attention.

You can't please a Leo for long if you are too eccentric. He likes a regular guy with established patterns, even though they may seem extravagant. He may be a passionate sex partner, but he prefers fairly conventional sex. Fixed signs tend to have fixed opinions, but Leo may be given to snap decisions based upon vanity rather than practical or rational considerations. It is very difficult for him to say "I'm sorry" or to admit failure. You should be adaptable and indulgent only to a certain degree with Leo men, or they may get too carried away with themselves. He needs to feel like a free agent, but he can benefit from your wise counsel if you temper your advice with complimentary introductions. Appealing to his pride, dignity, or generosity usually has the desired effect. You can even get him to accept the passive role in lovemaking if you let him know how good he is for you and praise his sexual talents. A Leo lover will always try to live up to your best opinion of him.

Keep him happy by displaying your affection and praising him for the genuine virtues he possesses. He has a wonderful, warm heart that needs to give and receive love and tenderness. You will have to understand his need for recognition from other men. He will flirt, but he feeds on the ego gratification he gets from it rather than from the sexual implications. Leo believes in true love and will feel a real emotional commitment to your relationship. He will be loyal and devoted to you, as long as you let him have the freedom to play for attention from the crowd. Leo will be eager for you to participate in his active social life because he likes the status of having a lover. Look your best and he will find it a compliment to his good taste and fortune if other men flirt with you. It will even enhance your desirability in his eyes.

Leo can be an engaging, boyish, affectionate, and passionate man—or a spoiled, lazy creature, too proud to end a relationship that no longer works. Though he thinks of himself as the dominant force in your relationship, you must be the one who has the strength to call it quits or take the initiative to make it work for both of you. He may not always be easy to live with, but there is a great deal of love in your Leo man.

VIRGO
August 21– September 20

♍

Symbol: The Virgin
Ruling Planet: Mercury
Colors: Beige and brown
Metal: Nickel
Natural House Rulership: Sixth House, the house of
    health and service
Sixth House Traits: Concern for physical health and
    desire for perfection
Motto: "I analyze"
Nature: Mutable sign (adaptation)
Element: Earth sign (material)
Qualities: Modest, conscientious, and critical
Capacities: Service to worthy ventures
Personality Key Words: Perfection, dedication, and
    sublimation

MAXIMIZING YOUR VIRGO POTENTIAL

Nothing is perfect in life, and yet your Virgo nature makes you dedicated to the ideal of perfection. Your sign comes at that time of year when the perfect days of summer are beginning to wane before the autumnal equinox. The Sun in Virgo symbolizes the point in personal development when one becomes aware of values beyond the self. The rulership of Mercury in an Earth sign causes you to be the natural critic in the zodiac, aware of the flaws of reality and determined to maintain order over chaos. The practical and material values of your Earth element combine with the mental and communicative powers of Mercury to give you great skills in comparison and analysis. Even love gets pinned down to the dissecting tray of Virgo examination, sometimes to your disadvantage. The symbol of the Virgin underlines the purity of your intent rather than your actual sexual condition in life.

Your goals in life are usually nothing less than perfection in both the material and spiritual worlds. Virgo's ideal of purity is expressed in his desire to keep life neat and ordered in tidy categories. You thrive on the mental processes of analyzing, categorizing, and criticizing, but the need for emotional input may be overlooked or miscalculated. You can be a caring lover, but in practical rather than emotional ways. Virgos take good care of all their responsibilities, from leases to lovers.

The Virgo man will set up exacting criteria for an acceptable lover or sexual experience. Your discriminating intellect causes you to keep your emotions "uncontaminated" and separate from your career, social life, and sexual needs. You can easily fall into a tidy pattern of brief affairs, as man after man fails to meet your criteria for perfection. You believe in the search for Mr. Right, but your analytical mind keeps finding little flaws in your potential Prince Charming. Falling in love is a matter of intellectual appraisal rather than emotional abandon for Virgos. You want to feel that your devotion and dedication to him will be a worthwhile investment with long-term potential. Your goal is a pure and perfect love.

There are so few people or situations that can meet Virgo's high standards that you are often disappointed. The drive for analysis and perfection can make you skeptical and activate the Virgo potential for pessimism. Your analytical skills break down into confusion when you are confronted with spiritual considerations. Your discriminating intellect is your strongest Virgo trait, and yet it can prevent you from enjoying life on a visceral level. Romance cannot be quantified, and you can lose the essence of experience if you are too busy weighing all the tangibles but ignoring the needs of the spirit. A cramped perspective makes you intolerant of the normal weaknesses of others and unreceptive to the values of imagination.

Your social life reflects the conscientious care that you devote to most aspects of your existence. Virgo will rarely throw parties that bring all of his acquaintances together. You prefer to deal with people in convenient categories rather than amorphous social situations. Sometimes your social life is affected by your dedication to health and fitness. Few Virgo-born health-food fans are to be found in bars (bad for the liver). You may be found in the gym, tuning your body in a meticulous manner, or on the jogging track. You enjoy pursuits of the mind, such as reading and museums as well as the stimulation of serious hobbies.

In a similar fashion, sex is a practical pleasure for you. Technique always takes precedence over passion. You are capable of a wide variety of sexual experiences as long as you feel emotionally detached from the physical activity. It is in the Virgo nature to analyze sex manuals and the techniques of your partners to learn all of the right moves. The result is a technical proficiency that is capable of providing physical stimulation, but not erotic satisfaction. The Virgo ability to distance yourself leaves you engaged in the mechanics of sex without the relaxation and recreation you need to keep your personality as positive as possible.

When all of the pieces fall neatly into place, you will find yourself in love. He will have to meet your physical, intellectual, and social criteria rather than sweep you off your feet emotionally or sexually. You place your faith in mutual respect rather than passion when you look for love. Virgo wants a lover he can serve and care for on a mental and physical plane rather than on an emotional or sexual level. If your definition of perfection in life includes having a lover, you will devote much time and energy to making the relationship work. Virgo recognizes the need for emotional stability as part of a well-rounded existence, on a par with proper diet, good grooming, and fiscal responsibility. Your desire for moderation and regularity leads you to seek a lover who will fit neatly into your existing life-style with a minimum of disruption.

Tender loving care can be the greatest gift you bring to a relationship. The mental stimulation and practical assistance you provide your lovers is the Virgo way of expressing emotion, devotion, and love. Once you have made a commitment, you are willing to serve your lover. You delight in presenting him with small, no-nonsense presents and doing favors that make his life easier. You want to know what he needs and likes so that you can provide for him, materially or sexually. The Virgo talent for technique will allow you to be a receptive sex partner who will cater to your lover's desires for physical intimacy with great skill. You offer your lovers dedication, attention, and consideration—important qualities for the success of any relationship.

The influence of nonsexual Mercury in a materialist Earth sign, symbolized by the Virgin, adds up to the sublimation of passion in the search for personality development. When faced with failure or rejection in the quest of love, you have the power to persevere and to compensate with your other interests. When your dreamboat turns into a tugboat in morning's light, you don't go to pieces. A Virgo thanks his lucky stars for his job, his home, his health, and all the things that keep him busy.

Your Virgo spirit may be undaunted by failure, but you never forget the lessons that teach you caution and reserve in making commitments. Don't let your concern with perfection prevent you from being the giving, loving man that lies within your Virgo self. Use your Mercury power of communication to keep yourself informed of your lover's needs and to articulate your own wishes and expectations. Be careful of your tendency to use people as pieces of a puzzle, of being too critical of inconsistencies and emotional weaknesses in others or in yourself. Pessimism is the one Virgo attribute that can color all of your relationships. With a lover you respect and admire, you can learn to be more tolerant, imaginative, and positive in your approach to life.

VIRGO & ARIES

Aries aspects your Eighth House—sexual mystery. You will be attracted to this natural man by his bright eyes and outgoing manner. Though he may seem very different from the men you normally meet, there is a definite sexual magnetism that draws you to him. If he's a typical Arian, his obvious butch sensibilities may cause you to hesitate, wondering if your neat life is worth messing up—and to whose benefit.

The men born under the sign of the Ram are Cardinal-Fire by nature—aggressive, emotional, and adventurous. He is also sloppy, reckless, selfish, demanding—and very sexy. It doesn't seem like the tidy Virgo cup of tea, but you two are joined by a search for truth and perfection in your sexual attractions.

Aries is the sign of primal ego, and you will probably have to confront his selfish enthusiasms as they disturb your orderly existence. He can come bounding into your life like a muddy puppy full of joy and friendship, unaware of the havoc he wreaks all around himself. Arians are generous souls but not very practical. He will offer to cut off his right arm or walk on broken glass to serve you when all you really want is someone to be punctual, consistent, considerate, and helpful without making such a big deal of it. When he does you a favor, be sure to express your sincere thanks. Virgo is into selfless service, but Aries needs at least a pat on the head to keep him happy.

An association with an Aries man will have to make you more tolerant, imaginative, and open to inspiration if it's going to last. A little more order and regularity in his life will be the real gift you can bring an Aries lover.

Though he is a man of large sexual appetites, he has a pure and perfect sense of the glories of love. You will have to learn to suspend some of your critical functions with him and give yourself up to the pleasures of intense sexual communion with this Arian bundle of bursting enthusiasm.

There are many sterling Aries qualities that will appeal to your Virgo sensibilities. He is honest, optimistic, and has an indomitable spirit. Even when you think him a naïve fool, he has the power to lift your spirits with his innocent charm. You can sublimate your critical urges through sex with your Aries lover, though he may be very demanding. Your reliance on technique is quite different from his straightforward desire for sex, and lots of it. If you are too fussy or reticent about sexual abandon, he may be less than faithful.

If you are pleased with other aspects of your relationship with an Aries man, you will be willing to allow him enough freedom to roam. He will always be honest about his need for freedom—perhaps more honest than you would like him to be. Arians love a challenge, and he may be wanting you to be more demanding of his attentions than he can express. You have the Earth-sign tendency to take your lovers for granted, but Aries needs proof of your devotion.

Fortunately your Virgo desire to take good care of your lover will be well received by Aries. He may actually need someone to button up his overcoat, but don't cramp his exuberant style. Appreciate his boyish charms for what they are and don't try to smother him with disapproval or demands for practicality. Virgo is the best fence-mender in the zodiac, but the Ram will never change his natural drives.

Let an Aries have his lead and use your own time alone to recharge your batteries in quiet pursuit of your more meticulous interests. If you let him blow off his Arian ego steam while you spend time relaxing in your own way, the times you spend together will allow you to really enjoy his company without feeling that you live in perpetual chaos. Virgo rules the nervous system, and an Aries lover can literally "get on your nerves" by just being himself. If it's love, you will go easy on the scolding—and won't think of yourself as a martyr, either.

Aries will delight in your gifts or unsolicited favors, and he will give to you in similar ways. Rather than becoming critical of his extravagance with presents or his overzealous favors, be specific in communicating the things you need, want, or wish for. Aries will always try to make your wishes come true, because he wants you to be more imaginative. He believes in miracles, and an Aries in love is always trying to pull off minor miracles.

One of the miraculous features of your love with an Aries is that you can let go enough to feel the protective bond between you, to appreciate his optimism, and to participate in his loving enthusiasm.

VIRGO & TAURUS

Taurus is the sign of the Bull, ruled by Venus—a combination of strength and receptivity that appeals to you. Since he is a fellow Earth sign, you will recognize certain affinities in your interests that are practical and material. He is Fixed-Earth, making him more possessive and much more stubborn than your own Mutable nature.

Virgo shares a basic trust with Taurus that centers around similar goals for security and serenity. You should certainly be able to find support for each other and develop your personalities within a loving relationship. With a Taurus lover you should be able to relax and enjoy his companionship without feeling overly critical of his values or actions. By the same token, he will appreciate your analytical skill and clear thinking. He will admire you for your mind, and that may be the highest compliment one can pay a Virgo.

Taurus is a sign of materialism and emotions related to security. He deals with the world on a material level as his approach to emotional security. He will be relieved to find that you are a man who understands the need for order and organization. You like his need to be goal-oriented and offer good advice on how to best achieve objectives. You will want to take good care of him, and he will strive to earn your approval. Romantic attraction combines with your practical natures to indicate a satisfying friendship and promising love life with a Taurus man.

He has a strong sex drive as part of his Earthy appetites. You trust him and therefore should be able to relax and enjoy the sensuous pleasures of sex with a Taurus lover. He does not demand an intricate lover but prefers simple sex on a regular basis. You don't have to worry about your performance, since Taurus expects gentleness and tender lovemaking rather than tangling with a superstud. Though Earth signs are normally not communicative during sex, the influence of your ruling Mercury will allow both of you to be open about your sexual needs. Don't be too sensitive when it comes to sex and his ribald sense of humor, or you will spoil some of the fun to be had with a Taurus lover.

Fixed-sign men tend to be dependable and faithful, so your romance should run a smooth course. He can be demanding, but you are very resourceful when it comes to pleasing the man you love. He is more emotional than you are, but he will see the ultimate value of your less passionate attitude toward life. Don't be too critical of him or he will begin to feel insecure and possessive. Bulls have tempers that are best avoided by being kind and consistent.

Taurus aspects your Ninth House—long journeys. You will be stimulated to making long-range plans and defining goals. With a Taurus lover, your life may become clarified in new ways that focus on a sense of purpose, education, and foreign travel. Your intellectual skills help to refine his organizational drives and overcome his tendency to be slightly plodding or prosaic in his approach. His creative talents are stimulated by the addition of your critical intelligence.

You can look forward to stability and solidity in an affair with a Taurus. He is honest and forthright, with a sense of values you understand. There may not be an overwhelming passion, but there is a mutual respect that you prize highly in your search for love and understanding. Conflicts will arise, but they usually can be resolved without pain if you go easy on the sarcasm. Both of you will try to avoid messy scenes. Even if the affair does not prove to be lasting, you probably will remain friends and confidants.

Taurus is prone to overindulgence, and you can help to keep him from going overboard in food, drink, and luxurious living. Though normally quite good with handling money and maintaining savings, he has a penchant for pleasure that is very different from your more ascetic tastes. It will take him some time to enjoy one of your ''hearty'' meals of alfalfa sprouts and bean curd, unless he can have pumpkin pie with whipped cream for dessert.

But Taurus also enjoys the quiet pleasure and comforts of

life at home. You will spend time together in relaxing entertainment with a few close friends rather than frequenting the glittering social scene. Home and hearth are sources of strength and security for both Taurus and Virgo. You will enjoy making your shared residence a haven for your Taurus, and he will make sure it is well decorated and comfortable.

Both of you are faithful in love. Taurus will be somewhat possessive of you, though you won't mind as long as he leaves you enough freedom to pursue your own intellectual interests. You will be protective of him, and he will like being cared for in such a practical manner. The aspects indicate a rewarding affair and a long-lasting relationship.

VIRGO & GEMINI

The Twins of Gemini are ruled by Mercury, your own planetary mentor, but in Mutable Air rather than Earth. Communication is the paramount issue between you as he inquisitively turns cartwheels in the Air and you keep his kite firmly anchored to the Earth. You have a way of refining his impulsive urges that gives Gemini a new clarity of purpose. He may rebel at being slightly grounded by your practical considerations, but he can learn a vital maturity and material sophistication under your care. There can be substantial rewards when you join forces with a Gemini lover.

You will be intrigued by his quick mentality and fresh outlook, though disturbed by his apparent superficiality. You will feel flattered by Gemini's intense interest in what you think about everything and anything. It will be a challenge to field the wild ideas he presents and put them into a rational perspective. He may seem a bit too radical for your

Virgo sensibilities but you are fascinated by his creative breadth and ambitious scope.

Activity and investigations are the keynotes of your attraction to each other. You read about and discuss a wide variety of subjects. Though you may disapprove of his opinions, he is quite flexible and open to alternative viewpoints. There may not be an initial sexual attraction, since the real bond between you is more mental than physical. Gemini can easily be seduced out of curiosity rather than lust for carnal pleasures.

If you care for him, you will be indulgent of his light-hearted attitude. He can get you to be more receptive to the humor in the world, rather than being a constant critic and pessimist. You have to let him have his freedom or he will simply fly away, both mentally and physically. You may even find his flirtations amusing in their naïveté as long as he is discreet. Let him go do the rounds with his pals while you spend some quiet time reordering your universe after his chaotic presence. He turns your world upside down, and your nerves are bound to get a bit frayed around the edges.

A little peace and quiet will help you stay on an even keel with a Gemini lover. Your sex lives should be basically tranquil and undemanding, for neither of you is driven by sexual passion, though both of you may be accomplished in the mechanics. Sex is a form of mental stimulation with you Mercury-ruled men. He is into fantasy trips and you can go along with his fun-and-games attitude as long as you understand his practical need for that kind of experience. When he is too involved in a new idea or you are immersed in some problem, both of you will look upon lovemaking as a distraction rather than a pleasure. Sex is confirmation of your power to stimulate each other mentally, rather than a physical expression of passion.

When the stars are favorable, you combine imagination, perception, and practical analysis in a dynamic partnership. Your administrative skills and his fund of ideas can lead to a very successful business relationship. Gemini has his finger on the pulse of society and only needs your practical advice to turn his sensitivity for trends into million-dollar ideas. Since he aspects your Tenth House—career—there is good chance of outstanding financial benefits with a Gemini lover.

When you get on each other's nerves, the issue will be lack of respect. The weapons will be words, sharp and to the point. Though he will shower you with sarcasm, you can usually get in quite a few well-timed licks that will take the wind right out of his sails. You are more susceptible to being hurt than he, but neither of you holds grudges. In the end there is a sense of duty to each other that will bring you to your senses and allow for forgiveness.

The older your Gemini lover, the more receptive he will be to your solid and stable virtues. As he matures, he comes to value you for the serious person you are, and the devotion you show him in so many ways. He will still maintain his youthful spirit and provide you with constant surprises that keep you mentally on your toes. You will be more tolerant of him if he has already proven himself as a man of achievement rather than being just a dizzy young cutie. Together you can have a solid base of mutual respect, enlivened by intellectual insights that provide for a special love between friends.

VIRGO & CANCER

Cardinal Water is his element, and a Cancer man will attract you with his clever conversation and charming manner. He's a sensitive creature, ruled by the inconstant Moon. You may find him too moody and changeable to understand, but he can be a very cozy, cuddly, and comforting love.

Cancer can get carried away with his overactive imagination, and he needs a practical partner like you to help him focus his energies. Your instinct is to protect him, and he will return your care with loving affection, as long as you aren't too strict or disapproving in your attention. If you nag or are overcritical, the Crab will retreat into his self-protective shell. If you remind him too often of his short-comings, he will become moody and withdrawn, losing the charm and grace you fell in love with in the first place.

Your Moonbeam man is basically romantic, kind, and considerate. These are qualities you value highly in a lover. Though he tends to be inwardly shy, if he is attracted to you, he will want to sweep you off your feet. Cancer is a Cardinal sign, and he is inspired to lead with his creative imagination. Don't be surprised if he sends you flowers, little notes, and other tokens of courtship. While it may seem extravagant to your more practical Earth-sign nature, you don't have to worry about him being a spendthrift. Cancer knows the value of a dollar—he is just temporarily carried away with you!

Cancer represents your Eleventh House—friendships—and you will trust him as a confidant and loyal companion. He activates your hopes and wishes, giving you a fresh and optimistic viewpoint. If you have been unlucky in love, meeting Cancer will give you new faith in the chance for a lasting relationship. Don't ignore his own real needs and indulge in mere wishful thinking. If you lose your heart and your head at the same time, you could become terribly disillusioned!

Cancer is not necessarily deceptive, but he is emotionally evasive. He is a man of secrets and secret feelings that even he does not fully comprehend. Your ruler, Mercury, wants to know, to analyze, to communicate. His Moon ruler understands that there are some things better left to the darkness of the subconscious. If you try to pry open his secret wounds, even though your aim is to cleanse and purify, the process will be too painful for him. He needs a man who will give him unconditional affection, regardless of his own doubts and fears. You can do that, Virgo, if it's love that you feel for this elusive Moonbeam.

You are a man of specifics and precision, even when it comes to your sexuality. You know what you like and how you like it; your tendency is to analyze your fantasies and find out how they operate. Cancer does not focus his sex drive in the same way you do, but he will be a willing and pliant sex partner if you articulate your needs. Learn to be more open to sexual variety under his influence; there are aspects here that indicate a continual development of your sexual style with a Cancer lover.

Style can be the keynote of your relationship. His diverse circle of friends will widen your horizons. With a Cancer lover your Mutable-sign qualities make you more flexible. You find that you are able to pick and choose what you like from a variety of new influences. Cancer's creative talents make you want to be more active and outgoing as a social personality.

Short trips, especially sojourns into the great outdoors, will lift your spirits immeasurably. Once you get out of the city, your cares will dissipate in the fresh air. A long walk by the shore or through the woods will serve to remind you and your lover of the really important things in life. The cycle of the seasons has a regularity and a purity that both calms and refreshes your troubled minds.

Trouble comes when you become too protective and he becomes too dependent. The best loves are those that make each person stronger, not weaker. Nothing is more miserable than a moping Moonbeam, and no one is touchier than a vexed Virgin.

Your relationship won't be neat and tidy, but it can be rewarding and fulfilling if you keep your wits about you. You are practical enough to be aware of his real virtues, and he is sensitive enough to appreciate your true motives. You can teach Cancer new ways of focusing his imaginative inspiration into practical experience. He can show you new ways to enjoy life to the fullest. Don't let the mundane world spoil the spiritual values you two can share as loving men and true companions.

VIRGO & LEO

Fixed-Fire Leo men are too passionate and extravagant for your Virgo instincts to trust, but you are still fascinated by them. You detect an air of mystery that captures your inquisitive mind. He represents a challenge to you, with undercurrents of fantasy and sexuality that make your temperature rise.

The ruling Sun of Leo adds warmth to your ruling Mercury, causing you to be more inspired and open to his charming optimism than critical of his egotism. You want to know more about him, even be more like him. You will get the biggest charge out of a Leo relationship if there is some clandestine element that increases the fantasy aspects. Often a Leo will come into your life when you are involved with another person. Questions of loyalty can be ignored or rationalized away when you fall under the spell of sexy Leo.

You both have qualities the other needs to be successful in developing your personalities. Leo is kind and generous, easygoing enough to take your criticism with a grain of salt. He has a sense of humor that will keep you from retreating into cool analysis, but he also respects your intellect. When in love with a Leo, you are aware of his wonderful potential and eager to make improvements. Remember, he is a Fixed sign, and making any changes will require tact and positive encouragement.

Appeal to his pride, support his ego through practical advice and loving concern, and he will be loyal. Leos want to protect their lovers and Virgos want to please their men. You both benefit from this kind of attention. Leo provides the devotion and you supply the dedication that can make your relationship deeply satisfying.

Leo brings out your domestic nature, and you will want to establish and maintain a home that will be a haven for him. His tastes are more flamboyant than yours, but the clean, efficient, and ascetic style you prefer will suit him in its majestic simplicity. You can refine his impulses and inspirations in a way that will bring both of you pleasure.

If he finds you attractive, he won't be shy about making it known. If he is serious about you, he won't try to rush you into a sexual situation. Leo has an innate respect for Virgo that allows you to receive his attention favorably rather than be put off by his typical Leonine traits. Leo represents your Twelfth House—mystery and hidden meanings—so you will be intrigued. Virgo will want to know why such a beam of sunshine should suddenly appear.

Leo's radiance can light up those elements of your life that need to be warmed by the Sun. Indications for a satisfying sexual experience are good if you accept his passion and refine it with a light Virgo touch of fantasy, gentleness, and technique. Make sure he gets plenty of rest and exercise. Leo expresses his physical and emotional well-being through love and affection. The better he feels, the better he will make you feel. Warm and safe in Leo's arms, you will receive some of the power of his confidence and courage.

Leo and Virgo reinforce each other's dignity and sense of obligation to give of themselves. Together you can devote time to a cause or project in the gay community that brings you even closer together. With a Leo lover, your status is raised through service of some kind.

When you find yourself at odds with his arrogance, vanity, self-indulgence, extravagance, or laziness, you will wonder just who needs whom and for what. Leo will have his serious doubts when you become hypercritical, cool, detached, nagging, and nervous. But your emotional ties will eventually overcome your differences. The way in which you please each other will go a long way toward making the moments of discontent bearable and temporary.

Leo may not understand your need for times of personal privacy. He takes everyone's feelings personally, so just be gentle, firm, and reassuring about your love but insist upon time to yourself to rest your nerves. You need to be healthy to cope with his emotional intensity. A Virgo can get ego burns from too much exposure to a Leo. When he's on his own, he will be faithful to you as long as you give him the attention and approval he craves.

Virgo and Leo have the power to solve the problems that arise in a man-to-man relationship with the combination of intellect (you) and inspiration (him). Between these two forces lies a vast field of emotion. You have access to emotional experiences with him that enrich your life. Leo's sunny influences extend the potential for growth and ripeness of Virgo into an Indian summer of the heart. If you can keep your Virgo personality tuned in to that mellow image of long, golden autumn afternoons, you will find a Leo lover a most enjoyable experience.

VIRGO & VIRGO

For two such neat and tidy personalities, the mess two Virgos can make of each other's lives is amazing. Attempts at maintaining compatibility will try your wits and fray your nerves. This is a high-energy relationship, as Mutable-Earth signs in association indicate communication in a material environment that calls for constant adaptation.

Earth signs feel a basic trust and a certain amount of comfort in each other's presence. You will appreciate his style, and you won't feel hesitant to say so. Your initial conversation will be about something intelligent and important to you, perhaps world news or local issues within your community. You can stay up all night talking to him and fall asleep in his arms without forcing the issue of sex. If sex does come first on his list, then you will doubt his intentions from the very beginning. Virgos distance themselves from emotional commitments with their sex partners by being very particular about the criteria for Mr. Right.

You normally want sex to develop out of your other mutual interests rather than be the focus of your relationship.

Neither of you trusts a relationship founded on a quick or intense sexual experience: It is not rational, not necessarily easy to analyze, and there are no sure lines of communication. You are afraid of hidden problems or unknown complications.

If your Virgo man does meet the criteria for your ideal, you will be dedicated to maintaining the relationship, to the point of suffering through unpleasant elements that may develop. The course of true love will rarely run smooth in a Virgo–Virgo affair. There will be constant analysis, and your relationship may become one continuous therapy sesson.

Keep yourselves active and involved in projects and amusements outside of your relationship. Gay community services can always use the aid of a Virgo or two. Treat yourselves to entertainment that will widen your interests rather than focus all your attention on each other. You will become too judgmental of him and will feel too scrutinized under his Virgo inspection. For some lovers in the same sign, the relationship is like looking in a mirror. With Virgo to Virgo, it can be eyeball to eyeball through a magnifying glass. The flaws can seem enormous, making both of you feel insecure.

Insecurity in Virgos will cause attacks of painful criticism that turn into sarcasm. Unhappy Virgos are not healthy, either. You can upset each other to the point where mutual support is no longer possible. At that point, you will agree that the relationship is no longer feasible and call it quits as efficiently and cleanly as possible.

If your need to be needed is stronger than your need to find fault or match wits, then Virgo lovers can overcome their differences. He has a fine, stimulating mind and a sincere desire to please you. There is a feeling of dedication that makes your relationship seem unique in a typically Virgo way. Passionate devotion will not be part of a Virgo–Virgo love affair, unless you both have several Fire-sign elements in your charts. Mutual respect is more important to both of you than smoldering desire.

You should enjoy his lovemaking because you like a partner who knows what he likes and who can satisfy you with a competent display of technique. You will be meticulous in assisting each other to orgasm, with just the right touch and proper timing. What may seem clinical to more passionate or emotional signs is actually Virgo's care, concentration, and consideration. You increase your sexual enjoyment, confidence, and competence with a Virgo lover.

Loyalty to your partner is important to Virgo—but you will not necessarily fault him for an occasional flirtation. You know that respect and mutual admiration are more important; you will want to work hard to make this a lasting relationship.

Get some fresh air into your relationship if you want your Virgo lover to thrive. Go hiking in the woods and expand the confines of your narrow Virgo interests. Keep bringing new elements into your mutual experiences and you can learn a great deal about yourself from a Virgo lover.

VIRGO & LIBRA

The Cardinal-Air nature of Libra men causes them to share your intellectual interests, but with a degree of imagination that you find very stimulating. The sign of the Balance symbolizes his dedication to justice and his openness to all ideas and experiences. Libra has a capacity to enjoy life that you can understand and appreciate because of its intellectual dimension. The influence of his ruling Venus adds new aesthetic dimensions to your practical vision that makes life much more pleasant in his company.

Gentle, inventive persuasion is the only way to reach a Libra man if you want to be part of his life. Romance may be the offing, but it will normally be at his initiative. Cardinal signs like to take the lead, and Libra is an active sign.

Let him set the pace of your involvement, and don't set any restrictions on it if you want a lasting relationship.

You are attracted to each other for different reasons. Libra finds you fascinating in a way that excites his curiosity. You find him interesting, but in a material way. He may impress you with the quality of his life-style rather than with any emotional attraction. You become more interested in possessions and finances than passion with a Libran companion. Your opportunities for advancement will increase, but you must be prepared to share your success with him or he will feel used by you.

A Libra man needs admiration and support more than critical advice. He takes you seriously, and that means you can restrict his creativity with your direct analytical reactions. You will have to learn to think about balanced evaluations rather than pointing out faults or a Libra will not stay around for long, no matter how intriguing he finds you. Libras need more affection than communication. Venus inclines him to feel, while Mercury impels you think.

Libra separates beauty from function in the same way you separate sex from emotion. Your practical outlook causes you to question his expenditures on aesthetic pleasures. With a Libra man as your lover you can learn to appreciate that beauty has a definite functional importance. Without it Libra loses his creative vitality and his wit turns to insincerity and indecision. Remember, he is an optimist and will always take to the sunny side of the street. If you keep casting shadows with Virgo pessimism and constant critiques, he will follow the Sun in search of a new chance for happiness with another man.

Libra searches for harmony in all things. Your ability to harmonize as sex partners will depend upon how receptive you are to his passionate and affectionate lovemaking. The warmth of his desire can add enough extra degrees to your Virgo coolness to make for a satisfying union. He likes variety in his sexual experiences, and your emphasis on technique will add to his erotic enjoyment. Offer to increase his pleasure with gentle Virgo touches, but never give him ad-

vice in bed or the game's over. Balance is a sensitive state
of existence, and the wrong word can send him into confusion and self-doubt. In a wavering mood he will turn to
anyone who offers him affection to soothe the sting of your
ill-timed analysis.

Libra represents your Second-House—money and possessions. His attraction to you is likely to be more romantic
and emotional than your interest in him. Be honest with
yourself about your feelings or he can be hurt by your materialist attitude. You are both idealists and can delude yourselves into believing that there is more emotional substance
to your relationship than really exists. You will expect too
much from each other unless you are completely open about
your expectations. Trading advice and understanding will
make your bonds with Libra strong and secure.

If you are careful and thoughtful, confrontations will be
rare because you share a gentleness of spirit and politeness
that prevents stormy scenes. He strives for grace while you
work toward simplicity. You please each other in your desires for peace and contentment, but too much passivity will
keep you from taking advantage of opportunities. This relationship needs stimulation and challenges to bring out the
best in both of you.

For you and Libra, the aspects indicate limited success in
love but broad success as partners in career or business. The
potential for friendship and happiness is always good with
Libra, but not always as lovers.

VIRGO & SCORPIO

Scorpio men exude sexuality through their Fixed-Water vibrations. Though Virgo normally shies away from such heavy sexual overtones, you will find him very attractive. Virgo wants to

get to know Scorpio better, as your ruling Mercury seeks to probe the mysteries of his distant Pluto. He has an equally inquisitive mind, and you may well come together over some issue or idea that you wish to explore in depth.

Scorpios are serious men when it comes to their relationships, and you feel that you may have found a high-minded friend in his handsome combination of intensity and cleverness. Neither of you rush into commitments, so there will be plenty of opportunities to gain each other's confidence before you take your involvement to a new level of meaning. Strangely, there is a definite compatibility between the nervous and restless mentality of Virgo and the more placid, intellectual intensity of Scorpio. He calms you down and you perk him up to a mutual feeling of relaxation when you start paling around together.

Scorpios have eyes that are deep pools, reflecting their power and mystery. They may scare others, but you sense their appeal for care and understanding. He is as aware as you are of the lack of perfection and purity in the world. In typical Scorpio fashion, he feels it as a secret sorrow or resents it as a cosmic plot against human potential. You want to soothe and comfort him, gain his trust, and help him apply his perceptive imagination to constructive purposes and long-range plans.

Honesty and integrity are important values to both Virgo and Scorpio. You can combine your love of knowledge with a sincerity of purpose that brings you to inspired levels of devotion. Friendship is definitely aspected in a relationship with a Scorpio. You form a strong bond that protects you from the outside world and its mundane disappointments. The sense of security you impart to each other gives you an opportunity to expand, relax, and even sparkle.

There is certainly fun to be had for you in a Scorpio romance. Travel is indicated, along with mental stimulation, writing, studying, and social connections. There can be a great deal of energy expended in good times, but you may wonder if there are any solid accomplishments. It seems as if there is hardly any time for evaluation and contemplation.

Scorpio energizes your life-style, and you accept new challenges with his self-confidence as your guide.

When your Mercurial energies become overextended, your
desire for quiet time alone may arouse his suspicion. He
may take your need for solitude personally, wondering what
or who has come over you and why you are avoiding him.
Sometimes you are fearful that he wants you too much, but
then you are truly comforted as well, by his protective ardor
and passionate devotion. Despite the inevitable conflicts between desire and detachment, trust will save the day in a
loving relationship with a Scorpio man.

The Earthiness of your latent sexual potential is enriched
by his Water-sign emotional intensity. You can blossom as
a lover in a Scorpio's embraces. He can bring you to heights
of passion that you never expected to experience. Sexuality
takes on a new purity with the love of a Scorpio man, encouraging you to enjoy sensual stimulation that defies analysis and silent criticism.

You have confidence in his devotion, since Scorpios prefer
to be faithful partners. Despite their reputation as the sexy
get-down devils of the zodiac, Scorpio men cease their sexual explorations once they find a man who satisfies their
need for stability and joins them in plumbing the mysteries
of sex together. Infidelity offends his self-image and indicates serious trouble.

With a Scorpio man the future looks bright to you. Your
life changes permanently with a Scorpio lover. You develop
new interests or gain a new circle of friends. People are
attracted to you as an interesting couple that enjoys life.
Virgo and Scorpio project a combination of practicality and
creativity that can be very impressive.

Scorpio represents your Third House—communication—
and the strength of your love for each other lies in the desire
and ability to keep the channels of mind, body, and spirit
in working order. Perceptive analysis and creative intellect
make this a strong friendship and a sincerely loving relationship for both you and your Scorpio man.

VIRGO & SAGITTARIUS

Keep your Virgo wits about you when the Mutable-Fire qualities of Sagittarius strike like a thunderbolt around you. Lightning never strikes twice in the same place, so one Sagittarius lover may be all you ever attempt. Virgo is ruled by Mercury, the smallest planet; Sagittarius by Jupiter, the largest body in the solar system. The difference in perspective is between your quick and practical attention to detail and his expansive vision. It is a continuous polarity that presents constant challenges.

His symbol is the Centaur, half man in his inspirations and half horse in his unbridled energy. Virgos hate halfway measures. You may find that a Sagittarian man turns you on but never really delivers. The Centaur can be an exciting adventure, but he won't come through in a long-term relationship. At least not in ways that will be easy for a Virgo to comprehend.

Jupiter's influence leads Sagittarius to constantly expanding social experiences. He likes to travel or at least work his way through "the scene," always open to chance encounters. Your Virgo sense of propriety is put a little out of joint by the fact that he takes chances all the time—and is often successful. Jupiter makes him lucky. No matter how bungling or clumsy he may seem to your perfectionist's eye, he lands jelly-side up. Sagittarius has a much richer, more exhilarating, more irresponsible attitude about life and love than your Virgo mind can compute.

Sagittarius slows you down and undermines your Mercurial talents. After the end of a Sagittarian lover's appearance in your life it will take time for you to recover, recuperate, and regain some of your quickness and brightness. You may feel that you have been overshadowed by the Centaur and his expansive power. You will dedicate yourself to the accomplishment of his ideals, but he won't really devote himself in the same way.

Virgo can wish upon the same star as Sagittarius, but you set to work, while he keeps on wishing and dreaming. His imaginative mind and cheeky manner may be endearing at first, but you have a much better time playing around together than getting down to serious tasks. You'll feel cheated and fooled, except when you remember the bright vision of his dream, a dream that you shared.

Share good times with the Centaur and he can be a rewarding and enriching friend. You should spend time out-of-doors, camping, hiking, and enjoying physical activities. Intense emotional involvement with a Sagittarian will confuse and confound you, but there can be a fine intellectual and physical relationship. He is an exciting sexual being, and your lovemaking can be very satisfying. If you want sex without emotional attachment, Sagittarius can be a real buddy. You can have a loving and open relationship with a Sagittarian that doesn't require the commitment to becoming "a couple."

There is much you can learn from him and give to him without becoming lovers or expecting a long-term involvement. Sagittarian men are at their best as partners you meet while traveling. Three days together on Maui or a dynamite weekend on the road will be a breathtaking experience. All the passion and excitement of love with the proper stranger will be exhilarating.

If you and your Sagittarian are older, you can have a mutually beneficial meeting of minds. Once Sagittarius has had plenty of opportunity to roam, he will be more open to appreciating your Virgo virtues. If the Centaur is younger than you, he will make you feel old. You will adopt all his responsibilities, and he will be free to indulge his whims while you are becoming a drudge.

Focus on the fun with this charming, sexy adventurer, but don't get caught in a demanding relationship with him. You can experience a wonderfully refreshing breadth of vision and imaginative boost from a joyride on the road of life with the Centaur of Sagittarius.

VIRGO & CAPRICORN

Your most refined Earth-sign sensibilities are aspected when you meet the Cardinal-Earth Mountain Goat of Capricorn. You feel creative and at the same time confused by the intensity of his demands for even more perfection than Virgo expects. Because he is ambitious, his level of desire is more powerful than yours. Make sure you are aware of the ground rules before you make a commitment. You can't be too meticulous when dealing with Capricorn.

These Mountain Goats usually will impress you with their reserved, serious demeanor and sense of values. His ruling Saturn imposes restrictions on your Mutable Mercury nature but also causes you to focus your interests. Patience is the key to dealing with Capricorn, since he takes a very long view of life. Slow and steady wins the race, and ultimately Capricorns are winners. Your relationship will develop slowly and steadily as you gain each other's trust.

Even if you meet in a casual manner, your subsequent dates will have an element of politeness. Though you are both Earth signs, you don't really have an Earthy relationship. You will often be hot to get it on with a Capricorn man, but he doesn't seem to want sex as much as you do. You are more interesting to him mentally than sexually. Capricorn can try your patience at the outset of an affair because you wonder if it will ever get off the ground. The Mountain Goat climbs slowly and deliberately compared with your quick grasp of matters. Your Virgo instincts are stimulated and you want to get down to business, but somehow Capricorn holds you back.

Plan the seduction scene at your place. Cook him a simple but ample meal with emphasis on the proper details—properly chilled wine, candlelight, a small bowl of flowers. Don't be extravagant in your preparations; it's not your style, and he won't appreciate flamboyant expenditure. Keep the atmosphere relaxed and comfortable. Let him put his feet up and encourage him to talk about the things that are really important to him: his career, his plans, his past experiences as they relate to the future.

You may spend the evening in quiet conversation, enjoying the security of each other's presence. You both respond to gentle, earnest feelings, and passion will not usually flare up in the Earth-sign combination of Virgo and Capricorn. You will both approach your eventual sexual union as gentlemen who bed each other, rather than guys who simply ''do it.'' You may even have to court him before Capricorn decides to accept a sexual dimension to your encounter. When you finally slip between your crisply ironed sheets, the physical experience may be very satisfying. There will be no shooting stars, but the levels of desire are well matched. Both of you are fastidious lovers, interested in the mechanics of physical stimulation. You will be the more aggressive partner with a Capricorn, wanting to express your attraction through sexual channels of communication.

Capricorn represents your Fifth House—romance and creativity. Your Virgo desire is to serve him through sentimental, loving attention. He will respond by opening up and loosening up in your care. You can share your secret fears and repressed joys in a spirit of Mutable trust. Sex will gradually take on special meaning, allowing you both to find much gentle warmth and intimacy in each other's company.

If you make a commitment, you will be dedicated to seeing it through. Both of you want a man you can count on to be there when you need him. You also share a willingness to provide just that kind of dutiful companionship for your lovers. There is an aspect of compassion in a Virgo-Capricorn relationship that brings out the best in your normally cool and detached personalities.

You will be faithful to each other as lovers, and loyal as friends. Even if your affair is short-lived, the trust you share can be incorporated in a new relationship that can grow stronger over the years. Since Capricorn men get better with time, you may get more response from a Capricorn who is considerably older than you. After fifty, these guys are at their best—accomplished, polished, men of achievement who desire to advance their partners to worthy positions.

If he has Capricorn rising, you may find him a gentle and considerate lover who responds to your attentions with a fond kindness. If he has a Fire sign rising, there will be enough creativity between you to make it an exciting and successful relationship.

VIRGO & AQUARIUS

It's all or nothing when you meet the Fixed-Air men of Aquarius. You are attracted to his friendly manner and intellectual conversation. He is symbolized by the Waterbearer and brings you ideas you can analyze. Aquarius is ruled by Uranus, planet of the unexpected, and unless you have interests beyond your initial attraction, this affair is too unpredictable for your Virgo nervous system.

Aquarius men are promiscuous, but socially rather than sexually. He is more interested in sex as a social experience than as an emotional one. The more unusual and unexpected the encounter, the more he will be attracted to you. Aquarian men are easy to meet, fun to play with, but difficult for a Virgo to live with for any length of time.

You will have the best time with an Aquarian if you can suspend a little of your practicality and focus on the intellectual and social stimulation he provides. You can learn about a wide range of eclectic subjects from an Aquarian buddy, from film to science, from pornography to palm reading. He loves mysteries and you love problem solving, so your inquisitive natures will be charged in each other's company. You may be a little edgy when you realize the mystery he's interested in is you!

Aquarius wants to probe your personality and your private life, but not with an eye to settling down. He loves the game of pursuit and conquest too much to get seriously involved in just one mystery or just one man. He will impress you with his attentiveness and gallantry, but you will not be the only recipient of his charms. Remember that Aquarius lives for the moment, and his moments are complex blends of unexpected elements. His restless search in life is for truth and knowledge through experience. The truth may be pure, but not perfection in your Virgo analysis.

Both Virgo and Aquarius tend to be romantics, but he is dreamy in love and you become even more responsible when emotionally stirred. Aquarius represents your Sixth House—service—touching the core of your Virgo instincts. You want to serve him, but the needs of an Aquarius man are more eccentric than you are used to coping with. Nervous strain will make you defensive in trying to keep up with his erratic desires. Don't confuse the intensity of his interests with emotional commitment or you will be disappointed.

The Sixth House also indicates matters of health, and Aquarius will benefit from your interest in diet and physical care. He will prefer to take his exercise in noncompetitive ways that conform to his need for the eccentric. Hang gliding, windsurfing, and skateboarding are wild enough to spark his imagination, though you might prefer a civilized game of tennis.

Fun and games are always in the cards with an Aquarius lover. He loves to travel, especially to places of historic interest. Aquarians get too bored on the beach with nothing but beautiful bodies to muse upon. He would rather be climbing the ruins or wandering the museums with you than baking in the sun any day.

Aquarius needs Virgo for the values of an informed critic. He will be loving and loyal as long as you understand his need for people, for a constantly changing grasp of the world that gives him strength. Aquarians usually end up giving more than they get from their lovers. Often what they give them is inspiration, if they get enough understanding and stimulation in return.

An inspired breakthrough is possible through your sexual experience with an Aquarian lover. Sex is always different with him, but each time will be infused with a passion that will put sex into a new perspective for you. You will revel in the physical expression of his need for you, and being needed is the easiest way for Virgo to feel loved. You bring communicative skills to his experimental imagination that win his admiration and allow him to express his gratitude and affection sexually.

This can be a true romance dedicated to the benefits and joys of feeling free to be in love. If an Aquarian affair features really satisfying sex, then you should use your Mutable skills to start adapting to his Fixed eccentricities, because with him your life is about to change, Virgo.

VIRGO & PISCES

Mutable-Water Pisces will attract you in the way that all opposites attract. Pisces men are the emotional counterpart of your Mutable-Earth qualities. Your interest in physically ordering the material world is mirrored by his concern with emotionally responding to the nonmaterial universe. His ruling planet, Neptune, is the lord of the wine-dark seas.

His symbol is the Fishes chasing their tails. Pisces is more intuitive and perceptive than your practical Virgo nature can quite grasp. His priorities are affected by his emotions, a situation you find quite confusing. Pisces is never quite sure of himself, and so he swims into disorganization. Virgo is never quite sure of himself, either, but you compensate by trying to control your environment. Your added strength may be just what Pisces needs to help him become a more creative personality.

Neptune makes the Pisces man secretive, but he will learn to be more open with a Virgo if you go easy on the criticism. Your intellectual flexibility can make you versatile enough to respond to each other without fixating on the difference between the spiritual and material worlds. Earth and Water elements blend harmoniously for Virgo and Pisces, symbolizing the potential for enrichment.

Through a Pisces lover your crisp Virgo intellect can be sensitized to emotional situations. Your ability to manage the real world gives Pisces the foundation for creative growth. You benefit from seeing the fruit of your labors ripen in the field of imagination. Pisces' subtlety, added to your refinement, makes you more perceptive and understanding in your critical powers.

You are naturally attracted and receptive to the Pisces man, but he is not an easy problem to solve. There is so much spontaneity that analysis may elude you. If you love him, you will feel perplexed and amused rather than vexed by his elusive, evasive, and dreamy charm.

Your Pisces man will seem most charming to you when he has gotten lost at sea. You can reassure him that the shore is not as far away as he feared. Finding fault with your Virgo edge is no way to keep him afloat. He needs your tender loving care more than any other man in the zodiac. You need his sensitive imagination more than any other man in the zodiac. If you are open to your shortcomings, as well as to your strengths, you can have an enjoyable love with a Pisces.

Pisces represents your Seventh House—partnerships—and teaming up with him as a lover may seem like a natural thing to do. Unless you two have a common dream, the relationship can drift along on swells of spontaneous energy with no direction. Work on focusing your blend of intellect and sensitivity with a sense of purpose. Expanding horizons by starting a business or renovating a house can bring much good fortune for you in a relationship with a Pisces.

Both of you embody aspects of selflessness in your love

relationships. You are the dedicated one, willing to work hard; and he is the devoted one, willing to sacrifice for the benefit of his love. You are the craftsman and he is the poet, even when it comes to lovemaking.

The sexual blending of Virgo and Pisces gives you the edge in technique and he the points of emotion. Together the aspects indicate pleasurable sex; sex that is comforting and loving in a way that makes you feel more secure and complete than with other men. He can unlock the doors to perception that keep you from integrating sex and emotional commitment. You can throw off your Virgo attitudes about sex and find a new freedom that makes you happier, more flexible, and more able to appreciate the virtues of Pisces.

Worry can nibble away at your contentment with a Pisces man because neither of you is a naturally happy-go-lucky guy. If you can surmount your worries, he can overcome his fears. As in all opposite-sign pairs you each have a secret weapon, whatever it is, that can hurt the other. But Virgo and Pisces also have the desire to forgive, even though there may be lapses of insecurity. You can hide yourself in your work while he lapses into fantasy or alcohol when things go awry. You can become compulsive about order in the face of chaos. Pisces should be able to help you increase your flexibility if he proves to you that his chaos can be a creative medium. Also, he gives your sense of humor a needed boost.

You have much to gain but also much to learn if you're in love with a Pisces man. The end result can be a rewarding experience that makes you a better person, even gives you a broader world vision. Order and chaos can join to form creativity under the combined loving care of Virgo and Pisces.

LOVING YOUR VIRGO MAN

If you are looking for a Virgo man, look to the pleasures of the intellect. Study groups, night courses, and theater clubs are all sprinkled with Virgos refining their minds and enjoying themselves. He doesn't stand out in a crowd, and it takes time to know him. Being casual isn't easy for Virgo, though his Mercury-ruled sensibilities appreciate spontaneous wit.

The typical Virgo Man of Life is well groomed rather than trendy. He likes denim if it's well pressed, leather if it's an Italian sport jacket. His criteria can be very exacting. You may be everything he wants in a man but fail to measure up because you have sideburns. If you aren't just the look he wants, he may not even try to get to know you. Virgos are dedicated to attaining perfection. He can't ignore "flaws" and becomes fixated on "weaknesses" in others. He likes his men well toned, trendy, or of some status. He's not a social climber, he just likes to associate with worthy companions.

If you get past his physical criteria, you can always interest a Virgo with intelligent conversation and clever repartee on a serious topic. But you have to be original, because Virgo can always spot a rehearsed come-on. If he responds right away to a sexual invitation, he won't really be very interested in more than a casual encounter. Virgo takes sex too seriously to call it "recreational," and he doesn't get deeply involved emotionally.

Virgos are susceptible to charm, and they like being courted. If you charge your approach with sexuality, he won't respect you as a person. If you treat him like a gentleman, you may uncover a gentle and loving man underneath his cool Virgo exterior. You needn't be flamboyant or extravagant in expressing your interest. Spending a lot of money won't impress him as much as small kindnesses and considerations. Since he has specific likes and dislikes, it is not hard to know how to please him.

Virgos are neat and clean types, in and out of bed. He is interested in technique more than passion, but he is very conscientious and eager to please. Virgo wants to serve his lovers in some way. If he is attracted to you, he will be loyal and even overlook certain disappointments for the sake of a relationship. When they forget the difference between service and sacrifice, Virgos can easily be used by insensitive lovers.

Virgo strives for perfection in others and in himself. His standards of performance are high, but he often meets them. He undermines his own security through his inclination to analyze and criticize. Virgo treats every issue, situation, and phenomenon as a matter to be solved rather than experienced. If he doesn't get enough intellectual stimulation, he becomes nitpicking, small-minded, and nervous. Though good at details, he needs enough variety in his life to keep fresh—he gets bitter and stale covering the same old ground.

Though he may be the critic of the zodiac, he is very sensitive to the criticism of others. Lack of perfection equals lack of worth. Virgo can become cynical and petulant when he feels insecure. He wants to be needed, to assure his sense of personal value. If you can live up to his expectations, he will be a loyal friend.

If you want a lover who can manage your life, you can find happiness with a Virgo man. You will have to conform to his systems; learn to like alfalfa tea and bean sprouts; shower before sex; and avoid being demonstrative in public. Virgo will take care of the household management or else take on the burden of worry. Either way he can be taken advantage of—up to a point. When Virgo makes a break, it is neat and clean, with a clinical air of detachment and a cynical remark to cover his disappointment at failing once again to find perfection.

Virgos are faithful lovers because they can't handle more than one relationship at a time. He may forgive you if you confess to the occasional lapse, but he will be outraged if you should deceive him or publicly embarrass him by your indiscretion.

Virgo is neither a sexual nor a social butterfly. Don't wear out his nervous system with large-scale social activities. If you want to enjoy quiet evenings at home, Virgo can be the man for you. Reading or playing backgammon by the fire, a few intimate friends, walks in the country, picnics, and simple pleasures all bring out the best in a Virgo man.

You will have to clean up your act to prove your commitment to a Virgo lover. He will respond with tender loving care. Keep his mind active and busy, and Virgo will be loyal, loving, and helpful. If he gets enough time on his own when he needs to be totally absorbed in some meticulous interest, he will try to be of even disposition. Short trips and changes of scene keep his inquisitive mind honed to a sharp edge and give him the kind of rest he needs from day-to-day cares.

If you want a lover you can count on, look to Virgo. It takes patience and faith to warm his heart, but the rewards are worth the effort.

LIBRA
September 21–
October 20

☲

Symbol: The Balance, or the Scales
Ruling Planet: Venus
Colors: Blue-greens
Metal: Bronze
Natural House Rulership: Seventh House, the house
    of partnerships
Seventh House Traits: Love of justice and need for
    beauty
Motto: ''I balance''
Nature: Cardinal sign (leadership)
Element: Air sign (mental)
Qualities: Diplomatic, compatible, and idealistic
Capacities: Matters of negotiation and comparison
Personality Key Words: Harmony, beauty, and
    justice

MAXIMIZING YOUR
LIBRA POTENTIAL

Libra men are ruled by Venus, the evening star, and you are certainly a star any evening you step out. Your nature is Cardinal Air, giving you style, wit, and poise. When the Sun is in Libra, the days and nights are equal, symbolized by the Balance. It's a nonorganic sign, yet it symbolizes a characteristic of the human mind, the balance between the two sides of the brain.

Libra is traditionally associated with the concept of partnership, and you believe in the intellectual ideal of romantic love. Harmony is the life goal of Libras. You seek harmony through ideas and experiences, but not emotions. Libras are blessed with intuition, but you need to pay more attention to your initial impressions to make them work for you. Balance is the key, and you must establish a goal in order to maximize your personality potential. Librans enjoy sex for variety and adventure, but self-indulgence will leave you feeling that your talents are being wasted. The physical and sexual gratification you achieve is a substitute for the intellectual and emotional approval you require from others.

Librans have an imaginative aesthetic sensitivity that needs stimulation to function in their best interest. Mundane or routine jobs will never hold you for long. You need plenty of money for the life-style you want, but it will have to be earned in some unusual fashion. Be innovative and don't be swayed by the opinions of others. If you count on yourself and keep up to your own criteria, any field you choose will lead to success.

Love means beauty and harmony to Libra, but excitement

is needed to spice the blend according to your taste. You tell yourself that love means a home and a handsome man to receive your affection, but you want adventure too. Passionate sex is the spark that keeps you interested in a long-term relationship. You would rather suffer emotional trauma with a dashing and dazzling lover than domestic boredom. Though you think you desire peace, quiet, and comfort in a relationship, you often invite conflict because of your need for stimulation. You are susceptible to flattery, and the attentions of other men make it difficult for you to decide upon any one person as your ideal. You always want to compare the men in your life, leaving you open to charges of insincerity.

The Sun in Libra gives you refined judgment in all matters relating to beauty, design, justice, and idealism. You are diplomatic and friendly, finding it easy to meet people. Your magnetic personality draws others to you. Your style is lighthearted and easygoing, giving you a gregarious charm but sometimes obscuring your intellectual qualities. Everything you do should be done in an imaginative manner and stamped with your unique personality.

Libran weaknesses come from the same sources as your strengths. Your creative imagination can become mere daydreaming. Indecision and a lack of tenacity are indicated as Libran sources of frustration. Consequently you can depend too much on the opinions of others to judge your self-worth.

The typical Libran social life revolves around your interest in people, ideas, and opinions. You have a way of bringing out the best in others and getting them to reveal themselves. Venus inclines you to be flirtatious, but only on an intellectual level. You enjoy the promise of sex in a stimulating conversation with an attractive man. You thrive on diversions and cultivate an active and regular social calendar with a few close friends and many casual acquaintances. You don't mix your friends, lovers, or casual acquaintances unless you are certain they will get along with each other. As always, you strive for balance, even if you sometimes overload the scales. Unless you have a lover, you prefer to entertain outside your home, balancing your public and private lives according to the mental activity involved.

Sex is one topic that you are not indecisive about. You love it. Lots of it. You are a gentle and affectionate lover and you want the same from your partner, but with a real intensity. Librans seek passion in sex as a balance for the lack of emotional commitment. It leads you to questioning the value of sex when it leaves you feeling empty after the thrill is over. As a Libra, you can get into kinky or bizarre sex because your tastes become jaded and you need more and more variety to get satisfaction. Your sex drive does not diminish very much with age, and neither does your ability to attract other men. Even when your physical beauty has begun to fade, your charm and social grace will make you an object of desire.

Nevertheless, in your Libran urge to balance, sex is never enough to keep you happy, even when you have captured an ideal fantasy figure. Partnership is your goal. You want a man who blends and balances your physical need for sexual variety and passion with emotional commitment. You want a lover who is masculine, passionate, and committed to growth within the liaison or you can't relate emotionally or sexually. If you and your lover have this, you will feel that the risk of time, emotion, and effort is worthwhile. But often you will put up with hurt and disappointment from your lover once you have made a commitment. A Libra in love can be intelligent about everything but his own feelings. You are easily hurt but will internalize your pain rather than jeopardize your love affair.

Thanks to the benefits of Venus, you have a great many things going for you, such as your ability to lead with your intellect and your sexual magnetism. You need approval and affection, even though you can seem very casual about love and detached from emotional experiences. Don't fool yourself by retreating from making decisions that propel you into life. You have to take control of the balancing factors in your career, social life, and emotional needs. Success will come in business and in love only when you accept the unusual means by which your future is advanced. You will always doubt your self-worth unless you "go for broke."

People want to be associated with you because you represent ideals of judgment or beauty that they value. Though you can seem flighty and unable to carry out the clever ideas you initiate, people who know you trust you. Many men offer to love you from split-second exchanges to lifelong obligations. You have the powers to compare and to choose endlessly, always in the direction of harmony maintained through movement, advancement, and creative stimulation.

LIBRA & ARIES

Your Libran love of masculine men is fulfilled with the Cardinal-Fire man of Aries. He is your natural male complement, being the sign opposite yours on the Wheel of Life. Aries is ruled by Mars, and your Venus nature appreciates his aggressive, masculine drive. Your Libran instinct is to balance his forceful ego with intellectual and sexual refinements that could make for a truly successful relationship.

Your Arian lover is impulsive and emotional, lacking the aesthetic sensibilities that color your life. You are attracted to his basic butch character for its simplicity, honesty, and sexuality. Your ideal fantasy figure is a very male archetype. Aries embodies the macho exuberance that answers your Libran need.

Aside from his boyish charms, you are attracted by the direct way he attempts to deal with life. You may even envy his ability to ignore the subtleties and nuances of a situation and go right to the heart of his wants and needs. When you first met, chances are he was the one who came on to you, flattering you with his attentions and obvious about his intentions. If you are typically indecisive, your Libran spirit sighs with relief whenever a man you find interesting takes the initiative. You can then concentrate on him rather than on your move and how to make it. You are often too studied, and you can learn about spontaneity from an Aries lover.

Since Venus and Mars are naturally attracted to each other, your initial sexual experience with Aries should be very exciting. The physical pleasures of love are highlighted in your stars. With an Aries man you have found a partner who enjoys the same kind of sex that you do: intensely physical but nonemotional. Both of you want a sexual experience that epitomizes man-to-man love. Though he may be willing to make an impulsive commitment to your relationship as lovers, you are both accustomed to a great deal of freedom. Let any kind of decision about commitment come with Libran precision and careful consideration rather than through Arian emotion.

An Aries lover can give you more energy and add a note of power to your relationship that makes for a dynamic blend of poise and potency. You have good ideas and creative sensibilities, and Aries has the initiative and drive to get moving on them. You can leave your emotional lethargy and reticence behind with an Aries at your side. New opportunities for public relations and publicity enhance your career and stimulate your talents through Aries' ability to encourage your best Libran traits.

Aries represents your Seventh House—partnerships. You see yourself in his eyes and you like what you see. The Aries Fire-sign need for action, excitement, passion, and aggression are just the stimulants you want to keep your life balanced. Variety, travel, and changing scenes keep you on your toes and preclude the boredom that is so deadly to both Aries and Libra. You may think you want to settle down and play backgammon by the fire, but you really want much more challenge in your life. He has an ego that needs to be cared for with typical Libran tact and affection. You want the best of everything and will work diligently to bring out the finest in your Aries lover's personality.

Aries is a romantic. Like you, he has an easygoing attitude about sex, but he really wants to find an ideal lover. He is extravagant in his need for, and expression of, love. A man of generous impulses, he will delight in giving and receiving presents that neither of you can afford. And your Venus-ruled romanticism will love the impetuous nature of Aries. You may even accept his occasional flirtation because it reinforces his masculine image—though you both will be better off being as faithful to each other as possible. Both Aries and Libra men are too susceptible to temptation, and letting each other fool around is playing with jealousy and self-deception.

Libras are inclined to partnership, and there is much mutual support and satisfaction indicated in an Aries love affair. You will need patience to deal with his high energy levels and impulsive emotions. Don't let your Air-sign detachment prevent you from enjoying the strong and direct pleasures of loving an Aries man.

LIBRA & TAURUS

Men born under the sign of the Bull are naturally attractive to you, since you share the rulership of Venus. He is the material manifestation of love as comfort while you embody the intellectual stimulation of romance. Venus, as the ruler of his Fixed-Earth sign, makes him more materialistic, possessive, and serious than the Venus of Libra.

Taurean men are interested in the pleasures of life. You will appreciate his taste for good food, relaxed surroundings, and sensuous sex. His initial attraction to you will be based upon your charm, grace, and style. A common interest in art or creative activities will often bring you two together with pleasing consequences.

A Libra–Taurus love affair will usually take root in surroundings that express harmony and comfort. Neither of you will skimp when it comes to personal luxury, even though he is much more money-conscious than you are. Taureans like to have a few good pieces that reflect their pride of possession and then forget about them once they are comfortable. You thrive on variety, but Taureans need the security of permanence to be happy. He may become unhappy about your desire to keep introducing changes into your environment.

Your Libran tendency to search for balance makes Taurus nervous, even though he agrees with the ultimate goal of harmony. As a Fixed sign he is devoted to organization. Your Cardinal-sign nature makes you more interested in initiation and inspiration. Taurus' resistance to impulsiveness will slow you down, but in a way that will allow you to be more creative and effective.

The aspects of Venus indicate an aura of respect and courtesy that allows you to be open with each other. Work on this natural sympathy to establish the ground rules early in your relationship and encourage Taurus to be more open about his feelings. If you can develop a framework that gives him security and at the same time allows you the freedom to experiment, there can be real happiness in a creative partnership between two loving men.

Even though you are as different as the morning and evening stars, the times you share between sunset and sunrise can be the sexual bond that keeps you together. Keep a balance between your love of the social scene and his fondness for quiet evenings at home. You can light up his life with your easy approach to sex, introducing a spirit of playful sensuality that will make him a very responsive lover. When it comes to sex, he's a meat-and-potatoes man, but your desire for inventive techniques can give him a taste of dessert. Likewise, Taurus men can be partners who will appeal to your desire for gentle and passionate sex.

The natural passivity of Taurus can combine with your tendency to procrastinate in a way that will leave you both open to charges of indolence or indifference to each other. This danger can be avoided as long as you have a common goal that gives the relationship a focus and a future. When he is feeling insecure or pessimistic, your job is to remind him of the dream you share and bring some Libran inspiration into his life. You can give your Taurus lover optimism that will increase his patience. You benefit from his practicality and his perseverance in matters that lead to mutual advancement through your creative efforts.

Taurus represents your Eighth House—mystery—and you will be drawn to him through a force that you don't completely understand. Patience is the key to lasting love with your Taurus man. You want to move, expand, and explore but he is dedicated to the safety of the status quo. If you are too speedy, he will become confused, mistrustful, and recalcitrant. If you can convince him that your love and affection is the only "sure thing" going, he may join you in risky enterprises, but you had better be willing to work hard.

Constant care and adjustment will result in harmony, but if the relationship becomes too stagnant, regular, and ordinary, you may be driven to romantic diversions. Your search for excitement with strangers will arouse your Taurus lover's possessive compulsions, forcing you to demand even more independence in an escalating battle between freedom and desire that exhausts your fund of affection.

Don't allow selfish impulses to destroy a loving bond between two men who are so capable of sharing deep affection. Emotional growth and material advancement are all indicated in a love affair between you and Taurus if you keep your mind on the pleasures of the present and the promise of the future.

LIBRA & GEMINI

Boredom will never be an issue when you fall for the Mutable Air-sign men of Gemini. He embodies a restless search for mental stimulation that charges your imagination and keeps you on your creative toes. The rulership of Mercury makes him quick, clever, and cute in a way that you may find both irresistible and exasperating.

A Gemini man will be attracted to your wit and charm. He is easy to talk to and eager to get to know you. You will be flattered by his attention to what you think and what you know. Both of you enjoy the fun of flirtation, making your meeting a suggestive and amusing situation that promises good times. Even if it turns out to be an encounter with no commitment beyond the moment, there is a bond between Air signs that allows you to enjoy the moment fully. Gemini men are not motivated by the intense sexuality you experience, but they often find Libras especially erotic.

As a romantic partner, Gemini will stimulate some of your best qualities. Since he is so restless and free-ranging in his interests, you will find that you attempt to balance his influence by being more stable. Your need for harmony causes you to realize that you have a responsibility to provide him with creative and constructive examples of Air-sign achievement. You strive to fulfill your potential, becoming less indecisive and more trusting of your intuition.

Dreams can come true with a Gemini lover, but only if you work toward making them real. You have much to gain if you take chances, improve your education, and increase your scope of activities. Your Gemini buddy will take you to new places and provide new inspirations that keep your love growing and changing.

The blending of two Air signs allows you to accommodate the need for freedom with a basic trust that prevents jealousy and possessiveness. Gemini may seem fickle and shallow to others, but you have the power to see the long-range potential in his energetic approach to life.

Sex will certainly be a lively area of common interest. Together you can really explore the dimensions of your sexual natures. He can be a master of technique who will certainly satisfy your need for variety. You may require him to be more masculine and aggressive in his lovemaking, but he is adaptable and eager to please. He will be quick to add his own touches of fun and fantasy to increase your pleasure. Toys, role playing, and costumes can become elements of your sexual repertoire with a Gemini lover. Your lovemaking takes on an air of abandon that adds to your desire. Unrestrained affection will be the crowning achievement of the sexual attraction between you and your Gemini man. The aspects for a lasting relationship are good.

Your patience will be tried by his incessant involvement with change, but under your loving care he will become less flighty and more capable of sustaining a serious relationship.

The most important bond between you and your Gemini lover is the sincere interest you have in each other. You can spend hours in constantly shifting kaleidoscopic conversations. Mercury makes him a born communicator, and you love the ideas, problems, and observations he brings to you for evaluation and clarification. Your need for intellectual recognition is fulfilled by the fact that he looks up to you for your intelligence and perception.

The life-style you develop with a Gemini lover will be tasteful and even trendy. You enjoy dining out, dancing, and his eclectic circle of acquaintances. You both keep up on the latest films and books, exchanging ideas and impressions with brilliance and wit. Make sure you get an occasional restful weekend in the country or you will begin to wear each other out.

If you blend the need for freedom with the desire for each other's company, the love you share with a Gemini man can be an enriching combination of experience and intellectual stimulation infused with affection.

LIBRA & CANCER

The Cardinal-Water Moonbeams of Cancer create an intellectual dilemma that can put you off-balance. He has your same quick mind but is more emotional and unpredictable than you are. You think when he feels, and that difference is the substance of your attraction as well as the source of tension in your relationship.

The initial attraction is romantic, but Cancer men take love and sex more seriously than you do. You are distressed by the idea of hurting him and may find yourself making a commitment you can't keep. Make sure you know what you want before you become involved with a Cancer man as your lover.

The rulership of the Moon, combined with your Venus influence, indicates attraction and harmony, but also responsibility. Unless you are willing to work hard, a Libra–Cancer love affair can be more than you bargained for and less than you hoped for. You will have to be the one who takes charge of the situation or you may drift into a half-hearted arrangement that satisfies neither of you.

What you need most in a coupling with a Cancer man is an open channel of communication to his feelings. He does not always understand his emotions and his reactions are not logical. Unless you encourage him to verbalize his feelings, you will be unaware of and unsympathetic to his needs. Tension grows as you find him evasive and he finds you unemotional.

Cancer represents your Tenth House, concerning career and ambition. A business relationship can be filled with positive excitement and trusting camaraderie. Your aspirations are refined by his insights, and you are more aware of your creative potential with a Cancer partner.

The difference between your active nature and his passive one will be apparent in your approach to sex. He will enjoy your skills as a lover and return your interest, but he may not have enough aggressive traits to give the edge of challenge and change you require. He is a capable and affectionate lover, but he is not as assertive as you would want him to be. Because he is often shy or inarticulate about his sexual needs, you don't really know what he wants. You may question your ability to satisfy him. You will begin to crave the excitement of your pals among the Beautiful People, the pleasures of the chase, and the joys of single life. Cancer will start to look for affectionate encounters that can somehow overcome his feelings of insecurity as your relationship drifts.

You both have a common desire to find a partner in life, but you want an intellectual companion and he seeks an emotional complement. The Cancer man focuses on the home as the repository of his heartfelt feelings. You will work with him to create an attractive and comfortable environment, but it will mean much more to him than it does to you.

Cancer's tendency to read emotional meaning into everything will disturb your Libran sensibilities. He is a man of moods, and you will find it difficult to be sympathetic and compassionate as a matter of form. You need to understand before you can offer your support, and often he has no explanation for the way he feels. When you try to analyze or comprehend his moods, you may feel inadequate. You just can't get a handle on something that has such elusive qualities. By the time you think you know what is happening with him, the Moon has changed phases and he is laughing instead of crying. You are mystified and vexed rather than intrigued.

You are optimistic by nature, but something in a Cancer relationship weighs you down. He isn't jealous or possessive, but he can be very dependent. His need for you is ultimately too restricting on your Air-sign desire for freedom. Cancer falls in love too deeply for you to achieve proper balance. As he increases his commitment you may find yourself increasing your detachment.

Cancer brings out the best in your public image rather than your qualities as a great lover. You can certainly enjoy a fun-loving fling with a Cancer, but you have to go slowly. Keep your wits about you or you may find yourself over your head in an emotional entanglement that prevents you from taking advantage of the creative and intellectual potential in a Libra–Cancer relationship.

LIBRA & LEO

The Lions of Leo are very attractive to you for their Fire-sign masculinity and sexuality. You can probably count quite a number of Leos as friends or partners. Libra loves the glamour that radiates from Leo's sunny personality, as well as his warmth and generosity. Your Cardinal-Air intellect fans the flames of his Leonine spirit in a way that can be both engaging and exasperating.

There is a natural friendship between you and Leo that makes for a truly enjoyable affair on a physical and social level, and the possibility of a challenging, long-term love relationship. It can be good sex and good times as you keep displaying your personas to each other and presenting them to the world. Nothing makes either of you feel as superior as an attractive and desirable lover. Unless you can develop a highly complementary relationship, there can be elements of competition that lead to jealousy and conflict.

Because you want a dashing man as your partner, Leo can easily sweep you off your feet. Your intellectual bent brings out his most noble instincts, and he will strive to make the best of impressions. The first blush of a Libra–Leo affair will fulfill all of your fantasies about man-to-man romance. He responds to your kindness and courtesy by being gallant and generous. Leo in love is a real Prince Charming in your

Libran eyes. Your attraction to his strength and virility will cause you to overlook his faults, or delude yourself into believing that he is perfect.

Leo always wants to live up to your opinion of him and to be as perfect as you want him to be. Between your fantasy image of the ideal lover and his attempt to live up to that image lies a wide gulf of reality that has to be faced. You have to be the practical partner in this relationship if you want it to work. The Libran power of emotional detachment is necessary for coping with Leo's incessant ego demands.

Both of you want to be adored by your lovers. He demands it and you expect it. But beware that while Leo will enjoy the compliments you give him, you may not get the same attention in return. He can get so involved in what he sees as his needs that you feel overwhelmed. You can become weary of bestowing your constant attention, cooling your feelings toward him. Then, just when you think you are least appreciated, your Leo man will surprise you with a thoughtful present or sincere praise that brings back all your affection.

As you can tell by now, it will be an up-and-down affair. You may tell yourself that you want a more tranquil relationship, but you really thrive on the pressure and variety that fills your life when you're in love with a Leo man. You would rather be angry or confused with the Lion than bored and unstimulated with a less demanding lover.

Boredom will never be an issue when you and Leo are making love. His warm affection becomes hot passion under your light touch and tender kisses. You want a man who can demand passion and excite you to new erotic highs. Both of you lose yourselves in sex, lingering in the afterglow of spent passion. Satisfying a Leo lover makes you feel self-satisfied as well. The masculine drive of a Leo man will bring out your own butch instincts in man-to-man sex. Though Leos can be rather conventional lovers, the quality of their passion makes up for the lack of variety. Don't be shy about bringing experimental elements into your love-making. Flattery and compliments about his sexual prowess are the keys to leading him into more adventurous techniques.

Leo represents your Eleventh House—hopes and wishes. He is just as much of a romantic as you are: in love with the idea of being in love. You adore the idea of having a man to share your life, and he is thrilled by the feeling of having a lover. You make each other feel worthy as companions, and it shows in the way you sparkle together.

Libra, the Scales of Justice, and Leo, the courageous Lion, are a powerful symbolic combination of high ideals. You are intelligent men, sensitive about your ego roles and insecure about the ability to give and receive love. A romantic union between you and a Leo man may exist on a very ideal plane that also allows you a new understanding of yourselves as creative personalities, with plenty of satisfying sex thrown in for good measure.

LIBRA & VIRGO

Though you may hit it off just fine with the Air-sign Mercury of Gemini, the Earth-sign men of Mercurial Virgo don't share your optimistic view of life, sex, and love. The aspects indicate a difficult path to true love between you and Virgo.

Virgo is inquisitive, and he will be attracted to your wit and intelligence. He's rather a clever lad himself and generally well informed. Like you, he has been searching for love and some understanding of emotion but has mainly had a series of brief liaisons that have left him unsatisfied. The difference is that you are an idealist and a romantic who believes in "true love" while Virgo is a practical realist who doubts the probability of the perfection he seeks. You go from rose to rose, inhaling the scent of each flower with hopes of rapture, and Virgo seems to dart from bud to bud, looking for the thorns.

In a practical sense you can develop a real appreciation of Virgo's virtues. You like the fact that he is peace-loving and meticulous. The first blush of your affair will focus on the way you two care for each other. Virgo wants to serve his lovers, to express his affection practically. Your aesthetic sensibilities will be pleased by the care he shows for keeping things neat and tidy. He will understand your need for a balanced environment and appreciate your touches of Venus-inspired beauty. The aspects indicate that there can be the harmony you crave to make you happy, but there are also potentials for abuse.

Since Virgo is so willing to be of service, you may take unfair advantage of him. You may let the situation drift into imbalance if you assume that your superior imaginative and creative powers are more important than his more mundane gifts. The domestic tranquillity you both treasure will crumble into scenes of bickering as he accuses you of being lazy and selfish. If you want to keep your Virgo lover, you will need to be more appreciative and considerate of him. With a healthy dose of Libran affection, you can give him a positive appreciation of his role in your life.

Your sex life can reflect the mutual desire of both Libra and Virgo to feel cherished. You have the power to bring out deeply held feelings for sexual pleasure in Virgo. He may be a master of technique, but you can supply the inspiration and imagination that transforms erotic proficiency into real passion. Exotic, experimental sex will be a heavy turn-on in your initial encounter, but your subsequent love life together will be more subtle and gentle. If you focus on the meaning of affection between two men, you can avoid the mechanical and prosaic lovemaking that may cause you to wander.

Fidelity may be a problem for you in a relationship with a Virgo. You are easily attracted to more dynamic types, and susceptible to the kind of flattery that Virgos rarely offer. Your imagination and your eye for masculine beauty make you prone to flirtations. And although you may occasionally stray, you want a man who will demand fidelity, who will challenge you to live up to your high opinion of yourself. Virgo will appeal to your sense of fairness, but not to your romantic desire for a man you can look up to.

Virgo represents your Twelfth House—hidden meanings—and you may find yourself drawn to him in ways you can't intellectualize. He can be a very loyal friend and sincere companion who will go out of his way to help you, even when you feel that you don't deserve it. He may seem like a nitpicker and a complainer, but you admire his sense of discipline and his powers of discrimination. The Virgo talent for refinement appeals to your own Libra tastes, even though he is not as imaginative or extravagant as you are. You can trust him, and he has a feeling of respect for you that can weather the storms of a love relationship and allow it to blossom into a fine friendship.

You two are a combination of high ideals, of romance and practicality that can bring lasting benefits to both of you. He needs some imaginative input in his life, and you can use some practical direction to give you a better perspective. Work together on your common desires for peace and harmony rather than trying to force each other into emotional roles that don't fit your deepest needs. Libra and Virgo can be loving brothers and helpful partners, above and beyond the transient pleasures of a romantic entanglement.

LIBRA & LIBRA

You would imagine that another Libra man would be sympathetic to your Cardinal Air-sign nature, ruled as you both are by the charming influence of Venus. There are certainly indications of compatibility, but two Libras in love can mean

too much Airy imagination, too much ego, too much indecision to fulfill each other's needs. Librans can be very
close friends, so close that the idea of being lovers seems
almost incestuous and certainly unfair to all the men in the
world that need a Libra man to "decorate" their lives.

It is certainly a favorable relationship for the things that
are closest to your heart. He can be a real good-time buddy
who matches your extravagant tastes for imaginative pleasures, but you may wonder if you can count on him when
the chips are down. Since Libras want to be lavish with their
lovers, he will buoy your spirits with fresh flowers and little
diversions, but you may feel that there is no solid foundation to keep your relationship on course.

You share a wonderful creative energy, but it only works
to your advantage when you have a specific goal. Without a
focus for your idealism the relationship will drift into frivolity and folly. It can be a fine little affair and an exciting
encounter that leads to an enjoyable friendship, even if your
sexual needs should find you wandering off in different directions.

You will like his unrestrained attitude toward most things
in life, as well as his little edge of cynicism, which lends
some perspective to his observations about the world and
its foibles—especially the world of romance. He is a romantic idealist, but his life-style has caused him to become
detached, which appeals to your own innermost sensibilities. Libra men are high-spirited but not naïve or gung ho.
He will like the idea that you take him seriously, without
compromising your sense of humor. Librans love to be
amused; it brings out their considerable charm and wit.

The Scales of Balance can be too heavily weighted with
dreams to find a practical and successful "happy medium"
when two Libras join forces as lovers. You can make big
plans but won't pay enough attention to detail to make them
reality. You begin to doubt yourself and him when there
isn't enough positive reinforcement from outside your relationship. Your egos need feeding with the beefsteak of
success and esteem rather than with the steady diet of larks'

tongues in aspic and cotton-candy compliments you two serve each other.

After the flattery of first looking in the mirror and seeing your Libra in the light of love, familiarity can breed a little contempt. After all, he probably shares your weaknesses as well as your strengths. Since you are both Cardinal signs, there is an insidious element of competition that can really throw you off-balance. Both of you want to be the leader, the man with the ideas, but you get bogged down by indecision. Your discussions can become endless rounds of "Listen to me!"—"No, listen to me!" that leaves you nowhere but up in the air with bruised egos and nothing substantial to show for it.

Problems of substance may also enter your sex life with a Libra lover. You will enjoy his tender and affectionate lovemaking, but there may be something lacking unless he has a Fire sign rising, adding a little passionate punch to his playful sexuality. Both of you are offended by coarse or brutish sex, but you like a very "masculine" man to stimulate your romantic fantasies.

Be honest with each other about your need to be admired by other men. Libras can be self-deceptive about elements in their personalities that they don't like. If you are caught carrying on outrageously, you will blame your lover for allowing it to happen. Don't start hurting each other with mutual recriminations that put too much cool detachment between you, or the affair will be over.

You can love a Libra man as much as you love yourself. Since you are both committed to personality growth, the older you both are, the better you can handle a same-sign lover. As men of accomplishment and maturity, you have a refined sense of who you are and what you want from life and love. As friends and lovers, Libra men are among the most desirable in the zodiac. The affection you need and the love you have to give can lead to a lot of happiness with another Libra in your life.

LIBRA & SCORPIO

If you find yourself teetering on the edge of boredom, the Fixed Water-sign man of Scorpio may just be your cup of tea, or else the tempest in the teapot. There's a smoldering sexuality about him that whets your appetite and perks up your imagination. The very fact that he is attracted to you, with his dark and handsome looks, is enough to start you fantasizing about his potential as a lover.

Scorpio men can provide you with amazing erotic and spiritual experiences, but there are difficulties to overcome as partners in love. Your ability to compromise, cooperate, and harmonize with your lover are all put to the test by the dominant powers of Scorpio men. You are attracted to his highly sexual vibrations and the promise of excitement but may find him too introspective and emotional to understand.

You are justice and he is revenge. You are love and he is sex. You are romance and he is mystery. It is natural that you should follow each other on the zodiac, but it doesn't follow that you can be lovers. Because you are so close in karmic development, you have a respect and fascination for each other that can be beneficial in friendship and in business. Romantic involvement may bring out tensions between you that obscure the positive pleasures of knowing a Scorpio man.

Libras tend to be optimists, especially about love. Once you gain Scorpio's trust by being honest and consistent, he will open up to your sense of humor and you can get him to be a little less serious about life. He is certainly attracted by your charm, wit, and social grace, but he takes you too seriously, makes too many demands on you, and ultimately drowns your shining personality with too much Fixed Water-sign intensity.

Your desire for erotic intensity will be fulfilled in exciting ways with a Scorpio lover. There is an element of relentless, driving passion that permeates his sex life. You are fascinated by his power and are willing to submit to his dominant urges, but sex with him may become too consuming, too demanding, and too emotional for your own pleasure. You want sex to be more fun, more playful, than Scorpio. As usual he takes it too seriously, and perhaps you don't take it seriously enough. You can get involved in some very intense sexual experiences with a Scorpio man, but you enjoy them for variety and interest while he uses erotic techniques to gain new levels of emotional sensation. Once is never enough for Scorpios, especially if it's good the first time.

The better you are in bed, the more possessive he will be toward you. The biggest problem between you as lovers is the fact that he can't help being jealous and you can't help needing to flirt. Well, not so much "flirt" as to feel free to be yourself, to enjoy the company of other men, and to know that they find you attractive. While your ego needs attention, Scorpio's ego requires nothing less than absolute devotion. He will accuse you of infidelity long before you commit any act you would identify as being untrue to him. Eventually he becomes so dominant that you have no logical recourse or power of appeal if you don't agree with him. Not having freedom of action is intolerable for all Air-sign men, especially Cardinal-sign Libras.

If you can get the brief affair out of your system, there is much to gain from close association with a Scorpio. He represents your Second House—money, income, and possessions. While a love relationship may restrict your freedom, a business contact with Scorpio will actually increase your independence because it increases your income. Pay attention, Libra, because love may be easy for you to find, but lack of money is often the major source of your unhappiness. If you aren't lucky in love with a Scorpio, you may well be fortunate in finances.

Patience is the key to dealing with Scorpio as a lover. You must weigh the benefits against the restrictions to decide what you want. Try to do this slowly, before you inadvertently promise him more than you can deliver. Libras can be self-deceptive, and Scorpios, though secretive themselves, will not tolerate any form of deception from their lovers. Rather than suffer the pain of disentangling yourself from a premature commitment to such a powerful personality, work on developing a Scorpio friendship that may turn into love as you come to know each other better.

LIBRA & SAGITTARIUS

Your Libra longing for purely physical sex is awakened when you come in contact with a Mutable Fire-sign man of Sagittarius. There is something lusty about his robust presence and knowing grin that appeals to your erotic imagination. He is ruled by jovial Jupiter, symbolizing the principles of his expansive personality and good intentions. Aside from the magnetic sexual vibrations between you, there is the likelihood of lasting friendship. You will treasure a Sagittarian man as a great drinking buddy, an enthusiastic conversationalist, and a generous pal.

You will be amazed and delighted at how well matched you seem in areas that are important to your Libran sensibilities. He is broadly funny—a complement to your clever wit. He is well traveled and well versed in a number of areas that fulfill your need for intellectual companionship. He is changeable and adaptable enough to keep you from being bored or vexed for very long. In short, he's the kind of man whose company brings out your best qualities and makes you look and feel good.

Because you are the Cardinal sign in this relationship, your Sagittarian will let you take the lead in most things. He prefers to keep his freedom rather than accept the restrictions and responsibilities of leadership in a relationship. Sagittarians are idealists, and his ideal love is a relationship between equals without the complications of dependency, dominance, or passivity, spoiling all the fun of being in love.

Your Venus rulership responds to the influence of Jupiter, eager and ready to party all night. He knows that sex can be fun and that you are in on the joke. There can be an almost conspiratorial camaraderie between you and Sagittarius as you stay up until dawn, talking and exchanging insights, information, and experiences.

Things may turn out differently than you plan if you count on a lasting love with a Sagittarius man. He is symbolized by the Centaur—half man, half horse, and born to wander. You are looking for partnership with a man you can count on to make your life complete. Sagittarius is more self-reliant and less interested in the limitations of long-term commitments. There may be a lot of fun and frolic with a Sagittarian, but it may not ever lead to anything more substantial than good times and fond memories.

Though he may take off to wander the world, the memory of his kisses will linger on in your sentimental Libran heart. You love the physical passion and intense masculine sexuality of Fire-sign men, and Sagittarius is the most adventurous partner of all the Fire signs. He can be almost fierce in his demanding passion, but he will respond affectionately to your gentle touch. There is no need to be shy or coy with a Sagittarian. You can verbalize your desires and Sagittarius will rise to the occasion time and time again!

You both enjoy people so much that you tend to split up at parties and mingle, enjoying the stimulation of new faces. For you, Libra, it adds a sparkle to your personality and an edge to your charm, which is an essential component of your social life. Though there might be a touch of romantic jealousy on your part, Sagittarius will be more amused than angered by the way you fall prey to the flattering attentions of other men.

Sagittarius represents your Third House—communications—and the lines are always open to forgiveness when you find yourselves at odds. Sagittarius impels you to communicate in creative ways as well. You work very well together on projects, as long as you make sure to follow through on the ideas he encourages.

The more exciting your life-style, the more likely that a Sagittarian buddy may be happy to "settle down" emotionally and make a commitment to you as your lover and partner. Both of you like to feel that you are "on the move." Libra and Sagittarius have the opportunity to share a romance that's built around the ideal of perpetual growth as loving men.

LIBRA & CAPRICORN

The men of Cardinal Earth-sign Capricorn present you with the opportunity for stability, but they also represent a challenge to your easygoing personality. If your hopeful optimism can balance out his cautious ambition, there is a good chance that you can be partners in friendship or in love.

There is tension indicated between Libra and Capricorn because you are both Cardinal signs. Symbolized by the Mountain Goat, the Capricorn man is dedicated to achieving emotional security through material success. He is interested in the tangible and practical elements of life, so you may find yourself at odds with Libra idealism and Capricorn realism. The combination of your imagination and his determination can spell success if you are able to overcome your differences and get down to business.

Capricorn is ruled by Saturn, planet of time and restriction. Your need for excitement may not be satisfied under Saturn's influence, but there are times when it is more important for you to accept responsibility than to seek stimulation. Capricorn affects your ability to think about the future, to define your goals, and to provide for your needs. It could mean an overhaul of your current ideas and life-style that will benefit you in later life.

Capricorn is at his best after forty or fifty. When he has attained the material success that allows him to feel secure, his personality comes into its own. He is a natural teacher and mentor who will offer you love and protection if you are a young Libra, or love and solid companionship if you are peers. If you want a real change to give your life meaning and direction, then a Capricorn lover can give you the support you need.

Living with a Capricorn isn't all nose to the grindstone. He is normally a man of creative sensitivity who appreciates fine art, classical music, and refined entertainment. You will appreciate his mature tastes because they complement your own interest in quality, though you are more open to innovative ideas in the arts.

If there is a bond of affection developing, you will see Capricorn as reassuring and gracious rather than stuffy or stodgy. There is an atmosphere of calm about him that can be soothing and comforting to your nerves. Though Capricorn may appear cool or aloof, he really enjoys your charm and intelligent conversation. He has trained himself to be serious, yet he yearns for the ease and informality you bring into his life.

Capricorn represents your Fourth House—home, security, and later life. You will be attracted to the idea of setting up a home with him or working toward a goal that provides security and commitment. You gain from the association by becoming more aware of details and more capable of accepting responsibility. Before you met Capricorn, you were cheery and optimistic about today and tomorrow but a bit depressed when you thought about your future. With Capricorn, you gain breadth of vision but lose a little of your sparkle in the exchange. Think of it as growing up rather than getting old, and don't lament for your lost youth.

Libras and Capricorns improve with age, becoming more and more secure in their sexuality. You will find that he has marvel-

ous powers of endurance in bed, though you may prefer a little
more fireworks than Capricorn is used to providing. As a lover
he is slow and deliberate but very sensuous, building to an intense climax. Your Libran imagination can "free" Capricorn's
personality from some of Saturn's stern restrictions, adding variety to his lovemaking. He will expect you to be faithful, but
you must explain your need for social attention and freedom of
action. Capricorn must learn to trust you if he wants to keep
your affection.

You can thrive in the companionship of dependable Capricorn. You feel the positive benefits of your intelligence
being tempered by wisdom about human nature. In return,
you give Capricorn a more humanistic view of life and a
feeling of hope. It is a relationship between equals that requires the delicate balance of your Libra qualities and flour-
ishes under his stable influence. Remember, Libra, unless
you are ready to settle down, you will not be ready for, nor
worthy of, a Capricorn's love. You have the power to engage
each other in a continuous education and exchange of insights that make you more fulfilled as individuals. There is
lasting love to share between the men of Libra and Capricorn, but only if you are willing to go the distance.

LIBRA & AQUARIUS

You are definitely turned on by the energy of Aquarius, your
Fixed Air-sign buddy. You have a natural affinity for many
of the same things in life but from differing points of view.
You both thrive on change, but the Libra of Venus loves
variety, while the Aquarian ruler, Uranus, makes him inclined to eccentricity. There is a kind of unpredictable magic
about Aquarian men that you find romantic.

Something unusual will characterize your first meeting,

and it will spark your imagination. You may meet him by the light of sunset, and in the glow of twilight's last twinkling he will appear incredibly romantic and dashing—and very sexy. Aquarians will want to be friends before you become lovers, but they often meet their friends through romantic encounters.

You are attracted to the obvious fun and games of an Aquarius affair, but surprises and sudden changes can leave you exhausted, unbalanced, and insecure. If you want a stable partnership that features cozy nights by the fire, don't look to Aquarius. If you want travel, unusual friends, and creative stimulation, then an Aquarian man may be just what you've been looking for, though perhaps more than you bargained for.

You need a certain amount of tranquillity to balance your Libran desire for variety; too much activity leaves you drained and cranky. Aquarius is much less sensitive than you are and may not realize the wear and tear his chaotic social existence is putting on your nerves.

The one element of a Libra–Aquarius relationship that calms you right down is the good sex that is generated by your Air-sign enthusiasm. You aren't aggressive or demanding with each other, but you both certainly fulfill your appetites for excitement and contentment. When your life-style becomes too hectic and you find yourselves at cross-purposes, sex puts the fun back in your romance and brings a peace of mind that reaffirms your commitment.

You are both idealists, but Aquarian ideals are broad and humanitarian rather than personal and romantic. He will admire your sense of justice, and you will find his tolerance an important virtue. Libra likes the range of Aquarius intellect, and even though you don't completely understand him, you find him fascinating. There is something excessive about your love for Aquarius that gives you a constant thrill.

Your social life with an Aquarius lover can be the kind of whirlwind you need to get your creative juices flowing. He knows a lot of people and has a lot of friends at different levels of society. You appreciate the opportunity to pick and choose new friends from such an eclectic assortment.

One of the issues between you and your Aquarian lover will be symbolized by the conflict between your Cardinal nature and his Fixed nature. You want to take the initiative, but you don't always know how to motivate him. Aquarius will accuse you of being bossy, and you counter by reminding him that he can be exasperatingly stubborn. He believes that there is a Truth with a capital T, but you are more inclined to compromise and then resent your capitulation. You may see him as impractical, but he can't help believing that his faults are really virtues. When you criticize him, he questions your loyalty. Though you receive much creative support from an Aquarian lover, he can make you feel insecure because you don't have enough control over the situation.

Aquarius represents your Fifth House—love, romance, and creativity. Falling in love with the Aquarius experience brings you success by channeling your intellectual and aesthetic talents into more humanitarian goals. You aim higher and you feel charged with positive personal magnetism. Aquarius, the Water-bearer, adds extra sparkle to your personality. You two are a blend of trust and freedom that come together in affectionate balance. If he moderates some of his eccentricity and you control some of your sensitivity, there is a dynamic and lasting love between the men of Libra and Aquarius.

LIBRA & PISCES

The Mutable Water-sign man of Pisces attracts you because of his gentle, sympathetic nature, though he is ultimately much more emotional than your Air-sign nature will comprehend. When Pisces enters your life, you will find a dreamy quality to his sexual magnetism that touches your romantic imagination.

You will not normally gravitate toward each other but

usually find yourselves thrown together by family, business, or other social forces. You share your romantic idealism, love of peace, harmony, and appreciation of beauty. Both Libra and Pisces men seek relationships in which they can make their partners happy, but contentment may be difficult to achieve. Selflessness without focus or ambition can leave you feeling unfulfilled.

Pisces is willing to serve you in some way, and you are flattered by his attention. He is ruled by Neptune, planet of illusion. In combination with your ruling Venus, the influence could indicate mutual self-indulgence and self-deception. Your Air and Water natures can create a fog of drugs, alcohol, and uncertainty that leaves you drifting into passive self-destruction. There is creative potential in a Libra–Pisces love affair, but you need common goals to work toward or you'll drift until you float away from one another.

Pisces is easygoing enough to please you and certainly affectionate, but not strong enough to balance your ego. He is emotional and sensitive, but doesn't know where to focus his energy. Because he is unsure of himself, you will feel forced to take a dominant role, even though you aren't comfortable being the sole source of strength in a relationship. His dependency and desire restrict your freedom, causing you to question the true value of a Pisces man as your lover.

With a Pisces lover, your active social interests are in conflict with his desire for an exclusive relationship. You need time on your own, away from Pisces' dependency that you feel dragging you down. Even though he may be romantically devoted to you, there is a feeling of sacrifice and obligation that compromises your image of ideal love.

Libra wants a partner who will complement his needs and desires in a harmonious manner. Pisces goes too far in accommodating you, and you have no check on your ego when he is so subservient. Ultimately it can be boring for you because there isn't enough intellectual and physical challenge to sustain your interest in man-to-man love and sex. You want more excitement in your men and in your love affairs.

Because he represents your Sixth House, the house of service, Pisces will want to make sacrifices for your benefit. Rather than working toward becoming a completely passive lover, you find yourself trying to overcompensate for him by being detached and demanding.

Ultimately, your Libran ideals of justice will tell you that this kind of relationship is unfair. Putting an end to a Pisces affair will be difficult. Neither of you will want to hurt the other, and it may take a long time to come to a decision, even though you are not happy.

There are important lessons to be learned from a Pisces. The love of a Pisces man can bring practical results rather than great romance. You can be friends with a Pisces at work or at play, but when sex enters the picture, things lose their equilibrium. You will certainly enjoy an occasional Pisces encounter for the gentle passion he provides. He can be most intuitive in the way he manages to please your sensibilities, but you may not want it as a steady diet.

These sensitive and sexy men are symbolized by the Fishes. Because they are in constant movement, it is difficult for you to balance and harmonize a Pisces relationship without tipping the scales. Be careful with a Pisces lover unless you know for sure what you want from life and are willing and stable enough to accept the love of a Pisces man.

LOVING YOUR LIBRA MAN

You can find a Libra man in pleasant surroundings that offer the opportunity for sexually charged meetings. They enjoy anyplace that allows them to interact with people, to talk and socialize with those they see as a "cut above" the rest.

It's not that they are social climbers as much as that they need beauty and a touch of luxury in their lives.

You can always gain Libra's attention by appealing to his sense of romance, aesthetics, or intelligence. He enjoys compliments and will even succumb to flattery, but it has to be clever. Libra wants to be liked for his talents and accomplishments, though he certainly won't mind being told how attractive he is as well.

Libra will be most responsive to you if you are classically attractive. Good-looking men as companions and lovers are a real ego boost to him. But he also likes clever conversation. Libra wants to know what you think, especially your attitudes about life and the lessons you have abstracted from your experiences. He has a fine sense of humor and he'll love it if you make him laugh.

If you want to please him with gifts, send him things that are well designed, refined, and unusual. If you give him something practical, make sure it is also beautiful. Flowers always elicit a romantic rise from Libras. Expensive chocolates are always welcome, and any extravagance in good taste earns Libra's admiration. He prefers things that are small and perfect rather than gaudy or ostentatious.

Despite his refined tastes, he is a hearty eater. Libras are both gourmets and gourmands, and they enjoy large portions of excellent food. When dining out, make sure you go someplace quiet and cozy, because Libras hate noise and distractions. He won't enjoy the meal if the restaurant is crowded and chaotic.

He can be almost eccentric in his desire for peace, beauty, and comfort, combined with his search for variety and intellectual stimulation. Libra likes the challenge of change but not on an emotional level. His life may seem chaotic to others, but he will cope with the consequences of his own mistakes better than he tolerates his friends or lovers creating emotional confusion.

You can keep a Libra lover happy by being consistent, honest, and fair. He has high standards of behavior, even though he is known for being nonchalant. Libra will not stay around very long if he believes you are deceiving him or treating him unfairly. He won't try to argue with you or appeal to you. He will simply pass judgment and walk out of your life. Librans are not known for their tempers, but their anger is awesome when you have violated their trust. He is not trying to hurt you, but simply attempting to express the depth of his indignation.

Avoid unbalancing this charming man of refined sensibilities and he will be a loyal friend and devoted lover. Libras love being in love, and he sincerely wants a partner to share his life. In typical fashion, he either will want to make a quick commitment to a relationship or else will deliberate and vacillate, wondering whether or not to get involved.

Once he's picked over a dozen daisies trying to decide if it's really love, he will put all of his heart into a relationship. Librans pride themselves on their ability and desire to please their lovers. His dedication to justice makes him a sincere believer in the Golden Rule. Libra men treat their lovers the way they, themselves, want to be treated—with kindness and consideration. Remember to be appreciative. He needs positive feedback if he is going to sparkle.

Librans have an inherent duality that comes from being a masculine, active sign, ruled by the feminine planet Venus. Their sexuality is affected by their desire for sensuality and their need for physical release. He wants to harmonize the polarities of peaceful, tranquil, comforting affection with the abandon and excitement of passionate sex. Libra wants to please his lovers, but he isn't passive. He is bisexual in the sense that he wants to blend masculine and feminine elements in his relationships. Libra wants a lover who can appreciate the need for tender loving care and the desire for intense physical experience. He wants to hold on and let go at the same time. You can make him weak in the knees and have him begging for more if you remember that he wants sex to be fun.

Equality is a very important concept to a Libra lover. He is the sign of partnership and he wants a partner he can respect as worthy of his love. With a weak-willed man Libra becomes too dominant. With a strong lover he becomes equally assertive, but in the spirit of companionship rather than competition. Libra likes a challenge but not on a personal or emotional level. Though he strives for harmony, he does not seek perfection, because then there would be nothing left to balance.

If you want to keep your Libra lover happy, you have to keep him interested by introducing new elements that intrigue rather than distract him. His mind is working all the time, and if life becomes tiresome, he will begin to wander, looking for new stimuli, in other men or in different situations that require his special talents.

A Libra lover will add elements of style and grace to your life if you can accept him for the blend of romance and intellect in him. He believes that harmony is beauty and that beauty is truth. Libra may be asking for a great deal in a loving union with you, but he is prepared to give as much as he gets. Appeal to his active mind, his love of beauty, and his need for mutual devotion and you have gone a long way toward success in loving your Libra man.

SCORPIO
October 21– November 20

♏

Symbol: The Scorpion
Ruling Planet: Pluto
Color: Dark red
Metal: Steel
Natural House Rulership: Eighth House, the house
    of sex, death, and transformation
Eighth House Traits: Desire to know the unknown
    and a need to control
Motto: "I desire"
Nature: Fixed sign (organizer)
Element: Water sign (emotion)
Qualities: Intensity, courage, and willpower
Capacities: Investigation and reorganization
Personality Key Words: Reserved, perceptive, and
    passionate

MAXIMIZING YOUR SCORPIO POTENTIAL

You are the Black Prince, the Great Dark Man, the Magician, and one of the most powerful signs of the zodiac, Scorpio. Symbols of mystery and transformation surround and infuse you with a mystical intensity and sexuality. You are Fixed Water by nature, an element symbolic of the primacy and strength of your emotions. You are intelligent and creative, but you act upon your feelings, and your feelings are easily hurt. Pluto, god of the underworld, is your ruling planet, according mysterious and awe-inspiring power to your personality.

You are "heavy," and it shows in the nature of your social relationships and your approach to loving men. Scorpio is the sign of sex, and your smoldering sexuality shows in your eyes. Other men are drawn to you because they sense your sexual power, but they rarely appreciate or understand the totality of the powers you possess.

Scorpio is symbolized by the Scorpion, which gives you the power to hurt not only others but also yourself, if you cannot externalize your passion and sensitivity. Love can give focus and meaning to your sexuality—and transform your personality. Scorpio is a dual sign, but the duality is a continuum that describes the bridge that leads from the Serpent (representative of the forbidden knowledge of sexuality) to the Eagle (symbol of the transcendent power of which you are capable). Whether you descend or soar depends upon the way in which you use your magical powers to be creative or destructive.

Integrating your powerful—and often warring—drives is a

difficult karmic task, and it makes you a very serious person. The young Scorpio finds it hard to cope with the responsibilities of his emotional needs. The fear of being unable to control your feelings makes you insecure and secretive. You crave power, and exercising control over others can be a substitute for your inability to be in charge of your own emotions.

Your deep emotions are combined with a relentless intellect that makes you determined to understand the nature of your knowledge and all of the mysteries of life itself. You are driven to investigate all forms of secret intelligence and taboo experiences in order to manipulate others. Your eyes are hypnotic, and you can convince another man that you can see into his very soul.

Your greatest need is for a lover who is complete in his submission. You can force your desire upon other men through the dominant nature of your personality and sexuality, but it is love freely given that you need in order to give your trust. Manipulating others is like using a magic potion. You know that you have created this kind of love as a mirror image of your own needs, and you fear that the spell may wear off, leaving you alone. Even as you seek out others to love you, the intensity of Scorpio's needs and powers can alienate them.

You are unswervingly interested in your emotional needs, and it causes you to be separate, detached, and curiously unemotional about the needs of others. Your understanding of power makes you suspicious of others; your ability to get your way makes you overbearing. Your extreme sensitivity and powers of observation give you intuitive insights, but they often make you vulnerable to hurt. Your desire to know everything can lead you on a lifelong odyssey, exploring the depths and heights of every imaginable experience— especially sexual experience—but leaving you feeling unfulfilled.

You are a very attractive man, and though you prefer to be alone, you may lead an extraordinarily active social life. You want to be a respected member of society, despite your feelings of separateness. Scorpio gays often have positions of importance in business or the community, but the desire for respectability and public conventionality can cause them to be closeted. You believe in the privacy of your personal life and demand the right to do whatever you want in your own environment, despite the pressures of society, gay or straight.

Your need for privacy and your tendency toward secretiveness extends to your sex life and even to your partners. People think Scorpios are sex fiends, but you rarely talk about sex even though you may think about it a great deal. You have had the opportunity to have many casual partners, but you really do not enjoy "recreational" sex. Like everything else in your life, sex is serious business.

When you do fall in love, the demands you make upon your lover are very strong. You want a man who will give himself to you completely. He must be strong enough to deal with your intensity without being consumed, and vulnerable enough to understand and sympathize with your need for selfless devotion. He must be absolutely faithful to you or the relationship is over. You are faithful in love and insanely jealous. Any relationship, especially a love relationship, is an all-or-nothing proposition to Scorpio.

In return for complete devotion you give your lovers an intense commitment that is expressed through magnificent sexual passion. You don't want sex all the time, but when you do, it must be a magical and transcendent experience. When you feel secure in love, you are generous with your power and very protective of the relationship. You want a stable home life and will work hard to provide the best of everything.

You are a very difficult man to get along with, and you are as hard on yourself as you are on others. You want to be strong emotionally, and you punish yourself for your insecurities. You need creative outlets for your emotions, or the poison of doubt will corrupt your potential for growth. You possess great power, but the responsibility that comes with it can be a crushing weight unless you use your magnetism to energize others.

You achieve your highest goals only when you learn to share your intensity. Through a loving and creative relationship Scorpio is able to realize that sharing increases the potential for personal gratification. You must explain your needs to your lover and work to be sensitive to his emotions instead of continually thinking of your own feelings and needs. Above all, you must learn to trust. Your karmic mission in life is to combine passion with trust in a process that yields love that purifies, heals, and gives meaning to the Scorpio devotion to the mysteries of existence.

SCORPIO & ARIES

When you team up with a man who is Cardinal-Fire Aries, there is both excitement and obligation, mixed with the elemental differences between Fire and Water. He is deeply attracted to your magnetic sexuality, and you are turned on by his direct approach and obvious desire.

Aries' instincts are masculine, and he sees himself as butch to the core. Your Scorpio desire to delve into mysteries will be activated because you can't believe he is as uncomplicated as he seems. Go easy on Aries. He may seem arrogant and self-possessed with other men, but his attraction to you is quite sincere. He may well be too naïve for a relationship with a man of your sophistication, but he can provide you with an exciting time while it lasts.

Arians are into sex as gratification on a short fuse. He likes it man-to-man, with plenty of action. On a sexual level you can really enjoy his company, but to attempt a lasting relationship could be traumatic for both of you. You react against the pressures of his attachment to you, sensing that they will restrict your freedom but not his. Without the opportunity to be in control, you won't be very interested in a love relationship with an Aries man.

Aries is basically insecure unless he has enough affection to support his large ego. He has a roving eye that will defy your authority and insult your sense of values. Quarrels will be volatile with a potential for violence, because he can't control his emotional outbursts. You have to be the responsible one in this combination and know enough to maintain your distance and keep your cool.

Despite your reputation for sex, you need much more going for you in a relationship than physical interaction. Falling in love with an Aries man is almost "unnecessary" for a Scorpio, because you can easily attain what he has to offer without making an emotional commitment. Basically, Aries men want love and affection with no strings attached. No matter how young you are, Scorpio, you know that nothing valuable is free or without obligations.

Aries men like "schoolboy sex." You are more serious in your attitude about sex and the power of sexuality. He likes plenty of sex and multiple orgasms, but you are willing to wait, to bide your time until you get a chance for exactly what you want. Aries is playing with firecrackers when it comes to using his sexuality, but you, Scorpio, are a nuclear submarine by comparison.

Aries represents your Sixth House, the house of service, work, and health. He wants to serve you, and you feel protective toward him, even though it is never a smooth and easy relationship. As friends, you join forces and close ranks if either of you is threatened or needs help. Aries is generous, open, and giving, but don't forget to be effusive in your thanks. Because he is less sophisticated and manipulative than you are, your Aries buddy will be hurt or disappointed in the vagaries of gay love much more often than you are.

There can be a spirit of gay brotherhood between you and Aries, once you two realize that a long-term affair is not in the stars. You could be roommates, coworkers, or drinking buddies. Again, there will be disputes over who has what kind of power and how he gets to use it, questions of who is right and who goes first. Remember, Scorpio, time is on your side because you know how to plan, wait, and then execute your plan at just the right moment. Arians are too impetuous and too easily distracted to stay angry or hurt for very long.

There is a spiritual bond that comes out in a relationship with Aries. He believes in miracles and you believe in the occult. Aries will want you to teach him more about metaphysical matters, and a common interest in spiritual healing or parapsychology may often surface as a focal point in your relationship. A respect for knowledge of the nonmaterial world is one of the things you can teach the hardheaded Ram of Aries. A Scorpio can also be a big help in giving an Aries buddy some clues about handling money in the material world, since you understand the process of getting and using it much better than he does.

Though you may find him exasperating and childish, or petulant and aggressive, an Aries man can also amuse you with his exuberance. If you pick up on his bighearted approach to life, you won't take him too seriously and lose the benefit of knowing him. Love may not come your way through the Aries experience, but there is a good chance for a mutually supportive friendship.

SCORPIO & TAURUS

The Bull is opposite your sign on the Wheel of Life, and you will be attracted to him for the ways in which he is able to complement your virtues and moderate your vices. Taurean men are strong and stubborn, which excites you; they are also loyal and sensuous, which delights you.

Taurus is characterized as Fixed Earth, and his karmic

mission is to deal with the material world. As a Fixed Water sign, you must plumb the depths of emotional existence. Though you are different in your concerns, there is an affinity between you that allows for love and respect, but not without conflict. Because you are both Fixed signs, there are indications of obstinacy and possessiveness in a meeting of Scorpio and Taurus. If he loves you, he will feel that he owns you, but Taurus treats his possessions very well indeed. Because you have the power to satisfy him sexually, he will treasure your love as the ultimate in personal luxury.

Because Scorpios are secretive and Earth signs are not intuitive, he may be confused by your deep emotional nature. Taurus will want to comfort you and care for you, but he won't know how. Overhearing an offhand remark, he may think you want something desperately and go out of his way to provide it for you. Be gracious about his attempts to lavish you with favors that you may not need, expect, or want. Because Taureans are materialistic, nothing hurts and angers them like unappreciated generosity.

Sex is the real key to your compatibility with a Taurus man. He has a capacity and endurance that makes him a very responsive lover to your typical Scorpion style. He wants a man who can give him sexual variety because he tends to be prosaic and even a little shy when it comes to his physical needs. Taurus will appreciate the way you initiate new elements into lovemaking that increase his own responses. He is so concerned about money, career, possessions, and problems of one kind or another that sex is an important release for him. You can get him to take his mind off the workaday world through the power of loving.

With a Taurus man you can also learn a thing or two about the more passive pleasures of sex. Though usually men of solid proportions, they are gentle and cuddly in bed. Public displays of affection tend to embarrass them, but Taureans can be very affectionate lovers. His favorite times are long, slow, and luxurious sessions that leave him completely drained and utterly fulfilled.

You are loyal to your lovers as long as the sex is good, so

Taurus should never have reason to be unduly possessive unless he misreads your secretive moments. He is also predisposed to fidelity within a relationship, and there should be few opportunities for you to display your notorious Scorpion jealousy. You may resent the attention he puts into his career, but other men don't really have a chance of catching his eye because you satisfy him. Taurus is cautious and he is happy with the status quo, always preferring a Scorpio eagle in the hand to some unknown birds in the bush.

There are times when Taurus will think you are almost an unknown or unknowable quantity in his life. He may worry, may have private doubts and fears, but like most of the early, or "young," signs of the zodiac, his character is basically simple. You are a much more complex person with a highly developed internal life. When you are feeling down, good old Taurus wants to put on a pot of coffee and talk it out, looking for practical and material solutions to your deep emotional problems. Let him know that there are simply times when you must be alone with your thoughts and he will respect your wishes; otherwise, he will become confused and mistrustful, not only of your affection but also of his own ability to contribute to the relationship.

When you and he are out of sorts, the result is usually a standoff. Taurus actually intrigues you because he is strong enough to stand up to you. Since you are rather even-tempered, there isn't much practical reason to go through the motions of power tripping, but you probably will anyway. When the smoke clears, there are usually good lessons to be learned, which will strengthen your bonds.

Since Taurus represents your Seventh House—partnership—there is good reason to trust him and to feel that he can help make your life more complete. Furthermore, Taurus inspires you to work at overcoming the obstacles and oppositions in your love affair and in your own personality. You find yourself changing, but it is not a threatening situation. There is a potential for growth and stability, combined with sexuality and excitement, that can make a Taurus lover your mate for life.

SCORPIO & GEMINI

Few signs of the zodiac are farther from the serious side of Scorpio than the Mutable-Air men of Gemini. You are compelled to seek the depths of any subject or emotion, but the Twins of Gemini are all on the surface—or so it seems. Remember, there are two of him, and he never sets his mind on any one thing for very long. If you find yourself attracted to a Gemini gay blade, you should try to imagine the eagle and the hummingbird as lovers. The probability for success may not be great, but the possibilities are certainly worth exploring.

Gemini finds you fascinating, and you are intrigued because he is interested in your personality rather than in your sexuality. Scorpios are supposed to be the sex masters of the zodiac, but Gemini can be a breath of fresh air if you are tired of being everybody's favorite sex object. Gemini is ruled by Mercury, the planet of communication, and he wants to know everything. He'll talk your ear off if you let him, but he also listens and learns.

Your love of mystery is activated by Gemini men. You want to know what depth there is behind the superficial image. Something tells you that there are lessons to be learned from him, and he enjoys the opportunity to try to develop abstract knowledge from his experiences. You turn Gemini on to thinking more highly of himself and his natural talents.

There is an unusual aspect to your getting together, because Gemini and Scorpio have different interests and hang around with different crowds. He is into the brunch boys of the gossip network; you are more likely to be found in the boardrooms or leather bars. Business or family connections will bring you together, and the magnetism takes over from there.

You may not be sure what you want from Gemini, but you

do want him. Beware of getting yourself too deeply emotionally involved. Gemini understands ideas and sensations but not emotions. You may try to communicate your emotional pull toward him through passionate sex, but the lines of communication are crossed; he won't realize you are pouring out your heart to him.

The problem is that he will never want to get as serious about the relationship as you do, no matter how good the sex may be, and the indications are for some pretty good sex. Gemini is Mr. Fantasy in bed—or on the sofa, on the kitchen table, in the elevator, or in the cellar. Give this man a scenario and watch him go to work. He likes skin flicks and most kinds of pornography and mirrors to increase his mental stimulation. You are no slouch when it comes to variety, and Gemini will certainly keep you from being bored.

Gemini will enjoy the experience of your wholehearted passion in lovemaking, but it isn't as meaningful for him as it is for you. When he laughs or jokes or camps it up in bed, you feel that your love has been rejected. You may become too demanding—and maybe too rough—to keep him as a partner for very long. You can teach Gemini many things, but unless he has a Water sign rising, he will not respond to the idea of such an emotionally intense and monogamous relationship.

Fidelity is definitely an issue between you and a Gemini lover. You are not going to like his expansive social life and circle of ex-lovers as friends at all. Jealousy is an inherent part of your commitment, but Air-sign men need plenty of freedom to be themselves. There is little room for negotiation on the matter of loyalty.

Gemini represents your Eighth House, the house of sex and mystery. He will be very attracted to you, but he hasn't the stamina to maintain the kind of commitment you demand from a lover. It's an odd coupling that astounds your friends and confuses you and your Gemini. It may have been made in heaven, but it can be hell to try to maintain here on Earth.

Your relationship has more potential as a creative arrangement, because Gemini encourages you to expand your interests. You learn a new breadth of vision to complement
the depth of your intellect. You experience new drives and
discover new potential within yourself. You may resent being dragged out of your status quo existence, but you can
definitely benefit from a little carefree Gemini companionship in your life. He can turn out to be a much more profound event than you imagined.

SCORPIO & CANCER

Men born under the Cardinal Water sign of Cancer are natural companions for your Scorpio intensity. There is a potential for affection and power in your relationship with him
that excites your dreams and touches your heart. He shares
your intuitive nature, and there is unspoken communication
between you that puts you at ease but also stimulates your
imagination.

Everyone talks about Scorpio and sex, but your affair with
a Cancer man will have a depth and dimension to it that you
have never experienced before—the element of romance.
You will feel the glow from the influence of his Moon ruler
and come to understand a new level of transformation. Cancer men need to be conquered because they are predisposed
to surrender.

He will surrender to your dark and handsome charms, but
because he is a Cardinal sign, he won't give himself away
completely. He will want to be the leader in some important
aspects of your relationship. Cancer's creative imagination
and need for recognition compel him to take the initiative,
despite his tendency to be dependent on his partners. If you
can settle the question of who is the boss, and under what

circumstances, then the relationship between you two has a good chance for success.

Cancers are moody. It's as much of an astrological axiom as the fact that Scorpios are sexy. It is often difficult to understand Cancer's swings from efficiency to melancholy, from joy to introspection, and back again. But you will be tolerant—even sympathetic—of his moods because you understand the need to be alone with your feelings.

Cancer will be hesitant at first because his intuition tells him that this attraction is something much deeper than sexual fascination. There is no need for a heavy seduction scene with a Cancer man. Cancer will be ready to meet your fervent passion with equally ardent affection. He can become a wonderful lover in your expert embraces, and his erotic imagination will provide you with some new experiences, even for a man with as many past adventures as you, Scorpio!

It's a good thing you take love, personal relationships, and sex so seriously because Cancer is very serious about the feelings he has for you. If you are hoping to find a man who can accept the intensity of your needs as a lover and fulfill them with an affection and devotion that challenges your capacity to receive the love you crave, that man will probably be a Cancer.

Water-sign men are homebodies, and you will want to settle down with him to a life of domestic tranquillity. But don't get too cozy, Scorpio, because there is still plenty of activity in store for you when you come under the Lunar love influences of Cancer. He represents your Ninth House—long journeys—and it will be a long and eventful road you travel together, full of plans and dreams that indicate future benefits. Things may not move quickly or smoothly, but with Cancer as your partner you are stimulated rather than apprehensive about the security in the relationship and in your life.

Feelings of jealousy, revenge, and possessiveness should rarely disturb the harmony of a Scorpio–Cancer relationship. He feels your Water-sign vulnerability as well as your strength, and he will never want to hurt you by being un-faithful or disloyal. In return, your instinct is to be protective of him, to shield him from the world of hurt and pain.

Your Scorpion strength allows you to repress the intensity of your emotions and direct them inward, toward your sexual drive. That process is the source of your legendary sexual powers. Cancer can't repress his emotions or they center on his stomach. He will get fat in the tummy or develop ulcers unless he has an emotional outlet. Often creative pursuits provide him with an effective and successful means of discharging his powerful feelings, but sometimes he just cries—just a few drops of Moondew around the eyes that say "Hug me!" loud enough so that only you can hear him.

Don't hesitate, Scorpio. After all the turn-ons and trauma of your sexual adventures, the love of a Cancer man may finally give you insight into your karmic mission of unraveling the mysterious connection between love, sex, and the transformation of the spirit.

SCORPIO & LEO

The combination of your Fixed-Water nature with the Fixed-Fire sign of Leo indicates a relationship that will eventually come to a boiling point, but may take a long time getting there. Both of you are men with powerful personalities but very different sources of energy and ego projection. The influence of his ruling Sun makes him an open, sunny, flamboyant person. Your Pluto ruler inclines you to be more reserved, less gregarious, but no less attractive.

Leo feels your secret magnetism and respects you for your power. You are drawn to his regal, Leo the Lion persona and are willing to accord him the same polite, yet distant, acknowledgment when you come across each other in social, business, or recreational situations. You run into each other at certain restaurants, theaters, bars; or you may work in the same field. You may well come to think of one another as "old faces" before you ever develop a personal relationship.

Just because you haven't spoken or introduced yourselves, it doesn't mean there is necessarily any ill will between you and a Leo man. As friendly strangers you consider yourselves equals and observe the Golden Rule. As lovers you will experience feelings that challenge and question his public image versus his private life. Along with feelings of competition comes resentment. You envy his luck, but you don't admire his talent. Once you begin to probe the mystery of Leo, the illusion disappears for you. He becomes a paper tiger, and he loses some of his precious dignity and nobility in your eyes.

The stars indicate a competitive relationship between two very different forms of male sexuality. Fixed-Fire Leo is as macho about sex roles as you can get. Fixed-Water Scorpio is "feminine" by nature but endowed with heavy butch influences from the rulership of Pluto. The combination of strong feminine intuitive traits with intense masculine energy is the secret of your sexual magnetism. Your sexuality relates to your attempt to understand the mysteries of the universe. Leo's sex drive is plugged directly into his ego. You may treat each other as equals, but you are also rivals.

The scent of challenge in the air whets your appetite for some potentially heavy scenes. It's your decision, Scorpio, because Leo men will rarely approach you. Your first move should involve sincere praise or believable flattery as the ticket of admission to Leo's world. You will play along with his ego games, but Leo will pay for the male arrogance you perceive in him.

You become fixated on getting Leo to surrender his invulnerability. You want him to admit his humanity and then you will concede him his price, but he will never do it at the cost of his dignity. You want to bring Leo down a peg or two and you can use sex to do it. You may even fantasize about physically overpowering a Leo man; not because you want to hurt him, but because you want him to receive some hot, masculine energy from a new direction with you as the administrator. Once the sanctity of his rosy virtue has been violated, the affair is probably over. If he enjoys your approach to sex, it's an indication of deeper compatibilities. In either case, a Leo relationship changes your life.

Getting together with a Leo man can symbolize a big career move. Leo represents your Tenth House—public standing and career—so that getting involved with Leo in a social or business relationship is probably going to include some potent combinations of sex, money, fame, and ambition. Careers may be at stake or be made in a Scorpio–Leo liaison. On an abstract level, you are reacting to Leo as a social challenge to assert your personality as being ready for success. Leo makes you ambitious and causes you to lose some of your inhibitions and abandon the security of the status quo. You decide to seduce, command, and dominate the world of success and fame when you have a Leo man at your side.

Scorpio is not prone to doing anything frivolously, so your motives for becoming involved with Leo should be seriously examined. There is such a lack of credence between your Fixed signs that you focus too sharply on the arrogance you see in Leo, rather than the generous affection he wants to display. Your Scorpio ego becomes too involved and your jealousy causes you to decide that Leo is not genuine. You may initiate the excitement of a casual affair, but you have little patience for his charms. This will cause Leo to wonder why you bothered if you don't even like him. He won't appreciate your emotional depths or dark desires. You can certainly benefit from the optimism and warm personality of a Leo lover, but you must want to enjoy his company, rather than desire to conquer him through sex.

SCORPIO & VIRGO

A relationship with those born under the Mutable-Earth sign of Virgo can give you a new outlook on life and love that is beyond the preoccupation of sexuality. It is a refreshing change for you, Scorpio, to be closely involved with another gay man who doesn't present a sexual problem. Sex can permeate your life, but Scorpios don't always have many friends. With Virgo men you can develop a relationship that is characterized by practical friendship.

Although there may have been an initial sexual attraction to a Virgo man, it will not be as strong as the attachment you develop for other aspects of his personality. It is rare for you to find a man you can talk to. Your Scorpio intuition tells you that you can be vulnerable with a Virgo friend and speak about your innermost thoughts. Virgo's friendship can hold the promise of clarifying some of your insights into yourself and activating creative ideas on a sound basis.

You can become lovers or lifelong friends, but not constant companions. The changeable nature of his ruling planet, Mercury, and the long orbit of your Pluto ruler indicate periods of intense and meaningful communication followed by separation and reunion, according to your need for each other. You will feel truly loyal toward a Virgo buddy; you will be willing to rush to his aid, because you know that he will always accept your collect call at three A.M., whenever you have to talk to someone who understands.

Virgo represents your Eleventh House, the house of hopes, wishes, and dreams. Scorpios are traditionally secretive, but you trust Virgo with secrets. Virgo affords you new perspective on yourself because he is not as emotional as you are. Even though you are a Fixed sign, you recognize authority in the Mutable nature of Virgo. He has the ability to cool your excessive passions and encourage your intellect, which makes for a strong psychic bond.

Because of the power of his personality, Scorpio often makes enemies. Your closemouthed or suspicious nature makes some people wary of you. With a Virgo relationship you become more aware of the benefits of having friends. Virgo's karmic mission is to serve, and you are impressed by his dedication and devotion to his friends. Your Scorpio nature inclines you to be manipulative in your relationships, but Virgo makes you realize that people will be your friend just because they like you and not because they want something from you.

Many men want you as a sex object because of your magnetic Scorpio vibrations, but Virgo doesn't see you as a sex machine. You are relaxed in his presence once you realize that he gets a lot of pleasure from your company, and it doesn't stem from sex. You can be lovers with a Virgo for a brief time, but the sexual attraction between you is not satisfying. You are too passionate and emotionally intense for a Virgo man to really enjoy as a bed partner. He is too clinical in his approach to technique to fulfill your lusty desires. You want to get down and get it on, but Virgo is more interested in you as a personality than as a lover.

Virgo highlights your ambitions and presents concrete ways to achieve your goals. Despite the fact that you are both characterized as "pessimistic" signs, you gain faith in your ability to succeed because your motives are more clear under the Virgo influence of genuine friendship and moral support.

When either of you is out of harmony with the other, arguments can be very intense. Since you know each other intimately, you have the power to hurt each other badly if you get carried away with your words. Your verbal skills and mental qualities can bring you together but can also split you apart. Virgo cynicism and Scorpio sarcasm can be deadly weapons when you two get into verbal combat.

Fortunately, fallings-out between you don't last long, unless you are lovers or roommates. You won't bear a grudge against Virgo because you realize he speaks in your own best interest, even when he speaks in anger. Hold on to him, Scorpio, because a Virgo experience can be one of your most important relationships in the entire zodiac.

SCORPIO & LIBRA

If you want a relationship with another man that will change your life, you can find it with a Libra as your lover. There is an element of fascination with him that appeals to your sense of mystery and compels you to delve into the affair with typical Scorpio zeal. The influence of his Cardinal-Air nature, combined with your deep emotional needs and his intellectual desire for balance and harmony, can lead to a relationship of lasting significance.

Although you may correspond to his fantasy of ideal male sexuality, it is you who feels the stronger attraction. You can meet anywhere that provides a refined environment suitable to Libran sensibilities. You will be attracted to his intelligence and charm, as well as to his physical appearance. Beyond the obvious, you feel an inherent magnetism toward Libra, especially aspected by the sexual ambiguities of your astrological natures. You are a feminine sign with a masculine ruling planet, Pluto, while he is a masculine sign with a feminine ruling planet, Venus. You may not be sure who does what to whom, only that whatever it is, you want to do it. You will have to take the initiative and begin to learn about Libran indecision and vacillation from the beginning.

Your sexual relationship will probably involve several possible aspects of your combined sexuality. Initially, Libra will be impressed—even overwhelmed—by your masculine sex drive, but as your sex life develops, Libra is more capable of emotion and passion that will be very satisfying. You can provide him with the powerful affection he craves and the imaginative variety of sexual experience that can keep him faithful, despite his past record. In return for the sexual satisfaction you give to a Libran man, he will provide you with tender loving care. Though he will enjoy the animal intensity of Scorpio sex, you must treat him with gentle consideration to fulfill his needs in areas beyond sex.

Your aggressive loyalty to your lovers and your innate possessiveness are often obstacles in your relationships. Libra may be initially surprised by your demanding devotion, but he will respond warmly to the feeling of being protected by your powerful personality. The positive aspects of your emotional strength are highlighted by a Libra lover because he feels his own personality becoming stronger under your influence. Librans are prone to indecision or indolence without a challenge, and the task of balancing and harmonizing your aggressiveness gives him a new feeling of ambition and direction, which improves his self-image and makes him more desirable in your eyes.

Though Libras are sometimes accused of being insensitive to emotion, as your lover he will respect your need for emotional stability and privacy. Therefore, the indications are good for the domestic harmony you both require. Both of you take living together seriously, and Libra is the sign of partnership. Without a harmonious home life he can become physically ill, and you can retreat into silent brooding that will destroy what you have built together.

The world you want to share with a lover must be based on trust. Your suspicious nature can prevent you from exposing your emotional life to those around you, unless you are sure that they will not take advantage of you. The kindness and diplomacy inherent in Libra's nature will allow you to confide in him. If you are secretive, Libra will not mistrust you, but he will feel personally inadequate because he thinks he is untrustworthy. He may feel that you are being unfair or unjust if you are less than totally open with him about yourself. You need not fear exposing your ego to Libra, for he will never use his knowledge to harm you. Libra symbolically offers you the opportunity for karmic insights that can free your personality from fear and insecurity because he represents your Twelfth House— hidden meanings.

A Scorpio–Libra relationship is highly complex because you are so karmically connected. The attraction and the bonds are unusually powerful because the relationship grows in strength over time. Your life changes slowly but inexorably with a commitment to the creative development of your personalities.

SCORPIO & SCORPIO

There is a great deal to learn about the power of your own personality when you become involved with a Scorpio man. The quality of Fixed Water indicates a deep emotional attachment or an intense experience that leaves you sadder, but wiser, in terms of self-awareness.

There is an aura of compulsion about a Scorpio–Scorpio love. You may be surprised by the magnetic, almost psychic pull that you experience when you first meet him. You may feel stunned by the force with which you are drawn to each other. Your strong intuition may give you brief intimations of trouble ahead, but the attraction will be so compelling that you have no choice but to go with the experience and accept the flow of energy that is passing between you.

Don't worry about what to say to Scorpio on your initial meeting. You can communicate with each other on nonverbal levels. His eyes speak enough to let you know that there is a mutual attraction. You are probably thinking the same things: a mixture of fascination, temptation, and stimulation, combined with a physical rush. Across a crowded dance floor your eyes meet, your bodies say "Yes!" and the rest of the dancers become invisible.

One of the potential problems in an affair with another Scorpio is the tendency to lock on to each other and create an isolated world of your own. Because you can communicate so well emotionally and sexually with him, you have little desire to admit other elements into the relationship. A Scorpio couple may decide to live a very exclusive existence. You may give up previous social patterns and acquaintances because everything and everyone outside the relationship seems unimportant once your life is "completed" with the love of a Scorpio man.

The coming together of two Fixed-Water signs symbolizes the importance of having a home. You will go about establishing a nest of scorpions or an eagle's aerie, depending upon whether you reinforce each other's darker instincts or your better qualities.

Sexual intensity is the most outstanding characteristic of Scorpio love, but the ideal manifestation of your desires is not just physical gratification. The insecure Scorpio needs sexual stimulation and fulfillment because he wants emotional assurance. A more evolved Scorpio uses sex to sound the depths of emotional experience. Scorpio can leave men of other signs paddling on the surface of sexual experience, afraid of drowning, but another Scorpio will instinctively understand your search for profound meaning in sexual mystery.

Scorpio men are often stereotyped as being especially macho, particularly in the context of contemporary gay lifestyles, even though this is a "feminine" sign. With a Scorpio lover you feel free to allow your receptive and submissive dualistic nature to express itself. If jealousy comes between you and your Scorpio lover, your relationship becomes poisoned with doubt, which can lead to brooding unless you establish open lines of communication. You are basically loyal and faithful partners, but you must learn to verbalize your feelings. Often your suspicion is based upon your keen observation of details and your fertile imagination, rather than objective situations.

Remember, Scorpio, the same magic that has attracted so many other men to you also works for your Scorpio lover. You can learn to trust him as much as you trust yourself. You share an enormous fund of integrity and sincerity of purpose that should be the solid foundation of your union. Scorpios are traditionally secretive, but no one will better share your secrets than your Scorpio man. As you get to know him better, you also have the opportunity to develop self-awareness and a new clarity of purpose in fulfilling your needs as a powerful and intense personality.

If you and your Scorpio lover can focus on your highest ideals rather than your deepest fears, the relationship can bring you new understanding of the meaning of love. The mystery of the transformation of desire into devotion will keep you bound to each other and allow for the exploration of the most creative and magically sensitive aspects of the Scorpio personality.

SCORPIO & SAGITTARIUS

A love affair between you and the Centaur of Sagittarius can be an experience that blends intense attraction, material gain, and spiritual insights that can benefit your entire personality, even though it may not be a lasting relationship. Sagittarius is a natural teacher, and he will want to expose you to the breadth of his experience and the depth of his wisdom.

He will find you very attractive in a mysterious way. You fascinate Sagittarius, but he is not intimidated by the strength of your personal magnetism. He is a man of the world who understands intuition and seeks to provide you with a new ability to accept and use your personal power in more humanitarian directions. Because he is the sign immediately following yours on the Wheel of the Zodiac, Sagittarius has a karmic memory of the Scorpio experience. It makes him sympathetic to your emotions in ways that men of other signs cannot be.

You can meet him in connection with travel, educational activities, or recreation. Sagittarius will probably be the one who initiates the relationship because he finds you intriguing, and his lusty appetites are whetted by your sexual magnetism. You are more likely to be impressed by his material accomplishments and the life-style he maintains with typical Fire-sign panache. He sparks your ambition, and to some degree you seek to emulate him as the model for material success. You will be quick to see the practical advantages to be had with a Sagittarius lover, but you must be aware of your tendency to use others for your own purposes. If you look only at the material aspects of this relationship, you will discover that you haven't taken anything away from Sagittarius that he wouldn't willingly have given you.

Your sexual intensity will excite a Sagittarian man to tremendous physical expression. Sex tends to be a very serious matter for Scorpio, but the Sagittarian man brings equal powers of jovial celebration to lovemaking. Scorpio sex is an emotional experience, but Sagittarius loving is inspirational. You both get carried away but in different directions. You will respond with particular intensity to the very maleness of a Sagittarian lover. He is kind but not necessarily gentle; he is very physical in a way that stimulates enormous amounts of passion.

Sex may bring you together, but it cannot keep you together because Sagittarius cannot meet your demand for fidelity. His interests are wide-ranging in a way that will arouse your suspicion and jealousy. This man is a traveler. He requires a broad range of intellectual and social contacts to charge his Fire-sign ego. Sagittarius is a Mutable sign, and he needs constant variety to keep him happy. Because of his need for freedom and your desire for security, this relationship may not last.

Sagittarius is an open book, and he presumes that others are just as candid as he. Given the private and somewhat uncommunicative nature of Scorpio, you will find this particularly painful. More than any other sign, a Sagittarius lover can unwittingly cut you to the quick with his well-known bluntness. His apparent lack of respect for your feelings of privacy can make you even more secretive, driving a wedge between you.

However, you can draw a lesson from Sagittarius' sometimes awkward teachings: consider the real importance of these "secrets" you hold so dear. Your never-ending desire to protect your emotions can be a barrier that prevents those who want to love you from getting close enough to satisfy and understand you. For once, with Sagittarius, try to open up a little. Let him get close to you; it's possible that some of his optimism and enthusiasm for life will rub off. The material success he has attained is a function of his love of life, which he shares so willingly. A Sagittarius lover shows you what can be achieved when you direct your energies and emotional depth outward, rather than investing them in your own ego. If you dwell on your suspicions and insecurities or project them onto your Sagittarian lover, you will cast a shadow on his optimism that sends him on the road again.

If you really learn to love him for his strengths, you can become a more cheerful person. Learning to relate to others from Sagittarius, the teacher, will prevent you from being left alone once the call of the unknown has taken his enriching influence out of your life. A Sagittarius love affair can be especially beneficial to the young Scorpio, but whatever your age, the lessons of the Centaur will serve you well in becoming a more open, generous, and optimistic person. Your magnetism and power can be used for positive goals in making you a better lover in future relationships.

SCORPIO & CAPRICORN

The men of this Cardinal-Earth sign tend to be cautious, conservative, and dedicated to long-range goals. A Capricorn will probably be more attracted to you than you are to him, but he will take his time in a step-by-step approach to gaining your confidence and eliciting your interest. Over a period of time you will find that there are many things you can learn from and share with him in a relationship as a friend or lover.

Capricorn aspects your Third House, the house of communications. You will find it easy to talk with him about serious subjects because he likes knowledge and wisdom learned from sober and thoughtful study. Your interest in solving the mysteries of life will find a sympathetic listener in a Capricorn friend. At the same time, he always looks on the practical side of things and he won't pry into your secrets or personal life. You will feel relaxed in his company, and it should be an easy and natural path from intellectual interest to sexual communication.

Capricorns are dedicated to material success and often repress their sexuality in the interest of advancing their careers. Once he has attained security in life, he is able to accept his sexuality for the real importance it has in his personal happiness. He will feel relieved—even elated—to meet a Scorpio like you who is obviously serious about sex. The intensity of your desire for sexual expression and fulfillment adds an emotional dimension to love that practical Capricorn has denied himself. If he is ready for the joys of sex, he can be a most satisfying lover even though he doesn't project the same sexual fervor that you do. Since Capricorn is an Earth sign, he has a highly physical approach to sex and a characteristic earthiness that excites you in lovemaking. Though reserved and even severe in his social behavior, a Capricorn lover can become a different man in bed, especially under the influence of your passionate nature.

Just as you bring your special talents for sexual expression and depth of feeling to the relationship, Capricorn can provide Earthy good humor as an antidote to your oversensitivity and pessimistic attitude about life. You will respect his humor because it is witty rather than foolish, coarse, or sarcastic.

Your creative imagination and single-mindedness—combined with Capricorn's practical approach, executive skills, and ambition—can lead to a successful business association as well as a solid personal relationship. As a couple you are not flamboyant or ostentatious in terms of affection, but you admire each other, and others also admire the stability you have achieved. You may be somewhat closeted, as you are both very conscious of your public image as men of substantial responsibility.

In some manner, family responsibilities will affect a Scorpio–Capricorn liaison. Both of you are very conscious of the obligations you have to your families and to close friends who fulfill familial roles. A love affair with a Capricorn will involve unavoidable responsibilities that give a serious tone to the entire undertaking. If you have been living a life of adventure and diversity, it may surprise you that this kind of relationship can have so much appeal.

The positive values of a Capricorn love are indicated by the fact that you are a Fixed sign. You need roots that Capricorn can provide in typical Earth-sign fashion. He needs emotional nourishment from a serious person that you can give in abundance, thanks to your Water-sign abilities. The jealousies and suspicions that have tainted your affairs in the past need not surface to cause confusion and mistrust between you and a Capricorn lover.

Questions of power will have to be settled early on if you want to avoid confrontations. He will want to be the leader, to set the material tone, but your Scorpio nature inclines you to be resentful of those who encroach upon your will. Over time, you will discover that he has your mutual interests at heart and that his goal is to benefit you as a couple. Success and stability should make for a lasting association, but the very solidity of it all may be its ultimate downfall.

Boredom is the worm in this apple. You probably initiated this affair and encouraged its exclusivity, but it is Capricorn who can keep it from becoming dull and stale.

Achievement as individuals, sexual satisfaction, and intellectual companionship can characterize this union between loving men. If you can maintain a sense of continuing accomplishment, the depth of Scorpio can experience the heights of success that Capricorn shares with you. Above all, you are friends, and the spirit of trusting friendship will always keep you close to him even if a lasting love does not develop.

SCORPIO & AQUARIUS

You may long remember your meeting with an Aquarian. These Fixed Air-sign men touch your life in ways that compel your attention, but seldom your devotion. There are indications of excitement and tension because of the eccentricities he displays so publicly and you keep hidden.

You will probably meet an Aquarian in some unusual or unexpected manner. You may have similar backgrounds and might be introduced through family, but normally you are not drawn to each other in the course of events. The course of your relationship will rarely run smoothly, but the experience can have positive results if you don't place too much importance on developing an emotional relationship with an Aquarius man. You are likely to achieve intellectual compatibility, rather than the romantic variety, with an Aquarius. You are both interested in the kind of knowledge that goes beyond everyday experience; you both like to delve into the powers of the human mind and the world of symbolic meaning—even, perhaps, parapsychology.

But you won't have to go to your tarot deck to know that there is an exciting sexual dimension to an Aquarian man. Like almost everything else about him, Aquarius' sex habits are eccentric and exuberant. He enjoys experimentation for its own sake and brings his eclectic spirit of investigation into bed. Your own desire for transcendent sex will be stimulated by Aquarian lovemaking. What you must realize is that sex is a physical, rather than an emotional, experience for an Aquarian. You are matched in your intensity as sexual beings, but the activity has little emotional involvement for Aquarius. He enjoys the thrill and the skill, but it is only a game to him.

Good sex may not mean a satisfactory love between you and Aquarius. The kind of exclusive coupling you require and demand will not be forthcoming with him as your partner. Aquarius loves his friends, and you will lose him if you force him to choose between you and them. His free-ranging and freewheeling social life will make you envious of the time and devotion he spends on others, not to mention your suspicion that he has slept with every member of his softball team. Your suspicion may not be correct, but there is very little chance that you can change him, since he is immune to your power and oblivious to your deep needs for emotional security, social responsibility, and exclusive devotion in a love affair.

Because you are both Fixed Signs, it will be difficult for you to appreciate his virtues. Your Scorpio instincts for privacy, precision, and practicality are offended by the way he seems to be driven to outrageous behavior that can anger and embarrass you, especially in public. You prefer to confine your eccentricities to the seclusion of your home, but Aquarius is an uninhibited personality—a real character. Fixed signs always see their faults or fixations as virtues, and Aquarius will attempt to turn your orderly existence upside down in his misguided efforts to free you from what he sees as your repressed personality. He doesn't realize that in undermining your security and assaulting your carefully cultivated public image, he is threatening the very essence of your emotional stability.

Aquarius makes you feel vulnerable because you have no way of exercising your will over him. Your attempts to force him to conform to your concept of normality and respectability may only encourage him to greater excesses. Confrontations will be stormy and difficult to resolve because you are both so stiff-necked and because Fixed signs find it almost impossible to apologize for being themselves.

Aquarius aspects your Fourth House—home and family. Problems may arise from your living situation or due to family responsibilities you have that Aquarius does not properly respect. If you are at all closeted, an Aquarian is the last man on Earth you would bring home to meet your family. You can't trust him because you have no way of knowing how far he might go in exercising his right to be "weird."

You can bring out the best potential for a successful Aquarius association in business matters. With practical objectives to focus your energies, Scorpio and Aquarius can find harmony through the attainment of financial security. He is very good at making the necessary contacts, and you are able to provide important skills in operating the monetary and investment aspects of business. But a get-rich-quick scheme with an Aquarius partner will never work because there is no time to allow a margin for obstacles or the unexpected events that seem to settle around him like a cloud of chaos. Don't be deceived by his eccentric image where business is concerned. Aquarius has the talent to make you rich in ways that might never occur to you.

SCORPIO & PISCES

A Pisces love affair has the potential to become the one great, fulfilling romantic love of your life. There are many benefits to be derived, but there are also important responsibilities that bring all your best talents to bear. Because you are both Water signs, Mutable Pisces presents an opportunity for emotional understanding and reciprocal feelings better than any other sign.

You share many mutual interests with Pisces and can meet him in any recreational situation. Unlike so many casual encounters, this stranger in the night may well become the permanent focus for the love and affection you are ultimately seeking. The spirit of romance permeates a Scorpio–Pisces relationship because Pisces represents your Fifth House—love, romance, and creativity. You will take the initiative, and you determine the ultimate success of this relationship by the amount of positive energy you invest.

The totality you feel in a Pisces coupling will be expressed in sexual compatibility and creativity. You will experience an ardent emotional response with a Pisces man that will give new meaning to your sexual desires. The emotional feedback you receive from him will give you a sense of security and trust that will allay much of the fear and self-doubt that have plagued you in the past.

Your sexuality is tied to your need for confirmation. In other situations, you use your sexual magnetism as a tool or weapon to increase your power and gratify the demands of your ego. These habits of self-defense and power manipulation are not at issue with a Pisces because you intuit the depths of his love and his willingness to surrender to you. Paradoxically, his ability to surrender poses a much greater challenge to you, because you must summon up all the lessons you have learned about yourself and apply them in a positive, trusting manner. Though the stars indicate real love, the success of a Scorpio–Pisces relationship depends upon your maturity. You have all of the power to make this either a creative or destructive combination, Scorpio, depending upon whether you are ready to accept the karmic tasks of completion and surrender.

The deep emotional reverberations present in a Scorpio–Pisces relationship need to be directed toward further knowledge and creativity. You share deep emotional feelings and intuitions that permit intensely personal communication. Misunderstandings that commonly harm your efforts at developing personal relationship need not intrude here. Pisces' sympathy and perception give him insight into your most deep-seated needs and secrets. Rather than feeling vulnerable because he understands you so well, you should realize that Pisces can relieve you of the fear and insecurity that can block your creativity.

If you let your past disappointments cloud your vision and fail to appreciate the positive potential of this liaison, there is a possibility that sadomasochistic elements can emerge to ruin the deathless love that can be yours with a Pisces man. You will be tempted to use him and abuse him because he is willing to trust emotions to you. But remember, he can swim deeper than you ever can into the recesses of his Piscean dream. This potential danger may cause both of you to become lost in a fantasy world of alcohol, drugs, or self-destructive sex.

Your practical nature is the key to preventing the waste of this gift of love and trust. Few men will be so compatible with your innermost needs, and it's up to you to decide what direction you want to take. Accepting the trust of a Pisces lover can humanize all your relationships. People will respond to you in a more positive manner, and you can achieve your goals without undue exercise of power or manipulation.

Interest and knowledge of the occult can come into play with a Pisces lover. It would not be unusual for you to have memories of previous lives shared with your Pisces lover. Time can be stretched in this relationship to allow for long separations without diminishing the affection between you.

This relationship is not your one chance for happiness in life, but it does represent a special opportunity for fulfillment. If you integrate your positive experiences instead of brooding on past hurts, then you can reap the benefits of accepting the love of a Pisces man.

LOVING YOUR SCORPIO MAN

If the promise of intense emotional involvement and passionate sex turns you on, then a Scorpio man may be just what you are looking for but more than you bargained for, across the board. A Scorpio affair is always unforgettable in one way or another because he never does anything halfway or frivolously. He works hard and plays hard. Everything Scorpio does is characterized by intensity.

You can pick the Scorpio men out of a crowd by the powerful gaze in their eyes and their aura of smoldering sexuality. They project a totally masculine image, but it is more profound than the boyish butch of Aries or the arrogant appearance of Leo. Look for him wherever money or power are integral to the activity. In business he gravitates to finance or positions of authority and control. Though he projects a conservative image in the world of business, when he is out with the boys, Scorpio calls attention to himself with heavy jewelry or leather accessories—anything that signifies both luxury and eroticism.

Scorpio takes his image seriously and works hard to create the effect he desires. Be sure to compliment him on the way he wears his clothing, whether it's supertight jeans or a finely tailored three-piece suit. Scorpio wants attention and admiration, so don't be reticent with flattery. Even if he knows you are not one hundred percent sincere, he appreciates being told how impressive he is.

Getting to know a Scorpio is difficult because he is a very private person, but getting his attention will not be hard. Meet his gaze and let him hold you in its grip. If he looks away, you can be sure it is not because you have stared him down, but because you do not interest him. Go no further. Scorpio knows what he likes and knows what he wants. He will ruthlessly ignore any man who does not spark the proper response. If you come on heavy to him anyway, in the hope of changing his mind, you are looking for trouble. Never play around with a Scorpio who says no, or he will appear to change his mind only to teach you a lesson. At best, he will toy with your attentions and leave you horny and expectant as soon as he spots what he really wants. At worst he will allow you to think you are seducing him and then subject you to the full force of his passion in a cruel or inconsiderate fashion.

If you do meet a Scorpio's gaze and he holds you in it, you may feel that you have been hypnotized. His approach is verbally passive, but his magnetic power is enough to summon those he has chosen. He likes his men the way he likes himself: studied, conservative, and masculine in appearance. If you come on campy or dizzy, you have almost no chance with a Scorpio. Though he can be democratic in his choice of sexual partners, he is demanding about the people with whom he socializes.

Public eccentricity or flamboyance turns him off, but his character is marked by private and personal eccentricities that surface in his sex life. Public or private, he has fixed ideas about what he wants and cannot be swayed or deterred from getting his way. If you try to thwart Scorpio's demands or desires, you had better be ready to defend yourself. He is slow to anger, but quick to use the threat of anger as a manipulative device. You have to find some way of agreeing with him if you want to get along with him. Praise always works much better than criticism with a Scorpio. He really wants to be liked, but he does not often differentiate between affection and respect.

Devotion and affection are the real keys to his personality. He requires large, constant, and demonstrative amounts to warm his heart and allay his secret fears. Scorpios are men of many secrets and are excellent confidants, but they will use their knowledge against you if you fall out of favor. If you want a Scorpio lover, you will have to be absolutely devoted to him or it won't work for very long. His worst trait is his jealousy and suspicion. Scorpios are the detectives of the zodiac, and there is almost no way you can keep any indiscretions from him in an affair.

If he is attracted to you, Scorpio will want to establish an exclusive relationship quickly. Don't accept unless you are willing to submit to his enormous willpower and his tremendous need for unquestioning affection. If you think that the added attraction of passionately consuming sex is worth the difficulties, you may find excitement. Contentment will be very hard to achieve unless you devote as much of yourself to maintaining the relationship as he does—and then some.

A Scorpio man is a homebody, especially when he has a lover. Social events or an evening on the town are fraught with the potential for disaster, even though he can be a fun-loving social companion. The problem comes from the fact that there are other people involved, and Scorpio sees everyone else as potential threats to the sanctity of his love relationship. If you enjoy yourself too much, he will accuse you of flirting or allowing yourself to be the object of someone's flirtation. The best activities to share are those you can do alone together. Quiet evenings at home are better than parties or bars. Vacations at busy resorts can be absolute disasters, but a solitary cottage by the shore will refresh his spirits and relax his relentless emotional energy for a while. Swimming and sailing give him great pleasure, as well.

There is a great deal of need in a Scorpio lover that will challenge your capacity to love. It is not easy, but it can be very rewarding if you want a man who will be totally devoted to you. It will mean surrendering some of your freedom and accepting the fact that love can be all-consuming in its intensity. If you want passion but not peace, then a Scorpio man may be the love you want.

SAGITTARIUS
November 21–
December 20

↗

Symbol: The Centaur, or the Archer
Ruling Planet: Jupiter
Color: Deep blue
Metal: Tin
Natural House Rulership: Ninth House, the house of
    education, long journeys, and wide associations
Ninth House Traits: Love of freedom and trust in
    luck
Motto: "I see"
Nature: Mutable sign (adaptable)
Element: Fire sign (spiritual)
Qualities: Honest, impulsive, and optimistic
Capacities: Exploration and perspective
Personality Key Words: Jovial, prophetic, and
    versatile

MAXIMIZING YOUR SAGITTARIUS POTENTIAL

You are the wanderer of the zodiac, symbolized by the mythical Centaur's restless search for experience. The Mutable Fire-sign qualities of Sagittarius make you devoted to the pursuit of wisdom in all its forms, through direct knowledge of everything the world has to offer. You pride yourself on your ability to move from one area of interest to another, to be the scholar, the teacher, and the traveler. The expansive power of Jupiter endows you with good fortune, intuition, and the desire to find the meaning of life by living it with gusto. You are a powerful personality, but you are often unable to focus that power into any one single activity or relationship. You sense that you were born to do great things, but you feel driven to roam the wide world in search of the keys to that greatness.

Your basic goals in life center on your need for the freedom to seek your destiny, wherever it may lead you. You feel inspired to think great thoughts and do great deeds, and your inspiration takes precedence over the comforts of home, family, money, or love. You distance yourself from emotional involvements because without distance there is no chance for attaining the perspective that is the object of your quest. Your need to roam is symbolized by the powerful body of the Centaur, which combines both animal and human desires. The human half of the Centaur is the Archer, who sends his flaming arrows of inspiration into the air and then follows their trail. Even though your goals are elusive, your dedication to the spirit of the pursuit imbues your personality with an all-powerful optimism that is your most winning trait.

The search for love is as important to the Sagittarius personality as the search for wisdom. Love is a social experience for you. You enjoy the company of men, and it is natural and easy to meet someone. You expect love to make you feel good, to be an expression of the good opinion you have of others, and, above all, to be fun. Emotionally complex affairs are boring and leave you eager to hit the road again. Freedom is an essential component of your ability to love. You are a physically demanding lover, but rarely jealous. The Sagittarian concept of love is romantic but active and searching, rather than passive. Though you are social, gregarious, and at your best in the company of lots of people, you have the secret loneliness of the vagabond in your heart. You need love to make your life complete, but it must let you feel free in order to make you feel happy.

Though your quest for wisdom may take you from one field of endeavor to another, you are not shallow. When you study, you study intensely. When you travel, you travel widely. You see life as one long journey, heading toward an ultimate knowledge that can only come through the continuous expansion of the self. You are hungry for experience, and your desire makes you a free and open personality that others find very attractive.

Your weaknesses come from the same source as your strengths. Your ability to cover so much ground means that you find it hard to settle into one job, one place, or one relationship. Since you are always on the move, you may never see the concrete results of your efforts and may therefore remain unsatisfied. The intuitive powers of Sagittarius tell you that there is always more—more to know, more to see, more to do, and more to feel. You often expend much more energy than is necessary without realizing the effect of your own strength. In speech it makes you blunt, candid, and verbally wounding to those who don't understand that you are exceptionally kind but not particularly gentle. Physically, it makes you a little clumsy, and sexually it makes you rather rough-and-tumble without meaning to be anything more than exuberant and playful.

Because you have so few ties to family or home, your social life is very important. Your broad-minded sense of humor, informal style, and fund of energy bring good times, good fun, and good companions. You have no regular hang-out, preferring to make the rounds. You can go from the chic cocktail lounge to the sleaziest bar because you are not status-conscious and move in all social circles with ease. People sense that you are an original and value knowing you because you are a self-made personality. Your travels or studies have often freed you from your origins, making you a citizen of the world.

Your sex life is as democratic and freewheeling as your social life. The same feeling of informality and congeniality characterizes your pursuit of pleasure. Sagittarians please their partners because they are an interesting conglomeration of all the men they have ever been with. You enjoy the game of pursuit and conquest, but you play it openly. Your broad sense of humor and blunt approach make you very up-front about who and what you like when it comes to sex.

Your ideal love relationship is long-term but completely open-ended. You are faithful according to the situation but not on principle. You really believe that if you can't be with the one you love, you should love the one you're with! The Sagittarian love instinct is not likely to be permanently bound to any one personality, place, or relationship. Your restless ego is the main thread that connects all the events and people in your life. You need many experiences to support your ego, and any lover must acknowledge the fact that he cannot be the totality of your existence. You want him to be faithful to you, rather than to the ideal of a relationship. You can be emotionally faithful and truly devoted to the welfare of your love, but you can't always be physically faithful. You are devoted only to experience on all levels, and occasional infidelities do not compromise your idea of commitment in a relationship.

You provide your lovers with a life filled with inspiration and events. You are a natural cure for boredom, and it is the gift your lovers often appreciate most. You can give off so much buoyancy and enthusiasm that your lovers are overwhelmed with the realization that they can't keep you all to themselves without losing the essence of your adventurous and independent spirit. They may look upon you as a real heel or see you as a true hero, depending upon whether or not they can accept the kind of love you have to give. Your ideal love is a man with a strong, independent personality, who is able to give and receive love in the same open and honest fashion as you do.

The key to maximizing your potential as a loving man lies in your ability to enjoy life to the fullest. Never doubt your basic capacities, even if the results don't quite live up to your expectations. You can be most successful if you work on short-term projects rather than enmesh yourself in routine that stifles your jaunty and expansive personality. Deal with life as a series of fascinating events and you will be on the way to being a real success on your own terms.

SAGITTARIUS & ARIES

Falling in love with an aggressive, enthusiastic, eager Aries man is not difficult for a Sagittarian. Arians are your Fire-sign buddies. Since he has a Cardinal nature, he will take the lead, but he will also look up to you as a man of the world. You can have a lot of fun together and a very exciting sexual relationship without the domestic obligations that cramp your style.

Aries aspects your Fifth House, the house of romance. You should find him attractive and easy to approach. You will be drawn to his physical presence because he exudes masculine charm and energy.

You can meet him in almost any situation, though your mutual interest in sports and fitness gives you plenty of opportunities to find an Aries friend in the fresh air and sunshine rather than the smoky darkness of the social scene. The aspects between your ruling Jupiter and his ruling Mars indicate a spontaneous attraction that can lead to the type of male bonding relationship that is very close to your ideal. There will be little delay between your initial meeting and your first sexual experience with an Aries man. He is always ready, and you are always interested.

There is a great deal of sexual energy between you and every indication that it will be athletic, boisterous, and enthusiastic. You both think of sex as fun, and though there may be some question of who does what to whom and how, you will both agree that it should be often and with a spirit of playfulness. Your Aries may be surprised at how well you can match the intense physical power that he brings to lovemaking. It should be rough-and-tumble in bed, but you also add a note of cultivated passion that focuses his more animal instincts. The two of you can spend all night and half the day making love, amazing and delighting each other with your capacities for desire.

Desire, rather than devotion, is the key word in this relationship. You can become close friends and constant companions, but good sex stimulates you to personal rather than sexual loyalty. Neither of you is content for very long with just one partner, but you are also forgiving when it comes to sexual infidelity. The spirit of adventure dominates your personalities, and you encourage each other to be optimistic and forthright but also to be a bit reckless in your sexual and social lives. If you try to settle into a relationship based on domestic harmony, you can stifle the best aspects of having an Aries lover.

A Sagittarius–Aries love affair can become one of the best ''open'' relationships available to either of you. There is a basic sympathy and compatibility that accommodates your need to travel or to seek your own company without arousing jealousy or possessiveness in Aries. You can have a lot of fun together as traveling companions, because Aries is known for his pioneering spirit and looks for unusual destinations that are more exciting than the run-of-the-mill vacation spots.

Your Sagittarian nature disposes you to be kindly and tolerant of the brash and careless behavior of the typical Aries. You can encourage him to emulate you in seeking more elevated and humanitarian goals, but you can also stimulate him to take on much more than he can handle. Overextension of energy and funds will put a strain on Aries that you may not always realize, because you can count on greater resources within your own personality.

Both Sagittarius and Aries are self-oriented personalities, but there is a potential for creative selflessness when you combine forces. This relationship will work if you try to understand what you have to give each other and what you need to find in other people. As socially active as you may be, you also need periods on your own to study and engage in activities that reflect your philosophical and humanitarian instincts. You can help Aries develop his generosity of spirit into something that goes beyond his ego. You can hurt Aries by being insensitive to his needs for ego gratification, but he forgives as easily as he bruises. You share a sense of humor that can always bring you back together again.

Combined with your mutual capacities for enjoying life, there is the potential for growth in this relationship that can make it a lasting friendship that never loses its sexual dimension. You and Aries may come and go without chafing under the ties that bind you together as loving men.

SAGITTARIUS & TAURUS

A Sagittarius–Taurus love affair can develop into a relationship that blends your Fire-sign need for freedom with his Earth-sign need for stability. You can enrich one another's lives with new dimensions of Sagittarian inspiration and Taurean practicality, but it is you who must be the adaptive partner. Taurus is a Fixed sign, and he knows what he wants. If you are willing to accept his demands for a measure of domesticity, he will be able to provide you with a sense of belonging that accommodates your need to travel and indulge in a comfortable and casual way of life.

You can meet a Taurus man through educational or business contacts, but you will have to take the initiative. His solid build will catch your eye, and in conversation you will be impressed by his commonsense approach and his Earthy humor. Taureans are sexually responsive to your Sagittarian charms, and you'll be attracted to him because it seems to you that he could use a bit more vibrancy in his life. You enjoy the game of pursuit and conquest, but you should be aware of the profound effect you can have on the placid lifestyle that Taurus prefers.

Because Taurus aspects your Sixth House—service—you want to be of help to him in some way, probably by energizing his life, getting him out of his rut, and giving him a broader vision of the joys of adventure. Use your expansive personality to create an atmosphere for growth, rather than goading Taurus into a more active approach to life. One of the ways in which you can encourage him to be more responsive to you is through the passionate quality of your lovemaking.

Taureans are very male and very strong but also quite receptive, sensuous lovers. He doesn't like rough stuff, though he will certainly be aroused by your active male sexuality. You can learn to become more gentle and more subtle through the Taurean sexual experience. Get into the pleasures of giving massages, concentrating on the neck and shoulder muscles, and your Taurean will respond with new degrees of passion that will increase your enjoyment and mutual pleasure.

If you want to further extend your mutual interest in each other and maintain your physical attraction, you can do Taurus, and yourself, a favor by getting him involved in some kind of sports or fitness activity, especially if you indulge in midnight raids on the refrigerator after making love.

A domestic arrangement of jogging every morning, dinner every evening, and sex every night will suit Taurus perfectly. So much so that he will not understand your wanderlust for foreign climes or other companions. His possessive nature is at odds with your need to roam, but if you are honest and willing to satisfy his basic need for stability, your Taurus lover will allow you enough freedom to pursue outside interests. A Taurus love affair will slow you down, but it need not put a complete damper on your natural Sagittarian style. You need to travel, and he can be an amiable partner on the road as long as there is enough comfort and culinary compensation to keep him content. Driving cross-country and living on fast food is his idea of hell on wheels.

Taureans are worriers, and the more reassurance you give him, the better he will try to understand your needs. If he is confused, he will become insecure and mistrustful of your motives because he feels his material world being threatened. At that point you may learn a great deal about the latent emotional fury of the Bull. You can be frank and candid with him and he will value your honesty, but your blunt habit of speech is bound to hurt him. Whether or not this relationship can survive and prosper depends upon your ability to understand his needs. You can always get back into his good graces with little presents that appeal to his Taurean materialism, but you must understand that extravagant gifts will offend his sense of practicality. A Taurus wants gifts that last—especially the gift of love.

The love you have to give a Taurus may not be practical,

but it can be inspirational; it can provide you with a new understanding of the benefits gained by assuming mature responsibilities in a relationship with another man. The love he has to give you can help aim your energies in directions that expand your capacity for understanding others. If you can learn the positive value of compromise, you can share a love that may not be freewheeling, but one that allows you enough freedom to grow within a loving relationship.

SAGITTARIUS & GEMINI

A love affair with a Gemini man will involve aspects of natural attraction through opposition. Because he represents your Seventh House—partners—you are drawn to him but in the manner in which opposites attract. The combination of your Jupiter with his ruling Mercury indicates expansive communication, but with a spirit of competition and a certain amount of confusion because you are both dual signs.

You can be struck by a Gemini man in any social situation because you are both gregarious and you both have a wide circle of acquaintances of a more or less intimate nature. Your initial attraction will not be completely physical, though his youthful appearance and magnetism will accentuate your interest in his lively conversation. Words will be an important element in any Sagittarius–Gemini duo. The nature of your communication with a Gemini partner will determine the way in which you accommodate the differences and the similarities in your personalities.

Gemini men can fill you with feelings of desire that are unlike any you have ever known, because they go beyond the physical or even emotional dimensions of your sexual experiences. You crave his energy. The dual Sagittarian nature makes you an inspired personality on the outside but

more weighty, thoughtful, and even brooding than anyone—
except Gemini—would imagine. With his quick mind, he
arouses you in the way he can articulate ideas about which
you have had only momentary insight.

The versatility and flexibility of the Gemini Twins, plus
the inspirational and physical characteristics of the Sagittarian Centaur, add up to a continuous three-way romp. At
least one of the Twins will respond to the Centaur as a
fantasy figure, and the other Twin will keep you guessing.
This element of fantasy in lovemaking fulfills your needs
and challenges your imagination. You and Gemini can resolve your inevitable conflicts and communicate your devotion through making love.

There is a lot of fun and stimulation for you in a Gemini
love affair, but be careful: Together you will entertain your
many friends with your stories, and your life with a Gemini
man will be an open book. You are surrounded by talk, even
gossip, from your circle of friends, who often will be jealous. You both will hear the worst about the other. Jupiter
with Mercury and Mercury's friends means too much idle
talk, so you and your Gemini must listen carefully and weigh
every word you hear before you react.

The issue between you will ultimately be the difference
between ideals and ideas. You want to know what things
mean; Gemini quickly wants to study what they are. You
can find yourselves at odds as partners because you will
often take Gemini too seriously, inferring meaning and
commitment from casual remarks.

You compete with each other over who is the predominant
personality—socially, sexually, and intellectually. You are a
socially active and physically attractive couple, and you each
can become jealous of the other's power to attract. You
compete for the attention or intellectual loyalty of your
friends and acquaintances. At first you may find this exciting, but eventually its very pettiness will force you to question the whole relationship. Even though you are drawn to
Gemini, the stressful aspects involved may never allow you
to be happy.

You may find it an exasperating experience, but a Gemini partner or lover can join with you to create big ideas and big plans that go beyond big talk. Together you can be extremely successful, because you have so many contacts and combined skills. Your thoughtfulness will add weight to his free-ranging intelligence. Gemini becomes less superficial, and your concepts become activated in ways that can earn money.

This is a complex relationship that can hold much excitement but will not be easy. You have the opportunity to gain knowledge from each other, but the path is strewn with confusing verbiage. You can make your ideas effective with a Gemini lover, but if the relationship is to succeed, you two will have to create your own language, which communicates the love and affection you have for each other as loving men.

SAGITTARIUS & CANCER

If you meet a Cancer while you are on the road away from home, this Cardinal-sign man will take the initiative and want you to stay. You will be fascinated by his many temptations, but ultimately you may find that you must continue your long journey alone. Your need for freedom and your questing nature can prevent you from accepting the emotional needs of Cancer in his desire to keep you happy and keep you home.

You may both be scholars, and the classical qualities of your attraction will be part of the intrigue and mystery that so draws you to Cancer men. The expansive emotions that surround your relationship may cause you to wonder, even to brood, over the nature of your attraction. He will woo you with good food, good sex, and the opportunity to make money. Because he aspects your Sixth House—service and health—he will want to provide for you and take care of you. You may accept his heartfelt hospitality without realizing the degree of emotional commitment that is involved in a love affair with a Cancer man.

You will find that his efforts to please you arouse a sexual response and spark your imagination. His obvious affection will flatter you and increase your desire to reciprocate. Sex may be your favorite activity with a Cancer lover. His erotic imagination and need for sexual variety are stimulated and satisfied. You will find new levels of satisfaction as well, because Cancer increases your appreciation of the emotional dimension in lovemaking. Your tendency to be hot and heavy is moderated by the warm and affectionate responses of a Cancer lover.

The attentions and affections of your Cancer man can turn into a clinging possessiveness in response to your desire for experiences outside of the relationship. Cancer is not above an occasional indiscretion, but he will be very secretive— even deceptive—about his flings. Your legendary candor will bring out his feelings of inadequacy and exaggerate his reaction to your wanderings. Cancer may try to reach your heart through your stomach, tempting you with the pleasures of the table if he can't keep you with the pleasures of the bed. Food is a source of solace to Cancers. If you can't keep him happy, he'll start keeping company with the refrigerator until he becomes as unattractive as he feels. You should try to keep him active. Exercise is a way of getting him to be more extroverted, and it is also an activity that you enjoy and can share with him.

The compatibility that may be lacking in a love relationship can work to your mutual advantage as partners in money-making activities. With Cancer you can learn the subtleties of the formula for success, and you can give Cancer expansive support and encouragement to actualize his creative ideas.

By encouraging Cancer to become active in projects that are outside the scope of his emotional obsession, you can help him to moderate his typically Cancerian mood shifts, governed by the inconstant Moon. Under your guidance, he can learn to take a broader view of his experiences and possibilities. Cancer secretly longs for the freedom that you take as a given in your life. He presumes that he can only be happy in a home that is modeled on the home of his family. You realize that there are many options to the domestic scene. Your own need for a sense of belonging to combat your inner feeling of loneliness can make you somewhat sensitive to Cancer's own desires, but you have no sentimental attachment to the familial home life that Cancer imagines. It is up to you to suggest imaginative alternatives that encompass his need for security and your desire for freedom. If he has come to trust you, his desire to serve and please you will motivate him to overcome his fears.

If you, as a couple, are able to realize your potential for earning large amounts of money, you might be able to have homes in several places or travel extensively together. Cancer longs to see the world through your Sagittarian vision, but he is only capable of enjoying your perspective when he feels secure in practical terms.

You may not always remain lovers, but there is still the potential for friendship with your attraction to him. But unless you are ready to settle down, you may not find the answer to your quest with a Cancer man as your lover.

SAGITTARIUS & LEO

You are the lucky sign of the zodiac, Sagittarius, and Leo believes in luck. A love affair with a Leo man holds promise for great gains in emotional and practical matters if your two fiery temperaments can be harnessed for your common good. Leo has the qualities of Fixed Fire and he is the embodiment of the warmth and intensity of the Sun. In combination with your ruling Jupiter, Leo becomes aware of his power and you find great inspiration in his company. Questions of ego are involved, but a respect for the individual gifts you bring to this relationship can keep you both excited and creative.

In your first contact with Leo, he'll attract your attention because he has seen you first and he wants you. These golden boys of the zodiac are not shy when it comes to shining for the benefit of the objects of their desire. Since you represent his Fifth House—love and romance—Leo is naturally attracted to you in a completely unaffected way that touches a responsive chord in your heart. His very eagerness is totally charming and easy to fall in love with. You will feel flattered by his obvious desire to make your acquaintance, and you may well be interested in something more enduring than a brief affair.

You will want to spend many nights together with Leo because the sex between Fire-sign men is bound to keep you coming back for more. The passion and pleasure that comes together in a Sagittarius–Leo love will involve some aspects of competition. You are both active male signs, and Leo is seldom eager to accept the passive role in your exuberant lovemaking. Over time, the Leonine devotion to pleasure, combined with a growing trust for your regard, will allow him to open up to the joys of variety in sex that you have to offer. The potential for more and more satisfying sex with Leo keeps you interested. You admire Leo, but you are especially attracted to the potential you see in him, which can develop under your influence.

This relationship can be successful on many levels because Leo has natural gifts and a strength of character that your far-ranging intelligence can help focus. This is your key to helping Leo out of his egocentricity; with your wide-angle viewpoint you can unlock the Lion's jaw-tight doors and help him see a larger, more humanistic view of the world and his place in it. This can give a firmer, more substantial underpinning to any goals you decide on together. But remember, for Leo to share your vision he must believe that your affection and optimism are also dependent upon his love.

You and your Leo lover can bring out the best in each other. The dignity and self-composure that is so attractive in a Leo man can be accentuated and extended with the vision of your Sagittarian nature. But your frank and unconventional sense of humor can wound his pride and make him awkwardly self-conscious and insecure. If this happens, he can become lazy, sulky, and careless in his personal appearance and manners. The secret to keeping Leo's pride intact is systematic flattery. You can guide him with praise by encouraging his best efforts and letting your natural tolerance for his foibles take precedence over pettiness.

A common goal or project is essential for a Sagittarius–Leo love to survive and prosper. Without it, your enthusiasm and energy can turn into impractical illusions and worthless ego gratification. This, in turn, can introduce personal rivalries and jealousies that sensitive Leo will find intolerable. You are most likely to understand the importance of a long-term dimension in this relationship. It is up to you to use your karmic maturity to assist Leo along the path to a future of accomplishment, aided by the luck of Jupiter but founded on the real talents that you two possess and share. He has ingenuity and you have dedication and discipline. He has talent and you have wisdom. He has tact and you have candor. The combination of your strengths can make a relationship that allows your love to grow as you both grow together.

SAGITTARIUS & VIRGO

A relationship with a man born under the Mutable-Earth sign of Virgo will change your life, give direction to your many talents, and allow for the ultimately successful application of the expansive energy you feel from the influence of Jupiter. In combination with his ruling Mercury, you will employ your talent in writing and communications within a community of interest that gives you a solid home base and a sense of belonging, but need not restrict your ability to explore all of your options.

You can meet Virgo through your intellectual interests, and you will be attracted to his critical powers and mercurial wit. There is something particularly "neat" about Virgo's appearance and intellect that contrasts to your sometimes careless or casual approach to life. The initial attraction may not be sexual, except that your nature is to want sexual communication with those men whose qualities you admire or come to appreciate.

Virgo men are often masters of technique, and his deft touch will appeal to you. A Virgo lover can refine your animal enthusiasm and spark your idealistic feelings about the power of sex to transcend the differences between loving men. Virgo will respond to your humor as long as it is not too coarse, and you can give him a new appreciation of pleasure in his life. This will not be a wild and crazy affair, but it can be satisfying for both of you.

While you may not be totally content with the physical aspects of this arrangement, you can both come to understand the primary benefits that make it worth maintaining. Virgo is discriminating enough to judge the relative importance of your many adventures, if you have assured him of a secure commitment to your common goals. He will not be jealous, but he can resent your freedom if it threatens the material benefits you gain through your association. Listen to Virgo. He has your mutual interests uppermost in his mind. You have the enthusiasm that can inspire others, but success often depends upon the attention to detail that is Virgo's forte.

The choice to combine with Virgo is a test of your own maturity. Like the Jupiter of myth and archetype, you scatter your seed too widely, sometimes even destructively.

Virgo can help you understand your power and its effects. Virgo's influence encourages you to assume the responsibility for worthwhile action that is part of your Sagittarian inheritance. Though there may not be the passion you often crave, there is a purpose that satisfies your needs and fulfills your sense of destiny. You can assume control with Virgo's assistance, rather than being a victim of your impulse to roam. When you work together, there is such a feeling of compatibility that you two are unbeatable. When you work at cross-purposes, you affect the larger community because of your influence as important models for success.

Virgo will appreciate your enthusiasm, inventiveness, and intuition because they are qualities that he lacks, and he sees their practical value. The ego confirmation you receive from Virgo improves your sense of the limits of your power. Your energy becomes focused and you take an active and prominent role in affairs of the world.

A relationship with a Virgo man will be your best chance for concrete success. Your optimism and his discriminating intellect are the keys to this process. There may be reverses, but you will both believe in the efficacy of your partnership. The strength of that belief is the faith that can overcome your differences. With faith in your relationship and in yourselves, there is a respect and a stature that comes to both of you. Many others will look up to a Sagittarius–Virgo partnership for its obvious achievements.

Whether you have a partnership of minds and talents, or an emotional communion that endures as lovers, depends upon the affection you generate and the degree of sexual compatibility. No matter what form a Sagittarius–Virgo relationship takes, it holds great promise for your development as individuals and as members of society.

SAGITTARIUS & LIBRA

A relationship with a Libra man holds the potential for affection and friendship over a long period of time. The combination of Jupiter's influence with Libra's ruling Venus indicates an expansive aura of beauty, harmony, and balance that appeals to both Sagittarius and Libra. You share common goals and standards because you are dedicated to truth and Libra is devoted to justice. You can speak freely with each other, and his gentle consideration will refine your bluntness in the same way that Libra's influence adds grace and poise to all your Sagittarian instincts. Above all, you will be friends who can make each other happier as individuals because you both receive a sense of completion from the relationship.

You will meet Libra through one of your many social activities, probably in surroundings that reflect Libra's desire for beauty. Art, theater, or entertainment will be the core of the social pleasures you share. Your raw sense of enjoyment becomes more cultivated through your lively conversations with Libra about the various aesthetic experiences you have together. You are attracted to him because of the social company he keeps, and for his clever conversational skills. His somewhat unusual physical appearance will appeal to your eclectic tastes. The men of Libra are not the rough-and-tumble types you are used to, but your Mutable-Fire nature mixes well with his Cardinal-Air qualities.

This is a relationship characterized by the aspects of friendship. Libra will pick up on your dynamic qualities and magnetic sexuality, enjoying the prospect of a freewheeling masculine buddy who also has a thoughtful side to his personality. His affectionate response and high esteem for you will evoke an equally friendly feeling. Libra aspects your Eleventh House—friendship, hope, and wishes. In some way you will feel that your meeting up with a Libra man on the road of life is a dream come true.

If you want a relationship with a Libra man, you may have to be the aggressive one. Your initiative will help to overcome his doubts and ambiguous desires for partnership, but you must be patient and kind in order to win his trust. Once he has accepted your sexual advances, let Libra take the lead. He treats his bed partners as he desires to be treated. In lovemaking he expresses his talent for nonverbal communication by being as affectionate and tender as he hopes you will be. Your desire and ardent passion will excite and please him, but chaotic, mindless, or clumsy sex will confuse him and jeopardize his sense of balance.

You can find him emotionally satisfying as well because he is capable of warmth without the intensity you find so threatening to your free spirit. The influence of Jupiter expands his capacity for romantic love, and the vibrations of Venus soften your more impulsive drives.

Neither of you will put a high premium on exclusivity, but Libra will demand absolute honesty, which your Sagittarian dedication to truth will find easy to accommodate. You can have a reasonable degree of freedom with a Libra lover, but you must learn to be discreet or Libra will feel that you are being disrespectful and unjust. Libra will not demand that you make an exclusive commitment to him, but he will expect you to honor the relationship in a dignified manner.

The biggest question in a Sagittarius–Libra liaison is how far to take it. You can be the best of friends or the best of lovers. Whichever you choose, Libra will attempt to keep his own sense of balance. He will hope for the love of a lifetime, but he will be just as happy with you as a close friend. The decision is up to you, Sagittarius. You may hope for a romantic attachment, but your dreams may obscure the reality of what can be most mutually beneficial. You can have many lovers, but close friends like Libra are rare. Few other men will value your intellect as much as Libra, and he will always speak the truth, whereas others may only flatter you. Both of you are blessed with the ability to communicate any and all of your feelings in an open and free manner. Fortunately, you are so attracted to each other, you suit each other so well, that the ties of friendship are really binding. If Libra turns out not to be your Man of Life, you can still be friends for the rest of your days.

SAGITTARIUS & SCORPIO

To be blunt, the relationship you may form with a Scorpio man as your lover is the most dangerous to your ego survival of all the sign combinations. The issues that attract and threaten you at the same time are matters of karmic mystery. The Fixed-Water nature of Scorpio indicates a depth and secrecy of power that your Mutable-Fire qualities cannot deal with. In fact, power is the central theme of this relationship. Working toward a common goal, you have tremendous potential. This potential is symbolized by the combination of your ruling Jupiter with his Pluto leadership, which means that the expansive power of the hidden forces of the cosmos permeate your coming together. It cannot be taken lightly.

You might meet a Scorpio man through your common interest in competitive sports or social situations, but whatever the circumstances, you will be irresistibly drawn to him by a force that fascinates you but which you don't understand. This will not be an unusual occurrence for Scorpio, and you may find yourself going out of your way to initiate a relationship with him. It can get very hot and increasingly heavy as you are drawn to the farthest edges of sexual experience. For Scorpio, sex is a power game, and this is something else you may not understand. You Sagittarians are often rough-and-tumble lovers, but you do not connect pain with sexual ecstasy, as Scorpio sometimes does. Initially you may be excited by the idea of all this hot sex, but Scorpio can take it beyond reasonable limits. The elements of mystery and compulsion are ultimately at odds with your uncomplicated need for carefree pleasure. The realization that you have become a sex tool can bring you a lot of woe.

If you make a commitment to a Scorpio man as your lover, he will demand absolute fidelity, something you are hard-pressed to maintain in most relationships. Scorpios are notoriously jealous, and even if you are trying to be completely faithful, he will question your honesty. He will read flirtation into every social situation, and your need for freedom will be stifled or compromised at every turn. Your Sagittarian optimism can keep you going for a while, but it is also the source of the self-deception that infects this relationship.

It might seem that this relationship has nothing to offer you, but the combination of your powerful personalities can lead to a life of adventure, speculation, wealth, travel, and high status that appeals to both of you. Your good luck and optimism, tempered by Scorpio's perceptiveness and practical nature, can be an unbeatable force in the world of business. You can gain worldly wealth, but it may cost you your idealism.

Despite the feeling of glamour and romance and passion, it is you, Sagittarius, who must realize the futility of these games of power and materialism. As your self-respect wanes, your broader cosmic vision of the purpose of life comes to your rescue and may allow you to fulfill your role as Scorpio's karmic teacher. His gift for the occult and mysticism, as well as his own feelings of frustration and illusion, will allow him to see that you have the power to help him transform his life. Some would suggest that the key lies in your humanitarianism and your desire to seek wisdom.

An affair with a Scorpio lover can be a worthwhile experience because it can teach you the implications of your words and acts. You can learn to be a better lover and friend if you learn the lessons of power, freedom, and responsibility that are so important in your relationship with a Scorpio man.

SAGITTARIUS & SAGITTARIUS

A relationship with a Sagittarius man will bring out some of the best and worst qualities in both of you, but you are likely to really enjoy each other's company. Because you are both Mutable signs, you are willing to adapt to his impulses, and he will show you an equal tolerance. The differences between you depend upon your rising signs, and your curiosity will stimulate you to know more about the ways he is unlike you. You find him as fascinating as you find yourself. The dual nature of Sagittarius may make one of you the scholar-philosopher while the other may be the wandering traveler. You will be able to appreciate each other's accomplishments without much jealousy, though there may be more than a little element of competition. A relationship with a Sagittarius man will work best for you if he is your equal in education or experience. You can learn a lot more about yourself and about the way you appear to others from your Sagittarius lover. He can be a brief and fun-filled fling or a special friend and confidant, even though the prospects for a long-term relationship may not appeal to either of you.

You can meet a Sagittarius man in any of your own favorite situations: traveling, studying, or engaging in sports. You could become jogging companions or drinking buddies as easily as sex partners. You are certainly attracted to his masculine type and broad sense of humor. The idea of bedding each other will probably strike you both simultaneously.

Neither of you free-spirited Centaurs of Sagittarius take

sex too seriously. In fact, you look upon it as a great deal of fun. No situation is sacrosanct when it comes to satisfying your mutual desires for unusual and exciting sex, as long as it is amusing. You may never be serious lovers, but you can be good partners. If there is an emotional commitment, it is not likely to be restricting or conventional. It will be mutually understood that freedom is essential to your happiness.

Fidelity is not your strong suit, and it will be rare that he would demand it of you. But his need for companionship and his subconscious fear of loneliness is something you can understand and with which you can sympathize. A sense of loyalty to the relationship you share will be more important than a commitment to sexual exclusivity. As you grow older you may find that he is the most important person in your life.

Any relationship with a Sagittarian man under the mutually expansive influence of Jupiter is going to be restless, reckless, and unpredictably extravagant in the short run. It may take a long time to figure out the dualities involved. He may be pensive and introspective when you are feeling your most outgoing, and no amount of teasing or daring will make him put down his book and join you on a pub crawl. On the other hand, the two of you can so inflate your own egos that you become bores among your friends.

When the going gets tough, the tough get going, and footloose Sagittarians hit the road. You can always go off in different directions, suffer through delays, separations, alarms and diversions, only to be part of a joyous return in an unexpected situation. Born under the lucky star of Jupiter, you have the gift to experience fortuitous meetings.

All of the energy you two expend in fooling around and endlessly amusing each other can be put to more humanitarian purposes that are also in keeping with the nature and spirit of Sagittarius. Any project you put your minds to can benefit from the power of your combined optimism and energy. Furthermore, a common goal that requires the serious application of your talents will strengthen the bonds between you as it improves your own self-image and your respect for your partner.

Yours can be the ultimate open relationship as long as your combined Fire signs don't consume your energies too quickly. In a relationship with another Sagittarian man you believe that the world is a prize for the taking, but the value of that prize depends upon the level at which you choose to live.

SAGITTARIUS & CAPRICORN

An affair with a Capricorn man might represent an opportunity for a successful relationship with an older man. Even though his Fixed-Earth materialism and the restrictive influence of his ruling Saturn can cause him to be critical of your extravagance, he will be inclined to be fatherly toward you in a benevolent way. He sees your potential for achievement and wants to help you focus your talents and energies. Capricorn is the symbolic executive of the zodiac, and he sees you as the bright young man who needs some direction, discipline, and encouragement to succeed. You have an opportunity to gain the financial stability that can allow you to indulge your desire for travel or extensive study. Capricorn can be stern, and he is noted for his ability to be single-minded, but he will be sincere in his devotion to you and his desire to see you advance yourself. In return you can give him some of your Fire-sign inspiration and optimism to alleviate the burden of his worldly cares.

A Capricorn may catch your roving eye in any social situation that is a cut above the ordinary. Classical music, fine art, and good restaurants all attract him. His social engagements often revolve around business dealings or fund-raising events, rather than simple amusement. Don't expect him to be the life of the party, but he can be engaging and humorous in a shy way if you take the time to talk to him. He has no interest in the trivial, and your opening remarks should reflect your own capacity for serious thought. You will find his conversation interesting, and your intuition will tell you that he is a man who can affect your future. He can be your karmic teacher and your lover, but he will not assume either responsibility unless you take the initiative and convince him that you are worth knowing.

Capricorn will be attracted to your mind, but beneath his conservative appearance he is also thinking about your body. If you can get beyond the image of the three-piece suit, you may be in for a more than pleasant surprise. His conservative manner disguises a sexual intensity that can last and last. His approach to sex is governed by his Earth-sign nature, indicating a sensuous lover. You may initiate the encounter, but Capricorn will follow through with a desire for a more lasting relationship. If you stick with a Capricorn, you will learn a great deal about endurance on emotional and sexual levels. He has risen to the upper echelons in his career through hard work, patience, and the desire to succeed. He will bring all of these traits to bed, with the added force of the erotic feelings he has repressed and channeled into his path to the top. Though he may be older than you, a Capricorn can teach you that one can get much better as one gets older.

Capricorn men are faithful to their lovers because it is consistent with their concept of appropriate behavior. Any commitment he makes to you will be the product of considerable thought and soul-searching. His Cardinal-sign sex drive indicates that he is not above flirting, but is serious about everything. While he may demand fidelity of himself, he may allow your occasional roaming to go unnoticed if he believes that you are fulfilling the other goals he has set for you in developing your potential.

Capricorn can be indulgent of your Sagittarian foibles to a certain degree, but your expansive nature may sometimes give rise to feelings of insecurity in him. He expects progress in the relationship, and your enthusiasm must never turn to carelessness or extravagance. Under the influence of Capricorn you will want to become more effective in your life. The practical insights you gain from him can permit you to see your goals more clearly. Becoming a success is the way that you can return the care that Capricorn has for you.

You have the ability to give him a new feeling of personal happiness to complement his other achievements. Respect and appreciation for his values and accomplishments can overcome his pessimism and make him happy. He has been a loner all his life. Despite your outgoing personality and social conquests, you also have some sense of loneliness. You can offer him companionship and optimism, to provide him with a new appreciation for life. You have the ability to combine your personality potentials in a relationship that joins the adventurousness of Sagittarius with the practicality of Capricorn, to create a strong and loving bond that grows in a spirit of progress and prosperity.

SAGITTARIUS & AQUARIUS

A meeting with an Aquarius man might be a casual adventure that turns out to be one of the best friendships you will ever know with any of the signs of the zodiac. He is Fixed Air in nature, and you will find his wide-ranging intellect an inspiration to your own search for wisdom. The combination of your Saturn ruler with his ruling planet, Uranus, indicates that he is more "modern"—or eccentric—than you, but you find him interesting and much more stimulating than most of the men you meet. His open-minded curiosity in anything new complements your knowledge and fuels your philosophical mind.

Meeting an Aquarius is often a surprise. It happens in unusual situations, and since you find yourself in odd spots in your wanderings, you may come across your fair share of men born under the sign of the Water-bearer. If you find him attractive, you will have to be the aggressor because Aquarius men are often more interested in your mind than in your body, though he should certainly find you fascinating enough. You are both good conversationalists and the talk should be easy, open, and filled with the exchange of insight. He is always eager to hear new ideas.

Novelty and versatility characterize the sexual habits of the Aquarian man. Because of his Fixed-Air nature, his interest in sex is more inquisitive than passionate. His interest, however, in new techniques and interesting positions will add to your pleasure. Experimentation is Aquarius' means of keeping his erotic interest fresh and free from emotional involvement. You will enjoy the fun-loving aspect of love with an Aquarian. Sex may take place in usual locations or in situations that add considerably to the imaginative, erotic context of your affair. A touch of adventure is just the spark Aquarius needs to get aroused.

Fidelity should never be an issue between you, simply because it will not be expected or demanded by either of you. Neither of you is the jealous type. Aquarius will give you the freedom you need because you grant him the independence he wants. You don't want a lover who is dependent upon you in any way that restricts your ability to act according to your inspiration, and Aquarius feels much the same way. You can have a good nondominant relationship between equals with an Aquarius friend or lover. He aspects your Third House—communications—and getting along with him seems natural and comfortable, even though full of unexpected surprises. In many ways you feel like a brother to him, and you may be close friends even if you don't remain lovers.

Any relationship you establish can be creatively chaotic, or else structured to your mutual agreement, with clear responsibilities spelled out to avoid conflict. Neither of you seeks to dominate in this combination because you focus on your ideals, hopes, wishes, and dreams rather than on reality. You will break all the rules in trying to follow your lucky stars and always be willing to forgive each other because you both understand the compulsions involved.

There can be so much stimulation and excitement that you give up some solid elements in your life to chase Aquarian rainbows. Remember, Uranus is the planet of illusion and things may never work out the way they seem. You can have a good time, but there is difficulty in concentrating or finishing projects you start with Aquarius. You get a lot of hot ideas, but you have to be selective or none of them will come to anything substantial.

Your Aquarius man will be sorry to see you hit the road because he will miss the fun of fooling around together, but you may need to be off on your own to regain your sense of values after an intense period. He will always keep a light in the window; you're welcome when you return. An Aquarian may look upon you as the embodiment of his ideal of friendship. He has the feeling that you have the power to make his wishes come true.

You and Aquarius often join forces in political and community affairs because you are devoted to truth and humanitarian principles. You are natural participants in educational forums or journalism on behalf of the gay community. Though you are both rugged individualists, you realize that your right to be free or eccentric can be compromised unless you support groups that advocate your rights and seek to protect your life-style.

This is a fine romance, Sagittarius, and a lasting relationship that allows you to be good friends. The bonds of commitment allow you the freedom you need and the independence he craves. You show each other the best sides of your personalities as loving men when you find an Aquarius to share your life.

SAGITTARIUS & PISCES

A Pisces lover is going to be a challenge because of the double dualities involved with the Centaur and the Fishes. There are multiple motivations going on all the time that will amaze and confuse you in your attempt to understand where the relationship is headed. He is Mutable Water in quality and his emotions are iridescent moods that play across his mind like rainbows. The Mutable-Fire nature of Sagittarius inspires you to chase rainbows, although you may find yourself running in circles with Pisces. There is a chance for a definite breakthrough here, Sagittarius, because the combination of your ruling Jupiter with his Neptune rulership indicates new beginnings that affect your life, especially in domestic situations.

Pisces aspects your Fourth House—home and your later years. You may meet him at a point when you have been "on the road," either literally or spiritually, for a long time. Getting together with a Pisces man inspires you to think about having a home and finding a haven. If you are both ready for a mature relationship, there is a strong possibility that you can begin a new life with Pisces.

You will have to take the initiative in a Pisces affair. He certainly may be willing, but Pisceans are naturally timid and eager to be wooed. There is the spirit of the sensitive romantic within Pisces, and he will see you as every inch the dashing man you are. You will indeed spark his erotic imagination, but you may also overwhelm him with your aggressive sexual presence. Reach into your fund of experience and remember all of the kindest, gentlest moments you have shared with other loving men. Use those experiences as the clue for making love to a Pisces man and he will respond with a depth of passion that pleases and surprises you. Pisces men are not good "quickies," so relax

and luxuriate in the experience if you want to get the best
out of making love with him.

The tension between your blunt and bold enthusiasm and
his dreamy, elusive sensitivity will color all the aspects of
your relationship. Unless you have decided to make a con-
centrated effort to be faithful, or the two of you set up
housekeeping on a desert island, you will be tempted to
engage in extracurricular encounters when the opportunity
presents itself. Your devotion to the spirit of truth will cause
you to be very casual about it, offhandedly confiding in
Pisces. He will not be amused. If he feels his affections are
being abused, Pisces can become withdrawn, evasive, and
self-abusive as his self-confidence wanes.

You are an up-front personality. You say what you think
and don't often consider the consequences. Pisces talks
about what he feels, and he thinks about all the ramifica-
tions before he speaks. What you may call deception is only
his way of making the truth more palatable to his sensitive
soul. He will ''adjust'' the facts in order to preserve the
privacy of his feelings or because he doesn't want to hurt
others. You don't really understand either of these motivations, but your brusque manner may be just as mysterious
to Pisces.

This is not an easy relationship for either of you to cope
with unless you have had previous lovers and learned about
your ability to relate to other loving men as creative personalities. You share a wonderful idealism with Pisces that can
overcome the inadvertent hurts and disappointments you are
capable of inflicting on each other. You are both easygoing
individuals who can forgive and even forget things that annoy you. Your faith in the future and your belief in the value
of experience for its own sake can activate Pisces' creative
imagination.

Eventually, the old wanderlust may come over you again,
but this time you can take Pisces along. With you as his
guide, Pisces may come to understand the joys of experiencing life as it is, but he will always magnify the reality
with imaginative additions from his own dreams. Learn to

appreciate the added sensitive idealism and romanticism and you will attain new levels of maturity with a Pisces lover.

LOVING YOUR SAGITTARIUS MAN

If you are looking for Mr. Casual and a lighthearted good time, then keep your eyes open for a Sagittarian man. He won't be hard to find because he either stands out in a crowd or appears as an obvious loner. Sagittarius is a dual sign, and the men born under the sign of the Centaur are often one of two types: the good sport or the wandering scholar. If you spend enough time at the gym or the library, you are bound to run into each other.

Jogging is a typically Sagittarian activity, or if you ride, it will be quite easy to come across a Sagittarian in the saddle. They like big dogs and the park is filled with Centaurs taking a romp with man's best friend. He enjoys competitive sports as well, but his object is playing the game rather than winning. If there is an active physical side to your personality, you will find a Sagittarian man very stimulating.

If the pensive, studious type is more to your taste, don't count on Sagittarius. When he isn't running his Great Dane in the park, he could easily be in the library with another Dane, Kierkegaard. He is interested in philosophy and all aspects of the life of the mind as well as the body.

A Sagittarius man is usually in jeans, and he looks his best in casual clothes that matches his life-style. Look for him wherever the living is easy and the atmosphere relaxed and informal. He doesn't like to wear ties, and he won't dress up to please anyone but himself. Sagittarians live life for whatever enjoyment they can find. They don't dwell on the past and they approach the future with a devil-may-care attitude that you may find quite appealing.

Sagittarians are almost always available with a simple, straightforward approach. If you are friendly, open, and natural about your attraction to him, you will get positive results. Formalities, indecision, coyness, or elaborate ploys turn him right off. A dramatically staged seduction will make him laugh rather than stimulate his libido. Sagittarians have a broad and sometimes coarse sense of humor, so be prepared to enjoy yourself and to be yourself. He is not immune to flattery, but he doesn't take it too seriously.

You can't take a Sagittarian too seriously either, when it comes to his blunt manner. Those born under the sign of the Centaur are notorious for putting their hooves in their mouths. He may hurt or embarrass you with an unwitting remark, but that is never his intention. He is simply so honest and exuberant that he has no sense of tact and not much discretion.

You may find his lovemaking to be just as thoughtless. He is kind by nature but not particularly gentle in his behavior. The burden of being metaphorically half man and half horse makes him a little clumsy, even in bed. He finds no pleasure in pain or cruelty, but he doesn't know his own strength and he can cause you discomfort without being aware of it. He is a Fire sign, and he just gets naturally carried away on waves of inspiration during sex. He enjoys all forms of face-to-face, hand-to-hand, and buddy-to-buddy sex. Sagittarians understand how to enjoy sex, and loving him can be a true celebration.

You can please him best by accepting him for what he is: a wild and wonderful mythical creature who can never be completely domesticated. He is born to roam the world, searching for experience and seeking the meaning of life. When he doesn't actually hop a plane, he hits the books, wandering in the world of scholarship. Sagittarius is the original "rolling stone," and he gathers no moss (but often much wisdom) in his restless search for stimuli.

If you want a Sagittarian lover, you will have to accept him on his own terms. You can't tie him down to a life of unrelieved domesticity and expect him to be happy. He needs to feel free, and he wants a man who will love him for who he is rather than for what he may become.

A Sagitarrian good-time Charlie is not always going to be sexually faithful. He is too attractive and too aware of the opportunities for casual romance to be an exclusive partner. Sex does not have deep emotional significance for him. The typical Sagittarian man sees sex as an inspirational high. He has no sense of shame about his sexuality, and he has little patience or understanding for anyone who is closeted. If you have secrets to keep, don't get involved with a Sagittarius.

The men of Sagittarius are great travel companions because they find excitement wherever they go. Meeting up with him on the road can be an almost mystical experience of sharing passion and trust with a beautiful stranger in an exotic setting. He can pack more fun, urgency, and desire into three days in another town than most men can handle in three weeks at home!

Because he has so few ties to home and family, he can be completely at ease in almost any social situation, though he prefers it to be a casual scene where he can feel free to be his naturally boisterous self. He's definitely one of the stars of the bars and a real drinking buddy if you are in the mood for an all-night pub crawl.

His greatest gifts are his optimism and his generosity. He always believes in the joys and pleasures of tomorrow, and there is nothing he won't do for his friends. Make no idle wishes in front of a Sagittarius buddy because he will go out of his way to make your wish come true in his expansive Jupiter-influenced style. Jupiter is the planet of good fortune, and he wants to share his luck with everyone.

What he wants from you as a lover or a friend is complete acceptance of what he is in an open-ended relationship. You can be his home away from home and his port in any storm, but you have to accept the relationship on his own terms. If you want security, a Sagittarius man may not be able to provide what you are looking for in a relationship. If you can imagine loving a sea captain or an airline steward, then you may find a Sagittarian lover fascinating and romantic enough to accept separation in return for the pleasure of his homecoming.

CAPRICORN
December 21–
January 20

ℑ

Symbol: The Mountain Goat
Ruling Planet: Saturn
Colors: Dark browns and grays
Metal: Lead
Natural House Rulership: Tenth House, the house of
    career
Tenth House Traits: Desire for success and need for
    security
Motto: "I use"
Nature: Cardinal sign (leadership)
Element: Earth sign (material)
Qualities: Practical, dependable, and ambitious
Capacities: Perseverance and concentration
Personality Key Words: Integrity, sincerity, and
    reverence

MAXIMIZING YOUR CAPRICORN POTENTIAL

If you were born under the sign of the Mountain Goat, you are a man of Capricorn and the natural executive of the zodiac. You are a Cardinal-Earth sign and therefore the highest embodiment of the practical power to deal with the material world. You have the power to succeed in life because you combine thoroughness with ambition. The rulership of Saturn makes you very conscious of time, of the principle of restraint, and the fact that the path to ultimate success is through denial. You repress your emotions and inspirations, focusing them into your life's work. You are always on the move, and the direction is ever upward.

Your understanding of time gives you great strength through patience and perseverance. You are passionate, but you hold that passion in check, waiting for the opportunity to lavish your love on one all-consuming desire. You are not fickle, but you always hold back from any commitment until you have a secure perspective. Though you are conservative and cautious, you are willing to undergo many unusual episodes on the road to success in business or in love, but you can internalize any experience that promises the nourishment of your goals.

The men of Capricorn need the respect, status, and material security of a career in order to realize their full personality potential. You need constant growth and development to feel content with yourself and any relationship into which you enter. You have a sense of being responsible to society, which makes you want and need a lover in a permanent relationship who gives you the affection you crave and often neglect to give yourself. You need a home that is orderly and well appointed to serve as a refuge and a haven for the deep love you feel for your partner. Without a feeling that everything you do is leading toward greater security, you have none of the peace of mind that is essential to your well-being.

Your path to success lies in any field or position where it is important to have a person who welcomes hard work, but in an executive capacity. As a Cardinal sign, you welcome the opportunity to assume the responsibilities of leadership. Your practical perspective gives you an overview that allows you to make effective decisions that benefit the entire organization. The same abilities and desires set the tone of your relationships with other men in your search for love.

You have a need and talent to nurture your lovers and direct them toward the practical goal of establishing and maintaining a secure relationship. But often you will not seriously consider finding someone and settling down unless you have first attained material success in your career. You are neither romantic nor speculative, but dedicated to the practical need for finding an appropriate man to be the recipient of the deep passion and affection you are holding inside you. Until you meet your Man of Life, you are willing to shop around, but you will never trust your heart to anyone without a great deal of thought. When you fall in love, it must be the love of a lifetime.

Your talents are many and varied, but they all center around your capacity for accepting responsibility and your clear vision of leadership. You have steadfastness of purpose that allows you to rise to the top. In any situation you are quick to see the most practical and efficient solution. Though you are conservative, you are often ahead of your time because of the perceptive way in which you analyze the tasks at hand. You learn the rules and then you look to see how they can be broken in order to get the job done more efficiently. Your friends and lovers benefit from your sound advice, which is always leavened with the Capricorn sense of humor: ironic and Earthy, based upon practical experiences in a not so practical world. Your values embody enduring principles of tradition, and your tastes run to the conventional in art and music.

Your weaknesses are related to your high standards. You have a poor self-image because you are so demanding. You are your own worst critic and tend to remember your failures for a long time, rather than emphasizing your successes. You can become blinded by ambition and even ruthless, usually to your personal disadvantage because it cuts you off from emotional attachments. Your material success can't buy happiness, and yet you feel driven to succeed, even though the path may be lonely. Fortunately, Saturn's gift to you is the gift of time. With Capricorn, older is definitely better. All the carefree pleasures that Capricorns deny themselves in youth come to them when they are mature and secure enough to enjoy them.

Your social life is as practical and purposeful as all the other elements in your existence. You don't enjoy shallow pleasures. You enjoy a small circle of friends, and in general, you are not flamboyant or extravagant. Often your social engagements revolve around business associates and personal obligations such as family ties. Capricorns enjoy sports, but only if they are geared toward fitness or recreation rather than competition. Your social life usually revolves around culture, art, and music with close friends.

The Goat is an ancient symbol of sexuality, and a Capricorn man has a strong sex drive. Though you are not particularly promiscuous (because it seems so "unstable"), you enjoy sex on a regular basis. Capricorns are not above using sex for personal gain, and you gauge relationships carefully in terms of what they can do for you. You worry about the implications of getting involved with partners who might jeopardize your life-style. You like practical, comfortable arrangements with men who respect your desire for privacy and propriety without involving emotional demands or intruding on your career.

When you fall in love, you want a lover who will understand your need for security, respect your achievements, and accept your desire to nurture him. Your lovers benefit from all of the affection you have craved and saved because you lavish them with love and devotion. You want a man who can be happy in a traditional relationship. He must accept your sense of obligation to your family, and you want him to relate to them as an important part of your life. Even if your family disapproves of your sexual preference, you want a lover who would be socially acceptable to them. You place a high value on fidelity because it represents the stability of the commitment.

Your lovers benefit from the constancy of your devotion. You provide them with real concern for their welfare and often assist them in advancing their careers. You are especially good with younger lovers, who bring out the best in your paternal instinct, which includes providing a good home and material comforts. With you, a young man can always find a sympathetic ear for his problems, and you give sound advice from your fund of Saturnine wisdom. Having a stable and loving relationship with someone who respects you gives you the sense of purpose that your career sometimes lacks. Your doubts and worries disappear when you finally find love, and your sexual desire increases as the relationship continues. You have the endurance and the desire to love him all night long, as if you were making up for lost time. Don't worry, Capricorn, you can take it slow. Thanks to the influence of Saturn, time is on your side.

You have the strength of personality to maximize your potential, and a very satisfying life can evolve because of this. Capricorn always goes the distance, gaining power as you head for the top. You might need to work a bit on improving your self-image. Have faith as well as endurance, Capricorn. You can be pessimistic in the short run, but Saturn tells you to look to the future as you build on the past. Having the right lover is often the key to maximizing the best in your potential for happiness. You need a receptive partner, a man who wants the gifts you have to give. The love and respect of a man who is committed to your mutual happiness can provide you with the personal feeling of success that gives even more meaning to your life than the material things you have achieved. The road may be long and hard, but the view from the top of the mountain is the inspiration that makes any Capricorn glad to be a loving man.

CAPRICORN & ARIES

Life with an Aries man is all ups and downs in ways that can both attract and exasperate you at the same time. Ruled by fiery Mars, Aries is also a Cardinal sign, and he won't like the restrictions your ruling Saturn will want to place on his exuberant and sometimes reckless life-style. He has a lot of energy that you can help direct toward worthwhile goals. This may not be a long-term relationship, but his innovative mind and free spirit can be just the spark you need to add some new dimension to your life, in love or in business. He embodies the spirit of the pioneer, and you can find new social and sexual experiences when you get together with men born under the sign of the Ram. Through the inspiration of Aries you can be introduced to new ideas that will make money for both of you, though Aries will want to spend it in extravagant ways that stagger your practical sensibilities.

You can meet an Aries man almost anywhere, but you can be sure that whatever the situation, he will be drawing attention to himself. You may hold back your interest, cautiously surveying the scene in typical Capricorn fashion. Before you realize it, he may be upon you, boldly greeting you with a familiarity that simultaneously offends, surprises, and delights you. He is usually so brash that you don't have an opportunity to get your defenses into place.

Before you know it—or even want it—you may find yourself involved.

Sex with an Aries man will be intense but over with too quickly to completely satisfy your desire for a good long session that ends in a feeling of complete fulfillment. Aries enjoys passionate lovemaking, but he loses interest if it takes too long. You are more interested in quality sex with plenty of subtle touches that increase the physical sensation, but Arians tend to go for quantity.

The kind of sex you share with an Aries man is often symptomatic of the differences in your life-styles. He is flamboyant and exciting, but he doesn't deliver the goods in the way you do. You appreciate his boyish charm and naïve energy, but you can't make the same demands of him that you make of yourself. You will want to be faithful in any relationship you develop, but fidelity is difficult for an Aries because he has so much energy and desire to experience everything and everyone. He is very appealing to other men because he projects his sexuality and his availability. If you see that he has made a real commitment to growth and development in other areas of your relationship, you may be able to indulge his roving nature. Stability is always going to be at issue in any endeavor you undertake with an Aries man, but if you can provide the framework, Aries will bring inspiration and energy to any association you have together.

Though he can be erratic in behavior, Aries men are loyal friends and generous with their time. If he feels your sincere concern for his welfare and advancement, he will be devoted to you. There won't be anything you can't ask that he won't do, as long as you understand his strengths and weaknesses. With his youthful and insecure ego you must remember to praise him for his efforts rather than remind him of his shortcomings. You must learn to appreciate his gifts and develop a tolerance for his well-meaning mistakes. Because he is so ego-oriented, he doesn't often realize the effects of his actions on others.

Arians are the very spirit of youthful optimism. He feels that the whole world is waiting for him with open arms.

With him you can enjoy many of the pleasures and exciting times that you have always denied yourself. You can participate in his hectic social life, or, if you are secure enough and feel like staying home with a good book, you can get a great deal of vicarious enjoyment from the stories of his on-the-town adventures. You can be a true confidant for him, providing him with a mature perspective on the chaotic events that seem to fill his life. When he feels overwhelmed, confused, and unsure of himself, you can be the sympathetic shoulder he needs to lean on. You will be angry at his foolishness and at the way he leaves himself open to hurt, but your heart will melt when you feel how much he needs you.

Aries aspects your Fourth House—concerning home—and he may well be a disruptive element in your home life, but you feel that somehow there is a purpose to knowing and even loving him. What you require from Aries is respect for the differences between you. He must observe your need for privacy and propriety, but you may actually enjoy the way he energizes your life with his lovable antics. If it is love, you will find his complexities endearing rather than enraging. It may not last forever, but you can genuinely treasure your moments together with an Aries lover.

CAPRICORN & TAURUS

Of all the men you may seriously consider as your Man of Life, Taurus is the most likely to make you happy. He is Fixed Earth by nature, and he embodies all of the respectability and desire for material comfort that you also strive to attain. Ruled by Venus, these men, born under the sign of the Bull, are gentle and loving and have a strong desire for a happy home. You have similar values and inspire a feeling of confidence in each other that gives you the security you need. A love affair with a Taurus man can soften the hard edges and cool exteriors that sometimes obscure your own capacity for inner warmth.

You might meet a Taurus lover through your business, and you may be as impressed with his financial acumen as you are interested in his sexual potential. Any man that is good with figures and has a typically sensuous Taurean figure is bound to get your attention. Your common interest could easily be music. An evening that starts off with dinner, continues at the symphony, and ends at your place may be the beginning of a highly enjoyable affair. Neither of you is prone to love at first sight or quick commitments, but you will both be eager and willing to let events take their natural course toward a close, and then still closer, relationship.

Taureans aspect your Fifth House—love and romance—and you may feel swept off your feet for the first time in your life. Falling in love is serious business for both of you, but it may also make you feel giddy and lighthearted, which will make your sexual communication even better than you can imagine! Sex with Taurus is an unusually sensual experience. He is receptive to your ardent lovemaking and a responsive partner from the beginning. Your initial sexual experience will delight you, and the best part is that it will probably improve. It can be very Earthy and physical and active, but as time goes on, your lovemaking becomes an even more satisfying experience. Sex opens the doors to affection and emotion that you kept under control for so long. You will find that your love for him gets deeper and deeper through the expression of your feelings with your Taurean lover.

The basis of your relationship with Taurus is the trust you share. It precludes questions of fidelity and allows you to shed some of your natural reserve. He shares your goals and admires your methods, providing you with the respect you need from a lover. You both want a home and the pleasures of a stable domestic life, surrounded by comfort and luxury. Taurus will make sure that the place you share is attractive and reflects your own desire for a refined environment. The trust and stability of your relationship will be expressed in your commitment to material possessions. You will purchase good furnishings and may even buy a house together.

When you fall in love with Taurus, your career will be affected to the degree that you now have a definite goal on which to focus your ambition. Taurus will be sincere in his appreciation of your efforts to be a good provider, and he will attempt to match them because he cares for you so much. You need praise for your hard work, but Taurus may not be as vocal as you would like. His high regard for you will be noticeable in material ways. Giving thoughtful and practical gifts, preparing your favorite meals, preparing little surprises, and having your pipe and slippers always ready by the fire are his way of saying how much he cares for you. Because he trusts and understands the way in which you share his goals, his normal rigidity is replaced by flexibility and even a spirit of adventure.

When you find yourselves secure on the domestic front and in your careers, your great capacity for adventure and enjoyment will surface. You can even coax the placid Bull out of the pasture and onto the road. Your job as the Cardinal sign is to keep Taurus from getting into a rut. The happier he is, the less he wants to change any of his life patterns. Your need for active goals should be directed toward projects you can work on together. Collecting antiques is a favorite Taurean pastime and something you can even turn into quite a profitable enterprise. Any activity that combines material acquisition and the chance for profit will give both of you a great deal of pleasure.

A love affair with a Taurus man should be a lasting relationship that has all of the growth potential you require to be a happy, secure, and successful loving man.

CAPRICORN & GEMINI

Keeping your wit and wisdom intact is not going to be easy when you come across the Twins of Gemini playing their games in your life path. The Mutable-Air qualities of Gemini are often too flighty and seem too superficial to satisfy your Cardinal-Earth desires. He is ruled by Mercury, the planet of communication, and your ruling Saturn is not congenial to the ever-changing pattern of his wide-ranging interests. It may seem as if he is never involved with any one single idea long enough for you to make sense of what he is thinking. You might have a fun fling with a Gemini man, but the chances for a long-lasting relationship will depend upon factors that are more complicated than the compatibility of your Sun signs alone.

You can meet a Gemini in business, especially in any aspect of communications or information processing. You can find him to be clever and cute, in a lightweight fashion, though it will probably be Gemini who ventures to flirt with you as a means of getting the relationship going. He is mainly interested in what's on your mind, and you may feel flattered by his attention.

Sex with a Gemini can be fun, especially if you enjoy a touch of fantasy. He likes to add mental stimulation to sexual pleasure in a way that is a refreshing change from the intense physical activity that you are used to with a lover. If you correspond to one of his sexual fantasies, he will cast you in a role that can be fun if you relax and play the game with an open mind. Whatever he is into, it probably won't be very heavy, and may include a touch of pornography, which you actually enjoy for its Earthiness. Gemini has a carefree approach to sex that may even bring out your sense of humor.

You may have a good time together and entertain the idea of having him around on a regular and continuing basis, but

Gemini will rarely be interested in settling down to your way of life. He is a man of the moment, and you can learn to enjoy his company on an occasional basis rather than being subjected to his restless influence in a long-term exclusive relationship. Because Gemini aspects your Sixth House—work and service—you feel that you can help him somehow, but it may not be through a relationship as his lover.

If Gemini is a friend in business, his quick mind, his ability to correlate information, and his uncanny sense of new trends can be of a great advantage to you. His intellect is broad, but you must use your power to analyze and select that which will be the most useful and most profitable for you. If you let him have free rein, he may overload your circuits and leave you running around in circles.

Gemini's finances are usually chaotic, and you can be of assistance in helping him sort out his affairs. Under your influence, he will get down to work and pay attention to the details of his life, but you may not be able to sustain his interest in order and practicality for very long. Gemini will come to you for advice, and you will be sympathetic and try to give him the best of your considered opinion. The only thing you expect in return is that Gemini follow your advice to the letter. Unfortunately, his opinion or resolve is only as firm as that of the most recent person he has consulted. You may feel hurt, used, and rejected by Gemini if you take his habits too personally.

As a close and lasting partner, you may find Gemini hard to get along with because he seems too flighty—from your solid, stable point of view. Your view of time is seen from a long-range perspective; he tends to live moment by moment. From Gemini you can learn to take a short-range look at what is going on in your life and in your career. There are times when you become downhearted at the thought of the long and weary road ahead to the pinnacle of achievement that is the legacy of Capricorn. A Gemini experience can be a real pick-me-up that gets you out into society and out of your brooding preoccupation with your future or your past. You can be too traditional in your methods, and a Gemini will shake up the assumptions of that tradition just enough to put them in a new light and set you on a slightly different road to the top.

Gemini may not be your Man of Life, but he can be an important man in your life if you let him be himself. You can't tie him down intellectually or physically, so you might as well enjoy him for his virtues as a free spirit and make the best of the moments you spend together.

CAPRICORN & CANCER

A love affair with a Cancer man can become a satisfying and enjoyable relationship with potential for a lasting involvement, or it may be too powerful to continue for very long. You are opposite signs of the zodiac and attract each other because you are so different. Cancer men are Cardinal Water, embodying the primacy of their emotional drive, in contrast to your Cardinal-Earth material ambitions. He is the sign of the Crab, symbolizing caution and security. You have elements in your personalities that can combine either to make a tight, secure bond or else frighten each other into looking elsewhere for love. The combination of your ruling Saturn with his Moon rulership indicates a mutual sensitivity about being close to another man and the capacity to be understanding of each other's needs as loving men.

Cancer tends to be shy, and you are likely to be circumspect, so there may be some difficulty getting the affair off to a spectacular beginning. If he isn't put off by your cool and reserved manner and you don't find him too insecure, there is a good chance that something can develop between you. He has a good sense of humor when he feels relaxed, and he will certainly appreciate your ironic wit.

Cancers are highly receptive and responsive sex partners. You won't have to tell him what you like in bed because he is naturally attuned to your needs. You will enjoy the slow pace and the extremely sensual dimension of your lovemaking with a Cancer man. His emotional concentration and your physical endurance can mean a long and satisfying session that leaves you both looking forward to seeing each other again.

There is every other possibility that you can be compatible on levels that will lead to a commitment to become lovers. Cancer wants a home, and you understand the need for a stable home life. You can settle down together in domestic harmony, and you probably won't fall into a boring routine that would stifle your Cardinal-sign needs for activity and direction. You want a relationship that is committed to growth and Cancer seeks much the same thing; however, he needs a day-to-day approach to keep his emotional drives in line. Cancer is secretly as ambitious as you are, but his desires often overwhelm his ability to organize his talents. He can only dream of success until you enter his life and show him a way to the top.

Because Cancer represents your Seventh House—partnerships and balance—you may find that you are more outgoing and become a less private person, overcoming the reserved nature that has kept you cool, calm, and quiet. You enjoy your social life more and do more things together with a Cancer lover. You will enjoy entertaining at home and find comfort in his companionship when you go out. Because you can make each other feel so secure, there should be no question about being "out" as a couple. You won't make any formal declaration on the courthouse steps, but it will be obvious that you are loving partners.

Questions of fidelity should not be a threat to the affiliation you establish with a Cancer man. Cancers are faithful as long as they get the feeling of security and affection they require. You are capable of meeting those needs and you will be faithful. A problem may arise because of Cancer's general moodiness. Ruled by the Moon, his moods are inconstant and he can be secretive about his feelings. You may suspect that there is something going on that you don't know about or that he is hiding something from you. He is embarrassed by the vulnerability of his feelings and seeks to sulk in his shell rather than confront the phantoms. You can help Cancer articulate his feelings by making him feel as secure as possible. He will still have mood swings, but they will not be unbearably intense or a threat to your life together.

Out of the strong bond you develop will come a new feeling of compatibility that allows for some fun and exciting times together. Your home can then become a base of operations from which you can go forth to travel and explore the pleasures of the world beyond the nest which you create with a Cancer lover.

You are unlike each other on the surface, but there are deep needs and desires that you can fulfill for a Cancer lover. He needs your stability, admires your strength, and shares your ambition from an emotional, rather than materialistic, viewpoint. All the things you have to give him come from inside you, rather than being the usual exterior proofs of affection that others may seek. With a Cancer lover you can find a man who respects you for your accomplishments but loves you for who you are.

CAPRICORN & LEO

Getting involved with a Leo man is going to be an unusual experience for both of you. The intense warmth and vibrant personality associated with his Fixed-Fire nature are not normally considered compatible with your cooler, more reserved Cardinal-Earth qualities. The principle of restraint symbolized by your ruling Saturn is restrictive of the expansive personality influences of his ruling Sun. This could be a lasting relationship as you rise to the challenge of coping with Leo's demanding character. You may complain about his arrogance, but at the same time you are fascinated by his talent for inspiring you toward unusual paths to success. Leo will admire the results of your systematic approach and cooperate and work harder with you than almost anyone else.

You are both aggressive, but your natural caution will force Leo to initiate your first get-together. You find him an intriguing creature, and he excites you even though his outgoing manner makes you a little suspicious. You will probably meet through business, family, or some unusual connection because you really don't travel in the same social circles. It can be adventurous but stressful and strangely compelling for you.

You detect an air of mystery about Leo, which turns you on. Leo aspects your Eighth House—the mysteries of sex—and your curiosity is definitely aroused. You should find him to be a passionate and energetic partner if you suspend some of the proverbial caution of Capricorn. His lovemaking technique tends to be impassioned, well practiced, and theatrical. Leos enjoy acting out the ritual of subtle seduction over and over again, and like any true thespian, he needs an appreciative audience. The more encouragement he gets, the harder he will work at increasing your pleasure. It is important for him to impress you, because he wants to earn your respect as well as your love.

Respect is a mutual need for both you and Leo. He expects it from others, and you work hard to earn it as well. But maintaining each other's high regard may be difficult because you are so much alike under your different personas that you often seem to annoy each other. You can agree on goals but not always on the means by which to achieve them. Though he is outgoing and optimistic in his flamboyant Leo manner, you may come to realize that he is quite insecure and vulnerable, even to slightly critical comments. Leo wants everyone to love him for who he is. You have similar insecurities, but you seek love and admiration for what you do. You can see him as superficial and feel that he relies on his charm rather than on solid accomplishments. From Leo's point of view you seem to be all practicality and no personality. You both must strive to understand the intimate person underneath the public postures. Admiration and accomplishment add to your feelings of well-being, and you should work together toward these goals.

Leo can expand your horizons in dealing with people, and you can give him a better perspective on following through with the details that make the difference in achieving real success. You can make Leo get to work and be more serious about it. He can add an extra dimension of inspiration and creative force to any project you work on together. You share a common interest in ballet, music, and refined entertainment. Leo will make a handsome companion who increases your self-image because he is such an attractive personality.

A long-term relationship with a Leo man is possible, but only if you come across each other at the right time in your lives. When you are younger, neither of you will have the maturity or patience to look beyond the facade. As more mature men, you should feel secure enough in your own personalities to realize that there is more depth to be investigated. You will like his youthful attitude, and both of you want to stay young at heart well into old age. Since you get better-looking as you get older, the same Leo who decided not to come on to you when you were twenty may be hot on your trail when you are forty.

The effect of time will have slowed Leo down enough to appreciate your more conservative talents, and your success over the years should make you more confident in dealing with such a demanding ego. There will still be clashes over money, extravagance, and points of pride. You both tend to be stubborn and temperamental, but you will be the forgiving one, and Leo will love you more for your ability to bend a little.

Loving a Leo man is never going to be an easy proposition for you, but the rewards make it worthwhile. Leo needs your strength to give direction to his exuberant personality. Once you understand that he needs you, the doors to your love are open to your Leo man.

CAPRICORN & VIRGO

With a Virgo man you can have the kind of sensible and practical love you want. His nature is Mutable-Earth and he will look up to you, for he idealizes the Cardinal-Earth qualities you actively embody. Your Saturn leadership combines with his ruling Mercury to indicate refined pleasures and the kind of polite social exchanges that make you feel comfortable. As you learn to relax in his company, your obvious compatibility will make for a deeply affectionate relationship. It may not have all the emotional passion you might hope for at first, but this is a pairing that improves with time and familiarity. You share the same goals and you both aim for practical success in dealing with the material world.

You can meet a Virgo man in any of your regular social rounds, though your common bond will probably be intellectual. You may be initially attracted by a particularly apt analytical remark that earns your respect. And Virgo will be impressed with the careful style of your approach. Your ironic wit is much to his liking, and he may find you interesting because he sees your creative approach to problems. Virgo can understand the innovative elements in your thinking that are often too subtle for others to appreciate. You may well respond warmly to a newfound friend and admirer.

The approach to sex will not be impulsive or impatient when two Earth signs get together, though the natural attraction Virgo feels for you will help him to be more recep-

tive to your advances. You are the Cardinal sign and the
dominant personality in this relationship. Your sex drive is
much stronger than Virgo's and though he is not as Earthy
as you, your intense sexuality will elicit an ardent response
from him. Though both of you appear cool and reserved in
public, your private moments together can be warm, intimate, and totally satisfying. This should not be an emotionally demanding relationship, because neither of you
communicate through your emotions. You show each other
that you care by being evenhanded, practical, and considerate.

Though you both may have had sexually active pasts, both
Virgo and Capricorn consider sex to be really appropriate
only within the context of a coherent relationship. Casual
sex makes you feel uncomfortable and is rarely satisfying
because it is so inhibiting. In a regularly structured relationship you both become less analytical and begin to open
up. The process is slow and sure, exactly the way you want
it to be. Time is on your side in all things, Capricorn, and
the longer a Virgo affair lasts, the more likely it will endure
as a stable relationship. Virgo represents your Ninth House—
long journeys—and you feel that an affiliation with a Virgo
man has the potential to go the distance.

Domestic harmony is virtually assured because you have
such similar values. He is good at home repairs and he likes
gadgets and all manner of time- and money-saving devices.
You will insist upon certain touches of comfort that Virgo's
more austere tastes may not require, but between the two
of you there is every indication of a happy home. If you can
learn to like health food and a regular diet, you will enjoy
Virgo's culinary skills as well.

Virgo is widely read and keeps up on current events and
affairs. You can get new ideas for practical application to
problems in business from Virgo. Your cultural interests
should lead to an active social life, and Virgo may release
you from your conservative pattern of attending conventional events as he introduces you to contemporary or avant-
garde entertainment. His skill at keen appraisal can give you

new insights for enjoying leisure time you spend together. You never like to feel you've wasted any pennies, but money spent on books will never be questioned. Intellectual and social pleasures will form the cornerstone of your relationship with a Virgo man.

Travel is indicated, but at your typical Earth-sign leisurely pace. You enjoy foreign study and learning languages together, giving you access to the literature, theater, and films of other countries. (It will also increase your ability to bargain while shopping in other lands.)

From a position of mutual respect, a relationship with a Virgo man can develop into a very satisfactory life-style that promotes your mental security because it is stable and practical. You have the freedom to develop your intellectual capacities because you don't have to worry about keeping the relationship in order. Virgo works as a true partner in supporting your goals and providing possibilities for the growth and progress that is essential to your happiness.

CAPRICORN & LIBRA

You will be naturally attracted to the style of a Libra man. Those born under the sign of the Balance are Cardinal-Air in nature and dedicated to the principles of active mentality. In some ways he complements your own Cardinal-Earth qualities, but there is also conflict over misunderstanding and motivation. Your Saturn rulership, in combination with his ruling Venus, indicates that you have a restraining influence on his extravagance while he adds a dash of style to your life. You combine to zero-in on career ambitions, and your common aspirations provide the overriding tone to the relationship.

A Libra man will impress you by his tact, diplomacy, and

ability to talk on his feet. His gift for clever conversation is very appealing to you, and he touches your sense of irony with his balanced judgments of human frailties. He may be attracted by your amiable reserve and whimsical observation, but Libra may not be the aggressor unless you correspond to his ideal image of male beauty. You share an interest in art, so invite him to a foreign-film festival, museum, or the opera. Libra will be impressed by your choice of aesthetic pleasure, and you may find that courting him is easier than you anticipated.

But much may depend upon Libra's mood. When he is feeling down and dirty, he may find your cool, refined approach just what he needs to keep his world in order. If Libra is feeling too high-toned and Airy, he may want to experience the more Earthy and physical side of your sexy personality. So while you may not find him to be your ideal partner, there is an elusive quality to making love with a Libra that can encourage you to keep on trying to reach a sexual plateau that pleases both of you. The proverbial endurance of Capricorn men should please him, and you may try to outdo each other in your attempts to achieve sexual harmony.

Fidelity may be a problem with a Libra lover because he has an eye for beauty that tempts him to stray. If your sex life becomes prosaic, Libra's feelings of boredom will cause him to entertain other arrangements. You are possessive of your lovers and may decide that the insecurity of dealing with him is not worth the effort. Nevertheless, a Libra lover will strive for harmony and you will both want to preserve the appearance of stability, even when the going gets rough. You are both status-conscious and you want the respectability associated with a permanent relationship. You could continue the affair for a long time, even after the passion has declined, because you both get other benefits from the arrangement.

There will probably be a great deal of emphasis on social ambitions with a Libra lover. His sign aspects your Tenth House—career and social standing. You can establish a home and use it for entertaining in high style. You want a relationship that has obvious growth potential, and a Libra partner will meet the criteria—for a while. Your involvement will start slowly and build to a plateau when everything appears to be in order. Your home is exactly as Libra envisioned it; your career is sailing along on a sea of dinner parties and social successes; your sexual compatibility seems fine; and the occasional indiscretion is handled very discreetly—but it all is precariously balanced and may topple at any moment.

You are both Cardinal signs, and taking each other for granted will mean that you begin to grow apart when the excitement of mutual discovery begins to wane. The bonds between you are strong, but not easy. There can be eventual separation, but Libra can be counted on in emergencies whenever you need him, and you will always have a special place in your heart for the intimacy you have shared.

You can have a lasting relationship with a Libra man but it must be dedicated to long-range goals that provide creative excitement that can sustain your interest and overcome your differences. If you can blend tact and determination, it may turn out to be a satisfying union, but it will depend upon the levels of maturity that you both can attain in learning to love each other.

CAPRICORN & SCORPIO

You can fall in love with a Scorpio man and avoid the sting of the Scorpion because you have a natural compatibility that supplies the trust and faith you both require. The men born under the sign of Scorpio are Fixed-Water, indicating the intensity of their emotional depth. The stability and ambition of your Cardinal-Earth nature appeals to his sense of values. Your ruling Jupiter finds much to admire in the serious, even somber influence of his planetary ruler, Pluto. There is a strong magnetic attraction that indicates sexual harmony with a strong social relationship. This may not be a lasting love affair, but you will remain friends with a Scorpio lover after the romance has worn off.

The initial attraction should be intriguing. Scorpio aspects your Eleventh House—hopes, wishes, dreams, and friendship. This dark, hypnotic beauty may be just the male type you have longed for in your private flights of fancy. You will feel the need to impress him, but the look in his eyes will tell you that you can have him if you want him. Scorpios are intuitive, and your cautious manner will not deceive him into confusing your natural reserve with uninterest. He senses the secret strength in your personality, and it excites his desire to know you socially and intimately.

You may be reserved, respectful, even cool toward each other on the surface, but the scent of passion is in the air. Scorpio comes on strong, but you match his creative sexuality with your Earthly endurance. He will normally play the role of the aggressor, but you have the receptive power to meet his demands for totally absorbing sex. As in all things between you and a Scorpio man, there are elements of power and control related to the strength of will you sense in each other.

The combined willpower of your signs should make for a strong bond of fidelity. You will be faithful because your good sense tells you that incurring the suspicion of the Scorpion is neither wise nor practical. You will enjoy rising to the challenge of satisfying his potent sexual needs, and it gives a dimension of growth to the relationship that keeps you both happy. If either of you should get caught in an indiscreet attraction to another man, the repercussions could signal the end of your love affair. Scorpio rarely apologizes and finds it hard to be forgiving. You can attempt to forgive, but you find it difficult to forget.

This potentially deep bond will complement your social life with a Scorpio lover. He enjoys your company and bolsters your self-confidence. You are both devoted to creating respectable public images that reflect your powerful drives for success, and you will enjoy making the rounds of parties and smart restaurants as a striking couple. There are indications of movement, creativity, and vitality that you find dazzling with a Scorpio companion.

You have fun, but you may wonder where it is leading you. If your crowded social calendar revolves around cultivating business contacts and entertaining clients, you have no qualms. If you feel that you are spreading yourself too thin, you will begin to question the potential for continued stability in a Scorpio affair. The intensity and creative stimulation may be exhilarating, but if you feel that the life you are leading is essentially superficial, you won't be able to relax and enjoy the scene with Scorpio for very long.

Whatever the outcome of your love affair, he will want to remain friends and so will you. If you have shared the passion and trust available to each of you, Capricorn and Scorpio can be very protective and loving as friends. The pressures of the social scene may be more than you can bear, but the emotional depth you experience from this relationship will give you new insights into the potential for personal growth that makes you even stronger and happier in your path to ultimate success.

CAPRICORN & SAGITTARIUS

You will find a Sagittarius man immensely appealing, but often exasperating, if you try to keep up with his exuberant and expansive life-style. Those born under the sign of the Centaur are Mutable-Fire by nature, restless and free-ranging in their search for inspiration. Your own Cardinal-Earth sensibilities tell you he is impractical, but also very exciting to be with as a friend or lover. You are ruled by Saturn, the planet of time, order, and restraint. His ruling Jupiter makes you want to get more involved in the humanitarian concerns Sagittarius embraces. You may not like his extravagance or his drinking buddies very much, but you will admire his philosophical interests and the untapped talents you see in him. You won't be able to change a Sagittarius, but you can help him with practical matters, and you learn to enjoy him for his free spirit.

You will probably meet him through his more studious activities, rather than through his interest in sports, though you may run into him if you do a bit of jogging. Whatever the circumstances, you should find a Sagittarius man quite fascinating. He is usually a handsome specimen of casual, masculine charm, but your attraction is more than physical. He aspects your Twelfth House—hidden meanings—and there is some undefinable quality of karmic memory that draws you to him. The boisterous bravado with which he approaches life is so very different from your reserve and caution that you wonder what you see in him, and yet you are truly intrigued.

Sagittarius will make the first move in any encounter. He strikes like lightning, without much warning or warm-up, so don't worry about any seduction scenario with soft music and candlelight. Sagittarian lovemaking is highly physical and plenty of fun. You will enjoy the masculine quality of his passion, and his stamina will match your endurance. There is an almost overwhelming feeling of power when you two make love that excites your imagination and spurs you on to ever greater efforts.

Enjoy him for the moments you share in each other's arms, because none of your efforts at possessing him ultimately will be effective. Sagittarius is born to wander, loves the thrill of flirtation, and won't be willing to enter into an exclusive relationship with you, even if he tells you he loves you. You can be his buddy and you can be his lover, but you can't get him to settle down into a monogamous relationship for very long unless it's true love.

Under Sagittarius' influence you can take a serious interest in community affairs and the politics of the gay liberation movement. You can use your concern and talents to become active in lobbying for human-rights legislation or working with peer-counseling groups. Whatever interests you develop with a Sagittarius buddy as your guide, you will devote your executive skills to contribute to the practical success of the enterprise. You can learn a great deal about who you are and where your skills and energy can be directed from a Sagittarius man in your life.

You can have an equally important impact on his life because you have the power to show a Sagittarian how to earn money. You perceive his potential and you can direct him toward making practical use of his inspired ideas and abilities. Sagittarians count on their gambler's luck to see them through, but you can get him to be more reliant on his skills to earn his way in the world.

An affair with a Sagittarius can be a real boost to your ego without becoming an all-encompassing permanent relationship as you imagine your goal. He brings a new breadth of vision and a new concern for things beyond your practical world of business as usual. Your life is filled with the intrigue of romance and the release of secret feelings that give an added sparkle to your personality. You can indulge your need to teach and your desire to learn when you team up with a Sagittarius as your loving man.

CAPRICORN & CAPRICORN

Take your time, Capricorn—you have plenty of it, thanks to the favors of Saturn,—when you meet another man born under the sign of the Mountain Goat. You are Cardinal-Earth, and the bonds you form will be deep and lasting, fulfilling all your cautious hopes and secret dreams. Capricorns do dream of finding true love, but only another Capricorn believes and understands the intensity of those dreams.

Other same-sign couplings have problems of self-image when they see their faults uncomfortably reflected in their lovers. They can exploit their weaknesses and compete for power in ways that make their relationship selfish and self-destructive. Fixed-Earth Capricorn men are remarkably free from these differences and difficulties because no other Sun sign strives so hard to be true to himself as you do.

You should meet him through your career contacts, but it won't be love at first sight. It never is with true Capricorns. You may find him very attractive, you may suspect he feels the same way about you, but it may take a long time to find out for sure. The more conservative your career, the more you conform to the expected standards of dress and behavior. You won't be able to tell if he is a potential lover by an exchange of winks across the conference table or by which back pocket has what handkerchief.

If you want to get to know him better, invite him to join you in any of the activities you most enjoy. Offer him an extra ticket to the symphony or suggest a visit to an art gallery. The courtship between two Capricorns can go on forever.

The sexual experience you come to finally share with a Capricorn man will be anything but casual. Remember, Saturn makes you a master of timing, and you will know when the right romantic moment has come. If it's love you feel, neither of you will want to engage the other sexually until you feel ready to make a commitment to a true relationship. You are serious men, and you have plenty of patience to wait for "the real thing." When you finally bed him, you may take the lead but he will be very responsive. When Capricorn men make love, there is an enormous and powerful release of pent-up emotion. Years of denial, self-discipline, and serious application to practical tasks at the expense of your need to give and receive affection are suddenly given new meaning in the loving embrace of another

Capricorn man. It may not be like an earthquake the first
time, but like everything else about Capricorn, the sex gets
better and better as time goes on. He is so serious, solid,
and stable that you can trust him with your most private
thoughts. He understands your need for financial security
and peaceful surroundings. He can give you the admiration
and respect you work so hard to earn and the praise you
secretly desire.

Your Capricorn man can be imposing, even stern, in his
public life, but he reveals his other nature to you in your
private moments. He has a wonderfully ironic sense of humor that brings out your own sense of whimsy as you smile
at the subtle things that amuse you about the fads and foibles
of the world. It may be hard to convince you that there could
be trouble in paradise with a Capricorn lover, but there are
a couple of things you should be aware of if you want to
stay happy.

Capricorn is a Cardinal sign, and there will be a question
of who leads whom. When you get into an argument over
this, the outcome may leave you both a bit bruised and
brooding. Also, your exclusive relationship, which centers
on home life and career interests, may become a closed
system with no possibility for creative stimulation. Too
much caution and exclusivity can stifle your creativity.

Time is your mutual benefactor in a Capricorn love affair
because you get more creative, more imaginative, and more
open to the joys of experience as you get older. Maturity
frees you to enjoy all the pleasures you have denied yourself
on the path to success. If you keep this relationship from
becoming carved in stone, you will be free enough to enjoy
the blessings of time and share the best years of your life
with a Capricorn man as your loving partner.

CAPRICORN & AQUARIUS

A relationship with a man born under the sign of the Water-bearer is not likely to be the great, consuming love of your life, but there are indications of other pleasures that are near and dear to your heart. The men of Aquarius are Fixed-Air by nature and can provide innovative money-making ideas that work well with your practical Cardinal-Earth qualities. The combination of your ruling Saturn with his Uranus rulership indicates the principle of restraint joined to the idea of the new and unexpected. You can put his abstract ideas and concepts to practical use for your mutual benefit. You become more interested in experimental procedures that give your career a new earning potential when you team up with an Aquarius as friend or lover.

Aquarians are unconventional and you are not likely to meet in any of the places you usually frequent. If you are too cautious or too shy and reserved to approach him, count on Aquarius to jump right in. He will find you intriguing and he is never slow to make anyone's acquaintance. You may find him rather bold, but he is an attractive personality who seems genuinely interested in getting to know you.

You may feel flattered by his attention because his approach is intellectual rather than sexual. Aquarius wants to know what's on your mind, and he wants to talk about his latest ideas rather than rush you into bed. His primary goal in life is the establishment of friendships. Capricorns normally have few close friends. Because you are a very private person, you don't warm up to strangers, but an Aquarius man can be so engaging in his unconventional approach that you let down some of your defenses.

You can bed him with relative ease if that is what you want, because sex is just not that important to him. You may not find it especially satisfying because he isn't all that emotionally involved in making love. Aquarians may be flamboyant or experimental in their love play because they need an intellectual handle to enjoy themselves. You may find him mildly amusing, even erotically stimulating, as a bedfellow, but the Earth will not move for you and the experience will not usually lead to a lasting relationship.

You are too possessive of your lovers to be happy for long with an Aquarian. He won't settle down easily because he needs his independence. Unless you want his extensive circle of somewhat crazy friends and former partners turning your home into a community drop-in center, his casual lifestyle is not parallel with your ideas of domestic bliss. If you do develop some form of enduring relationship or commitment, you will probably have to keep separate residences rather than compromise his independence or your need for privacy.

It will be difficult for you to relax around his odd collection of cronies or enjoy the unusual social situations that he participates in with such spontaneity. You like to know when, where, and how you are going, but Aquarius can take off at any time to look for some new place of undetermined character. You might come to admire his daring, but it is just not your way of life.

You can avoid an Aquarian tangle of sexual and social confusion if you concentrate on the real strength he brings to you: the power of his intellect. Working together, you can see the way in which his ideas are ahead of their time and think up practical ways to put them into action. Aquarius can be stubborn about anyone tampering with his ideas, but he will like it if he sees the practical results when the money starts rolling in. But there is another problem: You will save your dollars and invest them for tomorrow; Aquarius will spend for today and let tomorrow take care of itself.

From this union you can learn to appreciate the value of being open to the unusual, and he can learn new ways in which his mental energy can be harnessed and directed for mutual benefit. It may not be true love, but it can be a very rewarding friendship for both you and your Aquarius partner.

CAPRICORN & PISCES

An affair with a Pisces man can be a wonderful tonic to your spirit; light and engaging with a dreamy quality that is a new experience for you. Men born under the sign of the Fishes are Mutable Water by nature and very different from you in their laid-back approach to life. The combination of your guiding Saturn with his Neptune rulership indicates a combination of the principle of restraint with the power of dreams. Pisces men are dreamers, but you have the power to focus those dreams into something worthwhile that benefits both of you.

You may meet a Pisces man through your interest in art or perhaps through a shared study of extrasensory perception and other psychic phenomena. Your curiosity is aroused in a pleasant way that lets you drop some of your natural reserve and decide to get some form of communication going. It won't be difficult because Pisces will see a natural friend in you and be attracted to your strength. He is quite perceptive, and you should find it easy to get it on with him.

There is a hint of romance in the air between you and Pisces that stimulates a sexual response. Pisces might even be quite eager to get to know you as a bedfellow, and you can have an enjoyable encounter that will be gentle, imaginative, loving, and sincere. Your sexual endurance will provide him with long, sensuous sessions while you also satisfy his dreams of a stable and serious lover.

Pisces will look up to you and be faithful to you, but through the veil of his illusions rather than in the clear light of reality. If you want this to be a long-running show, there is a lot of serious work involved in keeping Pisces motivated. He has emotional depths and shallows that will be hard for your practical mind to understand. Don't fall into your usual pattern of accepting every obligation and duty that is thrust upon you. Pisces can let you take over his life, and it will seem natural that your strength should fill the vacuum and be his support. Pisces will cling to you for emotional security, but what will you gain from this relationship?

Pisces aspects your Third House—communication, short journeys, and short-term projects. You feel brotherly toward him rather than seeing him as your Man of Life. Your best bet is to enjoy the insouciant aspects of your encounter and don't get too serious. Pisces actually improves your sense of humor because he appreciates irony, whimsy, and a sincere smile rather than a backslapping laugh.

Pisces adds a note of playful amusement that is a refreshing change from your usual outlook on life. You can enjoy his company on trips to the zoo, excursions to the countryside, or visits to amusement parks. A Piscean affair would be an ideal extra added attraction on a holiday at a seaside resort. In the uncharacteristic or unreal environment of the vacationer's world, you can feel free to let loose and have a fling with Pisces. If you have ever wanted a summer romance, look for a Pisces man to share those sunny days and star-filled nights.

You may worry about hurting Pisces and think less of yourself for "using" him. If that is the case, you should think twice before you even start and ask yourself who uses whom in an open affair when two loving men come together to share passion and trust. Capricorns don't want to get "involved" with another man just for sex, but it is central to the issues with a Pisces man. He may live in a world of dreams, but he recognizes the value of living out one's fantasies as a path to self-actualization. You may be a fantasy figure for a Pisces man because you represent his Eleventh House—hopes, dreams, and wishes.

When you get involved in a transitory affair with a Pisces man, you have the opportunity to be loved as the man you are in other men's eyes. A Pisces lover can give you a completely new perspective on the potential for self-awareness as a loving man.

LOVING YOUR CAPRICORN MAN

If you ever fell in love with the president of your bank, your high-school principal, or your boss, you may be looking for a Capricorn man. He is serious and sincere as a friend or lover. If you want fireworks and passionate spontaneity, Capricorn is not going to fill the bill as your Man of Life.

You can find him wherever there are refined pleasures or serious business in progress. Capricorns like their amusements to reflect their elevated goals in life. Look for him at hit shows rather than at performances of experimental theater; in cocktail lounges rather than waterfront bars; at the symphony rather than a rock concert. His style is conservative, cautious, and conformist because he matches his lifestyle to his dark three-piece suit. He prefers formal dress to casual attire because it is a convenient framework that tells you immediately who he is and what he likes without having to talk about himself.

Capricorns prefer to call attention to their achievements rather than to their personalities because they put so much of themselves into their work. These men don't simply have jobs, they have careers; and they are dedicated to rising methodically to the top in their professions. You may meet him through his work, but don't come on to him between the hours of nine and five or he will ignore you. Invite him to join you on neutral territory if you want him to relax and be open to suggestions of further intimacy.

Take him to that perfect little Italian restaurant across town that exudes hospitality and conviviality. He will enjoy the unpretentious atmosphere and admire your choice of a reasonably priced menu. Capricorns are practical on principle, even if they aren't paying the bill! He always looks for good value because he works hard for his money. He certainly won't appreciate extravagant presents, so you should give him things that you have made or small tokens of affection rather than trying to impress him with your ability to spend money.

Capricorn prefers other men to be subtle in making their interest known to him. In a way, he likes to be courted because he wants to have control over the situation at all times. He has a good sense of timing, and when the moment comes for a seduction scene, he will let you know that he is ready for love.

Capricorns take love—like everything else—very seriously. He is looking for a permanent partner to share his life. The man he wants is someone who can respect him for his dedication and admire him for his achievements. In the course of his life he will be able to reach any material goal he aims for because he is ambitious and extra-demanding of himself. When he feels secure, when he has demonstrated his mastery of the material world, the only thing he needs is a man to share the enormous fund of emotion and affection that he has denied himself in order to reach the top.

Rather than becoming old goats, the men of Capricorn are the ultimate in late bloomers. Saturn has given them the gift of time. As children they are too adult, but in maturity they come into their full powers to be beautiful people and loving men. He actually gets better-looking as he gets older, and may even become young and gay in his attitude toward life. When he has achieved success, he has passed the test of Saturn and proven his mastery over the material world.

In a relationship, his lover benefits from his kindness and his desire to give the affection he craves in return. He can be very demanding because he wants to instill his values in people who are close to him. More than that, he needs to see growth, development, and the fulfillment of potential. He needs to see change and advancement on a steady basis or he feels that one's life is being wasted—and Capricorns abhor waste.

You can keep him happy by working up to your potential

and by praising him for his virtues. Capricorns can put themselves down for failing to meet their self-imposed expectations, but they don't pat themselves on the back enough. You can be a better lover to a Capricorn man if you work on improving his self-image.

As a lover, he will be faithful because he sees it as practical and even efficient, but also because he believes in the propriety of exclusive relationships. If you cannot be faithful to him, he will view it as lack of respect, which will probably mean the end for him. If you want to fool around, don't play with Capricorn. He will never show it, but he is inwardly vulnerable and easily hurt. He may be stern and serious on the outside, but there is a very tender man under his sensible exterior who longs for love.

Capricorn is not always easy to live with, but you can be sure that whether you are his friend or his lover, he will always have your best practical interest at heart. He always gives good advice that is based upon sound judgment. He will never tell you something just because you want to hear it. His compliments are sincere and hard-earned, and his criticisms come without malice.

Some may consider him cool, distant, square, or a stuffed shirt, but the really important qualities of Capricorn are not on the outside. He is a very private person because he is unsure of how others feel about him and he has repressed his emotions. Getting to know him better can lead to one of the most worthwhile relationships you will ever have. When you are old and gray, he will still be young and gay— and he never forgets his friends!

AQUARIUS
January 21–
February 20

Symbol: The Water-bearer
Ruling Planet: Uranus
Color: Purple
Metal: Aluminum
Natural House Rulership: Eleventh House, the house
    of hopes, wishes, and friendship
Eleventh House Traits: Desire for knowledge and
    love of experience
Motto: ''I know''
Nature: Fixed sign (organizer)
Element: Air sign (mental)
Qualities: Altruistic, intellectual, and eccentric
Capacities: Investigation and combination
Personality Key Words: Individualism, eclecticism,
    and humanitarianism

MAXIMIZING YOUR AQUARIUS POTENTIAL

If you were born under the sign of the Water-bearer, you are dedicated to the examination and exploration of the world of ideas as abstract concepts. The Fixed-Air qualities of Aquarius make you devoted to the principle of intelligence for its own sake, and you may seem cool or detached because you shy away from emotional involvements that can restrict your mental freedom. You pride yourself on your ability to deal in concepts and to be a progressive thinker, rather than a man of action. The eccentric power of Uranus as your ruling planet endows you with optimism and the belief that many problems will solve themselves in unexpected and unconventional ways if you let events take their course. Aquarians are classic nonconformists, and you are open to all kinds of ideas as you pick and choose those that fit your vision of the future. You think of yourself as being a thoroughly modern man.

Your basic goals in life are focused on your need for freedom to think without emotional or practical distractions and demands. Your desire to pursue all of your many interests makes you seem somewhat distant because you are interested in the present mainly for the clues it can give to the future. You can attain a degree of perspective, which gives an objective value to your intellectual gifts, but you may not understand the human values involved in relating to other personalities. You want others to trust your vision, but it is difficult for them to have faith in you unless you produce some positive proof of your ability to achieve real results as well as conceive of theoretical plans. It is difficult for you to work under other people because you don't want any restraints on your independence. Though you are altruistic in your goals and want to improve the condition of mankind, you don't like to be pinned down to any one course of action or train of thought.

Uranus is the planet of surprise and change, making you unpredictable. You want others to trust you, but they may not always feel that you give them good reason to do so. Aquarians are a rare blend of idealism, optimism, and compassion, but you can fall into periods of wishful thinking and idle musing with no thoughts of the practical consequences. At the same time your Fixed-sign nature can make you quite opinionated. Once you decide on something, you can become rigid, but then you discard the idea when you come across a new one that seems totally fresh. Aquarians may seem to have the answers to everything, but you only speculate instead of acting. You need direction to be effective or else you can live and work in a mental environment that is so chaotic and individualistic, it puts people off and they won't listen to even your best ideas. Your friends can accuse you of inciting negative reactions by being so ''up-front,'' and straight society may dismiss you as part of the lunatic fringe. Fortunately your Fixed-sign nature, combined with the power of Uranus, gives you the faith to persevere in your beliefs.

Your social life is usually very active because you enjoy the company of many people from all walks of life. You are always looking for new stimuli because you are more interested in experimenting with many relationships than finding one man who will fulfill all your needs. You enjoy the bars for the easy camaraderie and conversation.

The search for sexual companionship is not your primary goal. You are more interested in having friends than lovers. At the same time you want to explore sex; you just don't want to trap yourself in an emotional commitment that might be a mistake. You are not bound by traditional concepts of morality, and you are no stranger to all of the polymorphous possibilities in sex between men. You will try anything once, but you will not become fixated for very long on any one form of sexual experience. You like to keep all your options open, and you never know what to say when one of your partners asks you what you like to do. If you are bold enough, the typical Aquarian answer would be "Everything." Despite your history of sexual experimentation, you take the principle of a commitment to a lover very seriously. This is why you have such a hard time surrendering—you are not sure that either you or your potential partner can live up to your ideals.

Above all else, your lover would have to be your good friend. You will take a great deal of time to think it over and get to know him before you will contemplate a serious relationship. You must consider him socially and intellectually compatible and equal. Your lover must value your individuality, and you will be faithful to him in return for his understanding. He must share your interest in sexual variety and be receptive to experimentation. Freedom and trust, combined with intellectual stimulation, are the high price tags you put on your love.

You can give your lover a new understanding of the value of your life-styles as loving men. Aquarians are proud to be gay because they see themselves as part of the wave of the future in experimental human relationships. You are rarely depressed and often elated by the constant challenge that you are posing to society—to understand, accept, and tolerate your need to be different in any way you choose.

You can maximize your potential if you harness your vision to the causes you believe in. Be willing to work in community and social projects that express your ideals. You are blessed with versatility and intellectual talent, plus the ability to hold firm to what you envision as the Aquarian age in which we all can maximize our potential.

AQUARIUS & ARIES

An affair with an Aries man could well be a lively, dynamic experience that appeals to your taste for the unexpected and unconventional. Your Fixed-Fire qualities are activated by the inspirational force of the Mutable nature of Aries. The ruling Uranus of Aquarius combines with the Mars rulership of Aries to indicate energized ideas. His boyish enthusiasm and your visionary thoughts can be a powerful force. It might be too torrid to last very long, but you can be fast friends and fast-paced lovers.

You will be attracted to his youthful spirit and boisterous manner. Aries is athletic and competitive in his approach to everything; he is full of flash and dash and has the ego of a high-school hero. He may wonder what he will become when and if he grows up, and he may see you as a role model because of your wide-ranging interests.

Your individuality is based upon conscious choices rather than the fluctuating inspiration that motivates Aries. He will recognize in you a combination of his own pioneering spirit with more intellectual consciousness. The relationship will call for considerable self-awareness on your part because Aries will encourage your most outrageous tendencies as Air and Fire blend into a consuming bonfire.

Aries will be impetuous in his sexual advances, both ardent and flattering in the way he is obviously eager to get you into bed. You will be attracted to his masculine charm, his open mind, and the ease with which you get along in a casual conversation. Both of you are willing to combine social and sexual amusement in becoming acquainted, so there won't be any elaborate seduction scene. Neither of you will presume that romance requires a deep emotional commitment in order for it to be a satisfying experience.

While you are an essentially congenial couple, there are differences in your approaches to making love. He is much more direct and physical in bed than you are. Aquarian sex is more fantasy-oriented and multidimensional than Aries is used to, but he can certainly get into the spirit of things by performing with mirrors or toys that add just the right element of the unusual. You can lapse into your multifaceted imagination during lovemaking with Aries, but he may not notice because he is paying more attention to the intense physical thrills that are surging through his body. You may find him to be too quick or unimaginative. Aries may feel that you are too calculated in your desires.

Neither of you will be particularly faithful as partners, but you should be good friends, able to talk openly. Neither Aquarius nor Aries realizes how their actions affect others. Your lack of practical consideration for each other can be the basis of your conflicts.

Aries takes all criticism as a direct assault on his ego, so you should cultivate a light touch. Unlike other Fixed signs, you avoid confrontations and don't like to be argumentative. Aquarius' Fixed-Air stubbornness takes the form of dismissing or ignoring people or attitudes with which you disagree. Fortunately there is plenty of room for agreement with an Aries buddy, at least in terms of activities—he tends to be a man of action rather than ideas.

Aries aspects your Third House—communications and short journeys—and you will find it easy to get along with him. You can work well together on short-term projects involving advertising, promotion, or public relations. Vacations together will become legendary exploits and totally fatiguing experiences. Even your daily lives together will be lived on the run and rarely on time. Don't be surprised if he is just a little grumpy in the morning. Aries doesn't have a great deal of stamina, so your running around is going to make him short-tempered because he is frequently teetering on the edge of exhaustion.

An Aries love affair may not be the relationship of your dreams, but it can be the way in which you meet a wonderful playmate who will become a good friend. As such, an Aries can be a loving companion who is fun, loyal, gener-

ous, and sincerely devoted to the relationship he shares with
you.

AQUARIUS & TAURUS

An affair with a Taurus man can be an unusual blend of
home life and social activity that combines people from the
worlds of entertainment, fashion, and the arts. The Fixed-
Earth qualities of Taurus join with your own Fixed-Air nature to indicate an unconventional mixture of practicality,
luxury, intellectuality, and business success. Great ideas are
put into motion by mixing business with pleasure when you
and a Taurus man get together. Your ruling planet, Uranus,
affects his Venus rulership by adding visionary insights that
fuel his desire for attaining the good things in life.

You two spend a great deal of money on your social life
and personal surroundings with the objective of making the
proper impression on people who can advance your careers.
If you keep reminding money-conscious Taurus that it can
be a tax write-off, he may not be too insecure about the
cash-flow crises that are bound to occur. He may be very
difficult to live with when the bills come in, but he will be
a happy Bull when the tide starts running the other way and
he begins to see the rewards of your efforts.

Taurean men are solid citizens. His approach may seem
unnecessarily plodding to you, and he can be stubbornly
conservative. There are times when you think he is a drag,
but you also know that he has a good sense of humor, is
sincere about caring for his friends and lovers, and is un-
questionably loyal. Your Air-sign detachment may not make
you warm enough or sensitive enough to provide him with
the kind of love he needs, but you can form a dynamic
partnership that is beneficial to both of you.

You might be attracted to a Taurus man by his dark masculinity, which has an element of sensuous promise, thanks to the influence of Venus. If he seems somewhat quiet at first, it isn't because he is really standoffish, he is probably just shy. Your talent for conversation can bring out his winning personality, but it might be wise to take it easy and relax, or he might take fright and amble away. He is Fixed-Earth, and your Fixed-Air quirks of thought and manner are bound to make him a little nervous. Your Aquarian talent for letting events take their natural course will allow him to loosen up, and Earthy Venus will tell him that if he likes you, he will want to bed you.

Your first sexual encounter will occur at his place, which will probably be well furnished but not particularly modern. Taureans like mating rituals that begin with their favorite music, a meal with a good bottle of wine, and a continuously building atmosphere of sensuality. The candlelight-and-wine approach may seem a bit old-fashioned to you, but it can be a very refreshing change from the more offbeat experiences you are accustomed to. Enjoy it, and be sure to tell him so! Compliment his hospitality and comfortable surroundings because they are points of pride for any Taurus. When he feels completely comfortable, well fed, and well regarded, his thoughts will turn to physical pleasures.

As a lover, he has an easy pace that reflects his strength, kindness, and sensitivity. He may be quieter than you, but he won't mind the occasional encouragement or suggestion. Taurus is no slave of love, but he is receptive and sensual. Sex is best for him when he knows what to expect. He won't appreciate anything too bizarre, but he will try to please you. You can play around with a Taurus man, but you can't toy with his affections. He is serious about sex and doesn't take commitment lightly.

Taureans are possessive of their lovers and he may not understand your need for such an unorthodox collection of friends. He can become confused and even suspicious of your desire for freedom, but the potential rewards that come from your relationship can soothe his insecurities. Because

Taurus aspects your Fourth House—home—much of your career and social life will revolve around your environment.

Money—and the things that money can buy—make him happy and secure. Together you two can have very successful careers. You provide the inspired ideas from your uncanny sense of the future, and he has the practical business knowledge necessary to make them work. There will be conflict and tension over just how far to go out on a limb. Taurus will always be more cautious and conservative than you. Your Fixed signs indicate that compromise is difficult and apologies rare indeed. You can usually let him think he is getting his way and do whatever you want, as long as the end result is productive. If not, be prepared to face the wrath of the angry Bull. Despite the inherent problems, you can have a strong friendship and a successful relationship loving a Taurus man.

AQUARIUS & GEMINI

A love affair with a Gemini man can be a completely unique experience that defies convention and forms a very close bond between you. The relationship can fail or succeed in a spectacular manner that combines romance, creativity, long-range projects, travel, and a sincere devotion to each other. The combination of your Fixed-Air nature with his Mutable-Air talents indicates a strong mental attraction and much interaction between abstract ideals and trendy ideas. Your ruling Uranus affects his Mercury rulership to make for unusual forms of communication that break traditions in order to achieve new paths to success. The Water-bearer of Aquarius pours out ideas for examination, and the Twins of Gemini pick up on every one of those ideas in order to broadcast them without any restraint or censorship.

It will probably be Gemini who articulates his romantic interest in you. He will look upon sex as another adjunct to sparkling conversation, and it won't be difficult to continue your interchange of ideas on a physical as well as an intellectual level. You both enjoy sex, but it does not have an urgency or a wild, emotional content for either Aquarius or Gemini. You both look upon it mainly as just another form of expression and adventure, rather than the ingredient of deep commitment.

Gemini wants love to be fun and involve fantasy. He enjoys mirrors, pornography, voyeurism, and all forms of mental stimulation to get himself physically aroused. You also enjoy any exotic approaches because your Air-sign nature gives you similar needs. Gemini men can be an encyclopedic collection of every sexual technique and fantasy they have ever experienced. An affair with him should be long-lasting simply because there is so little likelihood of the fatal boredom that has ruined relationships for both of you in the past.

Neither of you will expect a rigid, monogamous commitment. Other people may think you have a terrible relationship, but when Aquarius and Gemini get together, you don't give a damn about what other people think. Both of you understand that monogamy is not a security blanket you need to cling to in order to have a loving and exciting affair that fulfills your mutual needs for intelligent companionship. You believe, in typical Aquarian fashion, that you are forging the pattern for the relationship of the future.

Gemini collects information from a wide range of sources. Newspapers, television, magazines, street talk, and gossip provide him with a deep fund of current thought on every imaginable topic from world events to next year's hemlines and hairstyles. You can use his breadth of scope to provide new input for your own vision. Gemini gives you the extra edge on what's happening tomorrow. It means you will take extraordinary chances that can lead to embarrassing disasters or fantastic successes.

There will be tension and conflict that relate to the pace

of your life-style, but Gemini should be able to understand you well enough to let the good times roll with the bad. You both can become irritable and cranky, but you also have a respect for each other that accommodates the need for privacy and freedom whenever you need it. There can be manic swings of mood, but they are like fast-moving clouds on a windy day that never produce the rains of despair. There is an implicit agreement that you are going to live your lives together at full-tilt with few explanations and no apologies.

Gemini aspects your Fifth House—romance and creativity. You may look upon him as your ideal lover. He is willing to make a long-term commitment that does not include the emotional entanglements that have spoiled relationships for both of you in the past. Your love life will have all the excitement you crave, and you will be faithful to each other in your fashion. This is a relationship that sets it own standards, and you both enjoy the notoriety and variety of being lovers who live for the moment with an eye on tomorrow.

AQUARIUS & CANCER

You can have a truly loving and caring relationship with a Cancer man, but it will not be an easy affair. Your perceptions of life are very different, and you can confuse each other unless you have made a commitment to be as open as possible about your mutual needs. He is a Cardinal-Water sign, and his fluctuating moods and emotions are often perplexing to your Fixed-Air sensibility. The combined influences of your ruling Uranus with his Moon rulership indicate the potential for sensitivity and the possibility that you can change his life through new intellectual stimuli. Aspects of harmony, combined with the excitement of romance, can make this a highly enjoyable relationship if you give it a chance.

You may meet through your mutual interest in the theater or in connection with a creative hobby. From the beginning you will notice certain differences. Cancer is interested in the past and tends to be a traditionalist, while you are more modern, if not more radical. You have a direct approach to problems, but those born under the sign of the Crab are more indecisive. You will be attracted to his apparent depth and his ability to work through problems. Cancer adds balance and humanity to your sometimes detached approach to difficult questions. He can be an excellent resource person who will sincerely wish to help you in any project you undertake as a team, and he will take you farther than you could go on your own.

Cancer men can be shy and unsure of their emotions. He may indicate his attraction to you, but you must be the one who acts if you want him for your lover. In other situations his Cardinal-sign nature might cause him to be the aggressive partner, but he may wonder how you really feel and hesitate until you declare your intentions. Both of you may hold back for some time until you feel that a real friendship is forming before you take the next step and explore the sexual dimension of your attraction.

Cancer men are physical and emotional lovers. If your Air-sign fantasies include a man who will smother you with tender kisses and bathe you in affection, then you'll enjoy the best of Cancerian lovemaking. He likes variety in his sex life and you can provide enough creative touches to keep him happy. His changing moods may confuse you when he switches from passive to active, but you appreciate the unexpected in most things, and it will add an element of unpredictability that keeps you interested and able to match his strong sexual needs.

Cancer will want to be faithful, but your need for freedom of action may cause him to question your emotional commitment. Cancer aspects your Sixth House—service—and so you will want to take care of his needs as best you can, but you must encourage him to articulate those needs. He feels more than he thinks, and often he is something of a mystery to himself. You can teach him to cope with human emotions, perhaps for the first time.

A liaison with a Cancer man can provide practical benefits that center on your career and home. If you want a secure domestic base, Cancer's nesting instinct may be just what you are looking for in a lover. Your expansive nature makes you careless with money, but Cancer will encourage thrift, foresight, and specific career goals. He has a creative imagination that can lead to successful joint business ventures when combined with your futuristic concepts. Cancer's insecurity about his talents can be assuaged by your unswerving belief that events take care of themselves as long as you are committed to taking the chance and letting the chips fall where they may. Cancer wants to believe, but he needs your Fixed-sign determination to overcome his inevitable worries.

Your ability to communicate your affection is the key to a Cancer love affair. You must be not only verbal but physical as well, or he will seek other men's arms to comfort him in his emotional confusion. Without the assurance he needs, a Cancer man can become secretive, deceptive, and a victim of his mood swings.

This relationship will require a mature perspective from both of you, but it can be a very rewarding experience. You can learn that there are human dimensions to the abstract truths you hold so dear. Cancer can profit by experiencing some detachment from his constant preoccupation with his emotions. Together you can overcome your weaknesses and join your strengths in a lasting and loving relationship that makes you both more creative personalities and more capable and happy as loving men.

AQUARIUS & LEO

A relationship with a Leo man is certain to be complex and exciting, because he is your complementary opposite on the Wheel of Life. His Fixed-Fire nature can be inspirational to your Fixed-Air intellect, but you have very different motivations and tend to be set in your ways. The combination of your ruling Uranus with his Sun rulership indicates an unusual combination of strong personalities. The fact that opposites attract is the core of your initial attraction to each other. Facing your strengths and weaknesses in a loving relationship with a man who is your astrological mirror image is also the source of the inherent conflict between you. Like two actors of different schools, you are both convincing and compelling, but Leo has a natural gift of intensity and earnestness that your more intellectual method does not convey. Although many are drawn to Aquarius, their hearts go out to Leo.

You are natural partners, but your partnership requires that you both receive your fair share of attention. You can become jealous of Leo because he has such an artless warmth and grace that makes you seem calculated and cool. If you don't let yourself become envious of his charms, you can learn to enjoy him as a friend or lover. If you can hold on to the feeling of admiration and avoid dissecting his every nuance, searching for challenges to your own ego, you can have an ardent, loving relationship with a man born under the sign of the Lion.

Leo is a real golden boy who is accustomed to the adulation of his friends and the admiration of strangers. Even though his looks may be conventional, he carries himself with an aura of grace and dignity that attracts people to him. He has an undefinable way of lighting up others that makes them willing to stroke his ego.

You bring the stimulation of Air to his Fire-sign nature,

and there are likely to be some sparks of mutual desire. Leo will seldom make the first move with any man he considers his peer, so you should take the initiative and chat him up in your usual friendly manner. Leo is used to men coming on to him with obvious sexual intent, so your intellectual approach should be a refreshing change. Talking about what is on his mind will be a new form of flattery that will certainly get the attention of a Leo man.

It won't be difficult to talk him into your arms, and you should find him to be an inspiring bedfellow. He is physically active, but kind and generous with his affections. He demands your complete attention, and his ardor will be dampened if you distance yourself by using him as a fantasy figure. You tend to fantasize too much in bed, and Leo can teach you the pleasures of the here and now and how to experience completely the joy of physical communion. A Leo man loves by instinct, and his passionate energy can turn sex into a celebration of life.

Leo believes in his natural nobility, but he needs to have more faith in himself. His ego is strong, but he is secretly fragile and needs your praise. You have the insight to sense his feelings of vulnerability, and your gift of love and friendship will be very important to him. As Fixed signs, you both have the tendency to take your lovers for granted. It can be a fatal mistake. Leo looks for the admiration of other men, and you might embarrass him in public by some thoughtless and outrageous act of nonconformity. The result will be a raging argument once you get home, or an icy detachment that will bring out all your Fixed-sign stubbornness and inability to apologize.

Fixed signs always see their own faults as virtues. What you describe as Leo's egomania, he will term his pride. What Leo sees as recklessness in you, you describe as vision. Together you can blend your best qualities to become a successful team with an enormous amount of creative force and charisma. You aspect each other's Seventh House—partnership—and there is the potential and desire to balance your personalities. There can be excitement and even contentment, though you may always be upstaging each other. More actors are born under Leo and Aquarius than under any other sign. Take your cue, Aquarius, and play this one for the Academy Award.

AQUARIUS & VIRGO

A relationship with a Virgo man can be a long-lasting, tried-and-true experience that goes beyond the vagaries of love and sex into a really satisfying companionship. Your Fixed-Air nature of intellectual idealism gains practical assistance through his Mutable-Earth qualities. The combined influences of your Uranus rulership with his ruling Mercury gives you an open channel to communicate visionary ideas and practical considerations. Virgo can be a valuable friend because he will be an honest critic who is sincere in trying to help you.

Virgo aspects your Eighth House—mysterious attraction—and despite your differences in outlook, you will feel drawn to become his friend. Virgo wants to serve you in some way, and he might become the best roommate you could ever have. Since neither of you believes that sex is the determining factor, you can make an excellent "odd couple." With a Virgo man in your life you can look forward to laundered clothes, hot meals, an orderly home, and an excellent foil for your intellectual interests. If it happens that the physical side pleases and satisfies both of you, all of the other ingredients for a long-term relationship already may be present.

You are not likely to meet Virgo anywhere in "the scene," because there isn't any one place he likes well enough to be a "regular." He may very well be on the board of the local museum, where you also share an interest. Your aesthetic tastes combine at the level of very modern art. Conceptualist or experimental performances and theater pieces attract the curious critic in Virgo, as well as the Aquarian search for the newest of the new. You may have friends in common who introduce you, but they will have to be quite eclectic to be close friends to both of you.

Unless Virgo is on a binge, the odds are that he won't be anybody's plaything. His partners have to fulfill a lot of requirements. There are too many things that Virgo wants to know, and he doesn't trust his first impressions. Since your own interest in people is largely intellectual, you may enjoy his company for quite a long time before you consider the possibility of romance. In fact, he may be the one who changes your friendship into something more. Your Fixed-sign qualities mean that you can become comfortable with one workable level and may stay there. Virgo may deduce that you need someone to help you organize your life or provide a home base. He may also decide that he could love you because you meet his special criteria without even trying.

Virgo has the ability to excel at the techniques of sex, and you may find that he can complement your fantasies with just the right details. Virgo's lovemaking is subtle. There may not be a lot of passion but he's eager to please, though he won't want surprises when it comes to time and place. Like everything else in his life, lovemaking should be neat, tidy, and well thought out, or Virgo just won't get into the spirit.

Virgo represents a special challenge to you. Your life has so many different people in it that you will sometimes skip over difficult ones. But Virgo's genuine desire to help you and to understand evokes a mysterious response in you. You may wonder how you can put up with all of his fear, criticism, and pettiness for very long. For you to overcome the constricting aspects of your relationship it is necessary that you have a common bond outside the eccentricities of your individual personalities. Though you may be from similar backgrounds, or you may have met in school, something apart from those similarities will have to serve as a catalyst to bring you together with a Virgo.

Before you can realize the potential you have to help each other, a common interest must give you some insight into the Virgo personality. Virgo's gifts are for details and for specific goals. He requires an environment that has the ascetic comfort that his own restrained Earth qualities demand. He is self-reliant but can be overwhelmed and get down in the dumps. Your expansiveness can be the right tonic for him—in measured doses. This relationship can work only if you have considered the effect you may have on each other's lives.

AQUARIUS & LIBRA

A Libra love affair may turn out to be a truly satisfying relationship that meets your requirements for an ideal man to share your life. Libra may be the stardust of your Aquarian dreams! He is a fellow Air sign, and you share an intellectual approach to life and a fascination with relationships. He is Cardinal by nature and combines with your Fixed qualities to give you a sense of direction and focus for your ideals. The influence of Uranus on his Venus rulership indicates a new sense of harmony and justice for your altruistic abstractions. There are aspects of travel and study that could broaden your horizons without scattering your energies.

You can meet a Libra in surroundings that emphasize beauty and charm. You will appreciate his poise and his wit, as well as his quick grasp of the nuances of your ideas. Because you are interested in each other's minds, the way is already paved for an easy and natural romantic encounter with Libra. He should find you to be a dashing and romantic figure; he will find your high ideals endearing, and that will be a factor in his attraction to you.

Sex with Libra is going to be a real pleasure for both of you. Libra always treats his lovers the way he wants to be treated, so take your cues from him. He likes a sensual environment and wants to spend a long time in bed, pouring out much affection. It is the kind of sex between loving men that you appreciate best of all, because it is physical but not intensely passionate or overly emotional. Libra makes suggestions through his actions, but he never demands. Your desire for experimentation can easily be accommodated by a Libra lover. He enjoys sex but can become bored with a predictable partner. It has to be different every time for him to maintain his interest and desire. Your diverse tastes and large repertoire are perfectly matched to his love of variety.

Libra wants to have a lover and a partner to make his life complete, but he will not be smothering or demanding. You shy away from emotional commitments that threaten your independence. But with Libra you may feel new and strange sensations that awaken a latent romanticism in your heart. Slowly but surely you two may begin to discover emotions in your typical Air-sign ways. Libra aspects your Ninth House—long journeys—and you may well decide to travel together on the road of life for as long as possible.

You gain a sound foundation with Libra and become more decisive. He is an emotional ally because he adds just enough to give you a new sense of equilibrium. You respect him for his sense of integrity and the way he helps you to choose among the many concepts that sometimes overwhelm your ability to act.

Libra will keep you from making too many commitments to too many people, but he won't restrict your social life. He needs the stimulation of others as much as you do, sometimes even more. You will enjoy your nights out because neither of you needs the security of acting as a couple in public. You will split up and spend your evening mingling with the multitudes, enjoying the company and not worrying about what the other is up to. Libra may flirt, but it's only an ego game and you know it. He has an eye for pretty things and handsome men, but he need not possess them as long as he knows he's going home with you.

You both benefit from this relationship. You get an understanding friend who loves you for your best qualities, and Libra finds a worthy person of his affections at last. New feelings of responsibility, romance, and an understanding of human values make this a love you will long treasure.

AQUARIUS & SCORPIO

A relationship with a Scorpio man as your friend or lover is going to be a difficult proposition. The combination of your Fixed-Air intellect and free-ranging life-style and his Fixed-Water qualities of emotion and possession are not really compatible. There is always a scent of challenge whenever you two get together. The unpredictable influence of Uranus confuses and disturbs the deep forces of mystery associated with his Pluto rulership. Scorpio's personality combines powerful, quiet emotion with a drive to exercise control over others. You could benefit from learning more about the strength of emotions, but Scorpio does not want to reveal his inner feelings or thoughts, because he thinks letting them out would make him vulnerable. You are equally firm in your optimism, your ideals, and the strength of your convictions. Communication will be difficult because you don't understand each other's motives.

You can meet a Scorpio in some unexpected manner, perhaps through business or family connections, but you might not be attracted to him in a normal social situation. Though he may be quite eccentric privately, he presents a very conservative image in public. This kind of double life is not usually your style, though you will be interested in sampling a Scorpio at least once. If you are interested, Scorpio is intuitive enough to respond by coming on to you, and you are experimental enough to accept.

Your curiosity will be more than satisfied with a Scorpio man. He is highly knowledgeable about sex, and he knows what he wants and how he wants it. You can get into the spirit of things for a while, but you won't like his dominant, forceful manner if he tries to come on too strong. You can get involved in the fantasy of making it with the Great Dark Man, but he may take your fantasies too far in the direction of intense emotion and physical passion. You may not understand what is happening to him during lovemaking because he retreats so deeply into himself.

If Scorpio should find it to be a pleasing experience, he might be interested in making it a more regular affair, but the demands he makes on his lovers are more than your free spirit will ever tolerate. He is suspicious of your wide circle of friends, and he'd rather you give them up and spend your time at home. You might not mind it for a short-term change of pace, but you will soon feel that he is more interested in sex than in the intellectual relationship you want and need. Scorpio needs to assuage his insecurities by possessing his lovers. You may be willing to devote your life to an ideal, but never to the demands of one man who does not even give credence to your idealism.

The best thing Scorpio can do for you is to challenge you to stand up for what you believe. Normally you don't get into arguments. Your tolerance for others' life-styles and opinions is quite extensive, unless they threaten you. If someone expresses an opinion you oppose, you are often willing to let it pass rather than try to convince the blind to see. You don't really believe that you can force anyone to change his mind. Scorpio does. Because he is a Fixed sign, he can't resist challenging your ideas and opinions. Scorpio makes you want to put your ideals into practice in order to prove that you are right. Because your own Fixed-sign ego is involved, you gain a new determination to be practical, organized, and goal-oriented. Scorpio accuses you of being an idle dreamer, and you rise to the challenge.

Love and friendship may not be easy to find with a Scorpio, and your basic Aquarian inclination is not to try. You have the world of loving men in your heart, and there isn't enough room to focus all your energies on one relationship. If you win the respect of a Scorpio man, he may become totally loyal to you as a person, but he will always feel confused and threatened by your high principles—until he learns to see outside of himself. You can point the way, Aquarius, but you may not be able to take him there.

AQUARIUS & SAGITTARIUS

Any relationship with a Sagittarius man is going to be a real affair of the heart. He can be both friend and lover who satisfies the need for excitement in your life. Your Fixed Air is heated by the inspiration of his Mutable-Fire nature. Men born under the sign of the Centaur stimulate your imagination. The combination of your ruling planet, Uranus, with his Jupiter rulership indicates an expansion of your ideals into new projects, travel, and experiments. The accent is on the desire for pleasure and new experiences in every direction with a man who appreciates the way you think and admires your nonconformism. There is ample room for spontaneity and idealism when you get together with a Sagittarian as a loving pal.

You can meet him almost anywhere in the world and tune right in to his free and easy personality. Your Aquarian sense of individuality will appreciate his casual style in dress and manner. Conversation will start with a joke and continue with a scintillating exchange of ideas and stories that range from the theories of Machiavelli to the latest Hollywood scandal. Sagittarius is a traveling man who has seen and done many things. He gets great pleasure from the opportunity to put his experiences into perspective. Your Fixed-Air intellectual capacities give him a framework for his thoughts and an attentive friend to share them with. You will admire his outlook on life because it complements your idealism.

There is an aura of fun-loving sexuality about Sagittarius that you will find alluring. You are both open to discussing your sexual experiences and preferences, without meaning to brag or dish. He understands your interpretation of sex as a means of communication, and it will be easy and natural for you to have a dialogue with each other very quickly. Your Aquarian curiosity will be aroused, and it won't take long for it to be satisfied, because Sagittarius is always ready for romantic entanglements.

You will definitely enjoy the cheerful sex play of Sagittarius. He will complement your fantasies and provide a direct approach to having fun in bed that is truly engaging. He is kind and generous in his exuberant spirit of erotic revelry. If he gets a little rough, it is only because he gets carried away. You two can tickle, tease, toss, and tumble all night—until you are weak from laughter and satiated with pleasure.

Neither of you is into heavy emotional commitment, and the accent will be on friendship and sharing good times together instead of settling down to any kind of traditional relationship. You are honest with each other about your needs for a lot of social contacts, though you can be very loyal friends. You can live together and be very loving roommates, but there must always be the acknowledgment of each other's need for freedom.

Sagittarius aspects your Eleventh House—hopes, wishes, and dreams. In some way you wish you could be like him, and he satisfies your requirements for an ideal friend. You can play practical jokes on each other, embarrass each other in front of strangers, and get into all manner of mischief, but you rarely get angry. Though you can be dreamers and mile-a-minute madcaps, there is a serious side to you both that is expressed in your combination of Aquarian idealism and Sagittarian humanitarianism.

You are appalled by injustice, and Sagittarius urges you to do something about it. You will take your beliefs to the telephones, the courts, the ballot boxes, and the streets to promote the cause you hold dear. Together you have the power to communicate and inspire others to follow your example.

When you get involved with a Sagittarian friend and lover, the horizons seem infinite. You travel together, you meet unconventional social contacts, you overextend yourselves and bloom in the challenge. You can be irresponsible, but your hearts are always in the right place. This is a very romantic and idealistic relationship that you will treasure for many years to come.

AQUARIUS & CAPRICORN

A relationship with a Capricorn man as your friend or lover will not be easy and carefree, but there is the possibility of beneficial change in your life. He is Cardinal-Earth in nature and much more ambitious, practical, and materialistic than your own Fixed-Air qualities of abstract intelligence. Your ruling Uranus, in combination with his Saturn, indicates a restraint upon your concepts that forces them into more practical channels. You may rebel against the restrictions but you can definitely benefit from the influences in a Capricorn relationship. If you can follow his direction without feeling that you have compromised your beliefs, Capricorn can help you make your dreams come true on a large scale.

Capricorns are conservative in their social habits, and you

will meet him in some unusual manner or someplace you have never seen before. He enjoys traditional pleasures and amusements rather than the somewhat far-out diversions you prefer. You may be attracted to him simply because he is so different from you and from the men you normally meet. If you want to get to know him better, don't try to impress him with your eccentricity. Engage him in a serious conversation; he will be interested in your innovative ideas and your concept of the future.

The immediate future may not involve a sexual dimension unless you take the initiative. Capricorns are slow to warm up sexually, but you may find that his coolness makes him even more attractive because you speculate about the sexy person beneath the exterior reserve. Don't let your inquisitive nature drive you to trifle with his affections. Capricorn men take sex seriously, as a prelude to a deeper commitment you may not be prepared to make.

If you go to bed with him, he may surprise you with his endurance as well as with his deep display of affection. On the other hand, you may be too detached and intellectual about the matter to enjoy his style of lovemaking. In either case you may still find that you fascinate each other. Capricorn may have an attachment to you that he can't quite explain, which makes him willing to continue the relationship in some form, though you may not become lovers in the traditional sense.

Capricorn wants a full-time, permanent partner in a love relationship, but his career comes first. Neither of you may be able to make a serious promise to an exclusive arrangement. Capricorns can be very possessive of their lovers, and you will instinctively rebel at any threat to your independence. You are honest and open enough to explain your need for freedom, and Capricorn will appreciate the fact that you know what you need and will respect your honesty—and respect is an important factor in Capricorn's emotional life. If he feels that you admire his achievements, he will value you as a friend and companion.

Capricorn is known as the executive of the zodiac, because of his practical skills and his ambition to succeed. He shares your concern with the future, but deals in terms of specific goals rather than abstract concepts. Capricorn may be conservative, traditional, and cautious, but he knows a good idea when he hears one, and you can be a mine of innovative ideas. If you are ready to accept well-intentioned advice and serious suggestions on making your dreams come true, Capricorn is the man to see. He knows how to take your visions and turn them into money-making propositions because he aspects your Second House—money and possessions. If you can accept the discipline he demands and are willing to work hard, he will help you become a success. All that he requires is a commitment to growth. He wants to see you making progress as the reward for his sincere concern and interest in your welfare. The step-by-step approach that Capricorn teaches is not easy, but it can give you a new dimension of power in applying yourself to the future you so vividly envision.

A Capricorn man may not be the great love of your life, but you will look upon his influence with tender affection and sincere admiration. He may seem stern and demanding, but he does have your welfare at heart, and he values the idealism you bring into his life. Treat him with affection, Aquarius, and you have a loving friend and dear companion for life.

AQUARIUS & AQUARIUS

Keep your wits about you, Aquarius, and hang on to your cowboy hat when you get involved with another Aquarian man. You are both so individualistic that you may wonder if he doesn't have the wrong birthdate. It may be hard to believe he is an Aquarian. Fixed Air joined to Fixed Air means that you both see your faults as virtues, and neither of you is going to budge. The joint forces of Uranus make this an effervescent and complex association that is filled with unexpected ups and downs, but you both keep your vision firmly fixed on the future. There may be aspects of competition as you strive to decide which one of you is the genius and which one the madman. When you are feeling compatible, you may decide that you are the only two sane people in a world of lunatics.

You will recognize each other immediately, and there could be an instant attraction if you are looking for a pal and soul mate. You probably will find his idiosyncrasies charming because you are usually very tolerant. You won't try to change him to your way of thinking, but you may think he is way off-base in a lot of his ideas. You both try to be thoroughly modern, but your interpretations of modernity may be very different, depending upon your family background and education. You may well be working in completely different fields, but find each other fascinating.

If there is a sexual attraction, it may take some time to develop. With an Aquarian man you can get into the romantic ritual of courtship for the first time. The process of getting into sex can be a long, drawn-out business. Dinner invitations, concerts, avant-garde art events, and long conversations will eventually lead to the building of a physical attraction.

As sexual partners you are admirably suited to each other. You will enjoy his carefree attitude and the spirit of experimental play that he brings to lovemaking. He won't be wildly passionate or intense, but he will be eager to please you with the techniques he has been researching. It will not be giddy and crazy but varied, erotic, and plenty of fun.

Just because the sex is good, he won't expect you to move in with him, because your personalities are so multidimensional that you may not be able to provide each other with the range you both need. Other men have important roles to fill in your lives, and you have too many outside interests to be willing to settle down for long.

You won't like the way he makes promises you know he can't keep, and you will be envious when Uranus comes to his rescue once again and pulls him out of an impossible situation. Your Aquarian lover can be a mirror image, a telescope, or a magnifying glass for all your best and worst traits. Aquarians like looking in mirrors, but they also want to gloss over the imperfections.

You may have your moments of communication breakdown, but your Aquarius lover can be your best critic because he understands where you are coming from and where you want to go. He realizes that you may miss details or be inconsistent because you are aiming at the future and it is easy to lose sight of some of the finer points of the present. But your basic differences stem from the fact that you are both individualists who keep trying to reform one another. Aquarians don't like to be judged, and both of you can be quick to take offense at personal remarks. Even though you may have periods when you are fixated on his weaknesses, or he seems intolerant of yours, you can accept these problems from an Aquarius because you treat each other as equals. You could never fall in love with a man who you felt was not your peer intellectually, socially, and sexually. You don't want to waste time explaining yourself, your motives, or your actions.

An Aquarius friend or lover can be a problematic companion. You like your life exciting, but your personal habits tend to be precise. Every Aquarian has a different set of little rules that give some semblance of order in a world of surprises. You can handle chaos—but only your own.

Finding a balance between your greater and lesser concepts of the universe is not going to be easy with Aquarius, but you will never be bored. In the end, the love you share with him may be expressed in an enduring friendship that embodies the highest of Aquarian ideals.

AQUARIUS & PISCES

An affair with a Pisces man will be an imaginative relationship that appeals to your desire for new experiences. Your natural instincts may make you a visionary, but it is Pisces who possesses true powers of perception. Your Fixed-Air qualities combine with his Mutable-Water nature to provide an intellectual framework for his imagination. Your ruling planet, Uranus, influences his Neptune rulership to create an aura of inventiveness and originality with a touch of wildness about it. You two can go to extremes because Pisces is even more tolerant than you are, and there are no brakes on the flow of ideas and perceptions. As an idealist, you encourage Pisces to make his dreams become reality.

Aquarians enjoy the latest in films and Pisceans love the fantasy of the silver screen. If you want to find a man born under the sign of the Fishes, you can meet one at the movies any night of the week. A coffee date after the film and a discussion of the ethereal quality of Garbo's face or the superiority of Antonioni's early work will always appeal to him. Don't assume that he is superficial, though. Pisces men are deeply emotional, and he will shy away if you come on too strong.

Neptune's qualities make him extremely intuitive, so your interest in him will be well understood before you suggest playing out a love scene. He is a real romantic and can bring out your secret affectionate nature.

Sex with a Pisces man will be good, bad, or beautiful, depending upon how you react to his emotional lovemaking. While he may not come up with any new twists for your repertoire, he is very responsive and willing to please you, and he will be receptive to your desire for erotic experimentation. Sex has a strong fantasy element for Pisces, and you can enjoy devising the roles you play with each other.

It can become very dramatic and inventive if you give free rein to your imagination.

Pisces will find you to be a magical figure and can easily fall in love with you. You are his neighbor in the zodiac, and he has karmic memories of the Aquarian personality, which allow him to feel safe and comfortable with you. In typical Aquarian fashion, you will want to distance yourself from the situation when you feel the confusing tides of his emotional nature beginning to flow. Pisces may want your coupling to be more permanent and committed than you do. Try to keep it light and easy in your usual style and Pisces should understand that you need more than one focus in your life until you are sure it is your ideal relationship. He is patient enough to keep the torch burning for a long time if you let him become a regular part of your life. Eventually he will understand that he needs much more tranquillity and security than you are willing to provide.

You can have a long and faithful friendship with a Pisces man once he realizes that you cannot be the rock he wants to cling to. You can be pals who go out looking for unusual kicks together, getting into some very bizarre adventures. Under your influence he develops a taste for fast company and new outlets for his secret fantasies. You can go through numerous life-style changes together—from Bohemian to butch, to spiritual conversions to political activism.

There is a spirit of serious play, but you can also get down to some serious work with Pisces. He can be so drifting and undirected that he makes you want to take on new responsibilities by the force of his example. He sees your potential and urges you to make something of yourself. On his own he may not be very practical, but with you, Pisces looks to details. He makes sure you get the recognition you deserve and that you get paid for it. You are in a unique situation where Pisces can serve you in ways he can't serve himself.

You will value your friendship with Pisces for the love and devotion he offers you. He may understand your goals better than any other sign in the zodiac, and he appreciates you for the special person you are.

Together with Pisces you can reach the stars you see in your vision of tomorrow. He shares your hopes for a glorious future and will gladly share your love. A Pisces friend or lover can be the man of your dreams.

LOVING YOUR AQUARIUS MAN

If you want a lighthearted, exciting, and intellectually stimulating love affair, you can find the man of the moment in an Aquarius lover. He loves everybody in general and is willing to love you in particular if you stir his mind, but he may not be a very long-term partner. You can always be friends with an Aquarius lover after the thrill is gone, but you will have to be friends beforehand as well if it is to be anything more than a one-night stand.

Aquarians are very attractive and have an unconscious charm that you should find very appealing. You can meet an Aquarius man in any setting that is extraordinary or offbeat. He enjoys music, the theater, and art but mainly in their most experimental forms. He is a thorough nonconformist, and a direct approach or studied line will not attract his interest at all. You must convince him that you are worth knowing, and he is always attracted to a good conversationalist rather than a handsome stud.

The men born under the sign of the Water-bearer are pouring out ideas to examine them for clues to the future. Often he is active in social and political organizations within the gay community, where he makes many of his closest friends. You can spot an Aquarius in the bars because so many people seem to know him and greet him. Aquarians are natural actors, and they enjoy playing to the crowd and then getting to know people one by one.

Many of his pals are former partners. Aquarians are not men with strong or passionate sex drives, but they are inquisitive and enjoy experimenting with the dedication of the true scientist. If you want to join his crowd of acquaintances, it won't be too difficult. You can interest him through his hobbies, such as astrology or astronomy, because he always looks to the future for his inspiration. If you want to appeal to his intellectual nature, remember that he is a Fixed sign and can be extremely opinionated.

He will enjoy the interplay of ideas, but you can't get him to change his mind by the force of argument. He may be a bit unpredictable, but his are original concepts rather than notions he has adopted from someone else. The best bet with Aquarius is to be friendly and open; feel free to be yourself.

When it comes to lovemaking, you should take the same approach. Aquarius will be open to most suggestions for sexual pleasure. He isn't a sex maniac, he just wants to know all there is to know about what other men like in making love. Often he has had a great deal of field experience and will add a few interesting twists of his own. Don't be shy about any amusing fetishes you have, such as an attraction to exotic settings or costumes.

You can expect just about anything from Aquarius except a serious emotional response. If it seems like you are becoming too involved, Aquarius will become Mr. Chill, distancing himself for fear that he will lose his precious freedom and objectivity. He can have a romantic streak and enjoy being courted, but it is all in a spirit of play. He understands love and the celebration of romance— Aquarians are happy to be alive and glad to be gay.

You can please him most by being a loyal friend and confidant, rather than trying to restrict him to a monogamous relationship. If the possibility is there, Aquarius alone must take the initiative or he will never be willing even to consider a serious commitment. He believes in the high ideal of long-lasting love, but he fears he can never live up to it or that he can never find a man as equally idealistic about the nature of a true relationship. Aquarius can be sexually faithful, but he must have complete independence to decide this issue for himself. If you demand his loyalty, Aquarius will be gone in short order.

Because he rejects the imposition of traditional values on his life-style, Aquarius is often far ahead of his time, and yet he feels he expresses what others would do if only they could accept the freedom and the responsibility. He can be an outrageous person in public or come on very low-key, depending upon the society he has chosen to reform through his personal example. You may never be sure what he will think of next, and that is definitely part of his charm. Uranus is the planet of surprises, and Aquarius can be full of them!

What he wants from you as his friend is a complete trust in his vision of the way things ought to be, and an unending tolerance for his beliefs. He will not force his opinions on you, but he must feel that you approve of his need to be an original. Knowing an Aquarius man can be a marvelous experience in which you gain new insights into your own beliefs and enjoy the benefits of an enlightening friendship for friendship's sake.

PISCES
February 21–March 20

)(

Symbol: The Fishes
Ruling Planet: Neptune
Color: Mauve
Metal: Platinum
Natural House Rulership: Twelfth House, the house
    of hidden meanings and desires
Twelfth House Traits: Desire for spiritual knowledge
    and need for affection
Motto: ''I believe''
Nature: Mutable sign (adaptable)
Element: Water sign (emotional)
Qualities: Imaginative, impressionable, and sensitive
Capacities: Belief and sympathy
Personality Key Words: Understanding, poetic, and
    spiritual

MAXIMIZING YOUR
PISCES POTENTIAL

Pisces is the sign of the zodiac that embodies the dual nature of the human self. Your symbol is the Fishes, swimming in opposite directions, always seeking meaning from the contradictions between reality and dreams. Your nature is Mutable Water, expressing the restless yearning of your emotional sensitivity to probe the meaning of life. Neptune rules the sign of Pisces, and he complicates your search for meaning by casting illusions, weaving dreams, and making your quest seem forever elusive. You are not the last sign of the zodiac, but rather "the one that comes before the first"—full of all the creative potential that gives humanity to the other eleven houses of the Wheel of Life.

Your goal in life is to actualize the symbolic gift of ego that Pisces has given to his fellow Sun signs. You can be selfless in your devotion to others and in your desire to help and serve. The overwhelming totality of your quest for meaning can make you feel insecure and insignificant. Even though you may receive encouragement from others, you can doubt your ability and your worth in face of life's enormous complexities. There is so much that you intuit, and so much more you believe there is yet to know, that you find it hard to set goals for yourself. You have many talents, but Neptune's dreamy influence causes you to wonder if the potential you have can ever be realized. You seek direction from outside yourself, hoping to trust your fate to others, and yet your task in life is to learn how to trust yourself. You are the most loving and giving of all the signs, and you must find an appropriate place on which to focus your wonderful romantic idealism.

Pisceans can be loners, even though your desire is to unite with an ideal to give your life meaning. The choices seem so myriad that you can be susceptible to escapism and solitude. You are at your best when you work alone in a creative or artistic endeavor that allows you to give free rein to your powerful imagination.

Your ability to give love is your outstanding trait. Pisceans are romantics, and your emotional nature causes you to idealize love and sex. You know that love is somehow connected to the mystery of life, and that being in love, giving love, and sharing love are somehow part of the solution. Love is a spiritual experience for you, but you tend to romanticize your sexual experiences, expecting a spiritual and emotional potential where none exists. If you're not careful, you can lose yourself in the search for ideal love.

Your greatest strength is in your compassion and in the depth and variety of your emotions. You have almost infinite options through your power of understanding and sympathy. You have the ability to believe wholeheartedly in your ideals and to devote yourself to worthy causes. You have the strength to renounce the material world for higher things and plunge yourself into any experience in the search for understanding. Your intuitive powers are very strong and can even be psychic. Intuition, coupled with a powerful imagination, makes you poetic, emotional, and extremely sensitive to people.

You are the most perceptive of the signs, but your gift of "second sight" can also be a source of weakness. You have to decide how to filter your perceptions, focus your imagination, and trust your intuition—or you may feel lost at sea. You may become passive and give yourself up to fate or to the stronger will of others because you often find it difficult to make decisions. You can become self-pitying and self-deceptive, unwilling to accept responsibility for your own life.

Your social life can revolve around your need for people

to accept your love or share your escapist fantasies. Pisceans can be particularly fond of alcohol, and you enjoy going to the bars with friends. Dancing is also a favored pastime because Pisces traditionally rules the feet.

Your sex life is often related to your social pleasures. You can seek to lose yourself in many sexual encounters, but you see that the numbers game is ultimately an empty pursuit. Pisceans take love and sex seriously. You can become disillusioned at the ease with which you give yourself to one prospective lover after another, and you take the emotional edge off the disappointment by mixing sex and fantasy. You tell yourself you want to let go and let loose, but you really want a reciprocal emotional experience rather than a sexual high.

Pisceans feel a strong need for a lover. You want a man who can accept your love and idealize your devotion. Your ideal lover must have some element of mystery to fuel your imagination and satisfy your need for romance. In practical terms you want a lover who can give meaning and direction to your life. You can become very dependent on any man who seems to have the answer. Your ideal Man of Life must be able to accept your love the way it is given, completely and without reservation, with a total emotional commitment.

Your most important need in a relationship with another man is devotion to growth and evolution. If love is the clue to the meaning of life, then having a lover must somehow advance you along the path to understanding. Emotional and financial stability are important to you, but you will forgo them in a relationship if you believe that the experience is taking you closer to unraveling the mystery of who you are.

When you are in love, you can be the most selfless and devoted of men. You give your lover sympathy and understanding in great measure. You believe that if you make him as strong as possible, the relationship will be lasting and secure. Your love can be boundless and even overwhelming in its intensity. You will work tirelessly toward the goals you have found through loving him, seeking to advance your mutual interests in any way you can. You idealize his virtues and minimize his faults. When you feel that you have found an appropriate place for your great fund of affection, you lose your insecurities and concentrate on the creative potentials that you have not been able to make work for you in the past.

You can give your love to others, but you must not deny your ego in the process. To love yourself you must find the same commitment to inner growth that you seek from a relationship. You should try to examine the facts of your life, as well as your emotions, to find patterns that reveal the meaning you seek. You have the imagination, the intuition, and the desire to deal with the enormous potential that is symbolized by Pisces. You need to develop faith in your ability to work with your gifts, and to trust your intuition. Realizing the difference between self-doubt and responsibility for yourself can be the key to maximizing your Piscean potential.

PISCES & ARIES

If you want excitement and adventure to spark your desire for romance, you can find it with an Aries man. He gets you out into the world of events, keeps you stimulated, and fires your latent ambition. Your Mutable-Water nature combines with the Cardinal-Fire qualities of Aries to generate imagination and inspiration. Your Neptune rulership influences his ruling Mars in ways that overcome limitations and instill confidence but also encourages self-deceptive bravado. Aries' natural enthusiasm is increased, and you can find yourself off on a joyride with no one's foot on the brake. It can lead to ups and downs, wild swings of fortune, and ultimate exhaustion unless you learn how to pace yourselves practically and emotionally.

You can meet an Aries man wherever the action is. He likes the bar scene because he feeds off the energy of crowds. You will be naturally attracted to his macho image and his direct approach. If he is attracted to you, there will be no ambiguity about his intentions. The more receptive you are, the more his ego will be satisfied. An Aries with a well-fed ego can be a real charmer. He can touch your sense of romance, and you will let him sweep you off your feet and into his arms.

An Aries man can be a titillating and passionate experience, though he lacks your emotional depth. You will have to encourage him to be more gently considerate of your needs and to relax and enjoy the sharing of pleasure. He can be too hot and too quick to satisfy your desire for a dreamy and affectionate lover. You want to feel protected and appreciated in return for your willingness to provide him with erotic pleasure. Aries is inspired by sex, but he is not as imaginative as you. Though he may be your equal as a romantic idealist, he needs to think more of what he can give to others as a lover than what love can do for him.

You can enjoy the flash and dash of Cardinal-Fire Aries for a while. He may not satisfy your need for mystery because he can be totally transparent to your Piscean intuition. He can be exciting, but also predictable. You want a relationship that is heading somewhere and growing, or else you may lapse into passivity or fantasy. Aries may not mind because he may not notice. He is not emotional, and he is rarely sensitive to the emotions of others unless they restrict his own freedom of action. Arians are as susceptible to the attentions of other men as Pisceans. You might both be tolerant of each other's chance encounters with an occasional stranger, but if it becomes part of the pattern of your relationship, you will lose the romance and security you need in a lasting involvement with another man.

Life may not be very secure with an Aries partner. He's an idea man who urges action, but he needs a partner who can follow through. You can provide creative input, but you may be easily discouraged if your projects get bogged down. You can combine your energies to work on short projects with quick payoffs, but they don't always work out the way you expect. Aries doesn't know his limitations, and you are the one who has to exercise caution and judgment. It will be difficult for you, but success will bring out new strengths in your character that enhance your personality.

You want to serve your lovers in selfless ways, and you can overindulge Aries to your mutual detriment. There may be times when you feel that he is using you, but material achievement may make it seem worthwhile. Aries aspects your Second House—money and possessions—and if you want a long-term relationship with an Aries man, you will realize that you have to bring home your own bacon.

Finding the right goals and maintaining focus may be difficult in a relationship with an Aries. There is a great deal of restless vitality, but you wonder if it is really leading anywhere. You can exhaust your energy and still feel compelled to keep working, even though it feels like your imagination is drying up. You need more relaxation when you are involved with an Aries man because you externalize more creative energy than you are used to. He brings you out of your interior world, but you definitely need vacation time of some sort or your world will become increasingly tempestuous.

Separate vacations should be the rule, or you will be taking the source of your chaos with you. Aries is too active to enjoy the peace and quiet of the country and you won't get enough of a breather by just going to another city. Your Aries buddy may love the idea of new streets to cruise and new bars to explore, but you absorb too much discord from your environment to relax in an urban setting, especially with Aries chomping at the bit. If you can't get away and commune with yourself at the seashore, you may have to take up yoga for relaxation. If you want to maintain a relationship with an Aries man, you need an occasional break—or a breakup is inevitable.

Whatever the final outcome of an Aries affair, you should be wiser, you may be richer, and you will have learned valuable new lessons about your basic needs and your inner strengths.

PISCES & TAURUS

A relationship with a man born under the sign of the Bull can be a very gratifying experience, filled with stimulating activities that lead to mutual growth. Your Mutable-Water nature has an enriching quality for the Fixed-Earth materialism and stability of Taurus. You add creative imagination to his life, and he is able to organize the relationship to your mutual benefit. Your Neptune rulership, combined with the Venus rulership of Taurus, indicates the potential for beautiful feelings and sensuous moods. You are in good hands with a Taurus lover. You should feel able to trust him. Though he can be very demanding, you will understand that he acts in your own best interest.

Taureans prefer serene, comforting environments, and they are fond of the tame outdoors. A stroll in the park or an afternoon contemplating the lagoon may end in meeting a Taurus man. Or he may be sitting on the edge of the meadow watching the sunset. Neither of you is quick to make the initial approach, but you should be able to intuit his interest. He isn't a fast talker, but his sense of humor will put you at ease. Taurus aspects your Third House— communications—and you should find it easy to exchange your feelings of romantic attraction.

A Taurean may well prefer to invite you to his place because he is rather fixed in his tastes and habits, and he's more in control in his own environment. You should appreciate the casual and comfortable style of his home. There are usually plenty of books and magazines, a full fridge, and all the accessories of a man who likes to spend time taking life easy amid creature comforts. Taureans are sentimentalists, so don't let the mementos of former lovers in the apartment throw you. He doesn't carry a torch for his ex-lovers, but he does have fond memories of the feelings he shared with them. Relax and enjoy the seduction scene. The soft music, candlelight, and wine are an important part of the ritual for Taurus. The more he likes you, the more time he will want to spend just enjoying your company, rather then getting right down to serious sex. With a Taurus you will spend many evenings either relaxing over a leisurely meal or just cuddling in front of the television set with a bowl of buttered popcorn. When he's feeling really cozy, then you will make your way into the bedroom.

Making love with a Taurus man is rarely a quickie! He is a sensualist and wants the sensations to last. He is receptive to passion, and you may be very responsive to his ardent and Earthy sexuality. Taureans may not be as imaginative or creative as Pisceans, but he will learn to appreciate your talents for the new dimensions of pleasure you can bring to him. Because he can be so passive, you may find yourself getting new enjoyment from taking the active role, but you might want him to be less prosaic and more open to some imaginative experimentation. Taureans have an Earthy sense of humor that often comes out in lovemaking. He can make you laugh at something you take too seriously, and you may love him all the more for it.

It may take some time for the affair to become serious. Taurus is cautious about making commitments, especially if he has had a recent failed romance. He wants to be sure he can trust you. Taurus is more vulnerable than he seems, and your Pisces perceptions should tell you not to arouse his affections if you aren't willing to accept a serious commitment from him. Taureans are possessive lovers, but you may not see this trait as a drawback. He can provide you with the kind of stable environment you look for in a relationship.

An affair with a Taurus man can provide the blend of romance and security you want and need, but it won't be too easy. He may stimulate and inspire you to use your talents actively. He pierces your emotional fog and insists that you avoid self-deception. It may hurt a little, but you will allow a Taurus to say things to you that would be crushing and intolerable from any other Sun sign. Take it slowly, and don't try to do everything at once in an attempt to get your life into shape. You must resist spreading yourself too thin in trying to please him.

Taurus will be sincere in encouraging you to channel your energies toward concrete results. If you are open to new viewpoints, you can be successful in a relationship with Taurus. He can get you to expand the limits you have imposed on yourself, but don't get carried away and lose your concentration. Making decisions is always difficult for you, but you gain strength from this relationship and can discover new potentials for deciding which elements of your myriad personality you need to develop. If not, you can become scattered, extravagant, and overly emotional.

Keep working on your need to exercise your imagination and gain more focus for your personal needs and you can be happy in a relationship with a loving Taurus man.

PISCES & GEMINI

You will be excited by a Gemini man because he can be highly entertaining and informative, but there may be hidden obligations in a relationship with a man born under the sign of the Twins. You are both dual signs, and the possibilities for confusion, or at least complexity, are abundant. You are both Mutable signs, but your Water nature and his Air nature are not truly compatible. He does not have your emotional dimension because Air signs think rather than feel. He has no need for intuition because he gathers concrete information. The combination of your ruling Neptune and his Mercury rulership creates a kind of fog through which you are attracted to each other, but communication is difficult to maintain with clarity.

You are likely to meet a Gemini through a mutual interest in art or theatrical events, perhaps behind the scenes, or in connection with his career in media. You will be impressed with his verbal dexterity, and he will certainly enjoy meeting you because Pisceans are among the best listeners in the zodiac. Even when you are bored, you try to be polite and attentive rather than hurt someone's feelings. With Gemini you rarely will be bored because he is full of interesting ideas. His motivation is not particularly sexual, but he won't be difficult to engage as a romantic partner because he doesn't attach great emotional significance to lovemaking. There won't be any commitment implied, and you will have the best possible time if you don't infer what isn't there. Listen to your intuition, but Gemini broadcasts on so many channels that you may not be able to read him very clearly.

Gemini understands sex as fantasy fulfillment, but as in everything else between you, it is on an intellectual level rather than on an emotional one. He is curious about sex and likes to explore and experiment with different kinds of erotic stimulation. If you get together at his place, he may have strategically placed mirrors to add a voyeuristic element. Your common interest in movies may lead to the VCR for a private screening of some erotic films to set the tone he needs to have a good time. You may find sex with a Gemini man initially stimulating, but lacking the emotional communication you want in a loving relationship.

Gemini aspects your Fourth House—home and environment. You may want to settle down with him, but it could be turbulent. If you make a commitment to a Gemini, you may have to be the one who works harder to maintain it. You keep thinking that a secure home life is just what he needs to give him some direction, but he may not agree or be willing to hold up his end of the responsibilities. You can be selfless and sacrificing in trying to establish security for a Gemini lover without getting any cooperation or emotional empathy from him. A relationship can be undermined by his gadding about, his career interests, or your own scrambling to keep all the systems working without much help.

You can develop new strength from this relationship, but ultimately it will be at the expense of your affection for your Gemini lover. The work is all on your shoulders. As is so often the case, you may learn to do for others that which you can't do for yourself. You will have to take the lead in establishing goals and direction or the relationship may founder.

Gemini benefits from your imagination and devotion, but what do you get, Pisces? It depends upon what you want and what you are willing to do to get it. You can put a lot of energy into an affair with a Gemini man, but it will be very difficult to establish the stable relationship you hope for as your romantic ideal. There is plenty of excitement, but it is restless activity for its own sake rather than the expression of a deeper bond. There are rewards, and there can be fun moments together, but you will not reach great heights. For example, after the theater, Gemini will talk about who was there and what gossip he overheard during intermission. You may wonder if he was paying any attention to the play. This difference in your personalities illustrates the basic problem with your relationship. He skims information from the surface, but he can be oblivious to what's underneath, which is obviously much more important to you. Gemini may pick up your signals that tell him you're unhappy and attempt to cheer you, but he isn't very interested in sharing the burden by examining what's wrong. The Gemini solution is to put on a happy face, but you still feel like Pagliacci. The lack of emotional feedback can lead you to escape inside yourself or to search for other shoulders to lean on. Gemini probably won't be jealous or concerned, and it will hurt you even more that he is so oblivious to your feelings.

There can be compensations with a Gemini lover, such as the sparkling social events associated with his career. But he will always come first, and you know it. The choice is up to you, but the experience will make you a stronger person.

PISCES & CANCER

The relationship you share with a Cancer man will have all the emotional intensity you crave in a long-lasting love affair. You both want many of the same qualities the other has to offer, and there is a spirit of harmony and creativity. Your Mutable-Water nature blends easily with his Cardinal-Water sign to allow for reciprocal affection, a sense of emotional purpose, and a creative desire to please each other. The Neptune rulership of Pisces is mellowed by the influence of his ruling Moon in a way that heightens your imagination and soothes your fears. Cancer will appreciate your need to serve your lovers, and he will want to return the feeling with protective care that provides the security you look for in a satisfying relationship.

You can meet a Cancer man through your involvement in any kind of creative discipline. Don't be surprised by the immediate magnetism because the Neptune–Moon combination indicates a definite physical attraction. You are both highly intuitive and he will know what is on your mind, so it should be easy to make his acquaintance. Cancers can be shy, but a smile from you may be just enough encouragement for him to make the first move. It may not happen the first time you meet, depending upon his mood. Cancers are sometimes prevented from acting because of feelings of insecurity they can't explain. No other Sun sign can empathize with his occasional emotional confusion better than you, Pisces.

Cancer aspects your Fifth House—romance and creativity. You are more than likely to fall in love with him, and the catalyst will be in the quality of your sexual partnership. You will find him comforting, calming, and very erotic. Your imagination is aroused because he activates all your fantasies about meeting a man who is easy to love and completely accepting, rather than demanding, of your affection. The Moon reflects the light that it receives, and your tender responses will be received with pleasure and returned to you in kind. Cancers need sexual variety, and you can complement his own amorous imagination with magic touches that lead to a fulfilling sex life.

You will be a loyal and faithful partner in a relationship with a Cancer man. He will not be shy in showing you how much he needs you. While other men may find a Cancer lover too clinging or even smothering, his devotion represents the kind of all-encompassing commitment your Piscean sensibility looks for but often despairs of finding. Men born under the sign of the Crab will want to keep you cuddled close in a stable home environment. If you get the feeling that he is thinking in terms of forever, you are on the right wavelength with your Moonbeam lover.

There will be ups and downs in paradise, but the compatibility and compassion between Water signs can smooth the troubled emotions. You know when he is upset because of one of his moods, and you understand when to back off and let him work it out by himself. Sometimes all he needs is a big hug to bring back his sense of humor. When you two are out of sync and in conflicting moods, Cancer will try to evade the issues that threaten depression. Let him go through it any way he has to, but stay out of his way because he can have a very sharp tongue. Let him internalize the words and externalize the activity until he comes around of his own accord. Once he is calm, he will shyly and tentatively apologize with a glint of a teardrop in his eye that will melt your heart. Your Piscean power and willingness to forgive is always available to your Cancer lover. Often the issues that come between you are very minor and would be overlooked if you both weren't the two most sensitive signs of the zodiac.

Your sensitivity serves you well in artistic endeavors with a Cancer man as your partner. He stimulates you to see projects through to completion and to undertake new responsibilities in areas that spark your creative abilities. Sometimes you may feel that you are burdened with work, but you are comforted by the feeling of evolution in your character and the commitment to growth in the relationship. You can believe at last that you are on the path to some form of personal, material, or spiritual completion, and it is very satisfying. There are times when you are afraid that life is a dream, but in Piscean fashion you decide that you would rather not wake up because the dreams are happy and exciting.

There is a magnetic attraction between you and a Cancer lover that can lead to a formidable union of creative personalities. You find yourself extending your efforts, keeping busy, sensing real progress in the commitment you have made to him. If you are ready for a romance, Pisces, this is where the Wheel of Fortune stops.

PISCES & LEO

An affair with a Leo can be a demanding relationship but also can be one that fulfills your needs for a strong lover to provide direction and a sense of belonging to something beyond yourself. Your Mutable-Water nature stirs his Fixed-Fire qualities to warm your affections and stimulate him to be a more magnanimous personality. The combined influences of your Neptune rulership with the Sun of Leo indicate the presence of glamour and illusion, as well as conscientious endeavors. You are willing to serve Leo and to work for his best interests. You worry about his health and his job, and you expect him to live up to the image of perfection he wants to project. There are elements of mystery, romance, and sentimental attraction that can bind you together despite the differences between your Water and Fire qualities.

Leo is the more extroverted personality in this relationship. You may meet through work that involves the entertainment industry or creative fields such as fashion and advertising. Whatever the situation, Leo will play the role of the star, but you will see him as a person with basic needs rather than be awed by his presence. You take a no-nonsense approach that somehow sparks Leo's interest. His style will be to sweep you off your feet with a dramatic gesture. Reply with a little creative flattery and Leo can be yours for the asking.

The nights you spend with a Leo man can be immensely pleasurable. He likes to organize and orchestrate his affairs with all the flair typical of men born under the sign of the Lion. He may take you out to a show and to dinner, usually someplace where he is known by the maître d'. Accept his invitation for a nightcap at his place and you can stay for breakfast. (But you will be the one who rustles up the bacon and eggs while Leo gets an extra twenty minutes of sleep).

The sexual experience with a Leo man may not be all that you imagined. Though he is strong on passion, you seem to be the one to provide all the sensitivity. Leos can be fairly conventional, ritualistic, and predictable in their approach to lovemaking. You may find it interesting at first but not very challenging after a while. Unless you can lift the experience with some of your more imaginative touches, you may fall into a pleasant, but familiar, pattern in which Leo is intense, passionate, highly aroused, but ultimately self-absorbed. You want your lover to be a fantasy figure. While Leo certainly can be star-fantasy material, you may get tired of the same old movie.

In an alliance you establish with a Leo man, his tendency is to be loyal because he values fidelity. He can be jealous, but you will rarely give him cause to be suspicious. Unless you are feeling extremely alienated, you would never flirt in his presence; and if you are unfaithful to him, you can be deceptive and discreet enough so that he may never know. Leo may be the dominant figure in the relationship, but you have a certain kind of power over him because he can become dependent upon you and the way you look after him.

At heart (and Leos are all heart), he can be a little boy. Despite the regal dignity he projects in public, Leo is often insecure and needs ego confirmation to maintain his charming style. You are tolerant and sympathetic because he shows his vulnerable side to you, but he can be manipulative and pompous in his demands.

Leo aspects your Sixth House—work and service. The Piscean tendency in this relationship is to be selfless and strong on the material level but dependent on his need. When you begin questioning the value of maintaining the arrangement, Leo tells you he can't live without you and you are hooked all over again. You can be in love with the idea of having a beautiful and desirable man as your lover more than you are in love with the man himself. You have to be strong enough to realize where your best interests lie, and it may be difficult to make decisions. Leo touches your emotions, but he can weigh you down rather than buoy your spirits. You have to see your way clear to decide if he demands more of you than you should give.

There is great potential in a Pisces–Leo relationship for warmth and tenderness. You can share a true spirit of generosity and give each other strength in a long-lasting and creative union. The course of your love may not run smooth, but there can be a rewarding blend of two very different personalities who learn a great deal about themselves as loving men.

PISCES & VIRGO

With a Virgo man you can learn more about yourself and the kind of love you have to give. He is your complementary opposite on the Wheel of Life. You can sense that he has qualities you can use in developing your personality and defining your goals. Your Mutable-Water nature blends with his Mutable Earth-sign qualities to produce endless potential for adapting to your differences. The combination of your Neptune rulership with his ruling Mercury makes it possible to communicate your dreams and understand his needs. Like other opposite-sign attractions, you may find yourself drawn to each other and then repelled over and over again. Nevertheless, you keep coming back for more. The relationship may not be one of enduring romantic love, but there is a karmic tie that can be mutually beneficial.

Virgo is symbolized by the Virgin, representing the ideal of purity and perfection through orderly material processes. Your own symbol, the Fishes, is also emblematic of an idealistic point of view, but you look for perfection in the emotional process. Virgo gives you new insights into grasping reality, and you provide him with the poetic imagination he needs to overcome his obsession with detail. You need direction and he needs vision. The potential for development as creative personalities is present if you overcome your outward differences and look to the real goals you aim for in life.

Getting to know each other will take time. You are cautious, evasive, and wary of committing yourself. Virgo is also shy about getting involved. He waits to see if his criteria for an ideal partner can be met, and you look for romantic clues that spark your imagination. Both of you have high standards for judging the value of a liaison with another man. You fear being hurt, and Virgo fears being deceived.

The differences in your natures can be clearly perceived in your sexual encounters with a Virgo man. You will find him to be technically competent, even skillful, but at a much lower level of emotional involvement than you. He certainly derives physical pleasure from your eroticism. Virgo is controlled, precise, and meticulous in trying to please his partner. You tend to let loose your fantasies and bathe your partner in waves of affection. Piscean fervor may confuse Virgo, because he doesn't understand the source of your emotions or his role in stimulating them.

When Virgo is puzzled, he seeks material order and intellectual precision to bring things back into focus. His meticulousness makes him the critic of the zodiac, always demanding that standards be established and adhered to. When you go to the movies together, he will analyze and evaluate the story line, character development, and production values; while you are caught up in the inspiration and heroic strength of the leading man in his devotion to honor in the face of awesome obstacles.

You both share a need to serve your lovers but in different ways. Virgo tends to be dedicated to working hard for the material and practical welfare of his companions. Your Pisces nature is to serve emotionally, to be selfless, and to relate to his perception of spiritual needs. Virgo can make you feel secure because he puts your world in order and looks after the mundane details that can depress you. You can provide Virgo with the chance to experience emotional security and true romance.

Virgo may not be the mysterious, ardent fantasy figure you idealize as your Man of Life, and the emotional release you need may not come from a sexual relationship with him. Your two signs are more capable of true platonic love than any others in the zodiac. A Virgo man can be a brotherly soul mate who picks you up when you are down and points you in the right direction. You can give him intuitive insight to feelings he doesn't know how to analyze. You can astonish Virgo with your flights of fancy and unstable emotions. He can sting you with his faultfinding and sharp tongue, but you tolerate and understand each other well enough to forgive.

A Virgo as friend or lover will often provide a lasting association that makes you stronger if you can find ways to look beyond your differences. You want to serve each other, but you can also serve others in your search for development as loving men and creative personalities.

PISCES & LIBRA

A relationship with a Libra man as your friend or lover brings a new emphasis on learning to discriminate between reality and fantasy. The Mutable-Water nature of Pisces and the Cardinal Air of Libra combine in imperfect ways to heighten your understanding of the differences between your ideals and his goals. Your Neptune rulership is influenced by his ruling Venus, indicating illusions of beauty and a desire for good taste and fine living. This alliance can mean unusual combinations of money and sex. You may want to show your creative talents to keep up with Libra's life-style or spend money on aesthetic trifles to earn his approval.

You may meet him through your work, especially if it involves commercial art or fashion. Libra aspects your Eighth House—mystery—and you will be naturally drawn to his poise. You may feel fascinated by him, want to know more about him, and also want to be more like him. Libra may zero in on your receptive eagerness, especially if he notices your dreamy eyes and their signals of desire.

Your intuitive powers will serve you well in a romantic encounter with a Libra man. You can extend his pleasure with your imaginative and affectionate touches as you look upon Libra as a fantasy figure. Air signs do not have Pisces' depth of emotion where sex is concerned. You may become very passive, and Libra will attempt to balance this by becoming more aggressive than he wants to be and blaming you for being too unassertive, but the real problem lies in the lack of compatibility between your sex drives and your emotional needs.

In a relationship with a Libra lover you will both strive to maintain harmony and a peaceful environment. Libra shares your desire for a partner to make his life complete. You may cling to each other even though the romantic security you want is really lacking. Libra thinks too highly of himself to hurt you by making a clean end of the affair. He will vacillate, weighing the possible alternatives and advantages to living with a man he doesn't understand and living alone. He may enjoy the challenge of coping with your unfathomable emotions, but not for very long. He craves excitement, variety, and social activity in a relationship, but you can't provide them when you feel unappreciated and misunderstood. Libra will go out alone, seeking the company of other men and social diversions, while you stay home indulging in escapist fantasies and watching late movies for emotional release.

As partners in business or creative efforts, Libra highlights feelings of inadequacy. He makes you feel insecure over matters of taste with his condescending attitude. If you rise to the challenge, it can cost you money. Libra will encourage you to be extravagant beyond your means. You want to demonstrate that you are imaginative and creative, and you strive to live up to the potential Libra sees in you, but there is no regard for the practical consequences. Libra can get you involved in get-rich-quick schemes that don't work and make you look bad. He awakens a feeling of vanity that is foreign to the Piscean nature and is detrimental to your self-image. Libra gives you direction, but it is the wrong direction. You overcome your reticence and accept his challenge, but it is the wrong challenge.

A Libra relationship can damage your idealism and make you feel gullible. You can appeal to his sense of fair play, but his values are obscured by the deceptive influence of

Neptune on his ruling Venus. There is beauty, but there is also disillusion and deception. Keep your eyes open with Libra. Ask yourself what he really wants from you and what you really have to give him as a friend, business associate, or lover.

PISCES & SCORPIO

You can find an emotional and soul mate in a relationship with a Scorpio man as your friend or lover. There is an intuitive understanding of each other's needs that can lead to a very satisfying affair. There can be enduring affection that brings out the best in your personalities. Your Mutable-Water nature is adaptable enough to accommodate the Fixed-Water intensity of Scorpio's emotions. The influence of your ruling Neptune, combined with the Pluto rulership of Scorpio, indicates an interest in mind-expanding experiences or metaphysical studies. You feel drawn to Scorpio, but there is an aura of romanticism rather than compulsion. Scorpio men have powerful personalities, but you feel no threat from him because your intuition senses his highest aspirations.

Wherever you meet, your Scorpio you will be attuned to his magnetic powers of sexual attraction. Scorpio men have eyes that draw others to them, and they usually have enough self-awareness to use them with discretion and accuracy. If he wants you, you will know what is on his mind. Meeting his gaze can activate your imagination, and you can see the fantasy figure of your dreams. Scorpio will be the one who takes the initiative. Though he can be quite aggressive with some men, your initial meeting will be very subtle, very romantic, and very seductive.

You don't really need words to communicate with each other because your Water-sign intuitions are at work, pro-

viding the assurance you need to trust and love him. Scorpio
is a master of sexual expression and you feel free to release
the emotional intensity that other lovers may not have reciprocated. The strength of his desire can be overwhelming,
and you will be willing to submit to him with a great affection that mellows the urgency of his erotic power. Scorpio
has no need to bend you to his will because your selfless
response to his lovemaking can defuse his need to over-
power you. Making love with a Scorpio man gives you a
feeling of completion through surrender that reflects the Piscean karmic task.

You will not hesitate to make a commitment to a Scorpio
man. He aspects your Ninth House—long journeys—and you
can imagine being bound to him in an increasingly deep
emotional relationship. You want to serve your lovers, and
you sense his secret vulnerabilities, his fear of being hurt,
and his desire to transcend the darkness of his insecurities.
Of all the Sun signs, you have the love most capable of
encouraging the positive potential in a Scorpio man by following your natural inclination to take the path of least resistance. You sympathize with his desire for self-knowledge,
and you want to see him take creative paths to personality
development.

Scorpio men are noted for their suspicion and jealousy in
love affairs. You will not give him reason to suspect you
because you appreciate his possessive love. Scorpio makes
you feel secure. You like the way he is a homebody and
prefers to spend his time with you in quiet pleasures rather
than pursuing an active and superficial social schedule.
Reading, working on improving your creative skills, or developing your interests in the occult will make for satisfying
evenings together. You share a desire to know the answers
to questions about the mysteries of life and the meaning of
dreams. Scorpio responds to your high ideals and your need
for a sense of evolution in a relationship. The basis for that
growth is the emotional stability you provide for each other.
Your love makes you grow in creative ways and fulfills many
of your ideal requirements for a long-lasting relationship.

In practical terms, a Scorpio lover can give you the confidence to pursue your dreams in concrete endeavors that advance your career. He can help you to define and refine your goals when you are feeling indecisive. He is a hard worker, and any project you develop together will benefit from his organizational skills as well as his creative input.

With a Scorpio lover you can feel strong enough to relax, to express your need to be loved, and to learn to live with your emotions. Scorpio gives you confidence in yourself because he wholeheartedly accepts your devotion. Your Piscean passivity can find a home in the heart of Scorpio because you offer him a love that he can cherish rather than conquer. Your relationship should be one that prospers as you blend your idealism in a search for self-awareness and mutual trust.

PISCES & SAGITTARIUS

A Sagittarius friend or lover will bring unexpected challenges that can have a beneficial effect on your career. Your Water-sign qualities of intuitive emotion are stirred by the Mutable-Fire inspiration of men born under the sign of the Centaur. Your ruling Neptune is influenced by his Jupiter rulership to indicate expanded responsibilities, which you can successfully accept. Sagittarius lacks your extreme sensitivity, and there are times when you find him inconsiderate and annoying, but you are buoyed up by his optimism and generous spirit. You join with his humanitarian goals and develop a more positive attitude about your ability to help others on a large scale. Sagittarius inspires you to look beyond your personal emotional concerns and see new ways of using your talents.

You will be attracted to the masculine style and confidence of a Sagittarian. His open, jovial manner will appeal to your romantic imagination. You may idealize his image as the dashing and daring personality you would like to be. He is outgoing, friendly with strangers, and easy to meet. If he finds you attractive, he will not be shy about introducing himself and getting to know you. In conversation, you will be impressed by the breadth of his experience, for Sagittarians have often traveled widely. You like the way he reflects upon his many experiences and the air of the philosopher about him. Sagittarius sparks your imagination.

Sex will be an easygoing experience with Sagittarius. He can be an enjoyable partner in a spirit of friendliness and fun, though he does not have the same emotional level you do. You respond to his natural Fire-sign intensity and passionate vigor. He likes to wrestle and tumble in a kind of male camaraderie that you should find very appealing. His manner is direct and physical without deep involvement but with kindness and a sense of play that allows you to relax and enjoy the experience. The sex is simple, and you should not expect him to get ultraserious.

Unless he is older, or has just made a long journey, he will not want to settle down with you or with any one man. Sagittarians value their freedom for the opportunity it affords them to explore the world without restrictions. Your intuition should tell you that there is no real possibility for a long-term commitment from him as your lover in anything but the most open type of relationship. He may care for you, but you won't be the only man in his life. If you demand that he be faithful to you, you will only be disappointed. He doesn't intend to alienate your affection, he is just not sensitive to your emotional vulnerability. Sagittarians have thick skins and they assume that they can dish it out as well as they can take it. He can wound you with his blunt remarks but he never intends to hurt; he is merely being honest.

Sagittarius can help you as a true friend if you trust his basic good intentions and use his insights in a creative way. You may not be able to be lovers in any traditional sense, but you can work together successfully on short-term projects and philanthropic goals. You can use his energy and ability to inspire others and promote your own imaginative ideas. There may be moments of confusion, but the luck of Jupiter often saves the day. You worry a lot, but Sagittarius always has high hopes for the future.

When you are operating at a peak energy level with Sagittarius, you may live in a chaotic world that both of you feed on as a natural creative environment. You will have to learn to accept more responsibility—especially where money is concerned—or you can be overwhelmed by the expansive habits that Sagittarius encourages. You might learn to become more practical because you have to look after the details he slides over.

Despite the fact that he can drive you to distraction with his restless energy, you appreciate the way he brings you out of your inward-looking personal and emotional life and urges you—even forces you—to be active and more outgoing. There are rewards in this unusual friendship, and your fondness for Sagittarius can survive his wanderings and cause you to look forward to his homecomings.

PISCES & CAPRICORN

A relationship with a Capricorn man can be a close association from which you gain a good friend. Men born under the sign of the Mountain Goat are proverbially practical, and you value knowing him for the sound advice he offers you. Your Mutable-Water nature seeks the stability of his Cardinal-Earth qualities because he can provide the sense of direction you need. Your Neptune rulership is affected by the restrictive forces of his Saturn ruler to focus your dreams and restrain your illusions. You may sometimes feel that he is too strict and too demanding, but he asks of you only that which you really seek for yourself in finding a worthwhile goal. Capricorn feels benevolent toward you, but he only understands your dreams when you make them specific. You earn his respect through real achievement rather than through imaginative ideas.

You probably will meet a Capricorn through a business connection rather than in a social context. He may often be in an executive capacity, and you may wind up working on a short-term project together. If there is a sexual attraction, you will find it difficult to express. Should Capricorn be attracted to you, he will be typically cautious and may seem unnecessarily distant. He is very aware of his position and the way in which others expect him to behave. Capricorn will not mix work and play or compromise his attention to his responsibilities.

Outside of work, Capricorn may be easier to approach, but he will still be circumspect. You will have to trust your intuition and make the offer of friendship without coming on to him, unless he seems obviously receptive. Capricorn aspects your Eleventh House—hopes, wishes, and dreams. You may be very eager to get close to him, but he may not comprehend your motives. He may not understand what kind of relationship can develop, especially if he is much older than you. If you do attract his interest, he may invite you to dinner or to the theater. It may be some time before you actually go to bed with him, because he is slow to get involved.

Sex with a Capricorn man will be down-to-earth with no fantasies attached. He will have a tender regard for you and be highly responsive to your affection and emotion. He will want to please you, but he will also take command of the situation. Your own desire to be receptive can lead to mutual satisfaction. He is intense and passionate but not without an ironic sense of humor that you will appreciate for its surprising warmth.

You may be very eager to commit yourself to a relationship with him, but you may not be able to live up to his demanding requirements for a lover. In love, he can be just as exacting as at the office. You may admire and respect him, but he wants you to show him your regard by emulating his approach to life. Capricorn will be affectionate and understanding, but if he is willing to become your lover, it is because he sees your potential and wants to encourage your development. He will accept the incongruities in your personality, but he needs to feel that you are working toward a goal at a steady pace. In return for your efforts, he will be generous and supportive.

Despite the high expectations he has for you, you can feel relaxed with him. Saturn gives him an understanding of time, and he won't require you to be an overnight success. If you are sincere in your efforts, he will be indulgent enough to let you set your own pace. You can go to him with emotional problems and he will give you the benefit of his wisdom, but he will be hurt and angered if you don't follow through and use his advice.

Though you may chafe under his restrictions, you realize that he is sincere in his concern for your happiness. He is a true friend in your eyes, and through his example you can learn to be somewhat more discriminating in your choice of friends and associates.

You may not be mature enough to sustain a Capricorn love relationship, but the aspects indicate that you may always be friends. You can feel secure in his affection, and he is the kind of man you can always depend on to have your welfare at heart.

PISCES & AQUARIUS

A relationship with an Aquarius man can provide you with an exciting partner who appreciates your imagination and your understanding of people. Your Mutable Water-sign nature combines with his Fixed-Air qualities to indicate a union of free-flowing ideas that can spell success in large letters. Your ruling planet, Neptune, influences his Uranus rulership to provide imaginative power to his unusual approach to life. Whatever you two do together is going to be touched with a bit of madness, but it will usually work to your advantage. Even though Aquarius is more abstract and less emotional than you, his idealism and constant search for originality will appeal to your need for stimulation. A prosaic relationship will bore you to distraction and withdrawal, but it will be anything but boring with an Aquarius man as your friend and lover.

You can meet an Aquarian anyplace that is new or unusual. He is often fascinated with avant-garde art, music, or film, and you probably will have creative interests in common. You can always start a conversation by asking his opinion because Fixed signs always have opinions about everything. He compares everything to his ideal standards, rather than judging anything on its own terms. His highest ideal is friendship, and an open, easy approach characterizes his style. It is often difficult for you to be direct, so take it easy and let him make the first move to get to know you better.

Sex may not be his primary motivation, though Aquarius is interested in new sexual experiences. If you invite him over to your place, he probably will expect your hospitality to extend itself into an overnight stay, but he won't be demanding. If sex is all you're interested in with an Aquarius man, he won't want to be your friend for very long. It may be momentarily interesting, but he will write you off as someone with nothing to offer him and go on his merry way, looking for somebody more worthy of his attention. Since Aquarius aspects your Twelfth House—karmic mysteries— you will want to know much more about him than a casual romantic experience will tell you.

You desire a lover who is a constant mystery in order to feed your fantasies, and Aquarius fills the bill. He always wants love to be a new revelation for his inquisitive mind.

You will enjoy his lovemaking because he fulfills and complements your fantasies. Aquarius will try anything once, and Pisces has the reputation of being the original "guy who can't say no." Together you can experience any form of diversion you can think up. There is no need to be shy with Aquarius, but you may have qualms about the level of his emotional involvement. Aquarians get mental and physical satisfaction from sex, but they are not highly emotional.

Air signs are more interested in things intellectual than visceral. Take it slow and easy with him. If you make an overwhelming declaration of your love and dependency, he will be lost to you. There is a fundamental difference between fascination and love that you can easily confuse, especially with your feelings toward Aquarius.

You won't be able to have him all to yourself. Aquarius needs many people in his life to feed his multidimensional personality. You can be a very important part of his life, but you will not be the only one. You share his high idealism, and you should be able to understand that there are ways you can serve him better than anyone. Pisceans want to serve those they love, and Aquarius can certainly benefit from your desire to see him get his act together.

Aquarius has great ideas, and you appreciate them more than any other Sun-sign personality because of their visionary quality. Pisceans are not known for their business acumen, but Aquarius brings out your abilities to organize his talents and promote concepts. You can be aggressive in taking care of his interests where money and possessions are concerned—much better than you can do for yourself. Because you are promoting someone else's ego, you lose your shyness and discover a new forcefulness and a feeling of competence. You will make sure that people of importance pay attention to Aquarius and that he gets well paid for his efforts and talents. You can convince him to be more serious about his career goals. Aquarians are often entertainers, actors, or inventors who have talent but can't get their ideas across to those who can make them successful. You can be his manager or agent and make sure he is noticed. You will be happy that you have found a way to express your caring for him, and he will become devoted to you for your perceptive understanding of his needs.

The material advancement you share with an Aquarius friend or lover gives you the security you both need for personal growth. It is the kind of evolutionary relationship you crave, and it fulfills many of Aquarius' needs for change, challenge, and sincere friendship.

PISCES & PISCES

A relationship with a Pisces can be a highly romantic, imaginative, and sensitive affair, but it will need a positive goal to give you both the direction you need to be happy. Without a common focus, you may find yourselves drifting in a sea of uncertainties and escapist fantasies. The combination of two Mutable-Water signs indicates a great deal of emotion, but it can be formless and confusing. The double influence of Neptune gives this relationship a strong, dreamlike quality that can drift into turmoil unless you strive to develop a practical purpose beyond the romantic attachment you feel astrologically.

You can meet a Pisces man in any of the places you normally frequent. He may be connected to the same organization you work for, hang out at the same bar, or enjoy the same kind of music and films you do. You can often spot him by his dreamy eyes. Your powerful intuition can tell you if he's interested in you, and his powers of perception will pick up on your attraction to him. Making the first move will be difficult, so you might as well be the one who takes the plunge, or you two might furtively glance at each other forever without getting acquainted. Don't be shy with him. Remember, he is as intuitive as you are, and he knows what's on your mind.

Once you are a little more relaxed with each other, he may admit that he has had a romantic interest in you for a long time but didn't know how to approach you. Though Pisceans are rarely direct, you should find that you can be open about your emotions with each other. Under the influence of a tentative feeling of trust and emotional confidence, drifting off to bed with him should be easy and very pleasurable. You can give free rein to your erotic imagination, and he will be agreeable and responsive. Romance calms the waters of your inhibitions, and the lovemaking should be gentle and passionate as he mirrors your desire to please. You can luxuriate in sexual empathy as you indulge each other's whims.

Escapism is often an important element of Piscean sexuality. It may further cloud your ability to decide on a positive direction for your relationship. You may use sex and alcohol to protect yourselves from your extreme sensitivity to the outside world and to shield your vulnerability, but you should not let yourself or your lover fall into the Piscean trap of self-pity and self-delusion.

With a Pisces lover you are pulled in at least two directions at once because you are both dual signs. You want romance but you also want security. You can confuse routine with security, and it will eventually make you edgy, discontent, and unfaithful. To be happy in a relationship you require a sense of growth. Without a goal that is beyond your relating to each other there is no focal point and no chance for individual development. Your creative imagination becomes stifled and you feel smothered. You want to serve your lover, but you don't know what he really wants. Despite the natural Piscean intuition, if you don't have a sense of yourself, you can't be expected to perceive anything but your own confusion.

You are both highly creative men but you both often question your talents. You can encourage him to develop his gifts, but Pisces' nature makes it difficult for him to believe that those closest to him can be fair judges. You can help him by disclosing his ideas to others who can give him encouragement. Compliments from strangers always mean a lot to a Pisces, so you are both susceptible to the attentions and opinions of others.

Making decisions is never easy for Pisces. With a Pisces man in your life the decision-making process can become very complex. Emotional factors and mutual insecurities can cast Neptunian clouds that will obscure your own best interests. You may not be able to decide if you really love each other or, for that matter, what movie to go to—or who should assume what degree of responsibility for making decisions in the first place. Knowing what you want out of a Pisces relationship is the biggest obstacle to overcome. Two men born under the sign of the Fishes can create so many possible permutations that effective action is difficult.

You can be as indulgent of your partner as you are of yourself, but it could lead to a long-lasting and ultimately unsatisfying relationship, unless you are committed to developing your potential. You may have more possibility for success if one of you is older, established, and mature enough to give your partner the wise counsel he needs. If you can help each other to grow, to use your perceptions and creative imagination outside yourselves, you have every reason to be the happiest of loving men.

LOVING YOUR PISCES MAN

If you are looking for a lover who loves to be in love, you may find your ideal in a Pisces man. He is a true romantic, all the way down to the tips of his dancing toes. Pisces men are easy to meet and easy to talk to because they are such good listeners. He is very emotional and will share your laughter, your tears, or your love with sympathy and understanding. He has a natural charm and an elusive quality that most men find instantly appealing.

Pisces rules the feet, and they are often good dancers. Look for him in the center of the crowd at any dance club. He loves the music and gets lost in the beat. For more relaxed entertainment he enjoys the bars. Pisceans are proverbially fond of drink. Theater and the arts are important diversions, and Pisceans are often film buffs.

Your approach should be sincere and friendly. He can be moody and shy, but he responds intuitively and you can often tell if he is interested in you by the look in his dreamy eyes. If he finds you attractive, he will often avert his gaze because he doesn't want to reveal the vulnerability of his feelings. Don't come on too strong or he will shy away. He is basically a gentle soul and needs encouragement.

Men born under the sign of the Fishes are blessed with great imaginations and active fantasy lives. He may look like your average cute guy sitting at the bar, but in his mind he may be Bogart sitting at Rick's Cafe in Casablanca. If Pisces casts you in one of his fantasy roles, he will want to explore the sexual potential of the movie-star quality he sees in you.

The Piscean sexual experience is usually very loving, affectionate, and responsive. He enjoys comfortable surroundings because he is so sensitive to his environment. If you are quick, physical, and intense, he may become quite passive—and you will lose the best of loving a Pisces. He enjoys making love in the most tender manner, to express emotional intimacy and the sharing of passion and trust. Sexual release is not his primary goal. He uses sex to reach deep inside his feelings and to give meaning to hidden sensations. Sex is mysterious for Pisces, and he explores the mysteries of life from the viewpoint of a romantic idealist.

Pisces is a man of many talents, and you can please him most by showing an interest in his creative potential. A

Pisces man may have a mundane job, but he often paints or writes poetry as an expression of his creative imagination. He may seem shy about showing his work to you, but he is probably eager for your comments and compliments. Pisceans have talents they keep hidden because they are insecure about seeking approval. They show great interest in others, and their selflessness can cause people to think that they have no interest in themselves. Without someone to encourage his potential, a Piscean can become too introspective and self-deprecating. You can do Pisces a favor by showing him that you appreciate him for the kind and caring person he is.

If you want to lift his spirits, a day in the country or a weekend at the seashore will have a wonderful restorative effect. Pisceans need time for nondirected contemplation in peaceful surroundings. He needs to be alone with himself and just experience the shimmering play of his emotions without feeling compelled to act. When he gets run-down or exhausted, your Piscean friend or lover becomes moody and hypersensitive. He can get upset over small matters that have nothing to do with what he really feels. Though he has many emotions, he often has no outlet for them.

Pisceans are idealists and can get great satisfaction from working for a worthy cause. The same guy who was still high on the beat at the disco in the wee hours on Sunday morning may spend Sunday evening as a volunteer in a senior citizens' home, bringing flowers and reading romantic novels to the old folks, or working for an AIDS hot line.

Pisces can be a man of many moods and contradictions, but he has the soul of a poet. When he is up, he can be inspirational; when he is down, you can almost see the cloud over his head. Love—and the search for it—is often the source of both his joy and his sorrow. Loving a Pisces man is not often easy, but the reward is the experience of sharing life with a true romantic.

Appendix
Rising Signs

Individuals may think like their Sun signs, but they may act like their Rising signs. The Rising sign, or Ascendant, expresses the way your personality is projected through your physical presence. It is determined by the sign of the zodiac that is on the Eastern horizon at the time of your birth and gives some specific focus to the general pattern set down by your Sun sign. The range of your needs, goals, and motivations may be determined by your Sun sign, but the way you act and other people's perceptions of your actions are indicated by your Rising sign.

After reading your Sun-sign chapter, check your time of birth in these tables and read the chapter on your rising sign. You will get a general idea of the factors that modify your approach to life and love. Do the same for your prospective partner or current lover.

The possibility for astrological complexity is immense, and environmental factors further expand the social dynamics. The charts that follow are generally accurate for North America, but you can only be absolutely certain of your Rising sign if you know the exact time of your birth and consult an astrological table for the day you were born.

ARIES

Birth Time	Rising Sign
4–6 A.M.	Aries
6–8 A.M.	Taurus
8–10 A.M.	Gemini
10 A.M.–12 noon	Cancer
12 noon–2 P.M.	Leo
2–4 P.M.	Virgo
4–6 P.M.	Libra
6–8 P.M.	Scorpio
8–10 P.M.	Sagittarius
10 P.M.–12 midnight	Capricorn
12 midnight–2 A.M.	Aquarius
2–4 A.M.	Pisces

TAURUS

Birth Time	Rising Sign
4–6 A.M.	Taurus
6–8 A.M.	Gemini
8–10 A.M.	Cancer
10 A.M.–12 noon	Leo
12 noon–2 P.M.	Virgo
2–4 P.M.	Libra
4–6 P.M.	Scorpio
6–8 P.M.	Sagittarius
8–10 P.M.	Capricorn
10 P.M.–12 midnight	Aquarius
12 midnight–2 A.M.	Pisces
2–4 A.M.	Aries

GEMINI

Birth Time	Rising Sign
4–6 A.M.	Gemini
6–8 A.M.	Cancer
8–10 A.M.	Leo
10 A.M.–12 noon	Virgo
12 noon–2 P.M.	Libra
2–4 P.M.	Scorpio
4–6 P.M.	Sagittarius
6–8 P.M.	Capricorn
8–10 P.M.	Aquarius
10 P.M.–12 midnight	Pisces
12 midnight–2 A.M.	Aries
2–4 A.M.	Taurus

CANCER

Birth Time	Rising Sign
4–6 A.M.	Cancer
6–8 A.M.	Leo
8–10 A.M.	Virgo
10 A.M.–12 noon	Libra
12 noon–2 P.M.	Scorpio
2–4 P.M.	Sagittarius
4–6 P.M.	Capricorn
6–8 P.M.	Aquarius
8–10 P.M.	Pisces
10 P.M.–12 midnight	Aries
12 midnight–2 A.M.	Taurus
2–4 A.M.	Gemini

LEO

Birth Time	Rising Sign
4–6 A.M.	Leo
6–8 A.M.	Virgo
8–10 A.M.	Libra
10 A.M.–12 noon	Scorpio
12 noon–2 P.M.	Sagittarius
2–4 P.M.	Capricorn
4–6 P.M.	Aquarius
6–8 P.M.	Pisces
8–10 P.M.	Aries
10 P.M.–12 midnight	Taurus
12 midnight–2 A.M.	Gemini
2–4 A.M.	Cancer

VIRGO

Birth Time	Rising Sign
4–6 A.M.	Virgo
6–8 A.M.	Libra
8–10 A.M.	Scorpio
10 A.M.–12 noon	Sagittarius
12 noon–2 P.M.	Capricorn
2–4 P.M.	Aquarius
4–6 P.M.	Pisces
6–8 P.M.	Aries
8–10 P.M.	Taurus
10 P.M.–12 midnight	Gemini
12 midnight–2 A.M.	Cancer
2–4 A.M.	Leo

LIBRA

Birth Time	Rising Sign
4–6 A.M.	Libra
6–8 A.M.	Scorpio
8–10 A.M.	Sagittarius
10 A.M.–12 noon	Capricorn
12 noon–2 P.M.	Aquarius
2–4 P.M.	Pisces
4–6 P.M.	Aries
6–8 P.M.	Taurus
8–10 P.M.	Gemini
10 P.M.–12 midnight	Cancer
12 midnight–2 A.M.	Leo
2–4 A.M.	Virgo

SCORPIO

Birth Time	Rising Sign
4–6 A.M.	Scorpio
6–8 A.M.	Sagittarius
8–10 A.M.	Capricorn
10 A.M.–12 noon	Aquarius
12 noon–2 P.M.	Pisces
2–4 P.M.	Aries
4–6 P.M.	Taurus
6–8 P.M.	Gemini
8–10 P.M.	Cancer
10 P.M.–12 midnight	Leo
12 midnight–2 A.M.	Virgo
2–4 A.M.	Libra

SAGITTARIUS

Birth Time	Rising Sign
4–6 A.M.	Sagittarius
6–8 A.M.	Capricorn
8–10 A.M.	Aquarius
10 A.M.–12 noon	Pisces
12 noon–2 P.M.	Aries
2–4 P.M.	Taurus
4–6 P.M.	Gemini
6–8 P.M.	Cancer
8–10 P.M.	Leo
10 P.M.–12 midnight	Virgo
12 midnight–2 A.M.	Libra
2–4 A.M.	Scorpio

CAPRICORN

Birth Time	Rising Sign
4–6 A.M.	Capricorn
6–8 A.M.	Aquarius
8–10 A.M.	Pisces
10 A.M.–12 noon	Aries
12 noon–2 P.M.	Taurus
2–4 P.M.	Gemini
4–6 P.M.	Cancer
6–8 P.M.	Leo
8–10 P.M.	Virgo
10 P.M.–12 midnight	Libra
12 midnight–2 A.M.	Scorpio
2–4 A.M.	Sagittarius

AQUARIUS

Birth Time	Rising Sign
4–6 A.M.	Aquarius
6–8 A.M.	Pisces
8–10 A.M.	Aries
10 A.M.–12 noon	Taurus
12 noon–2 P.M.	Gemini
2–4 P.M.	Cancer
4–6 P.M.	Leo
6–8 P.M.	Virgo
8–10 P.M.	Libra
10 P.M.–12 midnight	Scorpio
12 midnight–2 A.M.	Sagittarius
2–4 A.M.	Capricorn

PISCES

Birth Time	Rising Sign
4–6 A.M.	Pisces
6–8 A.M.	Aries
8–10 A.M.	Taurus
10 A.M.–12 noon	Gemini
12 noon–2 P.M.	Cancer
2–4 P.M.	Leo
4–6 P.M.	Virgo
6–8 P.M.	Libra
8–10 P.M.	Scorpio
10 P.M.–12 midnight	Sagittarius
12 midnight–2 A.M.	Capricorn
2–4 A.M.	Aquarius

ABOUT THE AUTHOR

Michael Jay was a student of astrology for more than twenty-five years, reading and writing about the stars and the events of our lives. His work as a journalist included several years writing a weekly column, "Cocktail Astrology," for the *New York Native*.

Michael was a Cancer with Cancer rising, Moon on the cusp of Aquarius and Pisces. He died in 1990.